The Last Resort

Studies in Evaluating the Children Act 1989

Series editors:
Dr Carolyn Davies, Prof. Jane Aldgate

Other titles in the series include
From Care to Accommodation
Parental Perspectives on Care Proceedings
Leaving Care in Partnership (forthcoming)
Safeguarding Children with the Children Act 1989 (forthcoming)
The Best-Laid Plans (forthcoming)

STUDIES IN EVALUATING THE CHILDREN ACT 1989

The Last Resort

Child Protection, the Courts and the 1989 Children Act

Joan Hunt
Alison Macleod
Caroline Thomas

Centre for Socio-Legal Studies
School for Policy Studies, University of Bristol

London: The Stationery Office

First published 1999

ISBN 0 11 322119 3

Published by The Stationery Office and available from:

The Publications Centre
(mail, telephone and fax orders only)
PO Box 276, London SW8 5DT
General enquiries 0171 873 0011
Telephone orders 0171 873 9090
Fax orders 0171 873 8200

The Stationery Office Bookshops
123 Kingsway, London WC2B 6PQ
0171 242 6393 Fax 0171 242 6394
68–69 Bull Street, Birmingham B4 6AD
0121 236 9696 Fax 0121 236 9699
33 Wine Street, Bristol BS1 2BQ
0117 926 4306 Fax 0117 929 4515
9–21 Princess Street, Manchester M60 8AS
0161 834 7201 Fax 0161 833 0634
16 Arthur Street, Belfast BT1 4GD
01232 238451 Fax 01232 235401
The Stationery Office Oriel Bookshop
The Friary, Cardiff CF1 4AA
01222 395548 Fax 01222 384347
71 Lothian Road, Edinburgh EH3 9AZ
0131 228 4181 Fax 0131 622 7017

The Stationery Office's Accredited Agents
(see Yellow Pages)

and through good booksellers

Printed in the United Kingdom for The Stationery Office
J69753 C10 1/99 9385 9685

Contents

Figures and tables

Figures

Tables

Foreword

The Children Act 1989 was implemented on 14 October 1991. At its launch the then Lord Chancellor, Lord Mackay, described the Act as 'the most radical legislative reform to children's services this century'. Shortly after the launch the Department of Health put together a strategy to monitor and evaluate the initial impact of the Act. Taking a tripartite approach, this drew on evidence from statistical returns, inspections and research to develop a rounded appreciation of early implementation. The subsequent strategy plan was published and circulated to relevant bodies, including social services and the major voluntary agencies, in 1993. This plan formed the backcloth for a programme of research studies commissioned by the Department of Health to explore early evaluation in more depth. It is these studies, some 20 in all, which form this new series.

The programme studies investigate the implementation of key changes introduced by the Act and evaluate the facilitators and inhibitors to the meeting of key objectives. A longer-term goal of the programme is to review the aims of the Act in the light of implementation with a view to reconsideration or amendment should this be felt necessary. Finally, a more general and important scientific aim is to consider how far change could be achieved successfully by changing the law.

There are several principles underlying the Children Act 1989 that permeate the research studies. An important strand of the Act is to bring together private and public law so that the needs of all children whose welfare is at risk might be approached in the same way. This philosophy is underpinned by the principle of promoting children's welfare. There should be recognition of children's time-scales and, in court cases, children's welfare should be paramount. To aid this paramountcy principle there should be a welfare checklist and delays in court hearings should be avoided.

The promotion of children's welfare takes a child development focus, urging local authorities to take a holistic and corporate approach to providing services. Departments such as health, education, housing, police, social services and recreation should work together to respond to children's needs. Children, the Act argues, are best looked after within their families wherever possible and, where not, the continuing support of parents and wider kin should be facilitated by avoiding compulsory proceedings whenever possible. Parents should be partners in any intervention process, and children's views should be sought and listened to in any decision-making affecting their lives. To promote continuity for children looked after, contact with families should be encouraged and children's religion, culture, ethnicity and language should be preserved.

Local authorities have a duty to move from services to prevent care to a broader remit of providing family support, which could include planned periods away from home. However, family support services should not be universal but target those most in need. The introduction of Children's Services Plans in 1996 has made the idea of corporate responsibility a more tangible reality and seeks to help local authorities look at how they may use scarce resources cost effectively.

The themes of the Children Act have relevance for the millennium. The concern with combating social exclusion is echoed through several of the studies, especially those on family support and young people looked after by local authorities. The value of early intervention is also a theme in the studies on family centres, day care and services for children defined as 'in need' under the Act. Further, the research on the implementation of the Looking After Children Schedules emphasises the importance to children in foster and residential care of attaining good outcomes in education. Lastly, attending to the health of parents and their children is another strand in both the family support and 'children looked after' studies.

To accompany the 20 individual studies in the research programme the Department of Health has commissioned an overview of the findings, to be published by The Stationery Office in the style of similar previous publications from HMSO: *Social Work Decisions in Child Care 1985; Pattern and Outcomes in Child Care 1991; Child Protection: Messages from Research 1996;* and *Focus on Teenagers 1997.*

The editors would like to express their appreciation to the members of the research community; professionals from different disciplines, and service users, among others, who have contributed so willingly and generously to the successful completion of the research studies and to the construction of the overview. Without their help, none of the research would have been written or disseminated.

Carolyn Davies
Jane Aldgate

Acknowledgements

The research reported here was commissioned and funded by the Department of Health. The project was supported by an Advisory Committee, initially under the chairmanship of Rupert Hughes and latterly of Elizabeth Johnson from the Department of Health and included officials from the Lord Chancellor's Department, the Home Office and the Department of Health, as well as representatives from practitioner groups and academics. We are most grateful for their advice and commitment.

Our thanks are also due to the President of the Family Division, Sir Stephen Brown, and to the officials of the Lord Chancellor's Department who arranged for us to have privileged access to the courts.

We owe an enormous debt of gratitude to the practitioners in all fields without whose time and assistance the research could not have been undertaken; the administrative staff in the courts and Social Services who helped us set up the project; the social workers, Guardians ad Litem and lawyers who agreed to be interviewed; the judges, magistrates and Justices' Clerks who permitted us to observe court hearings and gave us their time in interviews.

Above all, we need to thank the family members who, at a time of tension and distress in their lives, allowed us to be present in court and who talked to us later about their experiences in the interests of those who might stand in their place in the future. We are deeply appreciative of their generosity.

Past and present colleagues in the Socio-Legal Centre and in the School for Policy Studies have supported our efforts throughout, notably Mervyn Murch, Douglas Hooper and Paddy Hillyard.

Finally, we thank those who, at various times, formed part of the project team: fellow researchers Pam Freeman, Lynne Milsom, Judith Kent, Maureen Oakley and Pardeep Gill; Andrew Chalmers for his help with information technology; Catherine Brookes, Rosemary Nash and Tina Beattie for their support skills and administrative support. Special thanks are due to Doreen Bailey, our Project Administrator, whose unstinting assistance at all stages of the project has been invaluable.

1   *Introduction*

The background to reform

In a much quoted phrase the then Lord Chancellor, Lord Mackay, hailed the Children Act 1989 as:

> the most comprehensive and far-reaching reform of child care law which has come before Parliament in living memory.[1]

Its ambitious objective was to reform, simplify and codify the law relating to the care, upbringing and protection of children, sweeping away the previous inconsistent and fragmented statutory framework and replacing it with one which was coherent, integrated and based on a new philosophy about the relationship between the state and the family.

The main body of the Act has a dual parentage. The private law provisions, that is those relating to the regulation of relationships *within* a family, have their genesis in a thoroughgoing review initiated by the Law Commission in 1984, as part of their remit to monitor the development of the law. Wide consultation followed the publication of a series of working papers[2] producing, in 1988, final recommendations in the *Report on Guardianship and Custody*.[3] Parts 1 and 2 of the Children Act are substantially based on this report.[4]

Meanwhile, in a parallel and initially unrelated development, the public law relating to children had been subjected to a similar comprehensive scrutiny. Following the recommendation of a Parliamentary Select Committee in 1984[5] the government set up an inter-departmental working party with the aim of devising: 'a framework for developing the best child care practice and meeting more effectively the needs of children and their families' and producing: 'a clearer and more consistent body of law comprehensible not only to those operating it but to those affected by its operation'.[6]

The working party also canvassed opinion widely, through a series of discussion papers and seminars, producing, in 1985, a consultative document entitled *The Review of Child Care Law*.[7] The government's acceptance of most of the Review's recommendations was marked by the publication in 1987 of a White Paper, The Law on Child Care and Family Services,[8] which formed the basis for the public law provisions of the subsequent Children Bill.

The need for reform of child protection law in particular was also fuelled by the findings of a series of inquiries into deaths resulting from child abuse, most notably those of Jasmine Beckford,[9] Kimberley Carlile,[10] and Tyra Henry.[11] These had focused public attention on the inaction of child protection agencies. Events in Cleveland in 1987, when large numbers of children were removed from their homes following allegations of sexual abuse, in contrast generated public outrage at over-zealous intervention and highlighted the lack of safeguards against precipitate removal.[12]

In the wake of Cleveland yet another consultative document was issued, this time by the Lord Chancellor's Department,[13] canvassing reactions to the Inquiry's recommendation of an Office of Child Protection, one function of which would have been to scrutinise applications for compulsory powers. In the light of the generally negative reaction to this proposal, however, the idea was dropped.

The high public profile given to child protection issues over the many months that the Cleveland Inquiry sat undoubtedly helped to secure an early slot in the government's legislative programme for the Children Bill. The delay occasioned by the perceived need to wait for the Inquiry's findings also allowed the Law Commission's review of the private law to catch up and thus afforded a unique opportunity to integrate public and private child care law in one piece of legislation.

Monitoring and evaluating the Act

Thus almost all the reforms were the product of a detailed and lengthy consultation process and supported by a broad consensus among practitioner groups. The Bill's Parliamentary passage was also characterised by a remarkable degree of cross-party agreement. None the less it was accepted that it would be vital to monitor and evaluate the impact of such far-reaching changes.

The Children Act Advisory Committee, created to supervise the process of implementation, was kept in place, its annual reports on progress intended to supplement those to be provided by the Department of Health. A national network of Family Court Business and Services[14] Committees was established to monitor and respond to local implementation issues and to channel concerns to the centre through the Advisory Committee. The Lord Chancellor's Department created new statistical systems; the Department of Health extended its. The Social Services Inspectorate has undertaken a number of small-scale monitoring exercises.[15] A more detailed evaluation of the Act was inaugurated by the commissioning of research into specific aspects of the new legislation. The Statutory Intervention project,[16] on which this report is based, was one element in this programme.

The focus of the research

The philosophy of the Children Act is that children are best cared for within their families of origin without recourse to the courts and much of the Act is concerned with establishing a framework within which that can become a reality. None the less it recognises that there will be children whose care falls below that which is acceptable in a civilised society and whose interests require compulsory protection through the legal process. It is with these children that this research has been concerned.

The Act transformed both the substantive law governing state intervention, which will influence which families are taken to court, and the legal process, which affects their experiences once that decision is taken. There are, for example, new criteria for intervention both in an emergency and in the longer term and routes previously available to the local authority are closed off. There is an expanded range of interim and full orders. For the first time in English law it is recognised that delay in resolving issues relating to children is normally inimical to their interests and courts are given both duties and powers to prevent harmful delay arising. A system of concurrent jurisdiction allows cases to be allocated to the appropriate judicial level and for substantially the same remedies to be available in each.

The Statutory Intervention Project was set up to examine the impact of such major change on the use of compulsory powers of intervention by local authorities and on the management of such cases by the courts. Its objectives were to:

- analyse the decision-making processes by which compulsory powers are sought and determined;

- assess the extent, nature and effect of any changes in the use and management of statutory intervention;

- investigate how the legislation is viewed by those who operate it and the adult family members subject to it; and

- evaluate the operation of the legislation and what amendments or guidance may be necessary.

Within this broad remit we were asked to focus particularly on three aspects of change: the criteria for Care and Supervision Orders, the orders available to the court and the avoidance of delay.

Although nationally several thousand children are made subject to statutory intervention each year[17] such children are very much in the minority, even among those who come to the attention of child protection agencies.[18] Perhaps for this reason the legal process has, in the past, attracted remarkably little research attention. The poverty of information on care proceedings, for instance, meant that the Child Care Law Review had to commission a number of special studies.[19] The massive pre-Act research programme commissioned by the Department of Health[20] did not include a single study which looked specifically at this aspect of child protection. Though the authors and colleagues at the Socio-Legal Centre were able to contribute a certain amount of information from research on care proceedings,[21] this was focused on the representation of children, not on the operation of the court system. The decision to restrict local authority use of wardship was made without there having been any major research into its utility.[22]

Thus in contrast to the wealth of research evidence on the operation of the pre-Act child care and child protection system outside the courts, much of which had informed the process of law reform,[23] there was no equivalent fund of information on the functioning of the legal process against which the new law could be compared. To compensate for this empirical vacuum our research needed to incorporate a 'before' as well as an 'after' element, not only researching the new law but building up a comparative base of information on child protection proceedings under the old. This material is incorporated in the research report and was also separately reported to the Department of Health in an interim report *Child Protection Proceedings before the Children Act: A Case for Change?*[24]

As we explain in Chapter 2, because of the timing of the research commission it was not possible to undertake a fully comparative study. Thus the main emphasis of the research has been on the new law. We were also acutely conscious that the project presented a unique opportunity not only to chart change but to document the early stages of a new era in child care law. We have therefore sought not only to evaluate the Act but to describe its operation in sufficient detail to establish an empirical baseline against which future developments can be measured.

The breadth of the research made it unrealistic to present all the results in a single document. Accordingly the detailed findings have been recorded in three reports with the main themes and issues being encapsulated in a separate summary document.

The core of the project was a detailed comparative analysis of a sample of child protection cases going through the civil courts before and after the Act and interviews with key practitioners. This is the primary focus of *The Last Resort*. The second report, *Parental Perspectives on Care Proceedings*,[25] records the experiences of parents and other adult family members involved in a sub-sample of the post-Act cases. The third, *The Care Workloads of the Civil Courts under the Children Act*,[26] documents the findings of a survey of several hundred cases involving care or related proceedings before and after the Act in the study areas. It thus provides a statistical backdrop for the other two limbs of the project.

The full impact of the Children Act and its long-term viability may not be clear for some time to come. The theme of a still evolving system will be a recurrent one in this report. Indeed its organising principle is the image of a journey through the legal process. This serves as a double metaphor, first for the dynamic progress of the cases themselves through the courts, second for the growth and development of the family justice system under the Act. As we shall see in subsequent chapters, the eventual destination of our sample cases was very often unclear at the start and most were subject to change, disruption and delay en route. Much the same might be said of the new legislation.

NOTES

[1] Lord Mackay of Clashfern. *Hansard*, HOL, 6 December 1988 Second Reading Col 488.

[2] Guardianship (No. 91 (1985)); Custody (No. 96 (1986)); Care, Supervision and Interim Orders in Custody Proceedings (No. 100 (1987)); Wards of Court (No. 101 (1987)).

[3] Law Commission Report No. 172 (1988): *Family Law Review of Child Law: Guardianship and Custody*. HMSO.

[4] Bainham A (1990): *Children – the New Law. The Children Act 1989*. Family Law.

[5] House of Commons (1984): *Second Report of the All-Party Parliamentary Select Committee on Social Services*. (Session 1983–84): Children in Care (The Short Report). HMSO.

[6] DHSS (1985): *Review of Child Care Law: Report to Ministers of an Interdepartmental Working Party*. HMSO.

[7] Law Commission Report No. 172 (1988) op. cit.

[8] Cm 62.

[9] London Borough of Brent (1985): *A Child in Trust: Report of the Panel of Inquiry Investigating the Circumstances Surrounding the Death of Jasmine Beckford*. London Borough of Brent.

[10] London Borough of Greenwich (1987): *A Child in Mind: Protection of Children in a Responsible Society, Report of the Commission of Inquiry into the Circumstances Surrounding the Death of Kimberley Carlile*. London Borough of Greenwich.

[11] London Borough of Lambeth (1987): *Whose Child? The Report of the Public Inquiry into the Death of Tyra Henry*. London Borough of Lambeth.

[12] DHSS (1988): *Report of the Inquiry into Child Abuse in Cleveland 1987*. Cm 412, HMSO.

[13] Lord Chancellor's Department (1988): *Improvements in the Arrangements for Care Proceedings*. LCD.

[14] The latter were subsequently transformed into Family Court Fora.

[15] E.g. Court Orders Study (1992); Contact Orders (1994); Residence Orders (1995); Interim Care Orders (1994). HMSO.

[16] Statutory Intervention in Child Protection: the impact of the Children Act 1989.

[17] E.g. in the year 1992–93 there were 6,682 applications under Section 31. *Children Act Advisory Committee Annual Report* 1993–94. HMSO.

[18] DoH (1995): *Child Protection: Messages from Current Research and their Implications*. HMSO.

[19] E.g. of Interim Care Orders, Farmer E; Parker R (1985). *A Study of Interim Care Orders*. School of Applied Social Studies, University of Bristol; and of Place of Safety Orders, Dartington Social Research Unit.

[20] DoH (1995): op. cit.

[21] Representation of the Child in the Civil Courts. Research Project 1985–90.

[22] Hunt J (1993): *Local Authority Wardships before the Children Act: The Baby or the Bathwater?* HMSO.

[23] See, for example, DHSS (1985): *Social Work Decisions in Child Care*. HMSO; DoH (1991): *Patterns and Outcomes in Child Placement*. HMSO; DoH (1995): op. cit., 17.

[24] Hunt J; Macleod A (1993): *Child Protection Proceedings before the Children Act: A Case for Change?* Report to DoH.

[25] Freeman P; Hunt J (1998): *Parental Perspectives on Care Proceedings*. The Stationery Office.

[26] Thomas C; Hunt J (1996): *The Care Workloads of the Civil Courts under the Children Act*. Report to DoH. Centre for Socio-Legal Studies, University of Bristol.

2 *Methodology*

Research design: the rationale

The research was conceived as a study of the impact of law reform. Accordingly a comparative case study approach was selected as the most appropriate core methodology, based on samples of child protection cases proceeding through the civil courts before and after the Children Act 1989. This choice of approach determined the scale of the study; it not being considered feasible to undertake detailed, often qualitative, analysis of more than about 200 cases in all.

A key element in the research was also to examine the effect of the 1989 Act not only on decision-making processes within the local authority but on the court process. Logistical considerations were therefore important in deciding on the number of study areas since it would be necessary to gain access to and manage relationships with the social services department, legal department, Guardian ad Litem panel and three levels of court in each, as well as numerous firms of private practice lawyers. It was concluded that no more than three areas could be contemplated.

It was also decided that it would not be possible to deal with more than one court of each type per area; thus each would have to be de-limited by the catchment area of a single magistrates' court – a petty sessional division. In order to ensure a sufficient flow of cases throughout the research period, this meant that rural courts, which we knew from previous research[1] were only dealing with a handful of child protection cases even before the Children Act, would have to be excluded.

Thus it only remained to choose between medium to large city courts. Negotiations with courts and local authorities began months before the research was due to start; several magistrates' courts were prepared, even eager to take part, as were several county courts and local authorities; unfortunately not necessarily in the same area.

Eventually and somewhat miraculously it seemed to us at the time, everything fell, more or less, into place. We had three study areas, located within three court circuits, each in different areas of the country, representing different types of local government organisation, even distinct political complexions. In all three we had previously undertaken some court-based research and therefore had a stock not only of information but of working relationships with court personnel on which we could capitalise. Indeed without this springboard the process of negotiating access would undoubtedly have proved even more protracted.

As indicated earlier, we needed to limit the catchment area for the research to a single petty sessional division in each area. This meant that in one of our authorities, a shire county, cases were drawn only from social service teams within the urban districts. In a second authority the social services department, which was already involved in a number of other research projects, was anxious not to over-burden its staff. Accordingly we agreed to confine the research to a selection of offices. The districts, though not the cases, were selected by the authority to include an ethnically mixed population.

Access

From our current vantage point, with the data safely gathered in and analysed, it is easy to forget the difficulties presented by the access process. We emphasise them here, not to trumpet our success in surmounting them, but as a reminder to new researchers and their funders of the need for a long lead-in period and careful exploration of the potential hurdles.

As researchers whose primary experience lay with the legal system, we were very familiar with the formal and informal processes of acquiring consent and knew the likely obstacles and how to circumvent them. Social services research was relatively new territory, however, and we were fortunate to be able to call on the advice of more seasoned colleagues within the University.

The process of gaining consent within social services departments taught us a great deal about the importance of understanding the likely impact of different authority structures on the access process. The county and High Court systems, for instance, tend to operate on a command structure so that the key consent is that of the Lord Chancellor's Department with the support of the President of the Family Division; in the magistrates' courts access is controlled by the Justices' Clerk; lawyers make their own decisions.

Social services departments, however, are organised as a devolved bureaucracy, so that authority from the centre is *necessary*, but not *sufficient* to procure the co-operation of those elsewhere in the structure. Each authority, moreover, varied as to how many levels of the structure had to be penetrated before we could regard our position as secure; indeed there were a range of practices even within authorities and different requirements to be negotiated. For example, one district in one authority would initially only allow us access to files if parents had been informed and had not objected. This issue was not raised elsewhere.

In the course of the research other problems arose. In one of the local authorities concerned, (which we have unimaginatively identified as area C), the negotiating process was rather less prolonged than in the others. Scarcely had we opened the champagne to celebrate getting at least one study area safely into the fold, however, than the department was hit by industrial action. Given that the start date for the research was only a matter of weeks away, and neither of our other two areas was fully secure, we decided to stick with it, anticipating the dispute would soon be resolved. Sadly, we were wrong. This situation, which meant that the department was operating on much less than full strength for part of the research period, undoubtedly affected local practice. Attention is drawn to possible distortions in the data as a result at various points in the report.

In some respects, indeed, it is surprising that *any* court or local authority was prepared to sign up for the research. The project was due to begin shortly before implementation of the Act, thus at a point when a great deal of resources were being consumed in training and re-organisation. Moreover, as we explain in more detail below, agencies needed to make a commitment over several years, since there would be two major phases of fieldwork, separated by a period of analysis.

This two-stage approach brought renewed hurdles as personnel changed and some earlier 'understandings' had to be re-negotiated at several levels. Phase 1 of the research, moreover, had not involved us in contact with the judiciary, professional or lay; Phase 2 did and there were one or two nail-biting moments when it seemed possible that in some cases we might be denied access to court papers or court hearings. Fortunately, with the tactful assistance of the court administration, these problems were resolved.

Unlike the first part of the research, Phase 2 also involved direct observation of court hearings. This meant that access had to be negotiated with the families and professionals involved in each case before its first appearance in court. Without the fax machine, which enabled us to accompany our request to be present with details of the research, this process would probably have been impossible since usually we were only given notification of the hearing the day before. Although we had endeavoured to prepare the ground in advance by circulating local solicitors with details of the research and providing social services departments with letters to give to parents, experience soon showed that neither of these strategies was particularly reliable.

Due to constraints on resources the original research design did not include interviews with members of the judiciary. As the research was written up, however, it became increasingly apparent that this was an unfortunate omission and some additional funding was secured to add this invaluable dimension. However, negotiating access which had to go through official channels, though not difficult, was not swift.

The stages of data collection

Fieldwork was undertaken in two major phases with a third supplementary phase tacked on to the end.

Phase 1: Court proceedings prior to the Children Act 1989

Phase 1 of the research was designed to provide a comparative base of data on child protection proceedings under pre-Children Act legislation against which the reformed law could be assessed.

As indicated in Chapter 1, although by the time the Children Bill was introduced into Parliament a great deal was known about child care and child protection services outside the court system, there was very little information about the legal process. Some efforts were made, late in the day, to rectify this deficiency. In particular the Department of Health commissioned the researchers and colleagues to establish 'baseline' data on various aspects of child care proceedings. That short project (Children and the Civil Courts) provided statistical information on the duration of care and related proceedings in 14 magistrates' courts,[2] investigated the role of local authority legal departments by means of a national survey[3] and examined the use of the wardship jurisdiction by five local authorities.[4]

The Civil Courts project thus supplied some of the data which would be needed to assess the effectiveness of the new legislation. It was considered, however, that a more substantial data bank was required. Accordingly the first phase of this project was a detailed retrospective examination of 104 child protection cases[5] in which our three local authorities applied for compulsory powers in wardship, matrimonial or care proceedings over the period June 1989 to May 1990. This period was chosen on the basis that cases were recent enough to illustrate current practice while hopefully allowing sufficient time for most cases to have completed by the time the research began in June 1991.

These types of proceedings were selected as the major routes through which compulsory powers could be acquired under the pre-Act legislation. We had originally also planned to include a selection of cases in which the local authority assumed parental rights (under Section 3 of the Child Care Act 1980). None of the social services departments participating in the study, however, used this provision, a reflection of the injustice such administrative procedures were increasingly recognised to present.[6]

Constructing a research sample proved a far from straightforward task. None of the local authorities involved had developed information systems capable of identifying cases it had taken to court. For cases brought under the Children and Young Persons' Act 1969 we were able to rely on court registers in the juvenile courts which we were already scrutinising as part of our extensive survey of court workloads.[7] However, in the authority where only a few districts were taking part, it was necessary to go through every court file, of which there were several hundred, all inter-mixed with criminal files, to establish whether it fell within the catchment area.

Wardship cases were identified through the computerised returns made to the Principal Registry by each District Registry. These were less reliable than the juvenile court registers and had to be refined through scrutiny of court files, again plus checks with local authority legal departments.

For matrimonial proceedings there was no central data source which would allow us to differentiate cases in which the local authority had intervened and it was not feasible to scan the thousands of files involved. As far as two of our local authorities were concerned this was only a minor inconvenience, since their legal departments were confident such proceedings were rarely used. In the third, in contrast, we had been told that this was a relatively common mode of intervention. Tracking down even a small sample, however, proved a Byzantine exercise which owes everything to the perseverance and powers of recall of individual social workers, solicitors and above all one long-serving clerk in the legal department.

These methods gave us a sampling frame which, though by no means ideal, was the best that could be achieved in the circumstances. The sample cases were then selected to reflect the apparent proportionate use by each authority and by districts within each authority of each type of proceedings. The wardship and matrimonial cases had to be randomly selected. For the care cases, however, on which information was more easily available, we tried to stratify by ensuring the inclusion of a proportionate number of long cases and those in which the case did not end in an order to the local authority.

Inevitably the original sample had to be slightly adjusted in each area when files proved to be temporarily or permanently 'unavailable'. Potentially more serious was the stipulation mentioned earlier which required us to seek parental consent to the examination of files. This resulted in a loss of about half the original cases in this district (ten cases), either from objections or because of social workers' reluctance to allow parents to be approached. Most of the lost cases proved to be 'matrimonials' and no particular bias could be discerned among the care cases to which access was denied. None the less, the possibility of some distortion cannot be ruled out. Table 2.1 shows the distribution of the final sample.

Table 2.1 *Distribution of pre-Act sample*

	Area A		Area B		Area C		All areas	
	No.	%	No.	%	No.	%	No.	%
Cases involving wardship proceedings	11	27	10	28	22	82	43	41
Cases beginning in wardship	9	22	6	17	20	74	35	34
Cases involving intervention in matrimonial proceedings	11	27	1	3	—	—	12	12
Cases starting with matrimonial intervention	10	25	—	—	—	—	19	10
Cases involving care proceedings	22	54	30	83	7	26	59	57
(n=)		(41)		(36)		(27)		(104)

Data were extracted from court and social services files by means of one common pro forma plus separate forms for each type of proceedings involved. Harder, quantifiable data were recorded using mainly specific, pre-coded and computerised questions. This was supplemented by textual recording of more qualitative material, some of which was subsequently encoded.

As noted earlier each 'case' in the study includes all the children in a family subject to the same set of proceedings. This reflects the way practitioners and courts actually treat proceedings although in court statistics every application per child is recorded as a separate case. In order to manage the data on this basis, however, it was necessary to use one child per family as the 'index' child. Variable data such as relationships within the family, for instance, length of proceedings and interim orders were recorded as they related to this child, who was usually the one who was the focus of local authority concern.

Data collection in this first stage of the research was entirely a documentary exercise. This was considered to be unavoidable given the limitations of time and resources, and also the fact that while we were occupied in establishing a data bank on the operation of the previous legislation, social services and the courts were gearing themselves up for, and adjusting to implementation of the new legislation. The second phase of the research, however, involved a more varied methodology.

Phase 2: Court proceedings under the Children Act 1989

The sample

The 83 cases which comprised the post-Act sample were drawn from cases lodged in the courts over the first two years of implementation, that is from 14 October 1991 to 13 October 1993. Table 2.2 shows the distribution by area and year.

Table 2.2   *Distribution of post-Act sample*

	Area A	Area B	Area C	All areas
Year 1	15	16	12	43
Year 2	14	14	12	40
Total	29	30	24	83

In contrast to the ingenuity we had had to employ in constructing the earlier sample the process in Phase 2 was relatively straightforward in that only a single type of proceeding was involved and almost all cases would be initiated in the magistrates' courts, whose records, as we had previously established, were generally reliable. Checks were also instituted with local authority legal departments to ensure we did not miss any cases started in the higher courts.

Cases were selected for inclusion within the sample by two methods. The majority (53) were chosen *retrospectively* from a sampling pool derived from court records and local authority information, as described above. These cases started in the courts over the first 15 months of the research period. Because of the drop in the number of cases reaching the courts, which was characteristic of the first year of the Act, the sample in two of the research areas was smaller than we had hoped and comprised all the cases of which we were aware. In the third area cases were stratified by district, duration, court level and legal outcome and represented just over half the total cases.

Beginning in January 1993 an additional sample of 30 cases, ten from each area, were *prospectively* selected, in order that we could track their progress through the courts. For the identification of these cases we were dependent on referral by local authority solicitors and we are aware that this was not an entirely fail-safe approach. Further attrition occurred in those few cases where parents refused to allow us to be present in court or when we were informed subsequent to the first hearing.

Comparison of the post-Act sample with the data from our extensive survey of cases starting in the magistrates' courts suggests that the final sample probably represents around one in two of the children subject to care proceedings, varying between 41% in Area B, 49% in Area A and 62% in Area C. Since the extensive survey included beyond control as well as child protection cases the fraction of relevant cases represented will be somewhat higher than this, although precisely how much higher cannot be determined. It should also be noted that since fewer cases were brought to the court in the first year of the Act the Year 1 sample represents a larger fraction of the sampling pool than that from Year 2.

Sources of information

Data were collected on all these cases, as in the pre-Act sample, from social services files and records held at the relevant courts. A single pro forma was used, again combining pre-coded quantitative data with textual recording of more qualitative material. Direct observation of court hearings was undertaken in the 30 prospectively sampled cases, the researchers attending a total of 167 hearings.

The unexpected length of many cases substantially prolonged the fieldwork period. Indeed the last case entered into the sample, in mid-October 1993, completed too late for interviews to be conducted, although we did attend all the hearings. In all the remainder, plus 32 of the other sample cases, we interviewed a range of key practitioners, including Guardians ad Litem (27), social workers (40) and lawyers representing respectively the local authority (24), children (22) and adult family members (34). These interviews were partly case-based. Since we also wished to capitalise on the broader experiences of our interviewees however, a number of general questions covering various aspects of the reforms were included. Interviews with social services team managers (16), in contrast, were primarily aimed at their general experience. All interviews used a semi-structured format and were tape-recorded for later partial transcription.

Interviews were also completed with 35 adult family members in 25 cases. As explained in the previous chapter this material is being separately reported in detail, although key points from the data are used throughout this report.

Finally, towards the end of the research, we were able to add in the judicial dimension by interviewing 31 magistrates on the family proceedings court rotas, five Justices' Clerks and 14 judges and district judges. These interviews were entirely aimed at ascertaining our informants' general views on the new legislation and did not discuss individual cases. The researchers were also assisted, at the outset of each phase of the research, by the opportunity to have informal meetings with key representatives of social services management, court administration and the judiciary, in which issues relevant to the research topic and methodology were discussed.

Analysis

The report thus draws on three different types of data (files, observation, interviews) utilising 12 different schedules in addition to straightforward transcription of oral evidence. Data from the files' pro formas and court hearing schedules were analysed both quantitatively, using SPSS-X, and qualitatively. The interview material was mainly analysed by hand, though with some computerised assistance.

Illustrative material from the sample cases is used throughout the report, names and other identifying information having been changed to preserve confidentiality. Most of the cases appear on several occasions, thus as an *aide-mémoire* a list of text references is supplied in an appendix.

NOTES

[1] Representation of the Child in the Civil Courts. Research Project 1985–90.

[2] Thomas C et al. (1993): *The Duration of Care Proceedings: A Replication Study*. HMSO.

[3] Macleod A (1993): *Servicing Social Services: Local Authority Representation in Child Care Cases*. HMSO.

[4] Hunt J (1993): *Local Authority Wardships before the Children Act: The Baby or the Bathwater?* HMSO.

[5] The definition of a 'case' used in this study includes all the children in a family subject to the same set of proceedings.

[6] Adcock M; White R (1983): *The Administrative Parent: A Study of the Assumption of Parental Rights and Duties*. BAAF.

[7] Reported in Thomas C; Hunt J (1996): *The Care Workloads of the Civil Courts under the Children Act*. Research report to DoH. Centre for Socio-Legal Studies, University of Bristol.

3

Who gets to court?: a profile of the Children Act sample

- -

Tara O'Brien was 5 when her mother Vera finally left her violent husband and fled to relatives. The family were already well known to social services because of neglect and the police had been called many times to the home because of incidents of domestic violence. Tara and her four older siblings were eventually removed by the police and fostered. Some months later they were rehabilitated when Vera returned and went into a women's refuge.

From the time she entered primary school Tara's behaviour gave cause for concern. At 10 she was described as disruptive, aggressive and abusive. Vera had by then married Fred. When Tara was 11 she revealed that Fred had been sexually abusing her. Vera threw him out but neither she nor Tara told anyone outside the family.

At 13 Tara was arrested for theft and at 14 she was made subject to a Supervision Order. She was now presenting severe behaviour problems at home and school and was increasingly rejected by her mother and her siblings. The offences became more serious and at 15 Tara went into residential care. By this time she was drinking heavily and began to self-mutilate; she twice attempted suicide. After a series of fires in the children's home for which Tara was believed to be responsible she was referred to a child psychiatrist. Though noting a history of psychiatric problems in the family he found no evidence of major illness but described Tara as a very troubled teenager who was unwilling and unable to accept help.

When the local authority brought care proceedings Tara was 21 and her son Christopher, aged 4, had been taken into police protection for the second time in a month.

- -

The adults

Tara is a real person, not a composite character, and sadly none of the essential details of her story has been fabricated. None the less she exemplifies many of the characteristics of the parents we encountered in this research

(Figure 3.1). Of the 83 cases in our post-Act sample, for instance, 51 involved a parent who, like Tara, had been abused or in care as a child, 52 a parent suffering from an illness or disability (psychiatric disorder, learning difficulties, drug or alcohol dependency) which adversely affected their capacity to care for their children and 51 a parent with a criminal record.

Figure 3.1 *Who gets to court: the adults (n = 83)*

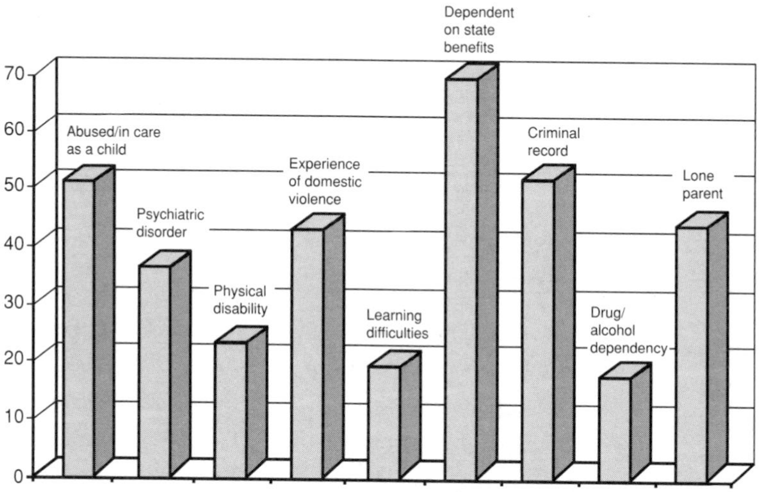

Like the majority of the case parents Tara was white and of UK origin although Christopher was one of the 25 index children of mixed parentage. She was also a young mother, having given birth when only 17. By this time she had returned home and Christopher's father Tomas was in prison. Although, as far as we could ascertain, only 11 mothers had not reached the age of majority when they gave birth to their first child, well over half were no more than 21. However most were considerably older than Tara by the time the sample court proceedings started, almost three-quarters being 25 or more.

On Tomas's release the couple lived together for a time although, like three in five of the other parents, they never married. The relationship was volatile and like half the sample mothers Tara was subjected to violence. By the time proceedings were brought she was struggling to bring up Christopher on her own (eight in ten couples were no longer living together and half the cases involved lone parents, all but one female). In company with another 71 families their sole legitimate source of income was state benefit.

A comparison of the families in this research with those in Gibbons'[1] analysis of child protection referrals demonstrates the more problematic profile of those who end up in the court system. Thus for example among families entering the child protection system:

- 13% involved mental illness (compared to 42% of the court sample);

- 27% involved domestic violence (compared to 51%);

- 54% were dependent on income support (compared to 84%);

- 36% were headed by a lone parent (compared to 52%); and

- one in seven parents had been abused as children (compared to one in three).

The children

It is a measure of the complexity and dislocation of many of these deprived and troubled families that of their 239 children 58% were not full siblings of the index child (49% of families). Almost a third (from 39% of families) were already being cared for outside the family unit.[2] However only 31 children (from 14 families) living in the same household as the case children were not drawn into proceedings. For the most part this was because of differences in age, gender or the quality of the parent/child relationship, although two 16-year-olds were able to give their own consent to accommodation under the new provisions of the Children Act rather than being subject to proceedings.

Of the children, 133 (61 male, 72 female) were the case children of the post-Act research. Typically a case comprised one (53) or two (17) children with only three cases in Area A and two in Area C having more than this. Eight of the 30 cases in Area B, however, involved three or more children (to a maximum of five). This is reflected in a higher mean family size of two compared to 1.4 and 1.3 in the other areas.

In the main these case children were young; mean age 4 years 10 months. In 50 cases the oldest child was under 5 and in 20 under a year (Table 3.1). Not surprisingly three-quarters were the youngest children in their families. However, 16 cases involved at least one child aged 10 or more and 11 *only* children of this age. Cases in Area C were particularly likely to involve older children: seven of the 24 cases brought by this authority related only to children aged 10 or more, and four of the six cases in the sample involving teenagers were from this area.

In spite of the preponderance of pre-schoolers, over a quarter of cases involved children considered to have special educational needs while in two-fifths some kind of health problem was recorded.

Table 3.1 *Age of children subject to proceedings*

	Area A	Area B	Area C	All areas
Oldest case child				
Mean (years)	4	4	6	5
% < 1 year	28	23	21	24
% 1–4	41	40	25	36
% 5–9	14	23	25	21
% 10 or more	17	13	29	19
Youngest case child				
Mean (years)	3	2	5	3
% < 1 year	38	40	21	34
% 1–4	45	57	33	46
% 5–9	7	—	17	7
% 10 or more	10	3	29	13
(n=)	*(42)*	*(50)*	*(32)*	*(133)*

Comparison with the pre-Act sample

The research suggests that the characteristics of families subject to proceedings have not changed substantially since the Act. They continue to be mainly poor, complex and dislocated families, known to both welfare agencies and the police. The differences in detail are usually small and may be the result of sampling bias. However the direction of the changes lends support to practitioner opinion that the Act is filtering out the less problematic cases, with higher incidences recorded of parents suffering from learning difficulties, drug or alcohol dependency and psychiatric disorders. The rise in this last category (from 27% to 42%) was most marked, suggesting there may be particular cause for concern. However the vulnerability of all these groups to compulsory intervention suggests a need to look more closely at the services available to help both the adults afflicted with such problems and the children who have to cope with their consequences.

The proportion of cases involving adults with a criminal record was high in both groups (around 60%). In the post-Act sample, however, the offences tended to be more serious: almost two-thirds involving incidents as serious as malicious wounding, grievous bodily harm, burglary, robbery, drug dealing, even single examples of arson, rape, blackmail and kidnapping.

Ethnicity

One of the factors the court must take into account when deciding whether to make a Care or Supervision Order is 'the child's background and any characteristics of his which the court considers relevant.'[3] An important consideration in setting up the study therefore was to try to ensure a reasonable number of children from ethnic minority groups. This was one of the reasons for locating the research in authorities with a sizeable urban population and specifically including inner-city areas.

Slightly over half the cases in the post-Act sample concerned children and parents who were of white UK descent. In 41 however, either a case child (40) or an adult still involved with the child (32) was not. As Table 3.2 shows, cases in Area C were most likely to involve a non-indigenous element, those in Area A the least, although the differences were more marked where the adults rather than the children were concerned.[4] Without a detailed analysis of the ethnic composition of the districts from which the sample was drawn it is not possible to say whether these figures indicate that a disproportionate number of ethnic minority families are subject to compulsory intervention. It would seem, however, to be a matter warranting further investigation.

The more detailed information recorded on the index children (Table 3.3) revealed that by far the largest minority group in the sample (25 children)

Table 3.2 *Ethnic composition of the sample*

	Area A %	Area B %	Area C %	All areas %
Case involves non-white UK				
child	45	50	50	48
adult	35	30	54	39
either	45	50	54	49
both	35	30	50	37
child only	10	20	0	11
Case involves non-European				
child	45	43	42	43
adult	35	23	42	33
either	45	43	42	43
both	35	23	42	33
child only	10	20	0	11
(n=)	*(29)*	*(30)*	*(24)*	*(83)*

were those of mixed parentage. Most of these children were first-generation racial mixes, with the predominant mix being white UK/other.

It will be seen that our use of the term 'non-white UK' defines a wide range of groups as of minority status, not all of whom would be commonly described in this way. The sample was therefore also analysed according to whether families were of non-European origin. These categories have been employed at various stages in the analysis to investigate any impact of ethnic differences and were also applied separately to adults and children, producing the multi-dimensional framework introduced in Table 3.2. Whilst it would be tedious to report the results on each dimension, important differences have been highlighted. However it should be borne in mind throughout that *numbers are small* and any apparent differences can only be indicative.

Table 3.3 *Ethnic origins of index children*

	No.
Single-race parentage	
White UK	45
Other European	1
African	3
Afro-Caribbean	2
Indian	2
Pakistani	3
Bangladeshi	1
Mixed parentage	
European mix	4
Non-European mix	5
European/non-European	12
Other/full details unknown	4

The children

The most obvious difference in relation to the children was that those from minority groups tended to be older. The mean age of the oldest case child in the white UK group for instance was 3.7 years, the youngest 2.3. Comparative figures for other children were 6.1 and 4.5. Cases involving children of 11 upwards were much more likely to involve non-European families, even more so when the child was a teenager. Concomitantly, such families were under-represented in cases involving children under 5. Even allowing for the age differential, we also found that slightly more children from non-European families were recorded as having special educational needs although the position was reversed in terms of health and disability.

The adults

The characteristics so noticeable in our profile of the adults were less frequently a feature of non-European families. These were half as likely to feature drug/alcohol abuse or learning disabilities (although the proportion suffering from a psychiatric disorder was only slightly less). They were almost three times as likely to have an adult in employment. The mothers tended to be older at the birth of their first child. Fewer were known to have been abused or in care as children and a much smaller proportion had a criminal record. In sum, on almost every one of a range of indicators of social morbidity it was the white UK families who presented the more troubled profile. As we shall see in the next chapter they also tended to have a longer period of enmeshment with welfare agencies.

Summary

The families caught up in child protection proceedings both before and after the Children Act tend to be drawn from the most vulnerable sections of society, victims of social inequity and personal misfortune. The majority of parents have been abused or in care as children; experienced fractured or abusive relationships as adults; are struggling with a range of psycho-social difficulties and living in straitened circumstances.

Those subject to statutory intervention under the Children Act present a greater concentration of problems than both the general population entering the child protection system and those subject to proceedings under previous legislation. This provides some supporting evidence that the filtering process has, as intended, become more rigorous. The adequacy of services available to particularly vulnerable groups, however, needs to be assessed.

The high proportion of children of ethnic minority or mixed parentage in the research sample may principally reflect the ethnic balance in the study areas. However the fact that the non-indigenous families presented a less problematic profile on all dimensions measured may indicate disproportionate representation. Ethnic monitoring of the use of statutory intervention would be needed to indicate whether there is system bias and, if so, what might be done to correct it.

[1] Gibbons J et al. (1995): *The Operation of Child Protection Registers*. HMSO.

[2] Forty-four children were in long-term care or adopted, 12 were with relatives or friends, 19 with another partner.

[3] Section 1(3)(d). Unless otherwise indicated, all section references are to the Children Act 1989.

[4] It should be noted that the fact that it was possible to establish these data on ethnic origin was a considerable improvement on the pre-Act situation where no information at all was recorded on over a fifth of cases.

4

Routes to court: the legal and welfare histories of the case families

Social work involvement

Families presenting the types of social problems described in the preceding pages are likely to have at least passing acquaintance with the child welfare system. Our data indicate that *even before the Children Act 1989* it was rare for cases to be completely unknown to social services (6; 6%) and that subsequently it has become even rarer (3; 4%) (Figure 4.1).

Figure 4.1 *Case current prior to events leading to proceedings*

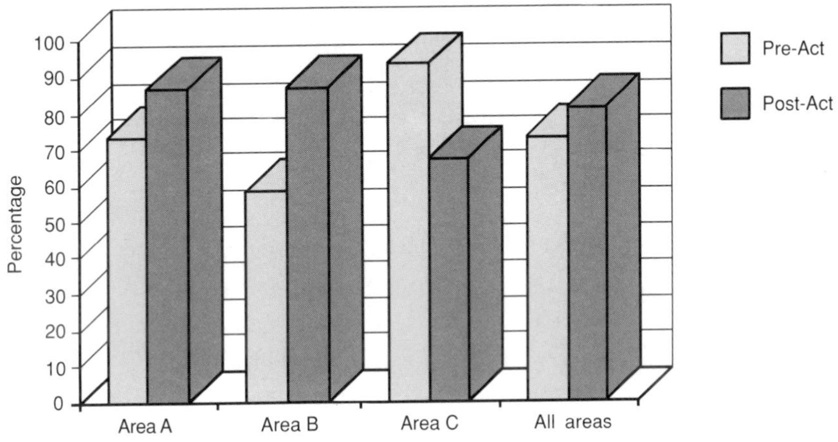

The proportion of families already being worked with immediately prior to the events leading to proceedings was strikingly high in both samples, at least three in four cases, though marginally greater post-Act. Children Act cases also tended to have been continuously worked with for rather longer (60% for more than a year compared to 54% pre-Act) the average period being 17 months in Area B, 22 months in Area C and over three years in Area A.

These aggregated figures, moreover, under-estimate the extent to which the legislation has affected practice. Prior to the Act, Area C had the smallest fraction of cases catapulting into court; post-Act the highest. The proportion of cases worked with for over a year also fell slightly, a reverse trend reflecting the prolonged industrial action in this area (Chapter 2). In contrast the proportion of cases going straight to court dropped dramatically in Area B whilst those worked with for more than a year rose from a third to a half. Even in Area A, whose cases tended to have been worked with longest pre-Act, there was a slight increase (Figure 4.2).

Figure 4.2 *Active cases: more than 12 months' continuous involvement prior to events leading to proceedings*

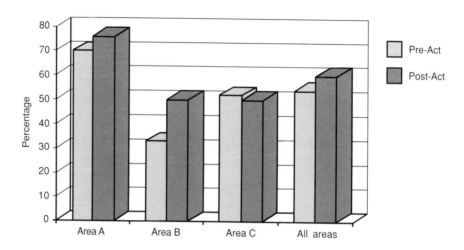

In a later section we look in detail at the efforts made to prevent the sample cases coming to court. At this point we shall note merely that post-Act active cases not only tended to have a longer 'run-up' to proceedings but were provided with more services in this period (Table 4.1). Ninety-four per cent of families (61) received some service other than contact with a social worker. Whilst this represents only a small global increase over pre-Act provision, greater change is evident when we look at particular services, for example domiciliary support, day care and family centres. Only in the area of financial/material help does the situation appear to be virtually unchanged whilst in terms of housing need the data suggest a deterioration.

Local authority records also note the refusal of other services in almost half the post-Act active cases (compared to under two-fifths of the pre-Act group). Thus the quantitative data suggest that the cases reaching court in the wake of the Children Act had problems which were proving *more resistant* to the welfare interventions on offer. This appears to be particularly the case in Area A where services were noted to have been rejected in half the pre-Act cases but nearer three-quarters of those initiated post-Act.

Table 4.1 *Services provided to case family in last continuous period of welfare involvement: comparative*

	All areas			
	Pre-Act		Post-Act	
	No.	%	No.	%
Domiciliary support	17	22	28	43
Day care	30	40	42	63
Day family centre	4	3	10	15
Care/residential placement (child)	29	38	32	48
Residential placement (family)	8	11	9	14
Specialist counselling/treatment (child)	15	20	17	25
Specialist counselling/treatment (adult)	22	29	32	48
Rehousing	15	20	8	12
Financial/material help	30	40	26	39
Other	8	11	19	28
Any of the above	70	92	63	94
(n=)	(76)		(65)	

Instances where requests for services are denied are less likely to be recorded in social services files and post-Act we noted only ten. There were, however, also a number of cases where it seems possible that things might have worked out differently had interventions been more timely, appropriate or skilful. This issue is explored further in Chapter 7.

Care experience

It will be evident from the previous section that most of the post-Act families were familiar with a range of home-based services. Many of their children also had experience of the care system. In both the pre- and post-Act sample, three in five families had had *at least* one child looked after by the local authority at some stage. Post-Act two in five had children currently looked after (some of them compulsorily) at the point the decision was taken to bring proceedings on the case children, compared to one in four pre-Act. Most notably in terms of local authority practice, as we shall explore later in this chapter, there was a fourfold increase in cases where the *case children* were already accommodated.

Child Protection Registration

Accommodation, like the voluntary care it replaced, is of course intended to be a service to families and some children may have been looked after for reasons which had little to do with child protection. The registration data, however, show such instances do not distort the overall picture. Sixty-four per cent (53) of the post-Act families had had at least one child on the Child Protection Register (CPR) even before the events leading to proceedings, rather more than pre-Act (59; 57%), while the difference in the proportions with children *currently* registered was even greater (45; 54% compared to 43; 41%). Children also tended to have been registered for longer: over half for a year or more post-Act compared to a third pre-Act.

As Figure 4.3 shows, the *majority* of case children, and again more than pre-Act, were *already* registered at the point court action was decided upon. In a further 16 cases (19%) the decision to register was made at the same time as the decision to proceed to court and in eight (10%) after court proceedings had begun. Surprisingly, 15 cases seem never to have been registered at all.

Figure 4.3 *Case children already on Child Protection Register prior to decision to bring proceedings*

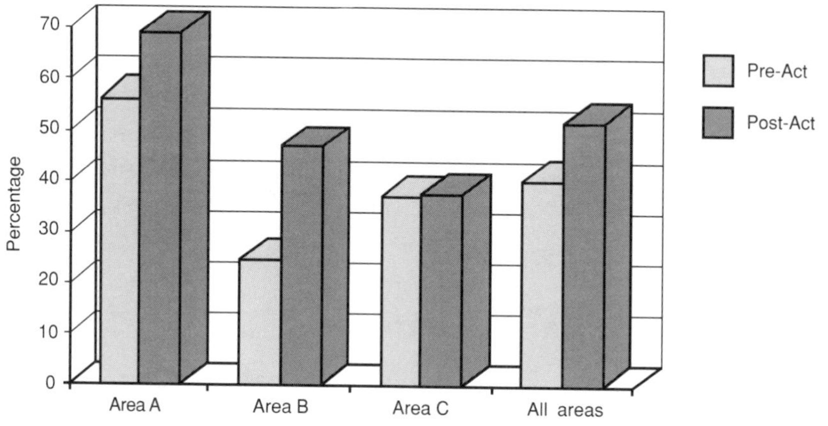

Previous compulsory intervention

Over a third of families taken to court under the Children Act had been through the whole process before (Figure 4.4). Some parents were at risk of losing their fourth, fifth or even sixth child. A further six had had children removed under some form of emergency protection although proceedings had not followed, while in an additional 21 cases care proceedings had been explicitly considered. Thus prior to the instigation of the sample proceedings the majority of post-Act families had already either been subject to or seriously considered for statutory intervention. This proportion (61; 74%) represents an increase on the pre-Act figures (62; 60%).

Figure 4.4 *Prior compulsory intervention in post-Act families (any child)*

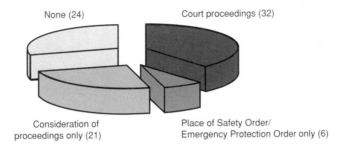

None (24)   Court proceedings (32)

Consideration of
proceedings only (21)   Place of Safety Order/
Emergency Protection Order only (6)

The percentage of cases where one of the case children had previous experience of child protection proceedings (Figure 4.5) was very similar in the two groups. However the proportion for whom proceedings had previously been explicitly considered was higher post-Act (21; 25% compared to 16; 15%); and highest of all in both periods in Area A (24% pre-Act; 38% post-Act).

Figure 4.5 *Prior compulsory intervention (post-Act case children)*

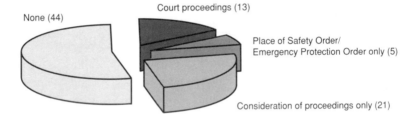

None (44)   Court proceedings (13)

Place of Safety Order/
Emergency Protection Order only (5)

Consideration of proceedings only (21)

Ethnic differences

From this brief overview of a number of indicators it will be evident that most of the cases subject to child protection proceedings before, and even more so after, the Children Act involved very troubled families who had been deeply and often chronically entangled within the child protection system. As indicated at the close of the previous chapter, however, this was rather less true of families involving adults from ethnic minority groups, particularly those of non-European origin (Table 4.2).

Most notably such families were less likely to be well known to welfare agencies. At the point the events leading to proceedings occurred, 95% of white families were either currently being worked with (47 cases) or had had previous periods of substantial involvement (6 cases). Only 20 (74%) of cases

Table 4.2 *Welfare and legal background: ethnic differences*

	Case involves non-European family %	Other cases %
Case current	74	84
Continuous involvement > 3 months	48	73
Non-case child care experience	4	23
Previous court proceedings	37	46
Seriously considered for proceedings only	29	50
Current CPR registration	52	70
(n=)	*(27)*	*(56)*

involving non-European families were current and none of the rest had had more than brief involvement. Current cases involving European families had, on average, also been continuously worked with for longer: 61% for over a year and 87% more than three months; the comparative figures for other families being 55% and 35%. Putting these figures together we found that one in two non-European families reached court within three months of their involvement with social services, *twice the rate* noted in the remainder of the sample. Non-European families were also less likely to have children other than the case children who had been or were being looked after, to have been involved in previous care or related proceedings, or to have been seriously considered for such proceedings.

Where such families were already being worked with, however, the case children were marginally more likely to be already on the Child Protection Register.[1] This fact may not be unrelated to the finding that despite their generally shorter continuous involvement with the welfare system, these families were in receipt of around the *same level* of service provision as the rest of the sample. They were also much *more* likely to have refused services.

Highways and by-ways

During the last continuous period of social work intervention the case children travelled one of seven main routes to court (Figure 4.6). The most direct was *Route 1:* such concern was felt about the parents' ability to care for a newborn baby that they were not given the opportunity to do so outside a legal framework. In all but one case this was because there had been major problems caring for previous children, usually resulting in removal.

Figure 4.6 Routes to court (n=83)

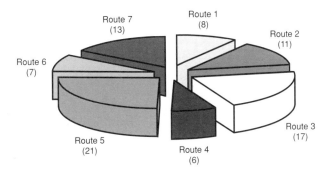

Route 7 (13) Route 1 (8) Route 2 (11) Route 6 (7) Route 5 (21) Route 4 (6) Route 3 (17)

Zara was Sandra's fifth child and Phil's second. Social services had been continuously involved for 11 years, ever since Sandra's first child Toby was removed on a Place of Safety Order when he was left unattended. Subsequent events are as detailed below, dated in relation to the start of the court proceedings on Zara.

10 years	Toby placed home on trial. Half-sibling Nicholas born.
9 years	Toby returned to care because of physical and emotional neglect.
7 years	Supervision Order substituted for Care Order.
3 years	Supervision Orders on both children (non-school attendance and neglect). Monique born, half-sibling to both the others.
2 years	Care Orders on Toby and Nicholas; Supervision Order on Monique.
15 months	Care proceedings on Monique following injury by Sandra's new partner Phil.
14 months	Programme of assessment of the prospects for Monique's rehabilitation breaks down. James born, Phil and Sandra's first child. Sandra and James admitted to a mother and baby home, later joined by Phil.
9 months	Proceedings initiated after Sandra and Phil leave the placement.
8 months	James subject to a Care Order and contact with Monique terminated.
5–4 months	Monique and James approved for adoption; Sandra, pregnant by Phil, lodges applications for contact and discharge of the Care Orders.

Two months later a pre-birth case conference recommended that the new baby should be removed immediately. Although subsequently Sandra said she would end her relationship with Phil and move into a mother and baby home, social services decided to pursue proceedings.

• •

In this group of cases, as Zara's case demonstrates, generally a great deal was known about the family, indeed in a sense the case got to court just because so much was known. In contrast knowledge was often very scanty in cases arriving via *Route 2*, none of which was being worked with prior to the events which led to proceedings; all erupted in some form of crisis, often accompanied by an Emergency Protection Order (EPO) or police powers of protection and were in court within a matter of days.

• •

Ahmed Khan came to the notice of social services when the police reported that in the course of enquiries into a matter in which his father might be involved, Mrs Khan had become very distressed and voiced fears of killing Ahmed in a variety of bizarre, highly specific ways. Ahmed appeared to be flourishing and there was no indication that Mrs Khan had ever done anything untoward to any child. However she did appear to be in the acute phase of a long-term psychiatric illness. The health professionals already involved were becoming increasingly concerned but had not thought it necessary to refer the case to the child protection system in the face of Mrs Khan's reluctance. There were known to be other children of an earlier marriage living with their father under a private law order.

Social services investigated and on the rather contradictory evidence available decided the risk was too substantial to be managed without greater support. Since Mr and Mrs Khan were not prepared to agree to alternative measures of protection an Emergency Protection Order (EPO) was taken.

• •

As we shall see later, cases arriving in court via this second route usually only did so because the parents, like Mr and Mrs Khan, would not agree to what the local authority considered to be adequate alternative means of ensuring the child was protected while investigations were completed. Thus as with the first group, though for different reasons, there was no intervening period when alternative ways of dealing with the problem were actually put in place. Together Routes 1 and 2 account for just over a quarter of cases in which there had been no previous proceedings on the case children.

In the majority of cases however the local authority *had* tried alternative options. In almost a quarter of first-time cases the children had remained at home while a range of services were offered (*Route 3*). Court action flowed either from the inability of such services to address the original problems sufficiently or from the emergence of new problems.

Routes 4, 5 and *6* together account for over half the whole sample and almost two-thirds of cases where there had been no previous proceedings. Here there was still an attempt to deal with difficulties on a voluntary basis but it was not felt safe for the child and parent to remain together in their home situation. Most commonly this involved separation (*Route 5*). There were however six cases where parent and child were placed together in some form of supervised setting, for example a mother and baby home, a residential family centre or – usually in the case of very young mothers – a foster home (*Route 4*).

Of course these categories represent a simplified version of reality. In seven cases the children, experienced both separation and a supervised setting (*Route 6*) and most children who had been separated had also spent some time at home. There were also the yo-yo children moving in and out of accommodation; those who moved from supervised placements with a parent back into the community and a few who seemed to be going round and round and back and forward repeatedly.

Finally there were the children who during this continuous period of social work involvement had been subject to previous court proceedings (*Route 7*).

- -

Sammi Collins was 3 when he was made subject to proceedings for the third time. He and his 4-year-old sister Tamsin were living with their parents Alice and Bill and Alice, still only 21, was again pregnant. Both children had been placed on the Child Protection Register as babies having being found unattended and several months later both were removed and care proceedings instituted after Sammi suffered what were alleged to be non-accidental injuries. They were returned home on Supervision Orders, by which time a third child had been born, unfortunately severely handicapped. She died two months later.

Sammi did not thrive at home where he was considered to be scapegoated and within a few months was again removed when social services applied to vary the Supervision Order to a Care Order. Following a positive assessment by an independent agency, however, he was returned home four months later; the application was withdrawn.

In the five months before the Supervision Order expired Sammi sustained minor injuries on 14 separate occasions. However, since his relationship with his mother was considered to be much improved and parental co-operation had been sustained it was decided that no legal action would be taken. The injuries continued, 10 being reported in the two months prior to the sample proceedings. Sammi and Tamsin claimed at least two of these were inflicted by Alice and medical opinion was that some injuries were unlikely to have been accidental and that the number of injuries was abnormal. Having concluded that Sammi was 'now receiving an unacceptable level of injuries whether or not they are accidental' social services asked for parental consent to accommodation, instituting proceedings when this was refused.

. . . .

Ethnic comparisons

The proportions of case children reaching court via most of these routes did not vary greatly with ethnic identity. Non-European children were rather less likely to have been placed in a supervised setting with their parent(s) en route and more likely to have experienced separation,[2] but the differences were small. They were also more vulnerable to compulsory intervention without any alternative being tried (Routes 1 and 2 combined). However there was only one example of a child from such a family being made subject to proceedings at birth (almost a quarter of the proportion of European families), whereas twice the proportion arrived in court via Route 2 (Table 4.3).

Table 4.3 Routes to court: ethnic differences

	Case involves non-European family		Other cases	
	No.	%	No.	%
Route 1	1	4	7	13
Route 2	6	22	5	9
Route 3	5	19	12	21
Route 4	1	4	5	9
Route 5	7	26	14	25
Route 6	3	11	4	7
Route 7	4	15	9	16
(n=)	(27)		(56)	

Points of entry to the court process

Care arrangements prior to any events precipitating court action

Immediately prior to the events precipitating proceedings[3] the majority of index children in the post-Act sample were living with at least one parent, usually at home. Just over a quarter were separated from any parent, while nine children had not so far been in their parent's care. The proportion of cases in which the child was still with a parent at this point was very similar across ethnic groups. However in non-European families this almost always meant placement at home, whereas several other families, though together, were in a supervised placement. Similarly, with one exception, children living apart from their non-European families were in local authority accommodation whereas other separated children formed a more disparate group which included new-born babies and children living with friends.

The use of accommodation as an alternative to court proceedings

Cases where the children were accommodated constituted a quarter of the post-Act sample. Clearly under the Children Act this has become a significant point of entry to the court process, particularly for children from minority ethnic groups, a third of whom were accommodated. Analysis of the circumstances in which the children were last accommodated[4] shows that in ten, i.e. almost half, this came about either in response to a parent's request (7 cases) or because of parental absence or hospitalisation (3 cases). While there were concerns about the family in each case in none had they reached the level where social services were considering *immediate* compulsory intervention.

In the remaining 11 cases, accommodation was 'negotiated' against a backdrop of possible court action. Although it was not always clear how explicitly parents had been made aware of the alternative scenario there were at least five cases in which the options had been plainly stated: agree accommodation or we go to court. In a further two it seems to have been the parent who dissuaded social services from a previously determined course. It should be noted that although non-European families were more likely to have children accommodated they were less likely to be subject to *enforced* arrangements. In all cases enforced accommodation was offered after the child was believed to have already suffered significant harm. Only one case might, in our judgement, have had difficulty satisfying the threshold criteria at that point: a case eventually diagnosed as Munchausen's Syndrome by Proxy in which a conflict of medical opinion might have undermined an immediate application to court.

Practitioners in all the groups interviewed expressed reservations about the use of accommodation as a diversionary strategy. These fell into three categories: issues of justice, lack of security and delay.

Natural and procedural justice

Concerns were expressed first about justice and fairness. Thus 'forced' accommodation was seen as basically dishonest, a perversion of the concept of accommodation which is intended to be a service to families. In this view if the local authority decides the child needs to be looked after and would take court action if parents do not agree then accommodation is not appropriate:

> My main anxiety is accommodation, I feel that is not really working. I don't know how you get round it; there's nothing illegal about it but social services are in such a strong position that parents have little option, if they don't comply with various conditions then the local authority will take proceedings. So social services manage to achieve the same result without actually going through court proceedings. In theory parents have complete parental responsibility; in reality they are quite powerless. (Solicitor)

> Accommodation is for those situations where parents need help and ask for help. But if the local authority would take proceedings if the family don't agree then they should take proceedings. I feel legal proceedings can protect families. I know they're very stressful and that has to be taken into account but they can also protect families against local authorities abusing their power. (Guardian ad Litem)

One might expect this position to be held most forcibly by practitioners within the legal system. However similar qualms were also expressed by some social services personnel:

> The fact that we have to go for accommodation with the threat of an application if parents don't agree, that's a much more subtle use of power than actually putting it before the court. I would have thought it felt more oppressive. Best practice would ensure you would use accommodation wherever possible but this is forcing accommodation. (Team manager)

For lawyers, as one might expect, issues of due process were central. Thus several cited the poor protection for the rights of parents and children within the *welfare* system compared to the sophisticated mechanisms which have developed within the *legal* system. Once a case gets to court parents have a right to be legally represented; they are entitled to legal aid irrespective of income; there will be a guardian to make an independent enquiry into the merits of the application. None of these protections exists within the welfare domain. Parental consent to accommodation may be neither informed nor freely given: while it may be good practice for social workers to encourage parents to seek legal advice, it is not compulsory and parents may not see the importance of getting themselves to a solicitor. Even if they do, the advice the lawyer can give is limited by the provisions of the Green Form scheme.[5] Local authorities may not allow the lawyer to attend case conferences or other crucial meetings. There is no equivalent of the Guardian ad Litem offering an independent social work opinion. Thus while decisions about accommodation may be made in the 'shadow' of the court[6] they none the less lack its protections.

Some lawyers also suggested that because local authorities achieve a measure of actual control over the child without having to satisfy any legal tests they may be tempted to 'negotiate' accommodation in cases they suspect to be evidentially weak, even though parents may be unaware of their doubts and agree thinking they are thereby avoiding certain court action. There was a little evidence from our research data that this does actually happen. However it does not appear to be widespread. As we shall see later, generally it has been the so-called *no order principle* that has made social services most hesitant about going to court, not the threshold criteria.

Another aspect of this concern about fairness was the fear that in all but very short periods of accommodation parents' rights will be diminished simply by the passage of time. Courts tend to be reluctant to disturb the status quo before the final hearing; by which time the outcome may be a foregone conclusion.

Insecurity

Other criticisms centred on the insecurity of the arrangement for the child, the carer and the social worker. Abolition of the 28-day notice period required by the previous legislation was the key criticism here, since it exposed placements to the threat of disruption. In reality, attempted on-the-spot removal may not be a very frequent occurrence; there was none in the sample. But the effect of fear itself should not be under-estimated. Thus a number of local authority personnel argued for the restoration of a notice period.[7] Interestingly so did one lawyer who argued that accommodation would be used more if there was a period of notice:

> The real weakness is that one can't prevent the parents' right to have the child home and undo, at very short notice, whatever arrangement has been made. I think in that situation it's understandable that the local authority say 'Well, yes, she can agree to accommodate, but for how long?' I think it would reinforce agreements if the accommodation arrangements could be such that . . . parents couldn't simply turn round and take them out of care without giving at least 7 days' notice.

Delay and drift

The third major issue highlighted by practitioners was delay. As one team manager put it:

> One danger is that the Children Act will re-introduce drift. There isn't any framework. We haven't any time-scales for children in accommodation within which time there has to be a long-term viable plan. So it's left to individuals and the whole question of leeway, what is reasonable, the whole thing seems to be fraught and unmanageable.

A solicitor illustrated his anxieties by describing a particular case of a seriously injured child whose parents denied any abuse but agreed to accommodation for purposes of assessment:

> I followed them through about three case conferences. I came in just after the first and was horrified about the time-scale of the local authority plan; they weren't thinking of returning the child for at least three months. This was a young child and there was already a worry about the relationship between mother and daughter because of the length of time the child had been in hospital, and I was also concerned about the level of contact.

> After discussion with the parents it was decided I would write what I hope was quite a conciliatory letter to social services . . . basically saying we didn't agree this time-scale was in the child's best interests and said if we couldn't amend it within so many weeks they would have to take it to court. It never went to court; they brought meetings forward and we went along and it was clear everyone was co-operating. I felt I managed to get that child home at least six/eight weeks earlier than otherwise.

What worried me was the time-scale they were looking at, what happened if at the end of that three months it all broke down, they'd then go to court anyway and you'd start the timetable of another assessment and meantime that child is losing its relationship with its parents.

Delay in the sample cases

Examination of the sample cases showed delay could arise in a number of ways:

1 Tardy social work decision-making in the absence of a clearly set timetable. Once the immediate crisis is passed, more pressing cases are likely to take over and the case can slip from sight. Accommodated cases may also be dealt with by the review process rather than case conference so that there is less external monitoring.

2 Reluctance to accept no progress is being made on a voluntary basis. Even where the case remains a priority it can be hard to accept that working on a voluntary basis with parents is going nowhere. Parents may therefore be given *one last chance* several times.

3 Anticipated difficulties in satisfying the statutory criteria. Lawyers seem to regard such cases as potentially being particularly troublesome.[8] Thus putting it to the test may be postponed.

4 Delay in implementing the decision to go to court. Legal departments are overstretched. Even when social services have taken the decision to bring proceedings and are supported by legal opinion the case may be constantly overtaken by other more pressing cases.

As Table 4.4 shows, by the time of the first court hearing the 21 accommodated children had spent an average of 38 weeks being looked after. Although just under a quarter reached court within 13 weeks the same proportion took over a year. These figures are particularly worrying given that all but two of the children were less than 5 and ten were under 2.

Moreover, as we shall see later, the court system hearing care proceedings had become increasingly log-jammed. Typically cases involving accommodated children spent a further 24 weeks in the court process so that by the final hearing, on average, well over a year had elapsed since these children embarked on their most recent period in accommodation. Those who were facing a future outside the family, usually adoption, could expect to contend with further delay and another set of court proceedings before their future was legally secured and, in all but one case (where the foster mother was to be approved as an adoptive parent), at least one more move.

Table 4.4 *Previously accommodated children:* the deferment of decisions*

	Period in accommodation** prior to proceedings	Duration of court proceedings	Total period looked after	Interval accommodation to final court hearing
Mean (weeks)	38	24	56	57
Range (weeks)	5–91	11–46	21–128	21–128
> 13 weeks	16	18	21	21
> 26 weeks	10	5	19	19
> 39 weeks	6	2	15	15
> 52 weeks	5	0	9	9

* excluding emergency accommodation   **last continuous period of accommodation

On a more positive note, we did find that both before and during the court proceedings these children had experienced a surprising amount of placement stability. Only two of the 21 cases had more than one placement during proceedings and none more than two; moreover there were only six cases where the children had more than one placement in total and none more than three. Thus at least, few were taking with them the experience of multiple short-term placements where there had been no possibility of developing attachments, even if the breaking of those attachments would be painful.

Parental perceptions of enforced accommodation

Interviews with a sample of parents of accommodated children[9] revealed that when faced with the offer of *forced* accommodation they felt under pressure, threatened, coerced and boxed in:

> They kept threatening me with an EPO if I didn't let them have their way. I didn't really agree to accommodation or reducing contact to one day a week.

> I signed it for a quiet life, to be seen to be co-operating but I thought to myself, am I signing something I will regret just to get them off my back?

As the second quote suggests, most parents agreed to accommodation in the hope that by doing so they would be able to keep their children, even if they had a worrying anxiety that by doing so they had actually signed the children away. As we have seen for this sample, those underlying suspicions generally proved correct; few children returned home. Parents therefore described feeling deceived as the period of accommodation stretched into months and ended with the local authority taking care proceedings anyway. Some suspected it had all been a deep-laid plot.

A worrying number of parents seemed unaware of their legal rights. Many said that with hindsight they realised they had needed more information and wished they had taken advice from a knowledgeable solicitor. Ironically, some said, their lack of knowledge was held against them in court. One father who was still trying to get his children back three years later told us:

> When we found out that because the children were in voluntary care we could have taken them home, social services changed and went for orders. In court the guardian said we could not have cared because we could have picked the children up any time.

Some parents were confused and bewildered about what they had to do while the children were accommodated in order to get them back:

> The thing is, you don't know what they want from you, what they are looking for, what they expect, what alternatives are there. Nobody tells you anything, they just carry on.

Others complained that goals were unreasonable but when they rejected them they were damned as being unco-operative. Distrust was compounded when goals changed. Most parents who felt their children were accommodated under duress spoke of feeling powerless and in one father's words:

> Social services don't listen to the Children Act; they don't work in partnership, they do what they like.

Of course, it could be said, why should we expect anything else? Parents who have been through care proceedings, particularly those who have lost their children, are bound to feel disenchanted and bitter. Moreover this study was concerned only with cases which reach court, the ones, therefore, for whom accommodation as a helping strategy has failed. Other studies looking at a broader spectrum of cases[10] suggest there are many other families who have had positive experiences and better outcomes.

The research data do not indicate that accommodation should never be used as an alternative to court proceedings. Like Owen[11] we recognise its potential value. As an alternative to an Emergency Protection Order it can provide a useful breathing space in which to explore alternatives to court action and, as we shall see in the next chapter, even where court action does result, it facilitates a more planned approach to proceedings. We would argue none the less that it has to be clearly recognised that accommodation in the shadow of the court is qualitatively different from accommodation as service. Indeed what parents had to say reinforced what practitioners told us, that it is a contradiction in terms. If accommodation is to continue to be used as a diversionary strategy it is necessary to devise some more stringent *safeguards* to prevent abuse and to prevent children drifting into long-term but insecure care.

Summary

Even before the Children Act statutory intervention rarely involved families who were completely unknown to child protection agencies. The majority were already being worked with prior to any event which precipitated legal action, while many had had children in care and on the Child Protection Register.

The Act has made it even less likely that compulsion will be an early response to family difficulties. Post-Act the proportion of previously known and active cases was higher, duration of continuous involvement longer; services provided greater. Families were more likely to have had children in care or on the Child Protection Register, while the case children themselves were not only more frequently registered but had been registered for longer. The voluntary approach was also more often persisted with in the face of difficulties: services had been refused in a higher proportion of cases and more had been seriously considered for court action at an earlier stage. Such findings indicate that the emphasis in the Act on exploring alternatives to compulsory intervention has had a real impact.

Families from ethnic minority groups tended to be less chronically and deeply entangled with the child protection system and to have a greater incidence of service refusal. It seems possible that difficulties in providing a culturally appropriate response to child protection issues may be exposing such families to a higher level of intervention. This issue warrants further investigation.

Families subject to care proceedings reach court by a diversity of paths. Seven main routes were identified, varying from babies protected compulsorily from birth or previously inactive cases which erupted in crisis and were in court within a matter of days, to those which had run the gamut of home-based services, residential placements, accommodation or previous court action.

Immediately prior to any events precipitating proceedings six in ten index children were living with at least one parent, usually at home. One in ten had not so far been in their parents' unmonitored care while over a quarter were separated, usually accommodated by the local authority.

Accommodation has become a significant point of entry to the court process, particularly for children from ethnic minority groups. The use of accommodation as a strategy to avoid or defer court action is controversial. While it can provide a breathing space to explore alternative options and facilitate a planned approach should proceedings prove necessary, it needs to be recognised as qualitatively different from accommodation as a service. Safeguards must be devised to prevent abuse and ensure children do not drift into long-term, insecure care. Periodic monitoring is recommended.

NOTES

[1] These figures exclude cases where statutory intervention was taken at birth.

[2] Figures arrived at by combining Routes 4 and 6 (experience of supervised setting) and 5 and 6 (separation).

[3] Therefore excluding placements made as the result of Emergency Protection Orders or alternative forms of short-term protection.

[4] These data relate only to the period of accommodation leading to the sample court proceedings.

[5] A publicly funded renumeration scheme under which solicitors can provide time and a limited amount of legal assistance.

[6] Mnookin R (1979): Bargaining in the Shadow of the Law: the case of divorce. *Yale Law Journal*, 88.

[7] Abolition of the 28-day notice period was not recommended by the Child Care Law Review.

[8] Eekelaar J; Dingwall R (1990): *The Reform of Child Care Law*. Tavistock/Routledge.

[9] Reported in more detail in Freeman P; Hunt J (1998): *Parental Perspectives on Care Proceedings*. The Stationery Office.

[10] Packman J; Hall C (1998): *From Care to Accommodation*. The Stationery Office; Thoburn J et al. (forthcoming): *Safeguarding Children with the Children Act*. The Stationery Office.

[11] Owen M (1992): *Social Justice and Children in Care*. Avebury.

5 *Triggering legal action*

Events leading to proceedings

The care arrangements for a child prior to intervention are a key variable in determining whether an application to court can be made in a planned way. Data on the post-Act sample cases show that where children have been living at home the decision is most likely to be crisis-driven and that the majority of proceedings initiated following a crisis (34 in 38) concern such children. Pre-Act, over three-quarters of our sample cases involved children in this highest risk group; post-Act just over half were in this category, whilst the proportion of children looked after by the local authority, the lowest risk group, had risen from less than one in ten to one in four. This almost certainly explains most of the parallel fall in the relative proportion of crisis-driven cases, from 71% to 46%. (Figure 5.1).

Figure 5.1 *Decision to bring proceedings precipitated by crisis*

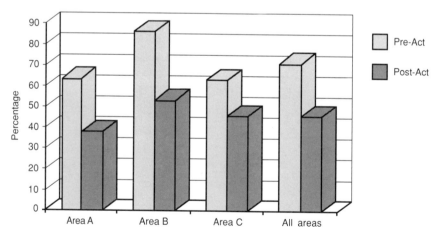

Disaggregating the Year 1 and Year 2 Children Act data suggests a continuing downward trend. However a degree of caution is needed in view of the differences in the way the two samples were collected (see Chapter 2). Since the Year 2 sample was dependent on referrals from the local authority, crisis cases may be under-represented, contacting the research team not being in the front of practitioners' minds when dealing with an emergency.

Cases arriving in court as the result of a crisis generally seemed to involve rather older children, the youngest case child being on average three years older than in other cases. Almost three-quarters were believed to be already suffering significant harm, usually as the result of physical abuse. Although differences are small it appeared that families in which either an adult or child was from a non-white UK group seemed to increase the chances of proceedings being crisis-driven. This is consistent with other characteristics of the minority families previously noted, the children generally being older, for instance, and a greater proportion living with their parents at home.

Initial protective action

The use of compulsory measures of protection

Although the research suggests that the chances of a case arriving in court in crisis are less under the Children Act than under previous legislation, they also show that in Areas A and C proceedings which did start in this way were more likely to have attracted formal measures of protection. Only Area B, which had a particularly high rate of cases beginning with compulsory emergency intervention pre-Act, showed a reduction. This area also had the highest fraction of post-Act cases in which alternative measures of emergency protection were arranged (Table 5.1).

Table 5.1 Post-Act crisis cases: initial protective action

	Area A	Area B	Area C	All areas
Voluntary				
Child at home	—	1	—	1
Supervised placement with parent(s)	—	2	—	2
Alternative placement without parent(s)	3	2	2	7
Compulsory				
Police protection	7	9	7	23
Emergency protection	4	4	3	11
(n=)	(14)	(18)	(12)	(44)

The use of compulsory emergency protection as a routine preventative non-emergency measure – for example to ensure that a child is not removed from hospital even when parents are not threatening this – was a common practice in our pre-Act sample. Post-Act it has become quite rare, only being used on three children, all babies in respect of whom pre-birth decisions had been made to apply for care proceedings initiated by an Emergency Protection Order (EPO) and where there was reason to believe parents would otherwise remove the baby.

Other than these three babies, there were only 11 cases in which post-Act emergency protection was initially provided by means of a court order. In a half of all crisis cases, and two-thirds of those attracting compulsory measures of protection, it was police powers which were invoked first (Table 5.1). However in contrast to pre-Act practice, none of these cases proceeded directly from police protection to care proceedings.[1] Most were followed by an Emergency Protection Order whilst in three voluntary measures of temporary protection were agreed.

As far as our sample cases were concerned, therefore, it seems that whilst court action post-Children Act was less likely to be precipitated by a crisis, where crises did arise in cases which proceeded to court they were *more likely* to be handled by means of compulsory measures of protection, in which police protection still played a substantial, if reduced, role. Yet, as the following section will show, this scenario does not fit easily with practitioner perceptions.

The approach to emergency protection under the Children Act

The majority view in all practitioner groups interviewed was that post-Act practice is characterised by a more measured approach to and minimal use of emergency protection. In consequence most Emergency Protection Orders (not simply those in the sample cases) were seen as justified, indeed unavoidable, even by solicitors commonly acting for parents. Only five solicitors and four Guardians ad Litem gave examples of dubious applications. Far more typical are the following comments:

> My impression is they've only been used when necessary. I haven't come across a case where the local authority acted totally unnecessarily. What has changed with the whole of the Children Act thinking is that social services aren't likely to go for an Emergency Protection Order unless it's absolutely essential. (Solicitor)

> It has clarified their thinking. In the past they used to go and get a Place of Safety Order at the drop of a hat. It has made their awareness greater and they are much more reluctant to remove children. (Guardian)

A range of factors were perceived to be pushing practice in this direction:

- the new legal criteria themselves are clearer, more demanding and stricter;

- the evidence is subject to more rigorous scrutiny by the courts;

- legal departments are more involved in considering the strength of the evidence before an application is made and are judged to adopt a cautious approach; and

- best practice under the Children Act is seen to be about partnership, negotiation, voluntarism and the importance of maintaining family links.

As a result we were told:

> We consider much more carefully; look at whether we've done things; whether there's any option. Trying alternatives; the emphasis is on partnership. (Team manager)

The picture of course is not black and white. There was evidence that in some area teams the pre-Act approach to emergency protection was already following Children Act principles; equally post-Act there was still some criticism of local authorities 'jumping the gun', or using compulsion without exploring the possibilities for agreement. But the overall trend of opinion in Areas A and B was clear, summed up by a team manager from the latter:

> The Act has led to better practice. In the past the Place of Safety Order (POSO) would have been in the front of our minds; the EPO is in the back. We look at alternatives first; the EPO is the last consideration.

Area C was somewhat anomalous. Pre-Act, we were told, few cases began with emergency orders and the departmental ethos discouraged such action. However industrial action and cuts in resources had generated a more crisis response approach, in which emergency protection, particularly police protection, had come to feature more strongly:

> We're using EPOs more; we rarely used Place of Safety Orders. Before the strike we did provide a Children Act service as near as dammit; what is disturbing now is we have the Children Act but we don't have the resources. So you move into EPOs whereas with the equivalent resources we might not have done that.

This may be sufficient to explain the data in this authority, particularly given the striking reduction in crisis cases in the second year, by which time the department was returning to a more normal operation.

One possible *general* explanation for the paradoxical post-Act proportionate increase in compulsory emergency protection is the continued prevalence of police protection. However there was no evidence in the data that it was police attitudes, rather than social services policies, which were driving practice. Examination of the circumstances in which police powers were exercised reveals this was done unilaterally in only two cases. In the remainder social services had either requested the police to assist (9), were jointly involved in decision-making (5), were consulted by telephone (1) or the decision was made in the context of interagency consultation on the case (6) sometimes involving provisional plans to take compulsory action.

There is no evidence that the discrepancy reflects practice changes between sample collection and interviewing. Although, overall, the proportion of cases starting with emergency protection was lower in our second year sample this was largely attributable to the declining proportion of crisis-driven cases.

Our preferred explanation is that for the most part post-Children Act practice has been characterised by more strenuous *attempts* to avoid compulsory intervention on an emergency basis and that the cases which did attract such orders were among the more intractable or serious. We have reached this conclusion on the basis of the following data:

- the increased proportion of post-Act cases in which the decision to seek statutory powers did not proceed from a crisis;

- the six cases in which the intention was to bring proceedings on notice but the plan was overtaken by subsequent events;

- the 21 additional cases in which non-compulsory measures of short-term protection were either agreed (9) or rejected by the parents (10) or other relatives (2); and

- the further three cases where although the immediate emergency was dealt with by police powers, agreement was subsequently reached with parents to secure the child's protection pending the first court hearing and a fourth where an Emergency Protection Order was sought only after such an agreement proved unacceptable to the children.

Of the 83 post-Act sample cases there were only 12 in which there was no evidence of any of the above. Even here one might deduce some possible reasons why there had apparently been no attempt to avoid compulsion. These included parents refusing (1) or unable because of mental illness (2) to discuss the situation with social services; two cases where previous voluntary agreements had failed; one where a Supervision Order was already in force; allegations of severe physical and/or sexual abuse (2); and two cases where the extended family was providing protection but it was unclear whether the Emergency Protection Order was providing security for them, the child or the local authority.

The remaining three cases, all in Area C, were previously inactive cases beginning with police protection in which the decision to seek an Emergency Protection Order was taken the same day. In one of these, which blew up on a Friday, there would have been little time for manoeuvre since the arrangements for continued protection would need to be in place by the Monday morning. In the other two cases, social services chose to apply for Emergency Protection Orders on notice. Since both crises occurred on a Wednesday it is possible that here too the decision-making process was dictated by considerations of timing, a point to which we shall return.

We would therefore conclude that although the bare quantitative data are at apparent odds with practitioner reports of post-Act practice, a careful case by case analysis can explain much of the discrepancy. This also confirms practitioner views that agency decision-making around initial protective action is case-specific rather than routinised and is influenced by philosophies, policies and practices which are at least formally hostile to compulsory measures.

There remain, however, questions about the degree to which social work practitioners have embraced or have been forced into voluntarism and whether the new approach places children at increased risk.

Conviction or constraint?

Disquiet about the move away from the use of emergency powers was voiced by a number of social services practitioners such as the team manager who said:

> We do all sorts of things now to avoid EPOs. But whether what we do is better, from the perspective of keeping children safe . . .

His anxieties focused particularly on the use of the *extended family* to provide initial protection, citing a case where the family agreed that a child who had been physically injured should be placed with his grandmother, who would contact the police if the parents tried to remove him. Under the old legislation:

> We would have taken a POSO and left the child with granny. I think that would have made the child safer. As it was it served its purpose but I would have felt more comfortable if there had been an EPO.

These doubts were expressed even more forcibly by a colleague from another office:

> I think the next child death will be that we didn't take an EPO and placed with other relatives.

Such anxieties may also be reflected in the small number of sample cases where relatives were used to provide initial protective action (7) and the even smaller number where such arrangements were not covered by an Emergency Protection Order (2).

The emphasis on working *in partnership* with parents was seen as another source of risk:

> There's a bit more hesitancy around due to the need to work in partnership; prior to the Act less attention would have been given to whether parents have been asked to co-operate on a voluntary basis. The decision may be risky or contentious but we have to ask first for voluntary co-operation.

A third theme was the need for *better evidence* to satisfy stricter grounds:

> I think the criteria are too strict, it feels like something has to happen before you can get an order; we need to have a child badly physically assaulted before you can protect them. I do get fearful that we might leave things. Many times when I'm tempted to take an EPO I feel I have to stand back and say well I'm not going to get it so I don't do it. I get worried that I will be too relaxed about situations.

This social worker cited a case in which he considered the child was left at risk because of anticipated legal difficulties in proving the grounds rather than a professional estimate of the balance of risk:

> We had a number of concerns about a family because of alcohol abuse and incidents of extreme marital violence and the child being exposed to that over and over again and mother failing to understand the need to protect. Then the child was involved in a fracas, she was held during an incident in which mother was hurt. We had everything arranged at conference level for removal but then we discussed it with legal and it didn't happen. It left me feeling

really unhappy. I felt really really uncomfortable with it. This was a man who changed extremely with drink, he'd been arrested many times for assault, waving an axe. A POSO would have been easier to get. The case conference members were really up in arms because we hadn't taken the Emergency Protection Order.

The influence of the legal department

Some degree of conflict between social services and their legal advisors about Emergency Protection Order applications was reported by social workers, team managers and local authority lawyers in all three areas. One of the more dramatic instances in the sample cases concerned Christopher O'Brien.

- -

When Christopher was 2 he and Tara moved into their own accommodation. Despite a range of supports things gradually began to deteriorate. While Tara's love for Christopher was not in doubt, there was increasing pessimism about her ability to provide secure and nurturing care. After a fire destroyed the house the situation rapidly degenerated: Tara was living a semi-nomadic chaotic existence and Christopher was witness to bouts of uncontrolled and violent behaviour when she was depressed or drunk. At intervals she attacked both his environment (home, school), people known to him (teacher, Vera) and herself.

Opinion among practitioners was reluctantly moving towards taking protective action when Tara dramatically slashed her arms. She was taken to hospital where, according to reports: 'she refused treatment, set fire to the casualty room and attacked staff'. Social services consulted their legal department about applying for an Emergency Protection Order but:

> had all sorts of problems. The advice was that mother doing such a dramatic piece of self-harm was not actually harmful to the child and social services couldn't apply for an EPO. There was an awful lot of argy bargy: social services felt there were sufficient grounds for an Emergency Protection Order and legal didn't. Social services thought the child was at incredible risk but that wasn't shared by legal. Consideration was given to sectioning mother because she was so out of control but it couldn't be done because she was intoxicated. So the police took an order because social services were being advised they wouldn't get it.

According to the social worker, who had naturally shared his frustration: 'The feeling within the office was that before the Act we could have got a POSO on the evidence easily.'

- -

Prior to the Act, the chances of such a stand-off occurring would have been infinitesimal. In all three authorities a high proportion of Place of Safety Orders were taken by the police and even where they were not, lawyers would have been consulted only in exceptional circumstances. Post-Act it is unusual for them *not* to be consulted, a point made repeatedly in interviews with local authority lawyers:

> We never got involved when POSOs were around, we usually stepped in once they'd got those and went for interim care. Now it's different. We're involved right from the start.

Indeed in one area the legal department had initially made sure of this by holding the application forms centrally! Whether this was necessary must be doubted; social workers appear to have been only too keen to get legal backing. In one of the sample cases, for instance, advice was sought from three lawyers before social services got the answer they clearly felt they needed in order to proceed.

The interview data suggest local authority lawyers see their role at this stage as not only establishing the grounds for the Emergency Protection Order but checking how far alternatives have been explored and attempting to ensure a calm assessment of the risks involved, a process, it was acknowledged, not always appreciated:

> Sometimes the social worker has rung up saying they want to go for an EPO and finds it difficult to understand when we ask what other options are available and they say we don't want to do that and it's not always the case where it would be appropriate for that to happen. Sometimes you have to play the Devil's Advocate and say you will have to respond to that in court; can you be satisfied that you can respond?

Ultimately, of course, lawyers recognise that the decision is not theirs and we were told of a few cases which did proceed to court against advice. Only one failed, confirming the prevailing view that: 'it's not the criteria, it's the way they are interpreted by legal.'

Taking risks

It would be over-simplistic, however, to see the dynamics of the decision-making process starkly in terms of anti-interventionist legal departments restraining anxious social work practitioners. Both groups have been influenced by the ethos of the Act so that in many instances social services were exercising their own restraints, even if, as we have seen, there were some anxieties about the consequences.

It was clear from the data that the way these social service departments responded to crisis situations had changed, with accommodation frequently being offered as an alternative to emergency protection. What was more difficult to establish was whether their threshold of risk had also changed so that children were being left exposed to harm following incidents which in the past would have led to their removal. Management of the crisis cases in the sample suggested the former, since only one child was allowed to remain in the same situation which had given rise to concern. Paradoxically in the pre-Act sample there were four. However if we look further back in the process things look rather different.

Of the sample cases which were already being worked with prior to the events leading to proceedings, thirty-five involved children still living at home. In 11 cases we identified previous incidents where emergency action might have been taken, but was not invoked. It is perhaps not surprising then that in seven of these 11 cases the crisis which precipitated care proceedings was responded to with compulsion. Nine of these 11 cases occurred in Area A, which may explain the proportionate post-Act increase in their use of such intervention referred to earlier.

• •

For 18 months social services had been working with Millie Smisson, who had left her husband because of his violence to herself and the children and long-term sexual abuse of Julie, now 16. Many services were offered to help Millie adjust to her new circumstances and care for her son Ben (6), although there were concerns about her excessive drinking and ability to care for and protect him. After a year these concerns had not been adequately addressed and Ben was placed on the Child Protection Register because of 'clear evidence of neglect' and the risk of 'all kinds of abuse'.

In the ensuing months Millie was drunk on numerous occasions. Ben continued to be neglected, dirty and smelly, frequently hungry, begging or stealing food and money. He was seen wandering the streets late at night. At home, which was poorly furnished and dirty, he regularly witnessed violence, the threat of violence and inappropriate sexual activity and was exposed to a whole range of dangers from the casual acquaintances whom Millie allowed in and with whom Ben was sometimes left. On other occasions he was left unattended. Pre-Act, the social worker told us:

> We would have intervened earlier, probably warded. We considered taking
> an EPO several times before we went to court and the child's solicitor
> pointed out two occasions when we could have got one.

This was confirmed in interview with this solicitor: 'The child had been at risk so long. They'd had people alerting them to the risks and they hadn't done anything.'

● ●

Even when social services reluctantly concluded that removal was unavoidable they did so by means of an application on notice, preparing Ben in advance of the court hearing at which they obtained an Interim Care Order. As illustrated by the next example, however, the danger of moving towards a more planned style of intervention is that the court may not grasp the immediacy of the risks to the child.

● ●

Colin and Antony Wyllie, aged 6 and 3, lived with their mother Grace, who suffered from chronic schizophrenia. Both children were wards of court although previous Supervision Orders had expired. Grace's care of the children had always been marginal even with considerable input from welfare agencies and in the months preceding the care application concern had mounted. There were a number of occasions when because of inadequate supervision the children placed themselves at grave risk, crossing a busy road, for example, and climbing up on a roof. 'Running around as they were, one day something was bound to happen' (team manager); 'It was only by the grace of God those children were still alive' (Guardian ad Litem).

Despite considering an Emergency Protection Order on a number of occasions social services eventually applied for an Interim Care Order on notice but at the first hearing the Judge refused the application on the grounds that 'I've read the papers and I'm not reading urgency.' The local authority decided not to appeal but to seek an Emergency Protection Order at the next opportunity, which arose ten days later. This incident was a good deal less serious than many earlier ones (and may not in fact have met the criteria). Under this threat Grace agreed the children should be accommodated.

● ●

Compulsory protection

Characteristics of cases attracting compulsory measures of protection

Analysis of cases which did begin with compulsory measures of protection in the main supports the view that decision-making around emergency protection is largely situation-dependent. The two factors most strongly linked with such action were (i) that the case was inactive at the point the events leading to proceedings arose and/or (ii) that those events involved some form of crisis. Age also seemed to be important even within crisis cases, with the youngest child in compulsory cases being, on average, more than two years older than those protected in other ways. Tests to associate the use of compulsion with particular characteristics of the adults concerned (for example physical or mental disability, addiction, criminal record, history of abuse or being in care as a child) showed that if anything these were protective factors, probably because their visibility meant they were already being worked with.

Ethnic differences

Families from minority groups however, as indicated earlier, more frequently came to the notice of the child protection system in circumstances which would render them vulnerable to emergency measures: they tended to present in crisis and were less likely to be currently active or previously well known. Thus there was less chance that the immediate crisis could be assessed on a sound basis of information. This is almost certainly part of the explanation for a higher proportion of crises involving ethnic minority families resulting in compulsory action.

The quality of the communication between parents and agency, however, is particularly critical in the assessment of emergency situations. Even where families and workers come from the same cultures, research shows this can be very difficult.[2] How much more so where they do not and the potential for mutual misunderstanding, for misreading the clues, is heightened. The case of the Khan family, introduced in Chapter 4, is perhaps a case in point.

• •

On being informed that an Emergency Protection Order had been granted Mrs Khan dropped her opposition to a psychiatric mother and baby unit and she and Ahmed were taken there that evening. Even while the arrangements were being made doubts surfaced about the seriousness of the risks and within days Mrs Khan *confessed* to habitually exaggerating her psychiatric symptoms and using them as a manipulative strategy. Her *fears* of harming Ahmed began to take on a rather different colour and her reports of Mr Khan's depression and suicide attempts were shown to be false. Within two weeks the family were reunited at home.

● ●

It is also relevant that the minority children subject to emergency protection were generally older; half the cases involving a child of 9 or more, compared to a third of the other cases. Thus we would hypothesise that the actions of the children themselves in drawing attention to the abuse and their wishes and feelings concerning the action to be taken might be an important factor. As we shall see later, in a number of cases they were certainly influential in the decision to institute care proceedings.

Police powers or court order?

As noted earlier, police powers still have a substantial if somewhat reduced place in the immediate protection of children under the Children Act. The case data reveal that social services were usually involved in the decision to invoke such powers while practitioner interviews suggest they may on occasion be exercised less than enthusiastically by the police. Policy in all the research areas was to use Emergency Protection Orders in preference to police powers where possible; indeed in one area concern about the unexpectedly high use of police powers had prompted discussion at senior management level resulting in directions to 'avoid police orders at all costs'. For front-line staff, however, these powers are seen as a vital part of their armoury, one practitioner going as far as to say that: 'If there weren't police powers of protection it would be nightmarish.'

Police powers may be positively justified where a child needs to be removed from an immediately dangerous situation or where the parent is or is likely to be violent. It seems, however, that they are also mis-used to circumvent court procedures which are 'unnecessarily cumbersome', 'bureaucratic', 'time-consuming' and 'inappropriate for emergency use'. Although revision of the much criticised Children Act forms has hopefully dealt with part of the problem, social workers also urged courts to be more realistic about the information they can reasonably expect in an emergency situation. In one study area serious tension had developed over applications for emergency orders within court hours:

You ring up and say you want an EPO. You then have to go through the whole history of it. The clerk makes unreasonable demands, he wants the papers right now. You give promises you can't possibly fulfil, like ten minutes when you know damn well it's going to take 1½ hours. They have to find magistrates and you have to find a court and by and large you might be able to get on in the afternoon. It can take hours and then the clerk might say he can't fit you in, you'll have to go elsewhere. The other day it took four phone calls till I found a court able to accommodate me. The adjective 'emergency' just doesn't apply.

However in all areas crises arising out of normal working hours were more likely to attract police 'orders' than Emergency Protection Orders. This may be understandable given that emergency duty teams provide only a skeletal service, social workers have no access to legal advice and in one area at least the telephone number of the duty clerk to the court could only be obtained via the police. To understand a phenomenon however is not necessarily to justify it. It has to be questioned whether the use of police powers should be determined by the day of the week or the time of day the need for protective action arises rather than the degree of risk to the child.

At a much more fundamental level the continued reliance on powers which can be exercised at the discretion of the individual police officer throws into relief the social worker's lack of equivalent authority.[3] It is surely illogical that social services are the main agency charged with the protection of children, but in situations where that responsibility is most acute they are dependent on another – one whose primary function is the enforcement of the law and which is principally identified in the public mind with crime and punishment. Given the negative press the profession has attracted in recent years the notion of giving social workers equivalent powers is unlikely to be countenanced. A more palatable alternative would be to seek to increase the responsiveness of the court system in emergency situations. If injunctions can be obtained in 1–2 hours why not Emergency Protection Orders? This is a matter which needs to be addressed by the Lord Chancellor's Department and the Department of Health on a national basis rather than being left to the idiosyncrasies of local arrangements.

For the foreseeable future, however, police powers will probably continue to play a significant role in the emergency protection of children. Yet this aspect of the process has been remarkably little studied,[4] a rather important gap in the child protection knowledge base, as this study reveals. It is recommended that research be commissioned into the topic.[5]

Emergency protection in the courts

Thirty-five of the sample cases were preceded by an application for an Emergency Protection Order; 14 as the initial form of protective action; the rest, as we have seen, following police protection. All these applications were made by the local authority,[6] almost all on an ex-parte basis in the family proceedings courts, most before a single magistrate (15) or a Justices' Clerk (5). One application was withdrawn after negotiations; all the remainder were granted. Only two orders were subsequently challenged, both were withdrawn. In ten cases the local authority applied to extend the order and although four were contested, all were granted.

Parental participation

Prior to the Children Act the emergency protection of children, whether by Place of Safety Orders or wardship, was always handled on an ex-parte basis. Under the Act there is a provision for inter-partes hearings[7] although the consensus among commentators[8] was that this would be little used. Our data bear out this prediction, 28 of the applications for initial orders were ex-parte. Examination of the circumstances, however, prompts some questioning of both practice and the legal framework.

Where an order is required to remove a child quickly from a dangerous situation the use of the ex-parte mechanism is understandable. However, very few of the sample cases fell into this category. As we saw earlier, in most circumstances police protection provides the real emergency provision; Emergency Protection Orders are best characterised as a stop-gap between police protection and care proceedings. Thirteen ex-parte applications concerned children already protected under police powers; a further five were already in a safe place although without legal protection. Even in the ten cases where removal was the objective there were few where the child could be said to be in immediate danger. Why then was there such a high use of what was intended to be an *emergency* procedure in apparently non-emergency situations?

The interview data provided only partial illumination. Social workers were not in general able to remember, let alone explain, the reasons for going down the ex-parte route. At a distance of many months this is perhaps not surprising. However the experience of the researchers putting the question was that the difference between the two approaches may not have been universally appreciated; indeed some social workers seemed unaware of the alternative. Local authority lawyers, more attuned to the requirements of the legal process, mainly blamed *poor communication*:

It's quite clear to me you should only go ex-parte if the child is not in your hands. The problem arises when the child is in police protection and somebody rings you up and says it expires in four hours' time. Really the parents ought to be there (at the hearing). I just feel social workers aren't terribly aware of needing to act. [Where there has been a Police Protection Order] social services obviously know because they've got the child but it's somebody putting two and two together and realising oh dear we've got to do something about this.

The case data reveal a third factor: time. The notice period for inter-partes hearings is one full day; police powers of protection last for a maximum of 72 hours. Thus an application on notice is only feasible when there is both excellent inter- and intra-agency communication (for example police/ hospital/ Emergency Duty Team; social services area team; legal department; court) *and* when the need for continuing legal action is unequivocal. Even where the most favourable conditions exist, however, the logistics of the court process have to be taken into account. Where police action is taken between Thursday and Sunday it would usually be impossible to arrange an inter-partes hearing. This factor alone would explain the use of the ex-parte route in over half our sample cases which were preceded by police protection.

Whatever the reasons for the minimal use of the on notice provisions there was evidence from two of the research areas that leave to proceed ex-parte was certainly not being granted automatically by the courts, though there was only one sample case where leave was refused. (Social services promptly sought the assistance of the police and the child, who was in hospital, was placed under police protection until the inter-partes hearing took place, which can scarcely have been what the court had in mind.) The rigorous approach of that court, particularly the stipendiary magistrate, was welcomed by several lawyers acting for families. Local authority informants were less positive, some questioning the approach of the particular court, others the whole notion of emergency protection on notice:

We are encouraged to go inter-partes but it makes nonsense of the emergency bit; either it's an emergency or it's not; if it's not you go down the road of Interim Care Orders. (Social worker)

In between the legally distinct variants of inter-partes and ex-parte hearings there were, however, in reality a number of cases which were neither fish nor fowl: hearings which were technically ex-parte but where parents were aware of the application and turned up, sometimes accompanied by a solicitor. Such cases pose legal and practical difficulties for all concerned, generating not only professional irritation but family distress:

> Social services got themselves into an awful muddle; they applied for an ex-parte order but then informed the parents. Then we had the ridiculous situation of the parents rolling up to be told they couldn't go in. So it was heard without them and we had a very angry parent waiting outside the door of the court saying they're taking my child away but not allowing me to say anything. (Local authority solicitor)

How does this appalling scene square with the principles of increased parental participation and partnership which underpin the Children Act? What message did it give to those parents about their status in legal proceedings and the value which would be placed on their views? Their exclusion was clearly not justified in terms of any danger to the child since social services had informed them of the application; it was purely a function of the legal framework. The question then arises, need this unfortunate situation continue? Would it be possible to devise a means of permitting parental involvement which will neither undermine their position nor clog up already over-burdened court lists with procedures which make the process even less suited to the purposes for which it was designed, the short-term protection of children? Since full blown adversarial hearings at this stage would be neither feasible nor desirable, what would?

The arguments against reform are substantial. Allowing parents to attend or even participate (perhaps by stating their position) in technically ex-parte hearings would not as the law stands affect their formal legal rights to challenge after 72 hours. These are only abrogated if they received notice of the hearing in accordance with the Rules as well as being present at the hearing. However at this point parents may have had little legal advice and may not be represented, so without great care on the part of the court and other participants they will in reality be considerably disadvantaged. If they do have legal representation the solicitor will have had scant time to familiarise himself with the issues and may therefore advise against attendance. Local authorities might consider it necessary to have legal representation themselves at all hearings; whereas in two areas social workers usually handled ex-parte hearings themselves. Courts would need to adjust both their working practices and listing arrangements. It is for others to decide whether these factors are determinative and indeed whether the problem is widespread. Fieldwork in our three research areas, however, indicates that this is an issue which was not recognised in the legislation and which needs to be addressed.

Ironically, the provision which *was* made in the Children Act to enhance the rights of parents, namely the right to challenge an order,[9] appears to be little used. The consensus among solicitors was that, though valuable in principle, it serves little purpose in practice:

> The procedure . . . is probably a little meaningless; I don't know anyone who has applied, there's no point. By the time you get the paperwork the seven days is practically up; you may as well get your case together and have a good go at the first interim.

Representation of the child at Emergency Protection Order hearings

The Act for the first time provided for the appointment of a guardian and solicitor to represent the child at the Emergency Protection Order application and any subsequent hearings. Pre-Act there was therefore much discussion as to how the guardian service in particular would be able to respond to requests for urgent appointments.

The data suggest that where initial applications were made on notice the panels were able to meet the demand: a guardian was present in five out of six cases. Attendance at extension hearings was also high (nine out of ten). However guardians were rarely present at ex-parte hearings, thus two-thirds of initial applications were heard without the benefit of their input. Nor was there evidence that lawyers were being used in compensation, indeed the child was even less likely to be legally represented at these hearings. Not only was there no single sample case in which a solicitor attended without a guardian, there were seven hearings at which the guardian acted unaccompanied. Interviews support these findings: 15 solicitors, for example, told us they had never attended an Emergency Protection Order hearing while guardians in Areas A and C said they were not normally involved until after the Emergency Protection Order had been made.

Does the lack of representation for the child matter?

Practitioners were not specifically asked whether representation for the child at the Emergency Protection Order stage was important and only a minority raised the issue, suggesting it was not a priority concern. This may principally reflect the perception that emergency protection was being used more appropriately and sparingly so that the lack of representation was not seen to result in any substantive injustice. There may also have been a degree of acceptance of the realities of resource difficulties. In Area C, for instance, which at the time of the research could not guarantee to have a guardian in place by the first hearing, attendance at the Emergency Protection Order was a forlorn hope. Finally there may be little either guardian or lawyer can positively contribute since, as one guardian commented:

> In most cases I've felt too ill-equipped to say one way or another and so I've instructed the solicitor to be as neutral as we can so we're not seen to be reaching any decision quickly.

Indeed it could be argued that representation for the child at this early stage could be dangerous, the *form* of procedural justice concealing its essentially limited *effectiveness*, leading to unjustified complacency or excessive weight being placed on neutral but insufficiently informed opinion.

None the less most guardians with experience of Emergency Protection Order hearings considered it *was* valuable to be there. Even on an ex-parte application, with no opportunity to speak to anyone before arriving at court, an experienced guardian, it was said, can find out a great deal in a short time, sufficient at least to check that the local authority is not acting precipitately. While her or his opinion may be of limited value unless it can be substantiated by some preliminary enquiries, the guardian can help the court by:

- ♦ offering an objective child-focused appraisal of the evidence;

- ♦ raising any issues that have not been looked at by the local authority;

- ♦ checking alternative options have been explored; and

- ♦ ensuring issues such as contact, short-term placements, schooling, etc. are looked at before patterns are set which may be harder to alter later.

Those solicitors who expressed a view would also prefer both guardian and solicitor to attend but where that is not possible legal representation was considered to be better than nothing: 'even though all you can do is check what they're doing isn't really off the wall.' Attendance at the hearing was also seen as useful for the child's representatives, helping them 'get to grips with the case' when matters are still in crisis and in ensuring that by the time of the first interim they will be in a position to make a positive contribution. Otherwise, as one lawyer put it:

> You're getting that lack of knowledge at the first interim. It's very frustrating for parents when the guardian says they're being neutral; the parents can't understand why their child has been in care for a week or more and they can't make a decision.

In an ideal world therefore it would seem the child *should* be represented by both a guardian and solicitor at the initial Emergency Protection Order hearing. This can probably only be achieved by some form of on-call system for both groups of professionals and a tight administrative system. In a less than ideal world whether the need justifies the effort is not yet proven.

Duration of emergency protection

None of our informants, whatever their professional background, mourned the loss of the 28-day Place of Safety Order. Sharp differences in opinion as well as considerable ambivalence, however, were elicited by the new 8-day Emergency Protection Order. The time constraints per se were not the problem, because 8-day Place of Safety Orders were previously the norm in all the research areas. It is the combination of the new mandatory time limits with the notice requirements for Section 31 applications, the need for written evidence, provision for challenge and local court timetables which have been found to present difficulties. The greatest hostility was expressed by social services staff and their legal advisors, the practitioners who were put under the greatest pressure by the time constraints. However three principal problems were identified by some members of all professional groups:

- the time available is insufficient to prepare properly for the first care hearing;

- work with the family takes second place to preparation for court; and

- the local authority may be forced into bringing care proceedings precipitately in cases where more time might have produced a different outcome.

These reservations might be summed up in a single phrase: 'the time limits are too short to do a proper job' (team manager).

The counter-argument, of course, is that if the time limits were longer the job would not necessarily be any better; the same processes would just take longer. It 'focuses the mind,' and 'gets everyone leaping around' were frequent comments, sometimes accompanied by suspicions that a lengthier timetable would lead to 'sloppy work and delay'. Getting the case into court as soon as possible was also seen as important given the high proportion of ex-parte orders.

The balance of opinion appeared to be that the time constraints are difficult but 'just about workable'. This may be partly because there are ways round the problem: extensions; application to issue care proceedings on short notice and the breathing space provided by the use of police powers of protection. None the less we consider that the time limits need to be reviewed. There was no evidence in the research to suggest that Emergency Protection Orders are now used as a routine way of starting care proceedings, which was found to be the case with Place of Safety Orders in some areas;[10] they are generally a response to a crisis situation when other options have proved fruitless. However once an Emergency Protection Order has been taken it seems care proceedings follow almost automatically, bearing out fears expressed prior to the Act.[11] Confirmation of this comes not only from the interview data but from our extensive study,[12] which revealed that 81% of successful Emergency Protection Order applications result in care proceedings, and also from research conducted by Thoburn and colleagues at the University of East Anglia.[13]

Two cases gave us particular cause for concern, both Asian families not already involved with social services. One revolved around alleged physical and emotional abuse of an 11-year-old; the other involved the Khan family. In each case the Emergency Protection Order would appear to have been justifiable and carefully thought out despite the high drama of the precipitating events. Within a very short time, however, both crises subsided, the children were returned home and each case concluded with an order of No Order. Such developments cause us to wonder whether with a longer Emergency Protection Order the juggernaut[14] could have been stopped before it even began to roll.

It may be argued that the facility for extension already allows for longer orders. However since this requires a hearing it means the focus remains on the court process rather than the family. We would suggest there could be a presumption of 15 days, the court retaining the power to make shorter orders, and that while little would be lost much could be gained. All parties already have the right to representation, a longer period would make this informed rather than token; any consequent proceedings would start from a better information base; the Guardian ad Litem, for instance, having had the opportunity to make initial enquiries. The right to challenge which is currently little exercised would provide a more meaningful safeguard against abuse. The court has the power to make directions about contact and other issues and there is a presumption of reasonable contact. Great care would, of course, be needed to ensure that matters do not just drift but that the period is seen as a time for intensive work to seize the potential for change which, as has long been recognised in psycho-social theory, a crisis can provide.[15] In this respect the guardian should provide an important safeguard.

Such a move would highlight some practical and legal problems which are obscured by current time-scales. Many panels, for instance, may have insufficient resource to ensure a guardian is in place for the duration of the Emergency Protection Order. Where, however, this is possible and the guardian considers that an application should be made in care proceedings but the local authority does not, what is to be done? Neither the guardian nor the court can force social services' hand. A rare though not unheard of situation at the moment, this would almost certainly become more common, providing yet another focus for tension between guardians, courts and local authorities. Neither problem, however, outweighs the advantages that might flow if the period of the Emergency Protection Order were no longer to be regarded as a holding operation but a time for constructive work and careful reflection.

Practitioner evaluation of the new provisions

Emergency protection under previous legislation was much criticised[16] particularly following the Cleveland crisis. If our research data suggest a less than wholly rosy picture now, we would not wish to deny the substantial improvements the Act has brought about at this stage of the legal process and their significance as safeguards against gross abuse. Only one of our practitioner informants did not regard the Emergency Protection Order as an enormous advance. Though individuals varied in what they chose to stress, the following aspects of this 'much less abusive process' were identified by all groups:

♦ the more rigorous criteria;

♦ the constraints on local authority autonomy;

♦ greater clarity both about what has to be proved and what can and must be done;

♦ a more appropriate time-scale;

♦ the right to challenge;

♦ the presumption of reasonable contact; and

♦ the greater involvement of parents.

We also found a broad measure of support for the way the provisions are being operated and interpreted, as this comment from a guardian indicates:

I was pleased to see the long POSO go and to have more safeguards. It's good magistrates have to consider in a more structured and thorough way and have to give reasons so if parents were able to absorb what has been said they would be able to understand and not be so much in the dark. Directions for contact are useful. Social services have to give more information. The EPO is more explicit about what has to happen and people are better at informing the parties. In the past POSOs could be made for 28 days and parents wouldn't know why or what was going on and they couldn't challenge. There's a lot more openness and fairness. If your child is taken you should know why, what the arrangements are and what is going to happen in the court case. So I think the Act has achieved an awful lot.

Placement and contact

For the majority of the children in the sample, emergency protection meant separation. There were only five cases (of 32) in which the child remained with a parent whose care was giving concern, all in supervised placements; and one where the children were removed from their mother and placed with their father. Even where arrangements were voluntary, separation was still the most likely outcome (8). Of the three cases where this did not occur there was only one where the children remained with parents in an unsupervised placement. Whatever the legal basis for protection children were least likely to experience parental separation in Area B. Moreover, even when separated from their parents, children in this area were more likely to remain within their extended families from the beginning. None the less in all areas relatives provided initial emergency placements in only a minority of cases (7).

Emergency Protection Orders were made in 29 cases involving separated children. Under the Act there is a presumption of reasonable parental contact so that a court direction is required before contact can be restricted. Such directions were made in 18 cases, with only one application dismissed. For the most part, however, social services were not seeking at this stage to deny contact (four applications, one refused), but to be in a position to monitor and control the conditions under which it occurred. Thus six orders directed contact at the discretion of the local authority and nine supervised contact in relation to at least one parent. Only three cases involved a more precise definition of the frequency, location or other conditions under which contact should take place.

Care arrangements at the start of court proceedings

Prior to the events leading to proceedings we found, as detailed earlier, that one in two index children was at home. By the time of the first hearing, however, as shown in Table 5.2, only one in seven was. In the next chapter we look at the concerns which brought about that dramatic change.

Table 5.2 *Care arrangements for the index child at the start of court proceedings*

	Area A	Area B	Area C	All areas
With parent				
at home	4	4	3	11
away from home	3	8	0	11
Separated				
placed outside family network				
compulsorily	10	7	7	24
voluntarily	12	7	12	31
Separated				
placed within family network	0	4	2	6
(n=)	*(29)*	*(30)*	*(24)*	*(83)*

Summary

Care proceedings under the Children Act are less likely to be instituted in the aftermath of a crisis than those under previous legislation. This is largely due to the rise in the use of accommodation and supervised placements in response to previous crises which might have led to earlier court action. Proceedings taken on children living at home are still most likely to be crisis-driven. Cases involving older children and ethnic minority groups are more likely than other cases to be precipitated by a crisis.

The reduction in crisis-driven cases largely explains the drop in proceedings beginning with compulsory emergency protection. Their use in crisis cases fell in only one area, rising in the other two. These data do not negate strong practitioner perceptions that the Act has changed the approach to emergency protection. Practice *was* characterised by more strenuous efforts to avoid compulsory powers; cases which did attract such orders were usually those where efforts were unavailing or inappropriate.

There was considerable anxiety among social work practitioners about the shift in emphasis and evidence of conflict with legal advisors who are much more likely to be involved at the point of crisis. There was no hard evidence that more children were being left unprotected when crises erupted. Rather crises which would previously have attracted a Place of Safety Order were being dealt with in other ways and no longer led straight to court action. It was the continuance of voluntary intervention, rather than the decision not to take an Emergency Protection Order, which was more likely to place the child at continuing risk.

Compulsory emergency intervention was most likely in cases which were not currently being worked with and involved older children. This explains much of the higher rate of use among ethnic minority families. A better appreciation of the family's cultural context might, however, enable some crises to be defused and keep more minority families out of the court system.

The police continue to play a key role in emergency protection. Very little information is available on the operation of police protection and further research is advised. The high use of police powers partly flows from deficiencies in the emergency protection procedures, particularly out of hours. The system is insufficiently geared to respond to crises, a matter which needs addressing.

The Emergency Protection Order is judged a vast improvement on the Place of Safety Order although there are reservations about the 8-day initial limit. Consideration should be given to extending this, encouraging the longer interval to be used for intensive focused work which might avert proceedings rather than using it primarily for evidence-gathering and preparation for court.

Parental rights have in theory been extended by the emergency protection provisions but in practice they were little exercised: there were few challenges, none successful. The majority of applications continued to be made on an ex-parte basis, often not justified by the urgency of the circumstances. Consideration needs to be given to how parents could participate at this crucial point.

The child's interests were very rarely protected by the presence of either a solicitor or Guardian ad Litem at the initial hearing. It is considered that an on-call system for both would be valuable although it was not established that this is a priority need.

By the first hearing of the care case six out of ten children were living outside their family network. Of those subject to Emergency Protection Orders over half were subject to contact restrictions though permission to refuse contact had been granted in only a small number.

NOTES
--

1 The most likely explanation for this of course is the reduction in the duration of police powers from eight to three days.

2 Cleaver H; Freeman P (1995): *Parental Perspectives in Cases of Suspected Child Abuse.* HMSO.

3 Such a power exists in some other jurisdictions. Diduck A (1995): Partnership: reflections on some Canadian experiences, in Kaganas F (ed.): *Legislating for Harmony: Partnership under the Children Act 1989.* Jessica Kingsley.

4 To our knowledge only one piece of research has been undertaken; an unpublished survey for the Home Office which concluded that further work was required. Borkowski's short article in *Family Law* (April 1995): Police Protection and Section 46, was based on a single interview.

5 Since this report was completed the Nuffield Foundation has made a grant to Prof. Judith Masson, of Warwick University, to examine the use of police powers of protection.

6 Under the Children Act anyone is entitled to apply for an Emergency Protection Order although it was always envisaged the local authority would be the main user.

7 Children Act 1989 Schedule 2(ii).

8 E.g. White R et al. (1990): *A Guide to the Children Act 1989.* Butterworths; DoH (1992): *The Children Act 1989 Court Orders Study: A Study of Local Authority Decision-making about Public-Law Court Applications.* HMSO.

9 It is of interest that this provision was not among the recommendations of the Child Care Law Review, nor was it mooted in the White Paper. Its introduction into the Children Bill appears to have been in response to the Cleveland Inquiry.

10 Packman J et al. (1986): *Who Needs Care?: Social Work Decisions about Children.* Blackwell.

11 Eekelaar J (1991): Parental Responsibility: State of Nature or Nature of the State? *Journal of Social Welfare Law*, No. 1.

12 Thomas C; Hunt J (1996): *The Care Workloads of the Civil Courts under the Children Act.* Report to DoH. Centre for Socio-Legal Studies, University of Bristol.

13 Thoburn J et al. (forthcoming): *Safeguarding Children with the Children Act.* The Stationery Office.

14 Smith P (1995): Child Protection Research. *Family Law*, 432.

15 Caplan G (1964): *The Theory and Practice of Mental Health Consultation. Principles of Preventative Psychiatry.* Basic Books.

16 DHSS (1985): *Review of Child Care Law.* HMSO; DHSS (1988): *Report of the Inquiry into Child Abuse in Cleveland 1987.* HMSO; Packman J et al. (1986): *Who Needs Care?: Social Work Decisions about Children.* Blackwell; Millham S et al. (1985): *Lost in Care.* Gower.

6 *Sizing up the first gate: the operation of the threshold criteria*

Standardising the criteria for statutory intervention

Before a court can consider making a care or supervision order under the Children Act it has to be satisfied that the *threshold*[1] conditions set out in Section 31(2) have been met. These require proof:

    (a)   that the child concerned is suffering, or is likely to suffer, significant harm; and

    (b)   that the harm, or likelihood of harm, is attributable to

        (i)   the care given to the child, or likely to be given to him if the order were not made, not being what it would be reasonable to expect a parent to give to him; or

        (ii)   the child's being beyond parental control.

Section 31(9) provides a gloss on the new terminology explaining that:

    ♦   'harm' means ill-treatment or the impairment of health or development;

    ♦   'development' means physical, intellectual, emotional, social or behavioural;

    ♦   'health' means physical or mental; and

    ♦   'ill-treatment' includes sexual abuse and forms of ill-treatment which are not physical.

Section 31(10) adds that:

> where the question of whether harm is significant turns on the child's health or development, his health or development shall be compared with that which could reasonably be expected of a similar child.

These unified conditions replace three main sets of grounds laid down in a plethora of prior legislation. Thus, as the *Review of Child Care Law*[2] pointed out:

- In family proceedings (for example divorce, adoption or wardship) a court could commit a child to care if there were exceptional circumstances making it impracticable or undesirable that the child should be entrusted to his parents or any other individual.

- In care proceedings under the Children and Young Persons Act 1969 the court had first to be satisfied that one of several specific conditions was met.[3]

- Under the Child Care Act 1980 a local authority could assume parental rights over children already in their care by satisfying one of another set of specified grounds.[4]

The formal impetus for standardisation came from the recommendation of the Short Committee[5] that: 'the present statutory conditions . . . be assimilated and simplified and subject to the same overall welfare condition.' While acknowledging that: 'it would be a major task to combine the degree of statutory protection which specific grounds give, with the degree of discretion [necessary] . . . to extend . . . protection to children who need it' they considered this was 'an essential step towards clearing a path through the thicket of child care law.'

The Child Care Law Review, to whom this major task was allocated, considered three principal options: a broad welfare test; an exceptional circumstances provision and specific grounds. The first it dismissed as too discretionary, concurring with the Committee that it was likely to 'lead to widely varying and subjective interpretations' and would not provide adequate protection against unwarranted state intervention. It also rejected an exceptional circumstances rider on the grounds that it added little to a broad welfare test and could also lead to inconsistency. Guidelines were deemed insufficient to direct the court's mind to the principles underlying restrictions on state intervention. 'Unless specific' it was concluded, 'guidelines would be little more than statements of the obvious, and if specific, would be open to many of the criticisms . . . of the existing specific conditions.'

The Review therefore concentrated on devising a test of *greater* specificity which was yet not *over*-specific. Rather than try to harmonise the existing specific grounds it went back to first principles developing an entirely new set of criteria reflecting a philosophical position on the justification for state intervention in family life, namely:

- there should be harm or likely harm to the child;

- the criteria should reflect the care which would be reasonable for the particular child;

- it should be necessary to show some substantial deficit; and

- the source of harm should be the absence of a reasonable degree of parental care.[6]

These principles were accepted by the government in its subsequent White Paper[7] and while the wording was debated vigorously during the Bill's passage through Parliament the criteria which passed into law essentially reflect the Review's recommendations.

Practitioner views on the reforms

A better framework?

Those practitioners we interviewed with pre-Act experience in general judged the new legislative framework a great improvement. The fundamental principle of the reform − standardisation and simplification of the statutory criteria − was well accepted, the previous proliferation of grounds and fora being described as 'ridiculous' and 'unfair'. Singled out for particular condemnation by each professional group was the injustice of allowing the local authority 'a second bite of the cherry' through wardship having lost a case in the juvenile court. The new criteria themselves were also on the whole regarded as a sensible *middle way*, avoiding both the narrow specificity of the Children and Young Persons Act and the broad vagueness of the wardship and matrimonial tests where 'you didn't have to show anything at all', and 'the judge could decide anything was exceptional circumstances'.

A number of key additional themes emerged with comments clustering around concepts such as focus, clarity, stringency and comprehensiveness. Somewhat surprisingly, the accusation of vagueness or woolliness was levelled not just at wardship but at the formally specific grounds in the Children and Young Persons Act which 'seemed a bit vague, a bit of a mop-up'. In comparison the new criteria were 'more focused', 'explicit' and 'better defined' as well as 'more straightforward' and 'easier to work with'. The concept of significant harm, it was said, allowed a broader approach:

> It's more comprehensive, especially as regards neglect; it's not just about immediate acts but the long term too. It acknowledges emotional abuse and issues about identity and culture. It was more difficult to look at those issues pre-Act. (Social worker)

At the same time the new tests were almost universally seen as more demanding to satisfy in terms of evidence and clarity of thought:

> We have to know more, give more detail, be much clearer. (Social worker)

> They're less glib, more difficult to meet, thought-provoking, more demanding in assessment and decision-making. (Guardian ad Litem)

It would of course be unrealistic to expect total consensus about such radical change and there were some dissenting views and reservations. For some social work practitioners, for instance, it was the Children and Young Persons Act concepts which seemed clearer and more straightforward. A lone team manager regretted the demise of parental rights resolutions; another argued the whole issue of emotional abuse and neglect had been 'pushed back by the Act'. The most significant reservations however, expressed primarily but not solely by local authority practitioners, revolved around the loss of wardship. In all three areas there were comments such as:

> There are occasions when I dearly miss wardship. It's where you think you know what is going on but are unable to prove it. If you're for a parent you say thank God they can't use wardship; if you're for the child or the local authority you might like to have the vagueness of wardship. (Private practice solicitor)

> Wardship really did offer a safety net . . . an underpinning and overarching protection that nothing else offers to the same extent. (Social worker)

> Like most local authority lawyers I suppose there are cases when I look back to wardship and think, if only. (Local authority solicitor)

This theme, of the sufficiency of the statutory jurisdiction and its appropriateness in comparison to wardship, is one to which we shall return at several points in this report. It should be said at this stage, however, that the restrictions on the use of wardship, though regretted by some, occasioned less disquiet in relation to getting cases to court than in terms of what could be done with them once they were there. Pre-Act concerns about how the system would work without wardship have thus far, as a number of commentators have concluded, in this respect proved largely unfounded.[8]

A workable and appropriate framework?

All practitioners were asked whether the criteria provided an appropriate and workable framework for decision-making in child protection cases. Again the response in all groups was generally positive and while a third voiced some reservations only one in ten was entirely critical. Given that these interviews were carried out after the Act had been in operation for three years, these findings, reflecting comments such as those below, would seem to indicate the new criteria are indeed proving acceptable:

> The Act has given us a framework in which to be very clear, about significant harm and other things which formulate and surround our practice. We've never had a framework like that before, it helps social work to become a much clearer, more thoughtful profession than it was in the old days, less fudging. (Team manager)

> I've thought about this quite hard and in all honesty I can't think of a better one. It seems to me it's the sort of test that catches all the problems that seem to have arisen. From the local authority point of view it is wide enough to catch most of the cases and from the parent's point of view it's wide enough to be able to argue it out. (Solicitor)

It was clear however that practitioners operating primarily in the court arena were feeling most comfortable with the new conditions. The high level of approval among Guardians ad Litem, of whom only two expressed reservations, was particularly striking. Several factors probably contributed to this: their role in the system as an independent second opinion; their familiarity with the operation of the criteria in the courts; perhaps also the fact that their pre-Act experience as guardians was confined to a single jurisdiction, the Children and Young Persons Act, which, as we saw earlier, most practitioners were happy to leave behind.

Social services personnel, on the other hand, generally with less experience of the court process under the new regime, were also in a position to compare it with the whole range of alternative frameworks. More fundamentally, theirs is a rather more difficult task, that of making the primary assessment of the degree of harm to a child. The much higher levels of discomfort experienced by social work practitioners (more than half expressing some reservations) are therefore understandable, particularly the ambivalence of team managers, who would usually carry the responsibility for making the final decision. It also seems logical that the views expressed by local authority lawyers, who act as the bridge between the welfare and legal spheres, should fall roughly midway between the extremes.

A comparison of the positive and more negative responses, however, also brings out that they were differentiated principally by the degree to which respondents could tolerate and work with uncertainty. The process of analysis required by the threshold criteria was seen as helpful but the concepts themselves were as yet devoid of content. Some accepted, even welcomed, this lack of precision:

> I can see they probably need to be as they are, fairly wide ranging and terribly malleable and not full of a lot of meaning because if they were too tight we wouldn't be able to use them in the way we can. (Local authority solicitor)

Others were very much hoping for the concepts to be invested with more precise meanings through practice, training or case law:

> What is significant? It seems vague and unclear. I feel very weak on that, I don't know enough of what it means. What is a reasonable parent? The concepts don't give me anything to hang onto. (Social worker)

> I'm unclear really how to apply the criteria to any particular case. I constantly approach cases thinking 'Ah quite clearly the criteria are met' and then thinking perhaps they're not. I suppose as more case law is reported we'll be happier when there is a body of decided cases to work from. (Solicitor)

However, as one local authority solicitor put it, perhaps the nub of the problem is less the inherent vagueness of the legal concepts than society's ill-defined expectations of adequate child-rearing:

> They don't provide us with any assistance as to what social services are meant to be doing. We're meant to be protecting children from significant harm but the threshold criteria don't tell you what that is and ideas about that change all the time. But I don't think the problem is with the law. There hasn't been a wide-ranging social debate on the whole issue of child protection, when children should be protected, when they should be removed and when remain and what the hell social services should be doing. That's the problem and it puts social workers in a really difficult position because even if they don't think that out the results of it come up time and again.

Once a case reaches court, however, it was said to be rare for these theoretically difficult concepts to create difficulties, a perspective strongly confirmed in our later interviews with the judiciary:

> I don't think the threshold criteria generally present a problem. We don't spend a lot of time agonising over where things fit within [them]. (District judge)

What explains this unexpected[9] dearth of legal argument? Is it that though significant harm might be hard to define and its nuances the meat of endless academic debate, in practice, as one magistrate put it: 'you recognise it when you see it'. Others, such as this guardian, testified to the self-evidence of the concept in practice:

> There was a lot of worry at the beginning about the definition . . . it seemed vague and subjective, but there is a fairly wide common acknowledgement of what is significant harm.

Perhaps it is that the cases are so severe that there is little room for argument, a common theme: 'I suspect there is a weeding out and they only bring in reasonably clear ones' (judge).

Other research supports this view. The criterion for placing a child on the Child Protection Register, for example, is also the risk of significant harm.[10] Hallett, writing about registered children, states:

> There is fairly widespread agreement amongst professionals that, in general, cases referred to or identified by the relevant agencies as child protection cases are appropriate and the thresholds of intervention being applied in practice are broadly acceptable.[11]

Thoburn's study[12] shows that even when the threshold had been crossed only a small minority of registrations led to care proceedings. The interpretation is also consistent with our own pre-Act data; both from this and a previous study,[13] which showed that very few applications would have had difficulty satisfying the threshold conditions. Thus in most cases one would expect that the issue concerning the court would not be the significance of harm but, on the one hand, the facts establishing the harm and, on the other, what is to be done.

Judicial interviews add further weight:

> You easily come to a conclusion that the child is at risk – the greater problem is how you are going to address that risk, which is the better route to see an improvement in the child's circumstances. But the existence or otherwise of circumstances which are prejudicial to the child, therefore need the threshold criteria, is not usually a problem. (Judge)

More worryingly, however, could it be that the issues are simply being evaded, either because they are too difficult or because they are seen as less relevant than the question of how matters are to be improved for the child in the future? There was some evidence for this contention too. Consider, for example, these comments from experienced practitioners:

> I've had no major dilemmas but I tend to duck similar child and reasonable parent; they're difficult. (Guardian ad Litem)

> I think one of the problems is people aren't applying the legal tests; they don't argue significance or harm or similar child. . . . People fudge around because they don't really know how to define it. At the start, on the training courses people did discuss harm, and whether it was significant, but when I think about it, people just don't bother. It's going by the board and what I think people are arguing is the orders. (Solicitor)

Then these revealing comments by members of the judiciary:

> I think it makes very little difference, quite honestly. A confession I suppose – most people really fudge it, or take a very poor view of the test; they look for the desirable outcome.

> I think there are times when all courts stretch them a little bit to protect the child.

All these factors are likely to have some bearing on the fact that in the early years of the Act the potential for dispute which was widely held to be inherent in the threshold conditions has not, in practice, been realised. Perhaps most influentially, however, such argument was explicitly discouraged by the President of the Family Division, Sir Stephen Brown, when he expressed the hope that:

> In approaching cases under the Children Act courts will not be invited to perform in every case a strict legalistic analysis of the statutory meaning of S31. Of course the words of the statute must be considered, but I do not believe that Parliament intended them to be unduly restrictive when the evidence clearly indicates that a certain course should be taken in order to protect the child.[14]

Without this very clear and timely steer away from an overly legalistic interpretation of the criteria it seems likely there would have been a great deal more litigation. Though the resultant case law would no doubt have been reassuring to some practitioners, a more prescriptive definition would not, on our evidence, be widely welcomed.

Areas of particular difficulty

If it is accepted that discretionary rather than prescriptive criteria are appropriate for care cases then it is inevitable that practitioners who have to gauge whether their concern for a particular child will meet the legal test will be subject to a degree of uncertainty and anxiety. Some types of case, however, were seen as particularly troublesome. Accommodated children, for example. Can the risk of significant harm be demonstrated by recurrent episodes of short-term accommodation or lack of reasonable parenting proved when parents resist moves towards permanency? What about cases where the child would be at risk if he were to return home but parents are agreeing to continuing accommodation and have never made any attempt to remove? Is the threshold crossed if there is no one with parental responsibility for the child because his parents are dead or their whereabouts are unknown? The decision in Birmingham CC v D & M [1994][15] suggested not, revealing a 'lacuna' of particular concern to authorities dealing with refugee children. Such cases were generally outwith the remit of the Children and Young Persons Act but could have been handled by parental rights resolutions, which dealt specifically with children who were in voluntary care, or by wardship. Indeed the need to regulate the position of children in voluntary care was one of the most frequent reasons for invoking wardship.[16]

Other reported problems were less about the *interpretation* of the criteria than the perceived greater difficulty in *proving* them. Thus the individualistic focus of the new criteria makes it harder, it was said, to prove the likelihood of harm to other children in the family on the basis of harm to one, to new-born children on the basis of harm to previous children, or to any child because of the presence of a Schedule 1 offender. Such cases would have been more easily, perhaps too easily, dealt with under Sections 1(2)(b) and (bb) of the Children and Young Persons Act.[17] Similarly, potential harm due to parental drug or alcohol abuse or psychiatric illness was said to be easier to get into court under wardship. While practitioners, in general, as we saw earlier, saw greater stringency as a positive, there were some concerns:

> about how easy it might be to adequately protect children in a difficult case. Whether it is because I don't have sufficient experience or whether it's anxiety because the legislation has changed but I suppose I have a fear as to whether what is good practice and challenging in the majority of cases might let the child down in a difficult one. (Team manager)

> I think if anything the Act might fail to protect children on occasion but I think we shall only build that information up. (Guardian ad Litem)

One recurrent theme in all practitioner groups was the continuing difficulty in proving significant harm where the concerns are about *emotional abuse* or *chronic neglect*. The threshold criteria in themselves have not exacerbated this inherent difficulty; on the contrary they encourage a broader approach. Rather it is the perception that the Act requires a more stringent testing of evidence altogether which has made social workers even less confident about going to court on the basis of the more nebulous, softer information which is often all that can be mustered in these types of case.

The impact of the threshold conditions on the use of statutory intervention

It was evident from the interview material that many social services personnel were anxious and uncertain about applying and proving the threshold criteria. Did this mean that cases which were judged to need a statutory framework were not being brought to court? In line with reports from elsewhere in the country,[18] there were certainly practitioners in all three areas who thought so:

> There are a lot of cases that are not going to court because you haven't got the evidence; I think we're putting children's lives in danger. You're always thinking about it; do we wait until something happens? (Social worker)

> A lot of cases are not being pursued because of the difficulty of making out the grounds. (Local authority solicitor)

In all, 21 practitioners (four team managers, eight social workers, nine local authority solicitors) said that they had had personal experience of such cases. The examples cited, however, generally seemed to reflect less an inability to take proceedings than the need to hold back until better evidence had been accumulated, a process confirmed by a wide range of respondents in each area:

> Some of the debate we are having at case conference is whether you go for it on the evidence you've got and maybe not get it or delay. There are a couple of cases where we've delayed; the child hasn't been at greater risk, more ongoing risk, you carry the risk for a longer time. We've decided what all the agencies have to do before the next conference to formulate tighter evidence. That's because we haven't wanted to take the risk of losing it. (Team manager)

> I haven't had any we haven't been able to bring because they don't fit the criteria; you can make them fit. But there are cases where I've said I'm sure the evidence is there but we haven't brought it out yet so I might suggest some sort of assessment. That's really affected the timing of proceedings rather than whether they're brought. (Local authority solicitor)

This stricter approach to the quality of evidence may be beneficial if it screens out ill-founded cases. Nor were we given any examples of cases where children had suffered serious physical injury as the result of a delayed application. None the less there are more subtle and ultimately perhaps more long-lasting forms of harm than physical abuse and these are the ones where delay seems most likely to occur because the evidence is harder to obtain. It will be seen later that the proportion of sample cases brought on the grounds of sexual abuse shows a substantial reduction on the pre-Act position. Some practitioners commented on the much greater difficulty of proving harm in those cases where:

> All your practice experience and gut feeling tells you the child is being abused but you're looking at pointers of behaviour and emotion and what's significant and what's not. It's the grave concern factor and you can't take it to court.

One team manager, for instance, cited a case of a mother suspected of sexual abuse:

> We wanted to take care proceedings a lot earlier than we did. The solicitor did go to the clerk of the court with the concern and the clerk took the view we didn't have the evidence for an EPO. The social worker was very concerned and rightly (as it turned out). That was one where the Act didn't help us because we had to wait for some major blow-up, for the older children to leave home and come to us with their concerns. Under the old legislation we probably would have gone for wardship.

Implications for social work practice

In this instance it is hard to see any alternative to a waiting strategy. Are there other cases, however, where as some interviewees suggested, a more systematic approach to case recording would enable social workers to be more confident about their 'gut feelings' or to see patterns of behaviour which persist over time?

> We do have a difficult case where I find it difficult to weigh whether the evidence isn't there or whether the social worker is not able to sort it out. I feel quite strongly that we need to intervene but the social worker is still very woolly about whether we would have the evidence. I'm trying to get him to sit down and sift from the file what he thinks is the evidence and then we can discuss it with legal. I think it's more his problem than the case but it's going to be very borderline. I'm sure if he actually wrote down the incidents he might well have a clear pattern of abuse and might be able to consider going for care proceedings because there clearly is a risk of significant harm.

But you can only prove that with a consistent pattern of things going wrong. (Team manager)

Such comments echo the reactions of the research team, having ploughed through the minutiae of social services files where case summaries only seemed to be produced on transfer to another worker and chronologies only for court proceedings. Yet a *running summary* accompanied with a *regularly updated chronology* would, we would suggest, be a relatively simple way of ensuring an overview of the case, useful in any event as a case management tool both for the worker and the team manager and invaluable if the case becomes one of the minority that eventually need to be taken to court.

The data also suggest that social workers need to incorporate an understanding of the legal framework more fully into their everyday practice and need more training, more opportunities to review their cases in the light of the Act and more assistance in doing so. No one should underestimate the difficulty the threshold conditions present to social workers.[19] The Act places a premium on careful assessment and acute judgement. A more analytical evidence-based approach,[20] properly recorded and regularly reviewed, would make the task of assessing the strength of the case for statutory action, should this become necessary, less daunting and render decision-making less subject to delay.

A critical element in this assessment is the role of the team manager and the quality and regularity of supervision, which, sadly, it was all too apparent, was variable and on occasion placed a child at totally unacceptable risk. If this cannot be securely established within the team structure, for whatever reason, then social workers, and the families whose lives are so critically affected by their judgements, have a right to expect that alternative arrangements are in place. We would urge that departments investigate how they might address this matter, perhaps through arranging consultation sessions with child protection specialists inside or outside the organisation. It also ought to be possible to devise ways in which the expertise accrued by guardians might be fed back into mainline practice.

Key decisions in case law

As indicated previously, in the early years of the Act there were surprisingly few appeals turning on the application of the threshold conditions, due in no small measure to early judicial guidance issued in the Newham case.[21] In that case the President also expressed the view that assessment of the likelihood of harm should not be made on the basis of the balance of probabilities, the civil standard of proof; in looking to the future the court has to assess the risk. This approach was confirmed by the Appeal Court in Re M[22] while in Re H[23]

Scott Baker J gave further support to a broad interpretation of the statutory conditions when he stated that in looking at the likelihood of harm:

> I am not limited only to looking at the present and the immediate future.
> If a court concludes that a parent, or carer, is likely to be unable to meet the
> emotional needs of a child in the future – even if years hence – my view is
> that the condition in S 31(2) would probably be met.

Subsequently, however, the decision in Re H and R[24] has identified difficulties with the interpretation of *likely* cases where the application depends on disputed facts. At the time of writing the implications of this decision and the confusion it is held to have created[25] as to the standard of proof to be applied remains to be seen. It may well, however, erode confidence in the flexibility of the new criteria and their capacity to provide adequate protection.[26] At the very least the fact that the case went as far as the House of Lords, and the verdict was split three to two, exposes a fundamental tension in the approach to the Act.

The decision in this case was delivered well after our fieldwork was complete and there was therefore no opportunity to canvass reaction to it. In contrast we were able to observe at first hand the impact of the Appeal Court decision in Re M.[27] The issue was the interpretation of the words 'is suffering'. During the passage of the Children Bill through Parliament the wording 'has suffered' was amended to 'is suffering' on the grounds that the original might allow intervention simply because the child had suffered harm at some point in the past which was unlikely to be repeated. As Eekelaar[28] argued, the point was weak, because 'proof of the ground does not of itself permit the making of an order'. It made it necessary 'for the courts to adopt the common-sense interpretation employed with respect to the expression "his proper development is being avoidably prevented" under the previous law'.

The initial decision in Re M however, did not adopt this 'common-sense interpretation' thus contradicting pre-Act judgements[29] which had established that it was not necessary that the harm should be continuing at the point the application was heard. Although the circumstances of the case were unusual, the implications of the judgement for the general interpretation of 'is suffering' created consternation among the legal practitioners we interviewed as it did nationally. In the context of the approach which had thus far prevailed it struck a discordant note, perhaps indicating a 'decisive reaction against what some may regard as excessively purposive interpretations of the legislation'.[30] The subsequent judgement by the House of Lords[31] which reversed the decision and restored the status quo was therefore greeted with widespread relief. The comment by Lord Templeton[32] that the case was:

an illustration of the tyranny of language and the importance of ascertaining and giving effect to the intentions of Parliament by construing a statute in accordance with the spirit rather than the letter of the Act

is further illustration of the non-legalistic approach to the Act which has generally characterised its implementation. The occasional punctuation points, however, are a salutary reminder that the potential for a quite different approach remains, indeed that the tide may already have begun to turn. Should this prove to be the case any relaxation in the screening process within local authorities could yet produce a field day for lawyers. Thus though on the basis of our research data we should pronounce the threshold criteria a substantial success we consider judgement may still need to be reserved.

The sample cases: factors causing concern

Although legislation will determine the particular way it is framed, serious concern about family functioning is the common element in all child protection cases proceeding to court. This section attempts to map the sources of that concern in the sample cases as a prelude to examining the translation of *concern* into *significant harm*. Our starting point is Table 6.1 which groups concerns into three broad categories. The first includes concerns because of alleged maltreatment of any child, not simply the case children. The second

Table 6.1 *Factors causing concern*

	Area A %	Area B %	Area C %	All areas %
Child maltreatment				
Pre-Act	95	100	82	93
Post-Act	90	87	88	88
Condition, development or behaviour of case children				
Pre-Act	81	47	48	61
Post-Act	48	33	33	39
Behaviour or circumstances of significant adults				
Pre-Act	71	67	78	61
Post-Act	76	90	88	84
(n=)				
Pre-Act	*(41)*	*(36)*	*(27)*	*(104)*
Post-Act	*(29)*	*(30)*	*(24)*	*(83)*

category covers concern about the condition or development of the case children only, while the third reflects concerns about the behaviour or circumstances of adults intimately connected with the child *in addition to* any alleged maltreatment.

Maltreatment

A very high proportion of both the pre- and post-Act sample involved allegations that at some point a child had already been maltreated (93% pre-Act; 88% post-Act). Whilst the proportion of maltreated *case* children was somewhat lower post-Act (77% cf 83%) it still accounted for more than three in four cases. Physical abuse and neglect were the commonest forms of maltreatment in all areas in both periods. Two changes, however, were noticeable under the Children Act (although it has to be remembered that numbers are small and the two samples not matched): an apparent *reduction* in the proportion of cases involving sexual abuse and the *increased* importance of emotional abuse.

More than three in ten of the pre-Act cases involved allegations that a child in the family had been subjected to sexual abuse; post-Act less than one in five. Perhaps more strikingly, the proportion in which such allegations were made in relation to case children had more than halved (from 27% to 11%). There were also fewer cases where abuse was recent (6% compared to 28%) and it was more rarely cited as the single form of maltreatment.

The fact that these changes were apparent in each research area suggests they reflected changes in practice rather than sampling differences. In the context of this research one can of course only speculate why cases involving alleged sexual abuse might not be reaching the courts so frequently. Does it, for example, reflect increased anxiety about the evidential basis for such cases (which would not be surprising in the wake of the Cleveland and Orkney enquiries)? Or is it that ideas of appropriate practice may have changed, so that more cases are being satisfactorily dealt with on a voluntary basis or by private law orders? Frothingham's findings, however, that post-Cleveland fewer children were registered or taken into care although the sexual abuse reported was more severe, are worrying, given the conclusion that 'a significant number of victims did not receive adequate protection'. [33]

The apparent increase in the proportion of cases involving emotional abuse seems to contradict earlier comments by practitioners on the continuing difficulty of substantiating such concerns. It should be noted however that it remains extremely rare for a case to be brought to court where this is the only concern. (In the pre-Act sample there was not a single case, post-Act only one). Thus while practitioners may have been encouraged to incorporate emotional harm by the broadening of the criteria[34] there is clearly no greater readiness to risk legal action without other evidence of ill-treatment.

Cases which involved physical abuse or neglect were much more likely to appear without accompanying concerns (35% and 32% respectively). None the less cases where only one form of maltreatment is believed to have occurred were in the minority, with 62% recording at least two forms and 26% more than two. The data also show that sadly, for a sizeable minority of case children, some form of maltreatment was not a new experience. Though the proportions in each authority varied, overall 45% of post-Act cases involved both past and present maltreatment of the case children, an increase on the pre-Act figure of 38%, with Areas A and C showing a substantial increase, and Area B showing a small decrease. These differences do not simply reflect the slightly higher proportion of cases where there had been previous statutory intervention. They therefore would seem to lend support to the view of many of our interviewees that post-Act statutory intervention, at least up to the point when this research was conducted, was occurring at a later stage.

Behaviour or circumstances of significant adults

In addition to allegations of maltreatment, a very high proportion of cases also involved concerns about other aspects of parental behaviour or circumstances (Table 6.1). This was even more likely to be the case post-Act. In both samples the most frequent concerns related to mental health, alcohol or substance abuse, domestic violence and accommodation problems. Concerns about mental health, domestic violence and criminal behaviour, however, seemed to be much more prevalent in the post-Act sample, suggesting a higher index of behaviour which was seen as problematic.

Condition, development or behaviour of case children

The condition of any child who has been ill-treated or neglected is likely to be a primary cause of concern. In many of the sample cases, however, there were additional, if not entirely unrelated, anxieties about the children, either because they had special needs,[35] were failing to develop properly or were displaying some form of disturbing or unacceptable behaviour.[36] The proportion of cases in which any such concerns were noted was substantially lower in the post-Act sample, (39% compared to 61%) largely because there were fewer children with special needs or displaying forms of challenging behaviour. The latter is likely to reflect the age distribution of the two samples. The fact that a higher proportion of children were already accommodated (Chapter 4) is also relevant.

The dimensions of concern: a summary

As Table 6.2 shows, in most of the sample cases there were multiple causes of concern with three-quarters of all post-Act cases recording factors from more than one of the three categories and a third from all three. A crude index of concern by which one point was assigned to each *type* of past or present maltreatment and each *form* of adult or child behaviour/circumstances causing concern brings out some of the complexity of the cases coming before the care courts. A mean of 5.2 factors was recorded in Area C, 4.5 in Areas A and B with over a third of cases recording between 6 and 11.

Table 6.2 *The dimensions of concern*

	Area A %	Area B %	Area C %	All areas %
No. of categories				
1 only	24	20	21	21
2	35	50	46	43
3	41	30	33	35
No. of concerns				
Range	1–10	2–8	1–11	1–11
% 5 or more	48	40	54	47
Mean	4.5	4.5	5.2	4.7
(n=)	*(29)*	*(30)*	*(24)*	*(83)*

Ethnic differences

The proportion of cases where some form of child maltreatment was already believed to have occurred was high across all ethnic groups although the lowest proportion was found in cases involving ethnic minorities, particularly non-European families (Table 6.3). It was however notable that maltreatment had occurred in all nine cases where only the children, but not the adult with care, was from this group. In all but one of these the children had also experienced more than one form of abuse. Less than half of the children in

Table 6.3 *Factors causing concern: ethnic differences*

	Case involves non-European family (n = 27) %	Other cases (n = 56) %
Child maltreatment	78	93
Condition, development or behaviour of case children	41	38
Behaviour or circumstances of significant adults	78	88
Number of categories		
1 only	33	16
2	33	48
3	33	36
Mean	2.0	2.2
Number of concerns		
Range	1–9	1–11
% 5 or more	37	52
Mean	4.0	5.0

non-European families had done so, however, compared to two-thirds of the rest of the sample. As a result the proportion of cases in which any of the main categories of maltreatment were noted was lower in non-European families though the relative incidence of each was broadly similar: physical abuse being slightly more common than neglect, followed by emotional abuse or neglect.

The fraction of cases in which the behaviour or circumstances of significant adults was an additional concern was also lower in these families. Balancing this to some degree we found that the case children appear to have been more likely than the children in other families to have suffered maltreatment in the past as well as in the present (47% compared to 36%) and their condition, development or behaviour was also marginally more likely to be giving concern.

Overall, however, the data presented in Table 6.3 again suggest that the non-European families reaching court might be considered to be presenting a rather less pathological profile than other families subject to the same proceedings. Moreover, although the numbers are of course very small, this pattern was similar across all three research areas.

From concern to significant harm

Assessing significance

In the absence of precise legislative or judicial definitions of significance how was the concept being operationalised? To our surprise (and dismay), neither social services nor court documentation was of much direct assistance in exploring this issue through the sample cases. Contrary to expectations[37] social work statements and reports were, with few exceptions, *descriptive* rather than analytical, with significant harm a label stuck on at the end, Q.E.D. That is not to say, necessarily, that a process of analysis had not been gone through, merely that often there was no record of this, even in the records pertinent to social services decision-making, for example case conference papers. This deficiency was also commented on by some members of the judiciary, as this specimen comment reveals:

> A lot of the local authority statements are just a regurgitation of their files, a historical note without really concentrating and saying right, out of this vast history, these are the five incidences we are relying on. They don't seem to deal with it in that way . . . you have to read between the lines, you can get to it, but it should really be there in the pleadings.

Nor were there many clues from in-court debate about the interpretation of significance. As we have already indicated, the concept itself rarely generated conflict. In most of the sample cases social services' interpretation of significance was not called into question in the subsequent proceedings; moreover most of the lawyers and guardians interviewed considered that on the whole these departments were getting it right.

In trying to assess what thresholds of significance were operating, therefore, it was necessary to devise our own framework for analysis. A basic division was first made according to:

- whether the case was principally based on current harm and might therefore satisfy the 'is suffering' test (41 cases) or would have to rely on proving likelihood (42); and

- the nature of the principal form(s) of harm. Although, as indicated earlier, many cases involved concern about more than one form of maltreatment, wherever possible a judgement was made about the primary form.

'Is suffering' significant harm

Physical maltreatment (19 cases)

The most basic measure of significance in relation to physical maltreatment is clearly severity of injury, employed by Bentovim, for instance, in his typology of levels of abuse.[38] Using this standard alone suggested very little was needed to cross the threshold since only three cases involved major trauma in the form of fractures or internal injuries (high significance); six involved severe or extensive bruising or burns (medium significance); five presented moderate or minor bruising (low significance) while five children had no detectable injury at all.

This rudimentary classification, however, has the strange effect that some children would be deemed not to have suffered significant *harm* at all, despite being seriously abused. Baby Jemima's father, for instance, was alleged to have placed his hands around her neck until she went red in the face and began to cough. On examination only three small red marks (not considered attributable to the father's action) were found on Jemima's neck and no other ill-effects were detectable on arrival at hospital. On a *seriousness of action* index, however, we would place this case, along with six others, on a higher level of significance, the ratings now reading five low, eight medium, six high. Linked to seriousness is the degree of *vulnerability* of the child. Since she was only 10 months old Jemima's abuse would attract a high significance rating,[39] as would that of three other children under 1 year old.

The fact that there was only one case in this group involving a single incident suggests that *chronicity* is another important dimension. In Jemima's case there had been several previous instances of what had been euphemistically described as '*rough handling*' by her father, who also had a conviction for cruelty against a previous child. Using this measure,[40] four of the sample cases were judged to be of low significance, six medium and eight high.

The *context* in which abuse occurs may also affect the determination of significance as a reflection of motivation. Abuse seen as a means of exercising necessary control over a child's behaviour, perhaps in a socially unacceptable but not excessively deviant way (2 cases) might be judged of least significance. A higher rating, however, might be attached to abuse believed to result from lack of control (8). Cases with an element of sadistic pleasure or callousness (5) have perhaps the highest motivational significance with those where the context has not been established (4) scoring only marginally lower. When Jemima was 6 months, her father was variously seen to unwrap her from a shawl by pulling one end and rolling the child across the floor; pick her up by the neck, lift her up by one arm, throw her into the cot and throw soil in her face.

All but four of these 19 cases were judged to have high significance on at least one of these indices. None was rated high on every one, but using a very crude scoring system eight cases did so overall, ten were assessed as moderate and one was borderline low to moderate.

The measures used so far could be applied to all the sample cases. In a number additional factors also seemed relevant. The *psychological effect* of the alleged abuse on the child for instance: in eight cases the children, mainly older children, were described as exhibiting high degrees of fear. Most had drawn attention to the abuse themselves, signalling that they had had enough. This measure would raise the significance levels of two cases.

The final dimension is again contextual. A bruise may be of low significance in terms of severity of injury or seriousness of action. Inflicted by a depressed mother at the end of her tether it may have only moderate motivational significance. But as an indicator that her coping strategies are breaking down it may be of high significance, an early warning that without intervention the child may be more seriously injured. On this *prognosticative* measure (for which there is support in the research literature and child abuse enquiry reports)[41] three cases which would otherwise be of low or low–moderate overall significance move onto a higher level. As a result 18 of the 19 cases would acquire a high rating on at least one measure while on the basis of overall scores nine would be rated high, ten moderate and none low.

This suggests that *even in cases involving physical abuse* a fairly formidable threshold was being operated by all three departments. The higher scores assigned to cases brought in Area A,[42] however, suggest that this authority was interpreting the test particularly severely. It was surprising, therefore, that the only case from here not rated high turned out to be one of the most borderline cases of the whole group. This case, involving 3-year-old Sammi Collins, experiencing his third set of care proceedings, was also the only one in this group in which a non-social services practitioner questioned whether the child was actually suffering *significant* harm.

Neglect (13 cases)

The word neglect does not appear in the new legislation although it remains one of the categories for inclusion on the Child Protection Register and it is clear from *Working Together*[43] that it is still intended to be recognised as a source of harm to children. Acknowledging that the categories for registration 'do not tie in precisely with the definition of "significant harm" in Section 31 of the Children Act', *Working Together* points out:

> With a case of neglect it will be necessary to consider whether it involves actual or likely 'significant harm' and whether it involves 'ill treatment' or 'impairment of health or development.'

Unfortunately while this poses the problem it offers no guidance as to how it might be resolved. Poor hygiene, for instance, is clearly neglectful behaviour but does it count as ill-treatment? Could it be said the child 'is suffering' harm, or would it have to be argued that it is likely to impair the child's health? Is impairment meant to be interpreted in the active sense of something which is done to children or passively as a condition of children? Such ambiguities, it is true, do not seem to trouble practitioners once the case is in court, even when different interpretations are implicit in the material presented to the court, sometimes even by the same person.

Given this apparent pragmatic approach and since we can see no logical reason why neglectful behaviour should be treated differently from physical or sexual abuse in this respect we have proceeded on the basis of including in the 'is suffering' group all cases where neglect[44] was a principal issue although in only nine was there any discernible effect on the children's health and development.

Four of these nine cases were categorised as high significance (on the basis of later expert opinion) including one of life-threatening failure to thrive. The rest were a mixture of gross behavioural disturbance and serious developmental or educational delay. In two of these cases, however, it was very unclear how much of the impairment was attributable to parental neglect and it was not the key element in the local authority case. There was no detectable impairment at all in three cases, while the remaining five appeared to be of low significance.

Applying a *seriousness of action* criteria produces a rather different picture. In one of the no impairment cases, for instance, the two Myers children, aged 1 and 2, were found with their seriously intoxicated mother in a car at the side of the motorway. In the case of Colin and Antony Wyllie the only detectable impairment was a degree of educational delay, but lack of supervision had resulted in the children putting themselves into life-threatening situations on a number of occasions. On this index we would rate seven of the 13 cases as of high significance.

Eight cases were rated high because of *vulnerability*. This has to be a rather more complex measure than simply age, reflecting individual inter-relationships between need and deficits in care. Colin and Antony Wyllie, for example, became more vulnerable to the effects of poor supervision with age and independence and more emotionally vulnerable to schoolyard taunts about being dirty and smelly. In contrast, for Robert Barnes, a premature baby, the likely physical effects of poor hygiene and inattention to his basic needs for warmth and nutrition were of particular importance.

The extent to which neglect is *global*, resulting in a failure to meet a whole range of needs or restricted to particular areas of care would also seem to be relevant to the assessment of significance. When she was not intoxicated Mrs Myers was considered to be providing a high level of care. In the case of Ben Smisson, however, which also involved alcohol abuse, it is hard to see that any of his needs were being met. Seven other cases were similarly rated as of high significance.

Eight of the 13 cases were also characterised by a high degree of *chronicity*. Four were rated as moderate in that either there had only been a few incidents or the neglect had persisted for a few months only. None of the neglect cases came to court as the result of a *single* failure of care.

As with physical abuse, no case scored high on all these indices. Twelve of the 13, however, did so on at least one and five on all but one. Again using a very crude scoring system, eight of the 13 cases were rated as of high overall significance, five moderate and none low. All these figures suggest a higher threshold for intervention than in cases based on physical abuse.

Area A again, remarkably, had both the greatest proportion of cases of high overall significance[45] and the one assessed, on this framework, as of least significance, which happened to be that of the Myers children. Yet though this case only reached the highest significance rating on one measure, seriousness of action, there would seem to be little room to dispute that, left in their mother's care, these children were likely to suffer injury or even death.

Sexual abuse (2 cases)

The relative rarity of cases involving any element of sexual abuse in the post-Act sample was commented on earlier. Even more remarkably, only two cases could be assigned to the 'is suffering' group and both involved the non-familial sexual activity of older girls, the *moral danger* scenario which until relatively recently would have been equated with Section 1(2)(c) of the

Children and Young Persons Act. Given that each involved exploitation by older men, in one case for money, and both involved genital contact/intercourse, a high significance rating would seem self-evident.

Emotional/psychological abuse or neglect (7 cases)

Little is self-evident, however, where these less tangible forms of harm are at issue,[46] with both highly specific and broad interpretations being advocated.[47] In allocating seven cases to this category we have adopted the framework in *Protecting Children*[48] with the addition of 'exposure to marital or family conflict and/or violence' which is there cited as a separate category of concern.

Montgomery,[49] writing before implementation of the Act, suggests that while professional opinion may be that emotional abuse and neglect is inherently damaging, without identifiable serious consequences legal action is unlikely to be taken. This would appear still to be the case. In three of the sample cases there was evidence of what was later categorised by independent professionals as severe suffering. For example, Jason, unable to speak at the age of 6, was described by the paediatrician as the most damaged child he had ever seen. In the other four cases the children were displaying less extreme reactions and despite rising levels of professional anxiety were only propelled into court because of other events (minor physical abuse, accidental injury in the course of domestic violence, lack of supervision). These became the pegs on which to hang the real concerns. All these children, however, were being exposed to seriously damaging experiences. Christopher's paediatrician, for example, expressed 'surprise' at the relatively moderate behavioural and psychological symptoms displayed by this particularly resilient[50] child and could only conclude that 'he must have considerable coping mechanisms' not to be 'showing more anxiety symptoms'.

In three of the cases in this group, although parents suffered from chronic psychiatric conditions, it was a recent acute deterioration which was impacting severely on the child. In all the others the child had experienced potentially damaging circumstances for a prolonged period. There had been a high level of professional and family concern, for instance, for at least a year about 11-year-old Jenny Grayson, whose mother's paranoia and childhood experience of sexual abuse made her grossly over-protective. When Jenny attended school (which was infrequently), her mother accompanied her into the classroom; she was not allowed to play on her own and if, rarely, a visitor came to the house she was always chaperoned. Yet it was only when Jenny herself began to rebel against her virtual imprisonment, resulting in violent conflict, that it was judged possible to intervene.

In Jenny's case, as in all but one of the others, social services intervened at the point the child appeared to be exposed to heightened levels of abuse because of a deterioration in parental functioning, usually linked with psychiatric illness. Thus in terms of short-term prognosis they would all be rated as of high significance. As far as the exception, Jason, was concerned, the level of abuse and damage was already so high that it is hard to see that anything worse could happen.

All seven cases were rated high on at least one index and two on all four. Most strikingly all seven cases reached a high level of *overall* significance. The fact that Jenny's case was rated as marginally the *least* significant and had been considered unlikely to satisfy the legal tests under either the new or old legislation is a cogent indication of the legal difficulties such cases are still believed to present. Even at the point of crisis after police protection was involved, local authority legal opinion was that there were insufficient grounds for an Emergency Protection Order and dubious grounds for care proceedings.

This attempt to quantify what might be regarded as unquantifiable is no doubt open to criticism. It does, however, lend support to the interview data in a number of ways:

♦ Statutory intervention in the first two years of the Act was certainly not being used to address 'minor deficiencies' in child care.[51] The parenting all these children were receiving fell far short of a reasonable standard. It was not a question of whether parenting was *good* enough, rather of whether it was *bad* enough to justify legal action.

♦ Where significant harm takes the form of emotional abuse the threshold is perceived to be particularly high.

♦ There was some variation in the thresholds operating in each authority with cases in Area A showing a higher overall level of significance for physical or emotional abuse and neglect.

Differences between the pre- and post-Act samples

One of the principal deficiencies in the Children and Young Persons Act 1969, and a major reason for the increasing popularity of wardship, was the lack of a general forward-looking ground. Thus in the majority of our pre-Act cases brought in care proceedings the children had recently experienced ill-treatment or neglect. However this was also found to apply in cases brought in jurisdictions which did permit anticipating the future. Thus the drop in the proportion of recently abused children in the post-Act sample (from four in five to one in two) cannot be attributed solely to variation in its composition.

The likelihood of significant harm

None of the 41 cases cited in the previous section would have been brought to court had the local authority not considered that as well as the harm they had already suffered, the children were likely to suffer harm in the future. In some cases indeed it was difficult to decide whether for our purposes 'is suffering' or 'is likely to suffer' was the most appropriate allocation. A similar problem arose with some of the 42 cases we assigned to the *likelihood* category but where there was *some* evidence of actual harm. For instance, when three children already in local authority care (because of neglect by their divorced mother) suddenly disclosed severe and persistent sexual and physical abuse by their re-married father, there was understandable concern about the welfare of father's new family. It was on this basis that social services went to court, rather than relying on allegations that at least two of these other children had also been abused. The case was therefore allocated to the likelihood group.

For purposes of analysis the 'is likely to' group was further sub-divided according to whether harm appeared to be predicted primarily on the basis of past harm to the case children (14), harm to non-case children (13) or parental circumstances/behaviour (15).

Likelihood based on past maltreatment of a case child (14 cases)

Nine cases assigned to this category involved accommodated[52] children and one a family living in a residential placement where, though there were concerns about the current borderline quality of care, the basis of the case was the likely recurrence of earlier gross neglect. Four other cases also primarily involved neglect, five physical abuse, three emotional abuse and one sexual abuse. Applying the same framework developed for analysing the 'is suffering' group seven cases were judged to be of overall high significance, seven moderate and none low. Levels of significance for each form of maltreatment appeared to be similar across the two groups, suggesting that for this type of case the existence of the 'is likely' provision has not resulted in an overall lowering of the threshold.

Previous abuse may be one of the best predictors of maltreatment, none the less the local authority still has to satisfy the court that without statutory intervention it is likely to recur, particularly when some considerable time has elapsed since the last episode (between six weeks to over a year and in nine cases more than four months). Again it was rare to find explicit argument in the documentation but analysis suggests implicit linkages were being made in a variety of ways because, for example, of:

- the continuation of the conditions associated with the earlier abuse, for example alcohol dependency (3 cases);

- allegations that abuse was continuing (1);

- the breakdown of voluntary agreements about behaviour, for example that the alleged perpetrator would stay away from the children (2 cases);

- professional assessments of the child's needs and parental ability to meet them (4); and

- parental recognition that they were unable to cope (1).

There were only three cases where none of these conditions could be relied on. One involved unexplained non-accidental injury which remained unexplained even after the child had been accommodated for three months, the second involved serious sexual abuse based on the child's evidence which was corroborated by his mentally ill mother but strenuously denied by the alleged perpetrator. Thus the thrust of the local authority's case would be that though it might not be possible to demonstrate that re-abuse was likely the fact that it was not possible to rule it out and the consequences for the child of re-occurrence given the severity of the earlier alleged abuse would be sufficient.

The third case, where the application was for a supervision order on 2-year-old Samantha, was an anomaly in the sample as a whole since the local authority withdrew at the first hearing, admitting that evidence they thought was there to prove the likelihood of harm, was not. Legal costs were awarded against them. We shall comment further on this case at a later stage.

Likelihood based on harm to a non-case child (13 cases)

Similar assessments of the likelihood of repetition had to be made in cases based primarily on the alleged or proven abuse of other children.[53] All except one involved maltreatment of another child within the family, six concurrently, seven at some time in the past. Six of these latter cases involved proceedings at birth; whilst in the seventh, mother and baby had been placed together in a specialist foster home for support and assessment some months prior to proceedings. The level of severity of these cases is indicated by the fact that in all but two (and all those involving past abuse) there had been criminal and/or civil protection proceedings.

In the six cases involving concurrent abuse of other children the assumption that in consequence the case children were also at risk was clearly not perceived as problematic and perhaps rightly so, although there were grounds for suspicion that abuse (in each case sexual abuse) had already occurred in only two. However there was one case where the gravity of the abuse, resulting in the death of a baby, seems to have overridden any other consideration, since to us the circumstances would suggest the other children were not vulnerable.

Where past abuse was concerned the grounds for action were usually the persistence of circumstances and/or behaviour patterns associated with previous events. Surprisingly the only one in which the likelihood of harm was seriously challenged was Zara's, whose future provoked intense uncertainty and conflict among practitioners from beginning to end. Alone of all the cases brought on new-born children, the firm intention was immediate and permanent removal and the local authority appeared to have no doubts that the threshold criteria would be met:

> We felt we had a very good case; there was a weight of evidence which indicated the child was very vulnerable; any child would be vulnerable in that relationship and there was plenty of evidence that supervision orders had been unsuccessful. (Social worker)

The child's solicitor had acted for the previous children and could therefore:

> well understand the local authority saying we've been here before, she isn't going to change, we've got to control what is happening to this baby.

The guardian, however, who was fresh to the case:

> had difficulty deciding whether the criteria were met. I disagreed quite significantly with the local authority and their interpretation of what sort of harm there might be. There was a history of physical injury but I felt it wasn't serious injury and that that was not the most notable aspect of this case; the harm was the harm the child might suffer in the presence of arguing adults. And I had discomfort about considering that to be significant.

The solicitor acting for Sandra, Zara's mother, expressed no doubts at all:

> I didn't think the threshold conditions were met. Simply because there's some kind of momentum once a number of children have gone into care, if another child comes along that's at risk and will go into care as well. It should be better now and if one had in mind the principles of the Act it shouldn't be happening.

Zara's case, complicated in so many ways, was simple in that there was no question of the parents, Sandra and Phil, agreeing to the local authority's plans. In other cases, however, where as yet there had been no harm to the child, parents were prepared to co-operate with protective plans. In such circumstances can the threshold be met? On the whole, lawyers tended to ignore such issues, concentrating their opposition on the need for an order when the argument would turn on the reliability of parental co-operation. In the only case we observed where the solicitor for the parents took a stricter approach and was proposing to challenge on this point at the first hearing the culture of pragmatism won the day. As he told us:

> I still think (my interpretation) was right . . . I was surprised that the child's solicitor didn't take the point on board. He thought I was being pedantic and legalistic; this was obviously a case where we should have an order and if I went down that route it would be heavily contested. I think I have to be honest and question how far that lay behind my decision not to contest it. When you're with someone who is more experienced than you are there's this inbuilt notion that they're probably right.

> But what swayed me was the mother. It was my stand not hers . . . . We'd made a lot of progress towards some kind of rapprochement with social services, a contested hearing would have meant a lot of evidence would have come out and the effect of that on her would have been for her to turn round and say bugger you lot, I'm not going to work with you if that's what you think of me. You can't afford to be too legalistic when the real solutions to the case aren't going to be found in a legalised mechanised approach. They have to be real solutions. It had to come from her, not this lawyer doing a ritual dance that wasn't going to achieve anything.

Likelihood based primarily on the behaviour or circumstances of the carer (15 cases)

Finally there were 15 cases where there was either no evidence that any child had ever seriously suffered harm or even if there was *some* evidence the primary argument seemed to be that the care *likely* to be given to the child would not be 'reasonable'. None of these cases would have satisfied the conditions in the Children and Young Persons Act; all would have been classic pre-Act wardships.[54]

The cases fell into two main groups. In the first (7 cases) the principal reason for proceedings was to make long-term plans for an accommodated child (6) or for a child in a supervised placement with a parent. Generally while there had been child protection concerns about these children before placement they had not suffered significant harm. However although rehabilitation plans had not worked out and the children had been away from their parents for an average of 47 weeks, the parent(s) would not consent to alternative plans or were inconsistent in their views. The likely harm was therefore argued to be the emotional consequences of impermanence.

In the second group the children were deemed at risk if they remained with their customary carers in an unsupervised setting (4 cases) or if they were returned from accommodation as parents requested (4). All but one of these cases involved carers with psychiatric disorders, the remaining case was a mother living with a violent partner whose attitude to the child, then accommodated, was negative and aggressive.

Significant harm: differences by area and ethnicity

The three study areas varied not only in the proportion of post-Act cases brought on the 'is suffering' ground but in their reasons for arguing that the case children were likely to suffer harm (Figure 6.1). A familial history of harm was the most common basis for arguing likelihood in Area A, parental behaviour in Area C and harm to the case children in the past in Area B.

Figure 6.1 *Significant harm: distribution between areas and categories*

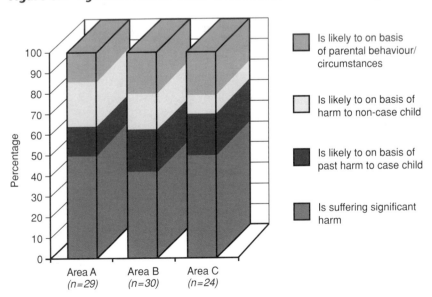

In all areas, cases involving minority group families were slightly more likely than others to be based on the 'is suffering' ground. Those brought on risk were also fractionally more likely than cases relating to white UK families to involve past harm to case children. In total in 73% of cases involving ethnic minority families (30) the case children were already believed to have suffered harm, compared to 62% (26) of other families.

In terms of the harm suffered, differences between ethnic groups were also small, the source being physical abuse or neglect in around three-quarters of cases, the proportions varying by only a few percent between the majority or minority groups. Of these two primary forms of harm physical abuse was commonest in all groups but tended to be more a feature of cases involving the majority population. Comparing levels of harm, however, marginally more cases involving non-European families were rated high. This was more marked where the harm resulted from physical abuse.

Not surprisingly, given the less chronic involvement of minority families with the welfare system, likelihood based on harm to non-case children was almost exclusively restricted to the white UK population. There was not a single case of this kind involving non-European families. Such families were, however, over-represented among cases primarily based on risk due to parental circumstances or behaviour. However we found no evidence to suggest that a lower threshold of risk was operating in these eight cases, all but one of which concerned very young and vulnerable children such as Ahmed Khan.

Unreasonable parenting

In addition to showing significant harm or its likelihood, the local authority must demonstrate the harm is attributable to: 'the care given to the child, or likely to be given to him if the order were not made, not being what it would be reasonable to expect a parent to give to him'.[55]

This second limb is clearly theoretically necessary to prevent intervention where the child is suffering harm which is in no way due to parental inadequacy. In the context of the majority[56] of the sample cases, however, where the alleged direct source of harm was ill-treatment, it appeared almost tautological and rarely received more than scant reference, even though deficits in parenting are central to most cases. The only cases in which definitions of reasonableness were explicitly argued were those involving physical 'abuse' in which a parent claimed to be exercising discipline and therefore acting responsibly. Since almost all these cases involved parents from ethnic minorities there was scope for dispute over cultural norms about appropriate punishment although none of the cases was dismissed on this ground.

Cases involving a parent who dearly loves their child but whose ability to provide adequate care has been adversely affected by events demonstrably beyond their control, psychiatric illness, for instance, or learning difficulties, are among the most distressing for practitioners to handle. Grace Wyllie for example, suffered from schizophrenia and it was clear that either because of her illness, or the medication required to treat it, the children were frequently left to their own dangerous devices, although there was no question about her love and concern for them. The reasonable parent test, however, is an objective one. The child's parents are judged 'by what a reasonable parent would do for the child in question', not by 'what can reasonably be expected of the child's parents in their circumstances and given their characteristics'.[57] None the less, while recognising that objectively parental care was not good enough, in some instances practitioners appeared to have difficulty separating this from the question of parental culpability. This could present a problem both before and after the case came to court. In Colin and Antony's case, for example, the guardian told us:

> We debated whether it was attributable to mother because of the mental illness. If mother had been blind or in a wheelchair? It was attributable to her lack of care but was it grounds for a Care Order? We concluded it was within her means to do something.

Attribution

Only two cases in the sample involved non-familial abuse (both involving sexual exploitation) as a primary source of harm; in each there were subsidiary concerns about ill-treatment or neglect within the family. In a further two, both involving lone mothers whose children had suffered severe physical injuries from an unidentified source, professionals appeared convinced the mother was not directly responsible but knew who was. One of these cases was appealed on the basis of non-attribution but given very short shrift by the appeal judge. In a further three cases there was some uncertainty as to which parent was responsible though usually one would be the main focus for suspicion.

Mothers (or in one case a female legal guardian) were believed to be directly implicated in the alleged harm or likely harm to the child in three-quarters of the sample cases (63; 76%), compared to fathers (22; 27%) and fathers or other male partners (31; 37%). This is scarcely surprising given that over half the cases (43) involved single parent households, all but one female headed. In dual-carer households the gender balance was more even: mothers were implicated in 63% of cases; fathers in 53% and fathers or male partners in 65%.

Cases revolving around issues of neglect and emotional abuse were most likely to arise from lone-parent households; physical and sexual abuse from households where mother was living with either the natural father or a new partner. Within dual-carer families harm arising from neglect and emotional abuse was also most likely to be attributed to women, physical and sexual abuse to men. These distributions reflect the general patterns revealed in the child protection literature.[58]

Only 17 cases involved an apparently non-abusing parent. There seemed to be some confusion among practitioners as to whether the case had to be proved against both parents. In the 12 brought on the 'is suffering' ground, however, it would not in general be difficult to show, if necessary, that this parent had failed to protect and was therefore also providing unreasonable parenting, although the issue could re-surface in considering the need for an order where the abuser was no longer present. Of the remainder, four cases were brought following the breakdown of previous protective measures using the non-abusing parent. The fifth case was that of the Khan family whose perceived unreasonableness began to look rather different as the story unfolded.

In attempting to analyse the application of the threshold criteria in the sample cases we confess to a certain sympathy with our lawyer informants who, while praising the principles of the new legislation, were scathing about its wording which was described as: 'cumbersome and long-winded', 'shockingly badly worded', 'strangulated', 'tortuous', 'verbose' and 'difficult to explain'. Like a number of practitioners we have also found the framework far from straight-forward to apply in any strict sense; the Act appears to lend itself to a logical flow chart type of approach[59] which is less clear-cut in practice. Were the courts ever to insist on a strict technical interpretation we would anticipate, as did numerous commentators prior to implementation, considerable difficulties.

Conversely, one has to question whether on their own the threshold criteria provide a high enough level of protection for families against unwarranted intervention. Our estimates of the level of significance in the sample cases support practitioner views that cases reaching the courts in the first two years of the Act were generally appropriate. However it is unlikely that this was principally a function of the conditions themselves. Rather the threshold criteria have to be seen in the context of the whole spirit of the Act and the new themes of voluntarism and partnership with parents which though unstated in the legislation are acknowledged to underpin it. These themes have in particular guided the interpretation of the key principle in Section 1 of the Act, which has been wrongly, but significantly, referred to universally as the *no order principle*. These issues form the subject of the next chapter.

Summary

The new criteria commanded a wide measure of support among practitioner interviewees who judged them not only viable and appropriate but a considerable improvement on previous legislation. Their interpretation has not proved generally problematic during proceedings nor for professionals practising primarily within the courts.

Social services staff have had more difficulty operationalising the criteria and assessing whether they have the evidence to satisfy them, resulting in uncertainty, anxiety and delays in bringing cases to court. Statements of evidence rarely applied the criteria to the facts, tended to focus on the actions or inactions of parents not the effects on the child and were chronological and descriptive rather than analytic. As social workers become more familiar with the legislation and common understandings develop confidence should increase. Further training is recommended.

Social workers should be helped to incorporate an understanding of the legal framework more thoroughly into their everyday practice and develop a more analytical evidence-based approach. This needs to be based on improved case recording. Maintaining a case chronology and periodic assessments of the extent to which the child's needs are being met should be a routine part of record-keeping, reviewed in regular supervision sessions.

The majority of sample cases reaching court before and after the Children Act involved multiple causes of concern. Most alleged more than one form of maltreatment and often repeated maltreatment. There tended to be additional concerns over parental circumstances or behaviour and often concerns over the welfare of the children apart from the consequences of maltreatment. Ethnic minority families presented a less pathological profile, again suggesting that they may be disproportionately vulnerable to statutory intervention.

Physical abuse and neglect remained, post-Act, the most frequent types of maltreatment alleged. The proportion of cases involving sexual abuse, however, was lower, suggesting changes in the pattern of response which might be a cause for concern. The incidence of emotional abuse was higher but it remained almost unheard of for a case to be brought to court on that ground alone.

Just under half the sample were judged to be principally based on the 'is suffering' ground with significant harm most frequently alleged as a consequence of physical abuse, followed by neglect, emotional abuse and sexual abuse.

A range of dimensions were developed to assess significance and combined to give an overall rating. Nearly all the cases were scored high on at least one dimension and almost two-thirds overall. None was judged low or borderline. This supports practitioner perceptions that only the more serious cases were being brought to court. All the cases involving harm as the result of sexual or emotional abuse were rated high, suggesting particularly testing thresholds were being operated, as were the majority of neglect cases. Overall significance levels were lowest where physical abuse was the source of harm.

Almost two-thirds of the cases judged to be brought primarily on the 'likely to suffer' ground were based on previous maltreatment either of the case children or other children. The proportion of cases based solely on predictions of risk because of parental circumstances or behaviour was slightly higher than in pre-Act wardships but still only amounted to less than a fifth of the whole sample. Non-European families were over-represented. Although there was no evidence that a lower threshold of risk was operating this finding warrants further investigation. Where harm was deemed to have occurred already significance levels were higher in these families, particularly cases involving physical abuse.

Cultural differences in parenting were on occasion used, though unsuccessfully, to challenge the second limb of the threshold criteria. Otherwise reasonable parenting was rarely an issue and received scant *explicit* attention. Attribution was similarly also rarely disputed: in most cases the source of harm was clear. Mothers were disproportionately implicated, a measure of the primary female responsibility for child-rearing and the proportion of female-headed households. Gender distribution was in line with that reported in the general child protection literature, physical and sexual abuse being primarily attributed to men, neglect and emotional abuse to women.

It was concluded that the threshold criteria, deceptively simple in theory, are exceedingly complex in application. The paucity of legal argument at the point the research was conducted reflects the tighter filter operated by social services and the common-sense, non-legalistic approach adopted by the courts during the research period. Were both these factors to change, this aspect of the new legislation could yet become a legal battleground. In this respect the jury is still out on the viability of the new test.

[1] The conditions are known as the 'threshold criteria' because they are not in themselves grounds for making an order. Rather, as the Lord Chancellor has emphasised, they are: 'the minimum circumstances which the Government considers should always be found to exist before it can ever be justified for a court even to begin to contemplate whether the State should be enabled to intervene compulsorily in family life'. Lord Mackay, LC (1989): Joseph Jackson Memorial Lecture. *New Law Journal*, 139.

[2] DHSS (1985): *Review of Child Care Law: Report to Ministers of an Interdepartmental Working Party*. HMSO.

[3] Children and Young Persons Act 1969 Section 1(2).

[4] Child Care Act 1980 Section 3.

[5] House of Commons (1984): *Second Report of the All-Party Parliamentary Select Committee on Social Services* (Session 1983–84): Children in Care (The Short Report). HMSO.

[6] White R et al. (1990): *A Guide to the Children Act 1989*. Butterworths.

[7] Law on Child Care and Family Services, Cm 62 1987.

[8] White R et al. (1995): *The Children Act in Practice*. 2nd edition. Butterworths.

[9] White et al. (1995) op. cit.; Cretney S (1990): Defining the Limits of State Intervention: the child and the courts, in Freestone D (ed.): *Children and the Law*. Hull University Press; Freeman M (1992): *Children, their Families and the Law. Working with the Children Act*. Macmillan.

[10] Home Office et al. (1991): *Working Together: A Guide to Arrangements for Inter-agency Co-operation for the Protection of Children from Abuse*. HMSO.

[11] Hallett C (1995): *Inter-agency Co-ordination and Child Protection*. HMSO.

[12] Thoburn J et al. (forthcoming): *Safeguarding Children with the Children Act*. The Stationery Office.

[13] Hunt J (1986): The Grounds for Care. Unpublished paper prepared for the DoH based on analysis of cases from the Representation of the Child in the Civil Courts, Research Project 1985–90.

[14] Newham London Borough LB v AG [1992] 2 FCR 119.

[15] 2 FCR 245, Thorpe J.

[16] Hunt J (1993): *Local Authority Wardships before the Children Act: The Baby or the Bathwater?* HMSO.

[17] DHSS (1985): op. cit.

[18] Kaganas F (1995): Partnership under the Children Act 1989 – an overview, in Kaganas F; King M; Piper C: *Legislating for Harmony: Partnership under the Children Act*. Jessica Kingsley.

[19] Harwin J (1992): Child Protection and the Role of the Social Worker under the Children Act; Parry M (1992): The Children Act 1989: a conflict of ideologies? *both chapters*, in Parry M (ed.) *The Children Act 1989: Conflict and Compromise*. Hull University Law School.

[20] DoH (1991): *Patterns and Outcomes in Child Placement*. HMSO.

[21] Newham London Borough LB v AG [1992] 2 FCR 119.

[22] Re M (A Minor) (Appeal) (No. 2) [1994] 1 FLR 59; Waite LJ. See also Re A (A Minor) (Care Proceedings) [1993] 1 FCR 824.

[23] Re H (A Minor) (S.37 Direction) [1993] 2 FLR 541 Scott Baker J.

[24] [1995] 1 FLR 643.

[25] White R et al. (1995): *The Children Act in Practice*. 2nd edition. Butterworths.

[26] White R (1996): Reasonable Doubt. *Community Care*, 8 February. Issue 1105.

[27] [1994] 1 FLR 73.

[28] Eekelaar J; Dingwall R (1990): *The Reform of Child Care Law*. Tavistock/Routledge.

[29] D v Berkshire County Council [1987] 1 All ER 20 at 33.

[30] Cretney S (1994): Comment on Re M. *Family Law*, February .

[31] Re M (A Minor) (Care Order: Threshold Conditions) [1994] 3 All ER 298.

[32] Quoted in Cobley C (1995): *Child Abuse and the Law*. Cavendish Publishing Limited.

[33] Frothingham T E et al. (1993): Child Sexual Abuse in Leeds Before and After Cleveland. *Child Abuse Review*, 23.

[34] O'Hagan, for instance, states 'the Act will compel practitioners, trainers, managers, solicitors and magistrates to widen their perspective on child abuse generally and to learn how to cope with emotional and psychological abuse in particular'. O'Hagan K (1993): *Emotional and Psychological Abuse of Children*. Open University Press.

[35] E.g. learning disability, chronic physical illness or disability, psychiatric illness.

[36] E.g. precocious sexual activity, delinquency, truancy, aggression, absconding from home, and being beyond control.

[37] O'Hagan (1993) op. cit. writes 'social workers will have learnt already . . . that it is insufficient merely to say that little Billy 'is suffering or likely to suffer significant harm' . . . Apart from any professional inadequacy this may constitute, courts are increasingly likely to enquire about what precisely is meant by this term: the type of harm? how is it inflicted? its immediate and long-term consequences?'

[38] Bentovim A (1991): Significant Harm in Context, in Adcock M et al. *A Significant Harm*. Significant Publications.

[39] High significance defined as under a year; medium 1–7 years; low more than 7.

[40] Low chronicity was defined as one previous incident; medium: more than one but not frequent or frequent but over a short period; high: maltreatment of the case children over a lengthy period or maltreatment of previous, non-case children.

[41] Stephanie Fox, for example, had suffered 30 known incidents of minor bruising before she died as the result of a violent assault. Corby B (1993): *Child Abuse, Towards a Knowledge Base*. Open University Press.

[42] In Area A, five out of six cases were rated as of high significance; Area B, two out of seven; Area C, two out of six.

[43] Home Office et al. (1991): *Working Together*. HMSO.

[44] This category includes neglect of physical care, (hygiene, nutrition, warmth and cloth-ing, medical needs) safety (lack of supervision, leaving alone, abandonment, exposure to danger) social and educational development. It follows the guidance offered by the Department of Health in 1988 in *Protecting Children: A Guide for Social Workers Undertaking a Comprehensive Assessment*. HMSO.

[45] Area A, three out of four cases rated high; B, three out of five; C, two out of three.

[46] Corby (1993) op. cit.; O'Hagan (1993) op. cit.; Goldstein J et al. (1979): *Beyond the Best Interests of the Child*. Free Press, New York.

[47] Wald M (1982): State Intervention on Behalf of Endangered Children – a proposed legal response. *Child Abuse and Neglect*, 6, 3–45; Garbarino J; Gilliam G (1980): *Understanding Abusive Families*. Lexington Books, Lexington, MA.

[48] DoH (1988): *Protecting Children: A Guide for Social Workers Undertaking a Comprehensive Assessment.* HMSO. In this document emotional abuse includes: rejection, lack of praise or encouragement, lack of comfort or love, lack of attachment, lack of proper stimulation (e.g. fun and play), lack of continuity of care (e.g. frequent moves), lack of appropriate handling (e.g. age-inappropriate expectations), serious over-protectiveness, inappropriate non-physical punishment (e.g. locking in bedrooms).

[49] Montgomery J (1989): The Emotional Abuse of Children. *Family Law*, 19, 25–9.

[50] Rutter M (1985): Resilience in the Face of Adversity: protective factors and resistance to psychiatric disorder. *British Journal of Psychiatry*, 147, 598–611.

[51] Lord Mackay, LC (1989): The Joseph Jackson Memorial Lecture. *New Law Journal*, 139.

[52] In the light of the House of Lords decision in Re M, that 'is suffering' relates to the point at which the local authority took protective action, which could be the use of accommodation, it is arguable that these cases should be re-classified.

[53] Principal form of maltreatment being neglect in nine cases, physical abuse in two, sexual abuse in three.

[54] Hunt (1993): op. cit.

[55] Children Act 1989, Section 31(2)(i).

[56] In 67 of the sample cases (80.7%) a parent (or in one case a legal guardian) was alleged to be directly responsible either for the principal form of harm or in a few cases, for ancillary abuse. This figure is only slightly lower than the 84.3% noted in the pre-Act sample.

[57] Eekelaar et al. (1990): op. cit.

[58] Corby (1993): op. cit.

[59] E.g. Adcock M et al. (1991): Examining the Threshold Criteria, in *Significant Harm*, op. cit.

7

Gate 2: establishing the need for an order

Compulsory intervention: the new approach

> Where a court is considering whether or not to make one or more orders . . .
> it shall not make the order or any of the orders unless it considers that doing
> so would be better for the child than making no order at all. (Children Act
> 1989, Section 1(5))

One of the key 'principles which guide the courts',[1] this gives effect in public
law to the recommendation of the Child Care Law Review that 'the grounds
should in future make a clear reference to the likely effectiveness of an order'.[2]
While acknowledging that already, under the Children and Young Persons
Act, if the primary grounds were proved the court still had to be satisfied that
the child 'is in need of care or control which he is unlikely to receive unless
an order is made' the Working Party's 'impression' was that:

> The test is often satisfied by proof that his needs will not be met outside care,
> rather than by positive proof that a Care Order or a Supervision Order will
> result in his needs being met or at least better catered for, and further that
> intervention will not do more overall harm than good.

One reason why courts were not applying the care or control test in the way
the Review thought necessary was that it was not clear whether they were
entitled to enquire into the use social services proposed to make of an order,[3]
an issue of particular frustration to Guardians ad Litem.[4] The Children Act
removes that impediment, requiring local authorities to specify their plan for
the child and the courts to evaluate it and decide (i) whether it will improve
the child's situation and (ii) whether it needs an order to be implemented.[5]

As Eekelaar[6] points out, however, Section 1(5), is only the 'final hurdle' the local
authority must clear, both the specific legislative changes and accompanying
official pronouncements reflecting 'political coolness towards the use of compulsory measures'. Thus the Act 'rests on the belief that children are best looked
after within the family . . . without resort to legal proceedings'.[7] Local authorities are directed to 'take reasonable steps designed to reduce the need to bring

proceedings'[8] and even when that need appears to exist, no longer have a *duty* to bring proceedings. 'Recourse to court should, as far as possible, be a last resort'.[9]

This concerted attempt to discourage court action emerged at the end of a decade in which the proportion of children compulsorily admitted to care rose substantially[10] while a raft of research studies demonstrated the deficiencies of state care.[11] Thus the thrust of child care policy, encapsulated in the Act, shifted to emphasise parental responsibility, the maintenance of the child within the kinship group, the supportive rather than the coercive role of the state. These changes were to be underpinned by a new style of working with families which has come to be known as *partnership*. The fundamental shift in attitudes required was encouraged by a range of government commissioned training programmes in which the emphasis was on communicating the *principles* as well as the details of the new law.

This pro-family, anti-compulsion strategy was never intended to prevent statutory intervention where this is the only appropriate remedy – the duty to safeguard the welfare of the child is there as a rider in all the guidance. In the initial stages of implementation, however, the emphasis on partnership and voluntarism combined with the presumption of no order proved a potent combination. All over the country the number of public law applications plummeted, stimulating an enquiry by the Social Services Inspectorate into local authority decision-making. This found: 'very little evidence that cases actually taken to court were failing because of partnership issues' but 'widespread concern that the "no order" principle could not be satisfied if parents were co-operating with the local authority'.[12] Similar reports prompted the Children Act Advisory Committee to issue guidance stressing that partnership and voluntarism were not synonymous and that if the local authority was in doubt about the need for an order it should issue an application and let the court decide.[13]

Our research was therefore carried out in a national context of uncertainty about the role of compulsory intervention with the initial strong emphasis on working on a voluntary basis giving way to a more muted cautious approach. These uncertainties and developments were very much in evidence in our interviews with practitioners.

Practitioner views

The presumption of no order

The principle that compulsory intervention had to be demonstrably better for the child was generally enthusiastically supported among practitioners operating primarily in the legal system:

> The no order principle is excellent, a final safeguard. . . . It encourages and really imposes a duty on the local authority to think creatively about the alternatives and to be really stringent in their assessment of families. We know care in itself is damaging and I think it is a very good thing that you ought to think twice. (Guardian ad Litem)

These twin themes of focusing on the benefit to the child of any proposed order and balancing the harm of remaining at home against the dangers of the care system also emerged in the otherwise more generally ambivalent comments of social work practitioners, for whom what was a laudable principle was proving difficult and uncomfortable to operate.

The test was also seen by most practitioners as a more challenging hurdle. Taken in isolation the differences between the care or control test in the Children and Young Persons Act 1969 and the *presumption of no order* may only be a matter of emphasis. In practice, as was crystal clear from our interview material, they are worlds apart. This was not primarily because of perceived differences in the legal requirements, although a number of court practitioners did point to a greater clarity and precision of expression. Overwhelmingly it was the fact that the new test was perceived to be taken more seriously that was seen to make the difference. There were, it is true, a number of cynical practitioners whose experience was of only token consideration being given to either test. Much more typical, however, were comments such as:

> The care or control test went on a nod and a wink; the no order principle really has to be discussed in court. In itself it doesn't really look that different; but it's come in with a very different ethos, it comes as a package and it is significantly different. (Guardian)

If these practitioners were correct that it is the spirit rather than the letter of the law which has made Section 1(5) bite in a way that the care or control test apparently did not, then over time these differences may well fade, a point made by one of the solicitors we interviewed:

> I don't know whether the no order principle will stand the test of time. When the law is changed it concentrates the mind and people look more closely at what they have to do but over time it slips. I guess when the care or control test came in it meant something and was applied rigorously but as time drifted on people knew what they wanted and it was a question of fashioning the law to fit.

As we shall see it is possible that even during our research period this process had already begun.

Impact on local authority practice

A dominant theme in interviews with guardians and private practice lawyers was that though Section 1(5) was a necessary test, in most of the cases coming to court under the Act the need for an order of some kind was evident. While in part this perception reflects the filtering out of the less serious cases by the threshold conditions, almost all practitioners made links, usually explicitly, with a *shift* in the approach to court action. As a result:

> You're less likely to get cases where the local authority hasn't tried everything.
> . . . The odd one pops up but most try quite comprehensive preventative
> work. (Guardian)

It was notable that despite this awareness of change, there were few explicit criticisms of the way the sample authorities had used the courts pre-Act. Indeed several practitioners were at pains to stress that it was more that ideas had changed about what was appropriate:

> I can't remember any cases pre-Act where I thought they had behaved
> outrageously. But after the Act there was almost a sea change in practice.
> I think what has happened is that pre-Act, they very often initiated court
> proceedings and then did the negotiation, at implementation they tried to
> do it the other way round: they tried to do the negotiation and only initiated
> proceedings when that had fallen apart. (Solicitor)

While the broad picture we have described was clear, it was not uniform. Many lawyers and guardians with experience of several local authorities commented on substantial differences in approach:

> The truth of the matter is it varies from authority to authority; e.g. in X they
> are more thoughtful, frequently we fight them but it's not bad practice given
> all the circumstances. Whereas you look at Y and Z and it's knee jerk reaction,
> they don't plan, they don't think through things, they bring proceedings
> without thinking.

Whenever any of our sample authorities were compared in this way it was always to their credit. However, within each, differences were perceived at the district and team level with some local authority solicitors reporting individual differences in coming to grips with change:

> Once social services have convinced themselves the threshold criteria have
> been reached they either overlook the no order principle or they apply it too

strictly. I've had both extremes, it depends on which social worker and which team. It depends on the managers and the training they've had which direction they're going in.

None the less, whatever their individual orientation, most social work interviewees with pre-Act experience were acutely aware of the changes brought about by the *philosophy* as well as the *specific requirements* of the legislation, with the need for a more careful, structured approach to decision-making being again a major theme:

> It's more considered, more about planning ahead so you don't just go for a Care Order to protect the child you go to court with a plan as to what you will do when you have the child in your care. The thinking is clearer, better, more planned. (Team manager)

That thinking was also seen to be permeated by the new ideas about partnership and minimal intervention:

> We are looking to agreements, looking to work with parents, looking at the principle of no order and not going to court. (Team manager)

The downside, however, voiced in each of the research areas, was the perception that 'we carry more risky cases now', and the acute anxiety this engendered:

> Local authorities are being put into an impossible position of having a whole set of partnership obligations while equally having a whole set of protection obligations to fulfil. I think it's quite dangerous really: my own worst fear is that this Act will lead to children dying because local authorities will overstep the need to work in partnership and fail to protect. It's such a delicate balance and the Act doesn't clearly demonstrate where that balance lies. (Team manager)

While none of our informants had personal experience of this worst fear coming true (and indeed most did not express their anxieties in quite such dramatic terms), the words they used: 'hoops', 'hurdles', 'fences', 'obstacles', 'feeling emasculated', speak volumes about their sense of frustration at *'having* to persevere with partnership at all costs', *'having* to try written agreements':

> When do you say enough is enough? You create a supportive package; you put in a lot of resources, a very comprehensive package and nothing happens. Do you go through it all over again? I agree you need to try and demonstrate

it's been done but someone somewhere along the line needs to say we've done as much as we can. (Social worker)

Local authority lawyers were neither oblivious to, nor immune from, these concerns, even while acknowledging that their advice was often seen as part of the problem:

> I expect there's a feeling that we just sit up here and say don't do it and they're the ones who have to take the risks and live with the anxiety and that's true. We're dealing with a higher level of risk now. But all of us get scared that we might have advised on a legal basis against a course of action when there might be a dead baby [as a result]. It's quite frightening at times and it doesn't get any less frightening.

As we have commented elsewhere, in the early years of this new legislation local authority lawyers have been crucially important in interpreting the Act for their client departments and have thus influenced decision-making about court action to a far greater extent than before. Nowhere has this been more evident than in the application of Section 1(5). The only case we were told of where a child had been re-injured demonstrates this very clearly:

> Mother had admitted physically assaulting the baby and agreed to go to a mother and baby home for assessment. Social services wanted care proceedings but because she was fully co-operating and had agreed to see a psychiatrist my advice was that we wouldn't actually satisfy the no order principle. The social worker was still adamant he wanted to go to court but the team manager accepted the advice that they should carry on as a voluntary arrangement and decide after the psychiatric assessment. Then mother hit the child again and at that point we went to court. So I suppose the team manager was primarily responsible for the decision but based very much on my advice. (Local authority lawyer)

On the whole the local authority lawyers interviewed saw the new test as not only valid in itself but a useful tool to test the strength of the case. There was a clear consensus in all three authorities that this was being done far more rigorously than hitherto:

> The really big difference is that we question social work practice much more than we did; what's been done and offered to the family. I can't remember being particularly concerned with that sort of thing in the past. It was almost social services came along and presented you with the case as it was, you didn't enquire so stringently about how they reached their present position.

The courts weren't concerned to the extent they are now, the courts didn't want to know. But now it is supposed to be known we've become a lot more enquiring about that and challenging about things that aren't being done properly.

The legal department in Area A was notable both for the consistency of its team approach and the strength of its explicit commitment to minimising court action by a social services department they perceived to be somewhat over-interventionist. In this authority there was a greater tradition of lawyer involvement in the decision-making processes and both legal advice and the legal team were held in high regard. Ironically, if understandably, it was here that frustration was most common. As one team manager reported despairingly: 'It isn't more difficult to get orders once you get to court; the difficulty is getting the legal department to put it into court.'

It was also from this area that the clearest signs emerged of a softening of approach, the lawyers themselves acknowledging their role in the changes noted by other practitioners:

We are now clearer about Section 1(5), that it's whether an order would be better for the child. My advice is better now; I'm happier to go for orders now. At the beginning we thought what we called the no order principle was stronger than it was; it was a feeling that grew up in the team, there was a strong emphasis on that in training. Now it's balancing out; it's found its rightful place.

For some private practice lawyers, however, this was not a more fitting homeostasis but a falling off:

It was different in the first year or so, the local authority bent over backwards to avoid taking proceedings. But my feeling is it's pretty much gone by the board now because they've grown in confidence that they will get the orders they want. There's quite an enlightened group of solicitors in the legal department who did their level best to go according to the principles of the Act. That very much informed the decisions of the social workers who were also making a genuine attempt. After a while I think they didn't feel so constrained any more by the principles and things have slipped back to the position that existed before, that they go for orders where they needn't.

Whatever one's perspective it seems clear that practice was changing while we were conducting our research. As social services become more familiar with the Act they should also develop more confidence in their own assessments and be less trammelled by those of lawyers. Thus more borderline cases may reach the courts. At the point this research was carried out, however, as we saw earlier, most lawyers and guardians considered the cases reaching court were appropriate cases for statutory action. Those who voiced reservations about local authority decisions were therefore far more likely to be concerned about attempts to work on a voluntary basis with unsuitable cases or 'soldiering on' beyond the point where this was reasonable.

Enforced accommodation is only a particular manifestation of the shift away from court action, thus the general points practitioners made about the defects of voluntarism echo those reported in Chapter 4. The dangers of delay and drift, of losing sight of the child's interests, were again primary themes:

> For some area offices it is absolutely the be all and end all that they go into every possible link to work in partnership . . . and at some point the children's needs get lost. In some cases it has been months and months before they have taken proceedings. (Solicitor)

'Wobbly and hairy voluntary agreements' were criticised as coercive to parents while jeopardising children's long-term welfare, even their short-term safety. Court proceedings, in contrast, provided an arena 'where solutions are considered on some sort of level footing' while 'wielding the big stick of court' can also bring about change in apparently 'stuck' cases. Even solicitors who generally acted for parents and whose priority under most circumstances was to avoid court action argued that often: 'It's the proceedings that gel the parents into carrying out the action they've agreed but not performed.'

Amid this ferment the sample cases were brought to court. In the next section we look at what social services could use to demonstrate that a public law order would improve the child's situation.

Justifying compulsory intervention in the sample cases

The objectives of intervention

By the final hearing, social services are expected to have firm ideas about the implementation and expected benefits of any order requested. Indeed the application form also requires them to state the plans for the child if a final order is made, implying that these will also be clear at the point proceedings are initiated. As our research data show, however, this is very far from the case.

In the analysis of the pre-Act sample we had been somewhat surprised to find that there was a firm welfare plan at the outset in only 49 cases, in the remaining 55 the final objective was seen to be contingent on developments during the legal process. This was in spite of the fact that 22 of this latter group had been worked with for at least four months before the decision to go to court and 15 for over a year. We concluded this finding went some way to explaining the long durations not only of wardship proceedings, where it was an expected reflection of the nature of that jurisdiction, but of care proceedings too, where it was not. Indeed we found the proportion of cases with contingent objectives was actually higher in care proceedings.

As reported in Chapter 3, more of the post-Act cases were already active prior to the events precipitating proceedings; they also tended to have been worked with longer. In consequence we had expected to find more cases in which the ultimate objectives of intervention were clear at the point proceedings were brought. This expectation was confounded: the proportion had actually dropped to a third (Figure 7.1) even though one in three of the remaining cases had been worked with for more than three months and around a quarter for more than a year.

Figure 7.1 *Objectives of intervention (all areas)*

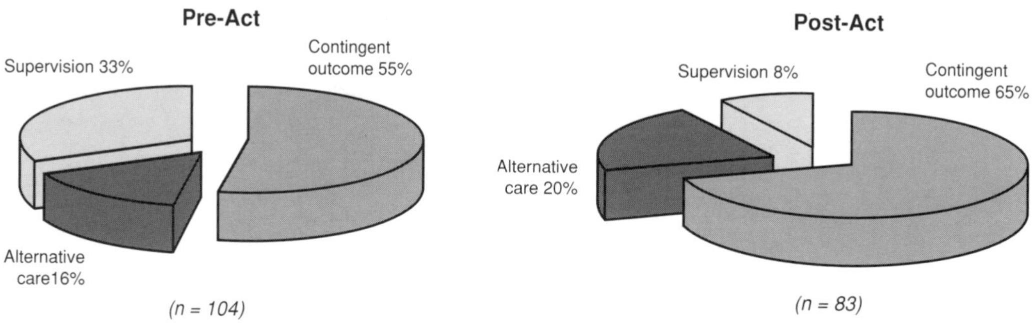

Pre-Act

Supervision 33%

Contingent outcome 55%

Alternative care 16%

(n = 104)

Post-Act

Supervision 8%

Contingent outcome 65%

Alternative care 20%

(n = 83)

A number of points emerged from further analysis of the comparative data:

1   The proportion of cases in which the objective at the outset was to provide long-term substitute care was higher post-Act (24% compared to 15%). This lends support to practitioner views that other options tend to have been explored more frequently. None the less it remains a rather low figure: both before and after the Act, social services were not generally intending from the start to remove children *permanently* from their parents.

2   The fraction of cases in which powers were being sought to supervise the child within the family has plummeted. As we shall see in a later

chapter this is consonant with widespread contempt for Supervision Orders by social work practitioners and their legal advisors.

3   There was variation between areas in the degree of change. Cases in which long-term substitute care was sought were only marginally more frequent post-Act in Area C, but substantially so in the other two areas. On the other hand, while C, and even more markedly A, appeared to have almost abandoned applications for Supervision Orders, this was less apparent in B. As a consequence of these differential shifts the proportion of cases with contingent objectives remained about the same in Area B but increased in the other two.

4   There was change over time (Figure 7.2). In the second year of the Act local authorities were much more likely to have firm long-term objectives (46% compared to 21%). The closeness of this to the pre-Act sample may suggest that local authorities initially dealt with their anxieties by being more tentative about their plans, subsequently becoming more confident and more definitive. Another possible explanation is that second year applications included more cases in which alternatives to court action had been tried, but found insufficient, the breakdown in voluntary agreements about which many practitioners spoke.

No consistent relationship was established between ethnicity and initial case objectives and any perceptible differences were minor. In cases involving ethnic minority families objectives were slightly more likely to be contingent although where they were firm substitute care rather than supervision was the usual aim. Most differentiated were families with a child, but not an adult with care, of non-European origin, where objectives were more likely to be clear and involve home supervision.

Figure 7.2 *The objectives of proceedings by year*

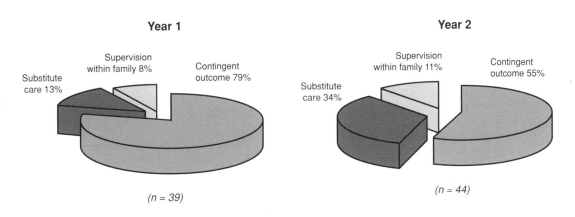

Year 1

Supervision within family 8%
Contingent outcome 79%
Substitute care 13%
(n = 39)

Year 2

Supervision within family 11%
Contingent outcome 55%
Substitute care 34%
(n = 44)

The need for compulsory intervention.

> *Prima facie* if 'reasonable parental care' is lacking . . . leading to a risk of significant harm to the child, *either* someone else must be shown as being able to supply it *or* the local authority should have the task.[14]

In this section we examine the sample cases in greater detail, focusing on what had been done to tackle the child protection issues prior to court, what alternatives to compulsory intervention had been explored and why the local authority considered an order was necessary to implement its plans. Since the issues raised by these questions vary according to what social services was seeking to achieve, for purposes of analysis the cases have been grouped on the basis of initial objectives.

Cases in which the objective was long-term substitute care (20 cases)

Most of the children for whom substitute care was the plan were young, all but six cases involving only children under 5. The families exhibited the most severe problems on all the indicators used in the previous chapter. None had been continuously worked with for less than four months and 14 had been worked with for over a year.

Supporting the family unit. With the exception of new-born baby Zara, in all these cases social services could point to substantial prior input aimed at keeping the child with at least one parent, a point acknowledged in Guardian ad Litem reports and by the practitioners we interviewed. As one mother's solicitor said: 'They had offered every support. No reasonable court could have come to any other conclusion'.

Accommodated children made up the bulk of the group (15). In 12 cases accommodation was itself preceded by alternative strategies (for example home support, residential placements, respite care, previous periods in accommodation) and in 12 there had been at least one attempt at rehabilitation. Only one child was accommodated without either. More typical is the case of Brian, who was multiply handicapped.

Brian's mother Paula has learning difficulties and spent all her childhood in care. Intensive support was given during pregnancy and after the birth both Paula and Brian were 'fostered'. Domiciliary support was provided on return to the community but there were concerns about Paula's drinking and two months later, after she had admitted shaking him, Brian was received into care. Nine months later he returned home after assessment at a family centre and phased rehabilitation. A range of support was provided to sustain the family unit which now included Frank, Brian's stepfather, although there were serious concerns and court action had been considered.

The family situation was approaching crisis point 17 months before proceedings were begun. Brian's behaviour had become increasingly difficult and the marital relationship more overtly conflictual. Respite care was organised after Brian suffered minor, but unexplained injuries and he was briefly fostered when Paula took an overdose. The level of family support was increased and after Paula made two more attempts at self-harm a shared care arrangement was established. Brian made considerable progress in this placement where he spent more and more time. It was converted into a foster placement eight months before proceedings began.

At this point the plan was still rehabilitation and the input into the family reflected this. However after four months the prognosis seemed poor. Brian's foster mother was unable to keep him long term and Paula agreed, reluctantly, that an alternative should be sought. In view of her co-operation care proceedings were not started. A month later Paula changed her mind and rehabilitation was re-started, again without success. Since Paula would not consent to substitute care the local authority applied for a Care Order. Brian was now 4.

In three of the remaining cases the children were at home although each had been previously subject to court action. The sample proceedings were brought only after efforts to support the family voluntarily proved consistently and seriously ineffective. A fourth case illustrates both the shift away from compulsion and the ineffectiveness of the alternative adopted.

For three months Louise Milsom (7) had been living at her grandparents' with her mother Janet, under an agreement that her father, George (a Schedule 1 offender pleading guilty to further sexual assaults on children outside the family), would have only supervised contact. Care proceedings could have been brought at the point the offences came to light and pre-Act almost certainly would have been. Instead social services tried to work on a contractual basis, offering the parents counselling and psychiatric help, only bringing proceedings, reluctantly, after the agreement was repeatedly breached, George had refused referral to the Gracewell Clinic[15] and a thorough risk assessment concluded that the prospects for safe rehabilitation to parents who were indicating their intention to live together again were poor.

The plan was to place with grandparents, reinforcing their position with a package of orders.

The decision to seek substitute care for Zara Butler was clearly an agonising one for some of the professionals most closely connected with her mother, Sandra. There was also some uncertainty as to the attitude of the court towards a plan which did not involve any attempt to preserve the family unit, although social services seem not to have doubted that there was enough to obtain the orders sought:

> The whole range of available resources had been previously run through. Our experience was that the longer the children remained with these parents the more damaged and insecure they became. With each set of proceedings we went further and further down the road. We hadn't felt safe with the previous child who had gone to the mother and baby home and there was no reason to believe there had been any change in the parents' relationship.

As we shall see in subsequent chapters, this confidence was misplaced.

The consideration of alternatives. Placing the child with a non-abusing parent was not an option in Zara's case nor in most of the others since all but one involved concern about the quality of care given by both parents, or by a lone mother.[16] Fathers were either out of the picture (5), implicated in the alleged harm (7), or otherwise considered unsuitable (5). Of the three cases in which the father's position had been insufficiently investigated, there was only one where paternal care was more than a very remote possibility and later events suggest the only effect of greater thoroughness would have been to delay proceedings.

This could not be said of the three cases in which the *extended family* had not been fully consulted, all of which ended with relative placements. Apart from these, however, when substitute care was the objective it seemed these local authorities had taken account of the duty to keep children within their kinship groups wherever possible and had investigated what relatives could offer.

As we shall see the earlier handling of several of these cases could be questioned. There were only four, however, in which this was relevant to the key issue of whether there was currently any alternative way to remedy the deficit in parental care. All other applications appeared to be very firmly based.

The need for compulsion. Assuming it could be proved that there was no other way of providing 'reasonable parental care' than the local authority's plan, demonstrating the need for an order in all of these cases would be fairly straightforward since parents were not prepared to agree. The court also has to be satisfied, however, as the Children Act Advisory Committee points out 'that they can deliver in this particular case'. This requirement is both theoretically[17] and practically impossible. Were it ever to be interpreted stringently it is doubtful that local authorities would ever apply for, or courts make, care orders where the intention is long-term substitute care. Although as Jane Rowe points out: 'If continuity can be achieved by a "permanent" fostering or adoptive placement which lasts, long-term outcomes are generally positive.'[18]

The research evidence shows:

> how difficult it is to provide a stable and positive experience for children or young people who are being looked after by local authorities for more than a brief period. . . . Premature endings and placement change continue to be prevalent.[19]

Even without such research findings courts will find little to reassure them from the cases that come before them: the proportion of parents who have themselves been in care; the delay in finding permanent homes for children removed in previous proceedings; the acknowledged difficulties in finding suitable placements. In one case in this group, for instance, the care plan stated: 'It could take 6–12 months before permanent substitute carers are found due to lack of resources in the department.'

Only one child was already placed in what was intended to be her permanent home. Thus in virtually every case social services started proceedings knowing the court would be asked to choose between the known specific risks of parental care and the generalised risk of the unknown. However, given the level of parenting problems evident in these cases and the fairly comprehensive elimination of alternatives, in effect the court would have little choice. It is only where the significance of the harm is more marginal or where there is some prospect of change, we would argue, that the balancing act can be performed in any meaningful way.

Cases where the objective of intervention was supervision within the family (8 cases)

On every index of severity these eight cases were less problematic than the previous group. They had also been worked with for a somewhat shorter period – six for under a year – although only one had been active for no more than three months.

Where the purpose of bringing proceedings is to protect the child in his or her home environment the key questions would seem to be first, is voluntary supervision likely to be insufficient and second, will the order sought (supervision orders in all but two) provide sufficient protection?

The likely *ineffectiveness* of voluntary supervision was, in our judgement, clearly demonstrable at the outset in five cases, either because parents were refusing social work involvement and/or because that involvement had failed to bring about the requisite change in behaviour. As one guardian wrote:

> Attempts to work with mother on a voluntary basis were continually frustrated by her lack of co-operation, refusal to accept the basis of concern and hostility towards social workers.

The evidence in the remaining cases was much weaker. Indeed in one there seemed to be every indication that local authority support would be welcomed and monitoring accepted.

• •

The Dinmore children had been seriously neglected in the past but currently their mother, Josie, was co-operating with a residential parenting skills programme. Funding to extend this having been refused, it was proposed to rehabilitate on interim care orders. This was opposed by the guardian and Josie's solicitor, who told us:

> It was very questionable. They'd waited a substantial time before they started proceedings; they hadn't started them at the time when all the concerns had arisen; they started them in the middle of an assessment

that was progressing quite well . . . Josie wanted social workers to be
involved; most of our clients can't wait to get them off their backs. If they
had persisted we would have really pressed home that they didn't have
the grounds to start proceedings.

On the morning of the first hearing the court was told that funding had been
agreed and the case was adjourned without any order.

⬤ ⬤

As to the likely sufficiency of the order and the plan, there was evidence in
three cases that previous court proceedings had produced some improvement.
As one of the guardians told us:

It seems clear that after expiry of the Supervision Order the family had said
'Ha ha you can't do anything to us now.' The children were definitely going
downhill and despite a certain amount of lip service from mother she wasn't
co-operating. As far as mother was concerned the only way she operates is
under coercion.

Two cases were unlikely to reach this point because of difficulties in showing
the need for an order while in a third the nature and degree of the harm was
not of the highest degree of significance. Thus the local authority plan to
leave the child at home did not appear to involve serious risk. In the remaining cases however there were doubts about the adequacy of the protection
plan; in one because previous Supervision Orders in wardship had not been
particularly effective while in the second, both the police and the extended
family were highly sceptical of mother's ability to change.

⬤ ⬤

Social services first became involved with the Phillips family when Sam, the
eldest child, was still a baby and there were serious concerns that his mother,
Joanne, was drinking to excess. After Sam had been left unattended on several
occasions he and his mother went to live with relatives and Joanne sought
treatment for her alcoholism. The case was closed.

Twins were born when Sam was 4. There were soon allegations that Joanne was
again drinking and leaving the children unattended, culminating in all three
being taken into police protection and placed with an aunt. Joanne agreed to
the children remaining there while she addressed her alcohol problems and a
contract was drawn up. Two months later she requested the children's return.
Although the terms of the contract had been breached and in the face of
considerable opposition from the extended family and the police, social services
agreed. The local authority lawyer consulted was reported to have advised that:

It is a reasonable social work decision to work with mother on a voluntary contractual basis as a first attempt to rehabilitate and keep out of care. It is difficult to predict how these type of cases will be viewed by the courts although usually they would be reluctant to remove unless there was a clearly established pattern of leaving unattended for prolonged periods.

A second agreement was drawn up and again not complied with and six weeks later Joanne was told court action would be taken. There was then a delay of six weeks during which, although Joanne attempted to change the decision, there were renewed allegations and her relationship with the social worker deteriorated. Social services then started proceedings but sought an adjournment without Interim Orders 'to give the other parties a chance to do an assessment and offer mother a further opportunity of working with us'.

●●

Cases where objectives were contingent on developments during proceedings (55 cases)

One of the reasons we don't get into court very often is that people do a kind of risk assessment on whether we're going to win the final order. You can't usually do that. What you should be doing is deciding whether you're going to get something useful for social services out of the first order. With an interim care order you're usually trying to maintain the status quo long enough to do an assessment. (Local authority solicitor)

Analysis of these cases reveals a gamut of reasons why assessment is such a common, almost a defining, feature of care proceedings. However they fall into two broad groups. First, cases where compulsory protection was deemed necessary before there was sufficient knowledge of the family to plan effectively. This includes new-born babies, inactive cases and those where work had started with the family but proceedings were begun before much had been accomplished. In the second group, although there had been substantial involvement, either the planning process was disrupted or proceedings were brought as a last ditch attempt to stimulate change.

Group 1

●●

James Pallister was 3 months when he was referred to hospital after 'a funny turn'. Examination revealed a cerebral haemorrhage and 11 fractured ribs, considered to have been caused on a number of separate occasions by severe shaking. There had been no previous concern about the quality of parental care either of James or his 2-year-old sister. His mother Natalie had, however, mentioned a bruise on the baby's chin to her health visitor two weeks earlier and two days before had consulted the GP because he was 'vomiting and grizzly'. Neither Natalie nor her husband David had any explanation, James had never been out of their care. They were 'devastated' by the diagnosis and 'co-operative' with enquiries. In view of their agreement to James remaining in hospital an EPO was not seen to be necessary.

By the case conference two weeks later James's injuries were still unexplained. Natalie and David agreed to a comprehensive assessment but not to James being accommodated for the requisite three months. Social services considered the parents' plan (that the family should live with relatives during this period), offered insufficient protection and might impede the assessment process. Proceedings were therefore initiated and Natalie and David were introduced to the prospective foster parents. By the first hearing a third option had been put forward by the parents and accepted, reluctantly, by the local authority and James moved to the care of his aunt under an Interim Residence Order with orders controlling parental contact.

● ●

Inactive cases (13). Contrasting criticisms might be made of social services' approach to James Pallister's case, for example for not exploring 'a perfectly good arrangement in the family', a point made in court. From another perspective, however, it could be argued that, given the severity of James's injuries and the obscurity of their source, not only was protection in a local authority placement an entirely understandable preference but the case should have gone straight to court. Pre-Act it certainly would have done and a Place of Safety Order would have been taken out as insurance against removal from hospital.

In terms of a baby's needs, however, separation from the primary carer, rather than the identity of the substitute, is the major issue. This area did not have a residential family facility which could have provided protection without separation. Area B did and in another previously inactive case involving serious injury to a baby (Liam Johnson) this option was offered although rejected. As with James no Emergency Protection Order was taken but even if the parents had accepted the residential place offered, the local authority (and all the other practitioners involved) had no doubts about the need for court action; there was no question of offering accommodation. Although, as the social worker told us, there were doubts whether an order would be granted in view of the parents co-operation to date, legal advice was that the seriousness of the injuries warranted a care application. This assessment was confirmed by both solicitors acting for parents. A striking difference in approach.

In total there was evidence that at least one alternative course of action was explored with the family in eight of these 13 inactive cases: accommodation (6); residential placement (2); the alleged perpetrator leaving (1); placement with relatives (1). In all but one the proposed action would have deferred proceedings until a more thorough assessment had been completed. It is noteworthy that opposition to voluntary arrangements in four of these cases came not from parents but from older children seeking the security of court ordered local authority care and that in each case the child's wishes weighed heavily in the local authority's decision.

To our knowledge the option of the alleged perpetrator leaving home was only explicitly mooted in one case although there appeared to be a non-abusing parent (two mothers, one father) in a further three. The fact that all three concerned Asian families perhaps ought to give us pause for thought. However the circumstances of each case as they appeared at the time do not suggest this would have been viable.

In two of the five cases in which no alternative to court action was known to have been canvassed the children were already staying temporarily with relatives and court orders were sought to maintain them there pending assessment. It was not clear from the documentation, however, whether a voluntary arrangement would have been acceptable to any of the parties. In the remaining cases, where again there was no indication of the acceptability of accommodation, in all but one the circumstances would support a strong need for the local authority to be in control. The exception was that of Joseph and his sister, which is examined in more detail later in this chapter.

The poor documentation of the exploration of alternatives in some of these cases is to be regretted: it may conceal a careful consideration of the available options in each area in every case. None the less the evidence we do have suggests that in almost all cases considerable efforts were being made to find non-compulsory ways of protecting the child while greater knowledge about the family was acquired and that court action was usually taken because other options were not possible or could not be adequately explored in the time available.

New-born babies (7). In inactive cases the main problem for the local authority in determining its long-term objective was lack of knowledge of the family. In this group, in contrast, social services had long experience of at least one parent. The key issue was therefore whether the parent(s) would be able to provide a reasonable standard of care for *this* child, given the removal of previous children (5); the marginal care of older children still at home (1)[20] or the parent's social circumstances and personal problems (1). In each, therefore, a period of assessment was proposed, either with the parent (4 residential, 1 at home) or via foster care (2).

The separation of parents and children in these latter cases is a measure of the pessimism felt by the workers involved. Indeed given the history and unchanged parental circumstances one might wonder why they were trying again when a whole range of services had been tried before and no new supports were on offer. Legal advice at a pre-birth conference on another case, however, suggests that anticipated difficulties in persuading the court to a more radical view were probably influential:

> In the light of the Children Act, social services would need to have been seen to try to engage mother and offer her a package of support; if there are legal proceedings the court would want clear details of attempts made to assist mother. Assessment is very important.

In only one case were proceedings taken at birth on a first child. The young mother, Nasreen, the only black parent in this group, had been in care as a teenager, becoming further alienated from her Muslim family and community when she became pregnant. Her 'nomadic lifestyle' and 'violent and uncontrollable temper' generated a high level of concern about the baby's safety, in response to which Nasreen agreed to live in a residential family unit both before and after the birth. This case had the lowest index of severity of all these seven cases suggesting that bringing proceedings might be rather extreme. This was strongly argued in court and initially, the guardian told us, she had 'felt social services were going over the top since Nasreen was co-operating and at the family centre'. However, she acknowledged that 'the social worker had done a lot with her whereas I had just become involved' and it was on the basis of that longer involvement that a pre-birth case conference decided that, despite Nasreen's co-operation, it was appropriate to bring proceedings. As the social worker explained:

> I'd been working with Nasreen for 12 months; it wasn't that we expected her to fail, we hoped she would succeed, but experience suggested that her co-operation would be short-lived.

This sometimes rueful prediction was the primary rationale for planning assessments within a compulsory framework in all the cases where previous children had been removed. Initiating court proceedings meant that should co-operation be withdrawn not only could the children be immediately protected but there would be less delay in providing for their long-term security. The advantage of this approach can be demonstrated by comparing two cases from the same authority.

Laurie was the third child of Gina, who was schizophrenic, and Matt, whose support was inconsistent and interrupted by periods of imprisonment. Gina still had contact with her older children, Marcus (4) and Abigail (2), living with relatives under Residence Orders. The family were adamant they could not take in another child. Prior to Laurie's birth Gina's mental health seemed somewhat improved, she was desperate to keep this child and agreed to a residential assessment, an option she had previously refused. Social services proposed to do this under Interim Care Orders and initiated proceedings when Laurie was only a few days old. Sadly things did not work out as planned and when Laurie was 9 months old the court made a Care Order with leave to terminate parental contact.

Court action had been planned immediately Stephen was born because of his mother Jasmine's chronic drug abuse and the fact that two half-siblings were in care awaiting adoption. Instead he was accommodated. After eight months in which Jasmine's plans oscillated between adoption and rehabilitation and she was sent to prison for a serious offence of violence, proceedings were begun, completing when Stephen was 14 months old.

Brief involvement with the case children (14). Social services had been working with 14 families on issues concerning the case children for no more than three months, although in two cases older children were in care and long before Robert Barnes was born there had been involvement in relation to his half-brother. Another baby (born drug-addicted) was also still in hospital when proceedings were brought. Only two other children were separated from their parent(s) at this point, both accommodated and a further two were with their mothers in supervised placements. The remaining nine were at home.

Social services input. Six of these cases had been referred so recently that few services had been put in place by the time the events leading to proceedings occurred. The Myers case, for instance, had been case-conferenced, a contract agreed and urgent referrals made to a psychologist and a family centre. Three weeks later however, when Mrs Myers was again found drunk it was decided the risks had become unacceptably high. In the rest considerable efforts had been initiated to preserve the family unit while problems were addressed.

Sophie Farrow, 3 years old, was taken into police protection after her parents, Lisa and Joe, were arrested for drunkenness and she was found alone. Although she was placed temporarily with her aunt none of her relatives was able to care for a longer period, nor was there a suitable foster home sufficiently near to allow adequate contact. Sophie was accordingly returned home with daily domiciliary support and a psychiatric referral made.

Within a week the family aide was so concerned for Sophie's welfare she felt it necessary to remain in the house overnight. Social services made a provisional plan to offer accommodation and called a case conference to which both parents were invited. However Joe turned up alone and drunk, reporting that Lisa had disappeared and he couldn't cope. The offer of accommodation prompted a very hostile and aggressive response which the social worker was unable to manage.[21] The police were called, Joe was arrested and Sophie again taken into police protection. This time an Emergency Protection Order and care proceedings followed.

The consideration of alternatives. Whatever the level of input, it typically involved working with the living arrangements current at the time the case was referred, only the two accommodated children experiencing change. It was the non-viability of these arrangements which led to proceedings. In most cases (11) efforts to work with the family on a voluntary basis were disrupted by some form of crisis, all but two of which were dealt with by compulsory emergency protection. None the less placements within the extended family were at least looked at, if not exhaustively explored, in nine cases, including two where placements were made, both protected by court orders. This, and the fact that at this stage only five families appear to have been offered alternatives which would have avoided court action, (compared to seven of the 12 new cases analysed earlier) suggests that even relatively brief acquaintance had made workers pessimistic about the efficacy of non-compulsory intervention or more confident this could be demonstrated.

At the point of crisis a non-abusing parent was in the picture in six cases: three fathers, three mothers. One mother and her surviving children moved to stay with relatives after the sudden death of the baby and father's admission of assault. The seriousness of the events alone appear to have satisfied practitioners of the need for legal protection since there was no evidence that a voluntary agreement would not have been both acceptable and effective while investigations were completed. The decision may also have been influenced, however, by the fact that at the time of the baby's death, a child pro-tection investigation was also underway into sexual abuse of an older sibling by her (estranged) father.

Another set of children moved to live with their recently separated father after mounting concerns over their mother's mental health. Although private law proceedings would have been a possibility in a less dire situation, the local authority considered mother's threats to kill herself and the children war-ranted more immediate action. In the remaining cases there were doubts about the non-abusing parent's ability to protect (3), or the permanency of the separation.

Group 2: social services involvement more than three months (21)

In 15 of the 21 cases in this group the children were living with at least one parent at the point the events leading to proceedings occurred, two at the home of a relative, the rest in their own homes. Of the six separated children five were accommodated, the sixth being cared for by a family friend. On average these cases had been continuously worked with for 23 months, in most the same range of problems had persisted over time; in four the case children had been returned home after earlier court proceedings. In only 11 was the timing of the decision to proceed to court taken in the aftermath of a crisis and only eight of these involved compulsory emergency intervention. The type of cases where, it might be thought, the local authority would be more likely to have a clear long-term objective.

A variety of case-related factors help to explain why proceedings were initi-ated before this stage was reached. Recent changes to which social services needed to respond, for example (3); parents in psychiatric hospital where the outcome of treatment was awaited (2); crises arising while assessments were incomplete (3). In most cases (13), however, it seems it was hoped that court action itself would stimulate some form of change in parental behaviour, for example in their co-operation with assessments, their willingness to divulge information, their motivation to seek treatment for psychiatric, drug or alcohol-related conditions. Thus the final order to be sought, or even whether any order would be needed at all, was dependent on how well founded this hope proved to be.

The prospects of 7-year-old Ben Smisson ever returning home appear to us to have been minimal from the outset, given that a high level of input over 17 months had failed to make any material impact on Millie's chronic alcoholism or capacity to care. In all but one of the others, however, there did seem to be a genuine hope, even expectation, that proceedings would help to unstick a case and the children would be rehabilitated. The Symons family was a case in point.

• •

Michelle Symons was 2 and her twin sisters 10 months. Her parents Claudette and Jake had separated when she was still a baby; there had been no recent contact. Since leaving care at the age of 16 Claudette has lived with her mother Betty with whom she has an ambivalent and turbulent relationship.

The concerns about insanitary household conditions and child care which pre-dated the twins' birth were substantially increased by their vulnerability. The family were persuaded to accept domiciliary help and a nursery place for Michelle.

An initial improvement was not maintained; all the children seemed under-stimulated and the twins were admitted to hospital with gastro-enteritis and severe malnutrition. Both made dramatic catch-up gains. All three children were placed on the Child Protection Register but there were considered to be insufficient grounds for court proceedings which were also seen as being too draconian at this point. A detailed written agreement was drawn up and the family warned that if it were not adhered to court action would be taken.

Claudette became more overtly uncooperative, denying admission to the domiciliary workers and threatening to kill herself and the children if anyone tried to remove them. After six weeks social services decided the care of the children was unacceptable. Claudette refused to consider either a mother and baby home or accommodation. An emergency case conference was called at which Claudette again refused to consider either of these alternatives and repeated her threat to kill herself and her children. While the case conference was still going on the children were removed into police protection.

• •

Social services' intention was to protect the children while more effective work was undertaken. Claudette's rejection of alternatives meant that this had to take place within a legal framework. Her repeated threats to kill herself and the children, which the case conference felt could not be ignored, meant that proceedings began in a confrontational way which was least conducive to future work.

The input into this group of cases was considerable. Ben's family had been rehoused, financial and material help given, multiple efforts made to address Millie's alcoholism, specialist therapeutic intervention arranged. The school offered term-time after-hours support and Ben was enrolled in a holiday playscheme. Other tenants on the estate kept a watchful eye as he wandered around unsupervised. There were no relatives in a position to help, and no non-abusing parent. As the social worker told us, 'by the time we went to court we felt we had exhausted all the possibilities'. Millie did consent to accommodation but this was vetoed by senior management on the dual grounds that to date Millie had co-operated better and to greater effect while court proceedings were in train (namely the divorce proceedings and subsequent Section 37 investigation) and (a measure of social services pessimism) this course of action could leave Ben stuck in care.

Apart from Ben's case, in all but two others alternatives to court action had either been tried or offered to the family and in one of these the local authority was seeking legal powers to enable the child to be moved rapidly to live with his father, who did not have parental responsibility. There was only one other case where at the point proceedings were brought placing with a non-abusing parent was a possibility – that of baby Jemima. Jemima's parents separated after the assault; the local authority was sceptical of the durability of this and therefore brought proceedings but in view of the change of circumstances proposed to use them as a test period. In all but three cases the possibilities of care within the extended family also appeared to have been explored. Thus although these cases might not have arrived in court with clear long-term objectives, they were very similar, in terms of service input and the exhaustion of alternatives, to those which did.

The justification for compulsory intervention: comparison with the pre-Act sample

One of the strongest themes in interviews was the view that local authorities were, on the whole, only bringing their strongest cases to court, those where there were no realistic alternatives and that this reflected a tightening up of practice. The sample cases tend to support these perceptions. Thus applying Section 1(5) to the pre-Act sample (excluding those already subject to a court order) we calculated that almost half would have been seen as less than cast-iron and therefore might well not have come to court as early as they did. This was not simply due to the more flexible 'tests' in the wardship and matrimonial jurisdictions. Almost half the cases brought in care proceedings were rated as potentially dubious compared to just over a third of the wardships.

The proportion of potentially problematic pre-Act cases was greatest among inactive cases (64%). In contrast, among the post-Act cases we considered there were only two where the necessity for court action was even arguable (17%). Similarly the arguments for bringing proceedings at birth were much stronger in the post-Act cases, only one of the eight cases being challenge-able compared to 57% pre-Act. Among cases which had been worked with prior to court action there was less room for doubt in either sample about the justification for action so that although the direction of change is the same it is less marked – 21% post-Act compared to 32% pre-Act.

None the less the data suggest that as many as one in six post-Act cases might have been diverted from the court process even at this late stage by a more vigorous pursuit of alternatives. Moreover, looking further back into the process, there was evidence of missed opportunities to prevent the deterioration in care which eventually brought the case to court.

Preventing the *need* to bring proceedings

The data so far presented indicate that at the point the post-Act sample cases were brought to court, social services were usually in a position to argue, with much stronger justification than hitherto, that there were no viable alternatives to compulsory intervention. Interviews with parents,[22] however, suggest few would agree with this assessment, a distressingly common theme being the lack of help provided to achieve what were perceived to be uncertain and unrealistic goals.

Not that parents generally denied services had been provided, although some did. Rather support was seen to be insufficient or inconsistent, inappropriate or wrongly targeted. Social work was seen as unduly skewed towards the children leaving the adults with unmet needs and therefore an impaired capacity to cope, a perception strongly supported by Farmer and Owen's research.[23] Many parents would have liked help which focused on their emotional needs, as a partner in a violent relationship for example, or a survivor of childhood abuse. Others suggested more attention to adverse environmental factors, particularly the stress engendered by poor housing.

It may be tempting to minimise these complaints as further displacement strategies for coping with an otherwise intolerable assault on moral integrity.[24] There were, however, a number of cases where it seemed possible that things might have been different had earlier intervention been more timely, intensive or differently targeted. As the Guardian ad Litem in one case commented in her report:

> The social worker and parents have worked well in partnership. The recent involvement has been intensive and thorough. It is a pity this did not occur when [the family] first came to the attention of the department; the outcome may well have been different.

Although this is technically irrelevant in terms of the legal process, in practice the previous handling of the case will be thoroughly probed, indeed in some cases the need to acknowledge natural injustices can distort proceedings to the extent that social services appear to be on trial. The local authority also has duties to prevent children suffering neglect or ill-treatment and reduce the need to bring proceedings and there is a public policy interest in minimising unnecessary use of the legal process. Thus some exploration of missed opportunities seems legitimate.

In all deficiencies in the provision of services were recorded[25] in 35 of the post-Act sample cases. Those in Areas B and C, the most severely affected authorities, were almost all related to staff shortages; those in Area A, where staffing was less of an issue, to more subtle questions about the quality or focusing of the input. The inability to respond to cases until they erupted in crisis, to monitor children on the Child Protection Register or supervise those on court orders was hopefully a transitory phenomenon in Area C, where almost all the cases receiving an inadequate service were those affected by the prolonged industrial action. The severe staffing problems in Area B however, evident in all our pre-Act research in this authority, appear to be more intractable. Cases here were also more likely to be affected by other resource difficulties, of which the next case is one of the more worrying examples.

• •

Karen's mother Tina has learning difficulties and spent much of her childhood in care. At the time of the birth Tina was living with Mark, the father, who was suspected of serious child abuse during an earlier relationship. Mark had assaulted Tina several times. The family were referred to social services when Tina was believed to be six months pregnant. A case conference decided, a month later, that although there were 'sufficient concerns to apply for an Interim Care Order' at birth, a residential assessment should be undertaken first. The next day Tina gave birth.

Despite some prematurity, Karen was discharged at six days and had to be placed with Tina in a children's home pending a more suitable placement, which took three weeks. Five days after moving to a mother and baby home Tina ran off in a highly distressed state, having discovered that Mark had formed a relationship with another resident. Karen was removed from her and placed with a foster carer, remaining accommodated there on expiry of the Police Protection Order. Tina moved in with her own previous foster parents and agreed to work with the local authority to resume care of her baby. After a wait of six weeks Tina and Karen moved into a second mother and baby home, considered to be 'more structured and supportive'.

Tina's care of Karen during the three-month placement was not without problems. Though 'improving slightly', she needed, it was concluded, 'a semi-independent unit where support could be offered 24 hours a day'. Instead they moved to a hostel for people with learning difficulties and from there to supported lodgings. Karen was placed in a day nursery. Amid mounting concern over Karen's welfare, five weeks after leaving the second mother and baby home Tina concluded she could not cope and asked for Karen's removal. Mother and child were placed temporarily with Tina's previous foster parents from which Karen moved to another foster home.

● ●

The local authority cannot have been satisfied that moving Karen and Tina around like parcels was the most helpful way to help a young lone mother (one moreover with learning difficulties and no consistent experience of family life herself) learn to parent a tiny baby. The Guardian ad Litem, though applauding the intention, was understandably critical:

> They tried to work in partnership with her from the time the child was born.
> . . . It was unfortunate they had difficulties finding a suitable place: to be placed in a children's home with a new baby was absolutely ridiculous although it was better than out in the community or removing Karen from her. But I felt strongly they should have provided a longer period of time at the second mother and baby home and really the breakdown which led to proceedings was due to lack of resources. It was quite clear she was booted out [of that placement] on financial grounds. It wasn't that they thought she was ready to go back into the community, it was that they weren't prepared to pay any longer.

A major theme to emerge from the Department of Health's child protection research programme[26] is that families who would be more appropriately helped by the provision of non-stigmatising support services have been drawn into the child protection system. Another sample case starkly illustrates the imbalance which has developed between the resourcing of the preventative and protective systems, requiring large sums of public money to be spent on court action once a child has been harmed while starving the services which might have prevented that harm occurring. This case, one of the first to be brought under the Children Act, had been referred prior to the events leading to proceedings but no contact made with the family. It was later the subject of a formal complaint.

Joseph (2) and Molly (6) were removed by the police after their mother Anna admitted losing her temper with Joseph over feeding difficulties and to have pushed Molly down the stairs a few days earlier. At the time the family were living in a refuge having escaped from Anna's violent cohabitee and, as the case conference was subsequently told, 'Anna had been asking for help for weeks'. The case however could not be allocated, despite referrals from the health visitor and school, despite the known domestic violence, despite the fact that Molly was on the Child Protection Register for emotional abuse. On the case file it was recorded that the health visitor was told 'to tell mother to come in if desperate'.

Anna *was* desperate; enough to take an overdose which got her away from her home and into a refuge where however she remained fearful of being found by her ex-partner. The refuge staff also requested a visit from social services but before any contact was made Joseph was injured. After she was arrested Anna is reported to have said, not without reason in the circumstances, 'To get a social worker you have to bash your kids.'

It is to be hoped that the subsequent shift in emphasis in public policy towards family support and implementation of the children in need provisions in the Act will reduce the likelihood of such cases ever needing compulsory intervention.

Failures of the child protection system

Alongside these inadequacies in service provision, however, there were also examples in each area of earlier failures in the child protection system. James Pallister and Liam Johnson both suffered bruising which primary health care practitioners did not consider worthy of further enquiry only weeks before they suffered major injuries. There were four other examples of similar failures by the health services to recognise abuse or to take appropriate action.

A further ten cases *had* been referred to social services but for a variety of reasons it was evident, with the benefit of hindsight, the risks had been wrongly assessed. Some of these concerned earlier investigations: in the only sample case involving a child death (in which father admitted assault) a sibling had told her teacher a few weeks earlier that the baby had been 'thrown onto the settee'. This was fully investigated according to child protection procedures but, in the absence of any other evidence, the parents' denial was accepted and no further action taken.

In other cases social services *were* working with the family, but somehow the original reasons for concern and the continuing risk to the child had become obscured. In the case of Louise Milsom, while commending the action taken to protect her once her father's new offences had become known, the guardian was scathing about previous complacency in the face of contradictory circumstantial evidence:

> I have difficulty understanding the lack of decisive action by the local authority . . . the series of indicators was strong enough to warrant certain actions of control being taken as a means of prevention. . . . The fact of a child taking her mother's place in a bed with a known offender should have been of extreme significance. . . . Belief in mother's ability to notify the agencies seems surprisingly misjudged; her limitations were well known but seem not to have been realised in the context of protecting children from abuse.

No doubt prompted by these points, the court, most unusually, also expressed concern at: 'the length of time that elapsed before the social services department took action to protect Louise in view of the significant indicators of probable harm'.

Of course it can only be a matter of speculation whether a more accurate perception of the risks would have allowed Louise or any of the other children to be adequately protected without involving the courts; in some it may only have advanced the point at which the case entered the legal process. As we shall see in the following section however, it is likely that in most there would have been *some* attempt to work with the family on a voluntary basis, even perhaps beyond the point at which that had ceased to have a realistic prospect of yielding results.

Postponing court action

Practitioner concerns about local authorities holding back from invoking the court process under the Children Act were amply borne out by the case data. Reservations about the length of time taken to get to court were expressed by at least one practitioner in 27 cases. There were also seven other cases in which the researchers judged there to have been delay. Cases in which the local authority was planning long-term substitute care were particularly vulnerable (14 of 20).

A Care Order was applied for after Marie (8) had been accommodated for six months. Her mother suffered from a long-term psychiatric illness and social services had been working with the family for years both on a voluntary basis and under wardship, providing respite care on a number of occasions. Unfortunately, as a psychological assessment confirmed, by the time Marie was accommodated for the last time she was displaying signs of severe disturbance. The guardian's report pointed out:

> The work done with this family has been extensive. Social work time, practical resources, in-home support, additional professional consultation and direct work have all been attempted in various combination. The professional and practical resources of the Health Authority and Education Department have also been extensively [deployed].

> If I have a criticism it is that all the help being offered may have obscured the Department's capacity to think about the repetitive nature of events, i.e. to stand back and think about this child's position in her family. Workers have been understandably sympathetic to mother herself, but this too may have resulted in the child's needs being neglected.

> There is now sound research evidence that parental compliance with support and services does *not* predict future success and mother has not always co-operated with local authority plans. Mother follows a high-risk pattern. Children in such families are very likely to be seriously deprived of any sense of permanency in childhood. The long-term damage caused in such families is well documented. These all pertain to this child. I appreciate that in situations where there is neglect it is difficult to judge when parenting slides over into not being 'good enough'. That point arose for Marie some time before [she was accommodated].

As we have seen, in terms of proving the need for an order, cases such as Marie's were the most securely based of the sample, considerable efforts having usually been devoted to maintaining the family unit and exploring alternative courses of action. It is evident, however, that such formidable evidence had usually been achieved at the cost of postponing the point at which long-term decisions could be made.

Of course not all delay was necessarily attributable to the Children Act. It is unfortunately not possible to make a direct quantitative comparison with the pre-Act position because of the inherent limitations of the data. But there were many pre-Act examples of attempts to work on a voluntary basis, particularly in Area C, and of a reluctance to admit when this approach was ineffective. Indeed in some of our post-Act sample the direction of the case had been set by pre-Act decisions, either by local authorities or the courts. Drift was not invented by the Children Act, nor sadly, lack of social work resources remedied by it.

Evidence of a causal relationship between delay and the new legislation was only found in 18 cases. In most of the remainder, however, we consider it not unwarranted to infer some linkage. Complaints about delay, for instance, were most frequent in cases where the children were accommodated and it appears to be the use of accommodation which reflects most notably the key Children Act principles of partnership and voluntarism. We might make similar inferences from the finding that in almost half the cases (41) there were earlier points where legal action might and in our view almost certainly would have been taken under previous legislation. This applied to 17 of the 20 cases where the local authority was seeking long-term substitute care, for instance; five of the eight where they were intending to supervise the child in the family; 13 of the 21 where work had been ongoing for more than three months and six of the 15 where it had lasted for less than this. Excluding inactive cases and new-borns this amounts to an astonishing 65%. Commenting on one of these cases the Guardian ad Litem told us:

> The local authority put up with such a lot, they really tried to be extremely helpful. It was quite extraordinary; it would have been *extremely* extraordinary before the Act.

For the social worker, however, this was accompanied by almost constant anxiety from the time the baby was discharged from hospital to the day, eight weeks later, when she and the police removed him:

> This was my first Children Act case and it has made me really upset. From my first visit I felt the baby was not safe there; the first time I went I felt I should have removed him. The hospital sent the baby home because they knew that if they went to court they wouldn't get what they were asking for. He shouldn't have left the hospital; the hospital knew that.

Pre-Act, all practitioners agreed, in view of the mother's bizarre behaviour in hospital and the degree of domestic violence, this child would have been warded shortly after birth and, according to the local authority solicitor, a direction sought for a residential placement. It has to be said that this approach would probably not have produced a different outcome in this case.

Had wardship proceedings been taken when baby Karen was born, however, she and her mother might well have been provided with more appropriate services. It is hard to envisage a judge giving leave for a ward to have six different placements in eight months or allowing shortage of resources to drive the case.

Although this can only be a subjective judgement we suspect there would only be a handful of cases (probably not more than seven in all) where the legal outcome would have been materially different if proceedings had been brought earlier. The postponing of long-term decisions, however, is likely to have diminished the life chances of many children[27] while in 22 cases there was some evidence that the delay had resulted in *direct* harm. As indicated earlier, linkages between delay and the new Act might be inferred in many cases and therefore the Act 'blamed' for damaging children, although a direct link could only be made in six cases. Indeed the most serious harm was experienced by children who had been rehabilitated following decisions in previous court proceedings; a salutary finding.

Our research, of course, was carried out in the early years of the legislation, thus capturing the most acute stage of professional uncertainty. Familiarity with the Act and official guidance may have encouraged a less hesitant approach, as this comment from a judge suggests:

> I did initially have concerns that local authorities were trying too hard to work with the parents and children were becoming harmed because they were delaying bringing proceedings too long because they may have been misinterpreting the criteria. I think that's gone although there may well still be cases across the country.

Others, however, indicated there was still cause for concern:

> What I do have anxiety about is the delay imposed by local authorities on themselves. . . . Their perception is that the Children Act is a brake on court proceedings whereas I feel it shouldn't be and isn't anything of the sort. . . . The resources which local authorities throw at families in an attempt not to engage the care machinery are in my view entirely misplaced and extremely dangerous for the children. Because when they finally [come to court] they are horribly damaged.

Thus the research findings indicate two equally uncomfortable conclusions. There were still children ending up in the court system arguably too early, though a much smaller proportion than under previous legislation, about one in six. At the same time there were delays in providing the protection of the court to other children who needed it, about two in five.

The Children Act did not invent this dilemma. Contrary to the dominant image of social work the majority of abused and neglected children have always been protected outside the legal system. Thus judging the viability of voluntary intervention is not a new professional skill which social workers are having to develop. However the new Act undoubtedly sharpens the dilemma and makes the exercise of that critical judgement more difficult and more dangerous for both workers and children. It is therefore vital that social workers, who are principally responsible for treading this particular tightrope should have the training, time, professional guidance and support to enable well-founded decisions to be made.

The importance of the quality of professional input through the child protection process was emphasised when the then Health Minister launched *Child Protection: Messages from Current Research and their Implications*:

> It is unrealistic to hope that professional interventions, however skilled and sensitive, will put an end to child abuse or eliminate harm or occasionally death at the hands of parents or carers or others in whose charge they are. What I seek is a professional input that uses that necessary blend of training, management, judgement, common sense and intuition, which will make hurt to a child or damage to a family less likely; which spots and remedies problems before they become crises; and which has the rigour to cope when a crisis has occurred.[28]

Local authorities and government, as well as social workers, have the duty to ensure that those conditions are met more fully than they appear to be at present.

Summary

Section 1(5), the so-called *no order principle*, gives legislative expression to the pro-family, voluntaristic thrust of current child care policy. In essence little different from the care or control test in the Children and Young Persons Act 1969 it has assumed much greater significance and was perceived by practitioners to represent a far more challenging hurdle.

The new test was universally welcomed by professionals practising primarily within the family justice system, who reported its dramatic effect on local authority practice, reflected in greater emphasis on exploring alternative options before resorting to court, an initial steep fall in the number of applications to court and more strongly based, better thought out, less challengeable applications.

For social work practitioners the new test has presented even greater problems than the threshold criteria, generating considerable anxiety and uncertainty about the appropriate balance between voluntarism and compulsion and fear that children's safety was being put at risk. It was clear not only that, influenced by notions of partnership, social workers themselves were seeking to work with families beyond the point at which they would previously have gone to court, but that decision-making was being significantly affected by cautious interpretations of the law by their legal advisors. There was evidence that even over the research period this interpretation was becoming less rigorous. After several years experience of the Act social services departments should have developed more confidence in their own assessments of the need for statutory action and be less dependent on lawyers' interpretations. Judicial interviews suggest, however, that although this approach was most marked in the early years of implementation it continues to give some cause for concern.

The sample data show that a higher proportion of post-Act cases were initiated in order to arrange long-term substitute care for children. This probably reflects the more cautious approach to bringing proceedings as a result of which alternatives had been more thoroughly explored prior to bringing the case to court. None the less such cases remained in the minority. Indeed in most cases the order which would be sought at the end of the day would depend on developments during proceedings. Most care proceedings, it was clear, are not primarily about getting a final order, they are about using the legal framework to produce a solution which is appropriate for the child.

Using a case typology developed on the basis of initial objectives, the evidence supporting the need for an order was analysed. It was found that at the point proceedings were initiated the justification for compulsory intervention was much stronger in the Children Act cases than in those brought under previous legislation. The case data confirm the view that greater efforts were being made to work with families on a voluntary basis although there were still a minority of cases which might have been diverted.

A common theme in interviews with parents, however, was of insufficient, inconsistent, inappropriate or wrongly targeted services. Analysis of the case material also revealed deficiencies in the provision of services in almost half the cases. The possibility that the need for court action could have been averted if earlier intervention had been different could not be discounted.

Alongside these shortfalls in preventative work, often linked with resource difficulties, there were also examples of deficits within the child protection system which exposed children to continuing maltreatment.

The widespread perception that the new legislation and particularly the no order principle has resulted in the deferment of court action was supported by the research data. There was evidence that some children had been harmed in the process, though not to the extent of serious physical injury, and others exposed to continuing risk.

The Children Act has sharpened the dilemmas inherent in the management of child protection cases. The importance of professional skills cannot be over-emphasised. Children have a right to expect that social workers have the training, support and time to reflect in order to enable well-founded judgements to be made. Local authorities and government have the duty to ensure that the conditions which allow that to happen are met more fully than they appear to be at present.

NOTES

[1] DoH (1989): *An Introduction to the Children Act 1989*. HMSO.

[2] DHSS (1985): *Review of Child Care Law: Report to Ministers of an Interdepartmental Working Party*. HMSO.

[3] Representation of the Child in the Civil Courts. Research Project 1985–90.

[4] Hunt J (1986): The Role and Practice of the Guardian ad Litem. Unpublished working paper.

[5] Eekelaar J; Dingwall R (1990): *The Reform of Child Care Law*. Tavistock/Routledge.

[6] Eekelaar (1991): Parental Responsibility: State of Nature or Nature of the State? *Journal of Social Welfare Law*, No. 1.

[7] DoH (1991): *The Children Act Guidance and Regulations, Volume 1: Court Orders*. HMSO.

[8] Schedule 2, Part 1, para. 7.

[9] DoH (1992): *The Children Act 1989 Court Orders Study*. HMSO.

[10] Social Services Committee: Children in Care in England and Wales. House of Commons Paper 88/89 No 84. Memoranda to Committee.

[11] DHSS (1985): *Social Work Decisions in Child Care*. HMSO; DoH (1991): op. cit; DoH (1989): *The Care of Children: Principles and Practice in Regulations and Guidance*. HMSO.

[12] DoH (1992): op. cit.

[13] *Children Act Advisory Committee Annual Report* 1992–93. LCD.

[14] op. cit.

[15] A specialist, and expensive, unit providing assessment and treatment for sexual offenders.

[16] The exception concerned alleged sexual and physical abuse by the father. At the time the alleged offences came to light the mother was acutely mentally ill and although it had been hoped to rehabilitate the child with her she made insufficient progress for this to seem possible within the time-scale of the child. Proceedings were initiated at the point when the father asked for this child's return.

[17] King M (1995): Law's Healing of Children's Hearings: the paradox moves north. *Journal of Social Policy*, 24(3).

[18] Rowe J et al. (1989): *Child Care Now*. BAAF Research Series 6.

[19] DOH (1991): op. cit.

[20] Social services had been working with this family for years but the care of the four children never rose above the barely tolerable. It was the birth of the fifth child and a deterioration in mother's mental health which tipped the case over the edge. Proceedings were initially brought on the baby alone, the other children being added in to proceedings after the Guardian ad Litem's concerns prompted a Section 37 order.

[21] This was one of a small number of cases where we wondered if greater skills in the handling of aggression might have defused the situation and allowed decisions to be made in less dramatic circumstances.

[22] Freeman P; Hunt J (1998): *Parental Perspectives on Care Proceedings*. The Stationery Office.

[23] Farmer E; Owen M (1995): *Child Protection Practice: Private Risks and Public Remedies – Decision-Making, Intervention and Outcome in Child Protection Work*. HMSO.

[24] Matza D; Sykes G (1957): Techniques of Neutralization: a theory of delinquency. *American Sociological Review*, 22.

[25] This is almost certainly an underestimate given that the research was not designed to address this issue and therefore data were not collected systematically.

[26] DoH (1995): *Child Protection: Messages from Current Research and their Implications*. HMSO.

[27] It is known for instance that it is harder to find adoptive placements for older children and that the risk of breakdown increases with age. DoH (1991): op. cit.

[28] Press Release 21 June 1995.

8 The gatekeepers: decision-making processes in the local authority

Inter-professional consultation

The multiple and chronic difficulties described in earlier chapters had usually brought the sample families to the attention of agencies other than social services. Indeed interagency concern had often been formalised in a case conference[1] even before the events triggering proceedings. The decision to take court action was thus almost invariably made in the context of interagency consultation, there being only two cases, both concerning accommodated children, in which there was there no evidence of this. Inter-professional dispute about court action was recorded in only two cases.

Most typically, decisions were taken at, or immediately following a case conference which made either a specific (45) or provisional recommendation (7). Six conferences were held after the application was made but before the first hearing. Where court action was precipitated by a crisis a conference was less likely to have taken place *before* the decision was made and emergency protection further reduced that likelihood. As noted earlier the crisis cases in our post-Act sample were more likely to have been subject to such intervention. Correspondingly they were also less likely to have been subject to formal interagency discussion. Since these factors were more in evidence in cases involving ethnic minority adults, it is not surprising that such families were least likely to have been subject to a case conference relevant to the decision to bring proceedings.

Although overall the proportion of cases subject to formal interagency consultation was higher post-Act the fraction of crisis cases reaching court after a case conference was lower in all areas. Our data provide no clear explanation why this should be so although one might speculate that the increased demands of the court system – for written applications, for notice, for statements, might have some relevance. So too might the changing practices around parental participation. It would indeed be ironic if reforms which were intended to make the process fairer for parents had resulted in this development.

Chairing of case conferences

Crisis cases were least likely to involve a case conference in Area A, where the differences between the pre- and post-Act sample were most striking. Part of the explanation may lie in departmental policy in this area that all conferences have a chair independent of the office bringing the case, which may have been difficult to arrange in the time available. All conferences in this area were chaired by a team manager from another district within the authority. In Area C, however, conferences were usually chaired by the district manager or a centrally based child protection officer; while in Area B, which was trying to move towards independent chairing, 17 out of 24 conferences were still chaired by the team manager responsible for the case. Such variation is a nationwide phenomenon.[2]

Professional attendance at case conferences

At the 53 conferences on which details were available a total of 532 professionals were in attendance, an average of between nine and ten people in Areas B and C, 11 and 12 in A, though at individual conferences attendance could be as low as four or as high as 18 professionals. As Table 8.1 shows, staff connected with social services accounted for 44% of the total membership with health professionals making up just over a quarter. In all cases either the social worker or the responsible team manager (usually both) attended. As other researchers have found,[3] health, education and police were the other key agencies most frequently involved. At least one health professional attended 94% of conferences, compared to 59% with a police presence

Table 8.1 *Principal professional groups attending case conferences*

	No.	%
SSD social work staff	170	32
SSD ancillary staff	36	7
Local authority lawyers	29	6
Community nursing staff	86	16
Other health professionals	51	10
Police	43	8
Education service	37	7
Institutional staff	37	7
Other professionals	43	7
Total	532	100

and 53% with someone from the education service. These ratios were very similar across all three authorities apart from a much greater police profile in Area A (81%). The overall frequency of police attendance was substantially lower than in Farmer's study of initial case conferences which is probably explicable in terms of differences between the two samples in the proportions of children still living with their parents when the case was conferenced.

The prevalence of health professionals partly reflects the age distribution of the sample, health visitors being the most regular non-social services attenders. At least one health visitor attended 75% of all conferences (compared to 59% in Farmer's study) and only five were invited but unable to be present – a 91% attendance rate. In comparison only 30% were attended by any doctor and a mere 15% by a GP (general practitioner) (even lower than Farmer found). The overall attendance rate for all health professionals other than health visitors was 52% (compared to 67% for education practitioners and 75% for the police). GPs and paediatricians had particularly low rates of attendance: 24 GPs and 19 paediatricians were invited to a case conference but only eight from each group attended.

Had all the professionals invited been able to attend the average size of the group would have risen to between 12 and 13 people. An intimidating experience for any non-professional to face, let alone a parent whose capacity to care for their child is being called into question.

Family participation in decision-making

Parental attendance at case conferences

In accordance with the principles of partnership which are now seen as integral to good practice, governmental guidance stipulates that excluding parents from case conferences should be exceptional and has to be specifically justified.[4] Although this research did not explore social workers' attitudes to parental attendance, since only a few voiced reservations we have no reason to question the findings of earlier research indicating they are broadly in favour.[5]

It is an approach, however, which required changes in practice in two of our three study areas, only Area B having adopted this policy pre-Act. Post-Act we found that in all areas it was unusual for at least one parent not to be invited to a pre-court conference and almost as unusual for neither to attend though there was some variation in both rates. It was notable, however, that although families involving ethnic minority adults had the highest invitation rate (93%) they had the poorest rate of attendance (50% compared to 89% of other families). Families including non-European adults had the poorest rate of all indicating that there may be greater difficulties engaging such families in formal processes. Only in Area C were attendance rates equal across ethnic groups.

Parental exclusion from *part* of the conference was the norm in all areas, a finding which echoes Farmer's pre-Act research.[6] Details were available on all but one of the 26 conferences attended by parents which specifically recommended court action, the conferences therefore which were most significant in terms of local authority decision-making. Only two parents stayed throughout. Seven attended only the beginning, three the end, two were brought in at the beginning and end, while the remaining 11 were known to have attended in part but further details were not recorded.

Partial justification for this exclusion, which parents resent,[7] may lie in the conference's wish to take legal advice. Local authority lawyers were present at 17 conferences attended by parents. Only the legal department in Area C had a policy of not attending in these circumstances (a policy which changed in the course of the research). The others followed Law Society guidance[8] that advice should not be given in the presence of other parties. Significantly, this 'weatherhouse' principle was usually interpreted to mean that parents and their advisor should withdraw from the conference at this point rather than social services and their advisor.

On occasion, it was reported, some members sought to use the opportunity for less inhibited discussion:

> It's a bit unfortunate when other members of the conference see that as the time to say what they really want to say. That is a real problem. You can understand why they want to do that, they feel uncomfortable. Social workers are more used to saying unpleasant things to people or in front of people but health visitors and teachers don't see that as part of their role. It's very tricky. Sometimes the chair will say 'this isn't what's meant to be happening now'; sometimes the chair will join in and encourage it. Sometimes I will step in but then I'm also interested in what people have to say. (Local authority lawyer)

Such comment reveals practitioners struggling to adapt to 'the requirement for professionals to work in a much more open manner and change some of their current practice' and highlights the key role of the chair in reminding conference members that 'all relevant information must be available to the conference'.[9] It also prompts speculation as to how these issues are dealt with when there is no legal advisor at the conference to provide a legitimate opportunity to exclude parents. Is the conference in reality no longer the real forum in which inter-professional discussion takes place, as some interviewees suggested? Or, as others told us, are decisions made at conference insecurely based on partial information and the avoidance of conflict with parents?[10]

> Generally I like parents there but I do think some people back off saying what they should say, which leaves the social worker feeling really set up. We've had to reconference several cases where things have gone really well and then outside another professional will say I didn't like to say in there but I have noticed such and such and you have to go through the whole thing again. People are quite wary about being the person who may be responsible for further action happening. But it's no good telling us outside. If they can't say it in the conference for God's sake write it down. (Team manager)

This process may partly explain why the case conference recommended that on expiry of the first Police Protection Order Christopher O'Brien should return home:

> Tara was quite disruptive. I think that made people very uncomfortable and they were less able to say what they felt. They become very anxious and almost frozen when people behave like that, muttering, threatening violence. . . . They didn't convey their anxieties adequately. It was perhaps one of the times when it's not a good idea to have the parents there. I had plenty of feedback afterwards. Hence the police agreeing to act as soon as possible. We were waiting for the next incident. I think if this had happened before the Children Act the whole flavour of the conference would have been different. Tara probably wouldn't have been there and people would have been a lot more open and felt less threatened. I think that would have resulted in earlier action. (Social worker)

Advice and advocacy

Perhaps because of their lengthier pre-Act experience with parents attending conferences, Area B seemed to be more comfortable with the idea of them being accompanied by lawyers:

> Once parents get a solicitor we are happy for them to attend meetings or case conferences before ever we go to court. Initially I think we were a bit nervous but now it has become almost standard practice. I don't personally invite solicitors but I would say to parents 'look you can invite them to come as a support'. We work with solicitors early on and I think now we find this is a good thing. We are also getting some good co-operation from solicitors. Some

of our more challenging child care solicitors are at the front line of saying to parents 'let's negotiate an agreement, let's co-operate'. (Team manager)

In this sample, however, lawyer attendance was most unusual (five cases). Some parents, of course, would not have consulted a solicitor at this stage. Others may have been unaware of their rights or their lawyer discouraged by the poor remuneration. Two of the parents we spoke to, however, said they had not been allowed to bring their lawyer. While none of our solicitor informants reported being refused permission to attend in the sample areas, several had experienced this elsewhere:

> That is something I do have a grievance about. Time and time again local authorities are dismissive of the right of the parent to be accompanied at a case conference. Frequently I have to refer them to *Working Together*.[11] A case conference is one of the most overwhelming situations a parent would ever find themselves in concerning their children. They're faced with lots of professional faces, many of whom are hostile to them. They are often inarticulate. Some tell me they have felt intimidated and badly treated. I have had clients who've been to a case conference and have said they didn't know I could have gone with them or even said they asked and were told they couldn't.

Virtually all the solicitors interviewed took the view they ought to be able to attend pre-court case conferences and would wish to do so, despite encountering some hostility and even if their role was confined (in line with official guidance) to advice and support. Views on whether participation did and should extend further than this were rather varied but some lawyers had clearly taken a very active part.

From our interviews with four parents whose lawyer did attend it was evident that this was very much valued and that parents felt empowered as well as supported. Even those accompanied by a non-legal professional or a lay person were generally more positive about the whole experience. The parents who attended alone (over half the group) were much more dissatisfied, finding the experience 'daunting', feeling 'overwhelmed with long words' and 'unable to speak'. Those who did speak complained 'they don't listen', 'your point of view never gets heard or understood', echoing exactly the feelings of the parents in Farmer and Owen's pre-Act study.[12] While parents who had attended smaller planning meetings felt more involved and able to participate, the majority of those attending a case conference found themselves intimidated by its size, depersonalised by its coldness, patronised and humiliated.

Farmer and Owen estimated there were only a tiny minority of conferences in which parents were able not only to express their views but to participate in exploration of issues. Interviews with parents in this study gave us no reason to believe that they would have been deemed to have participated to any greater extent or been any less affected by the 'social, cultural, organisational and linguistic' constraints identified by our colleagues. Our findings therefore support their conclusion that there is a 'great need for parental advocacy' at case conferences. Who should exercise that role must be a matter for debate. Lawyers might argue that their existing knowledge, skills and ethical base make them the most obvious candidates while others counter that this represents a further unhelpful colonisation of the welfare sphere by the legal.[13] A lawyer's presence does carry the risk that what was originally conceived as a mechanism to share information and plan interagency strategies will be hijacked and turned into a quasi-judicial forum, as some informants had experienced:

> I've had a couple of cases involving lawyers, both people who do a lot of criminal law and they treated it like a contested criminal trial. They were very aggressive, dominating, would not allow parents to speak or answer questions in case they implicated themselves. In a way it forced social services to go to court because they couldn't establish how much the parent was able to work with them. (Local authority lawyer)

On the other hand, a different approach can, it was reported, work to the benefit of everyone:

> I had one case where the children had been abused but mother was co-operative and asked if I would attend the case conference. I contacted the local authority and said I would be there. When I got there . . . the chair's hostility was made very obvious . . . why did I think it was necessary to be there? My position was made very clear that I didn't have the right to represent her.

> It's a little bit like being a duty solicitor at the police station; one has to think how to deal with it and my philosophy is that you get far more bees with honey than you do vinegar so rather than digging my heels in and trying to stand my ground forcibly I bent over backwards to make it clear that my client was willing to co-operate and that any suggestion they could make which was clearly in the interests of the children would be warmly received, supported and followed.

> During the course of the conference the hostility began to diminish and in fact certain suggestions were made to mother, and when it was seen that I was

actually encouraging her to go along with them at the end of it I was thanked and my support was valued. I think local authorities and particularly social workers still have this view that solicitors are there to cause trouble so I do think it's something they do need to address.

More broadly, the whole issue of parents' access to independent advice, advocacy and support before the case reaches court needs to be tackled.[14] Disempowerment was a major theme in our parental interviews, whether relating to being walked over at meetings, having suggestions ignored or being 'boxed in' to agreeing to accommodation and written contracts. We have also already reported lawyers' concerns about accommodation and voluntary agreements and highlighted the paucity of independent advice and advocacy in a welfare system which lacks the due process of court proceedings but within which equally momentous decisions are increasingly being made.[15]

The lawyers we spoke to tended to assume that social workers had been remiss in not advising parents to consult a solicitor. Our information would not generally support this. Moreover whatever social workers' private opinions might be about the legal profession we found that they were generally much more conscious of the need to encourage parents to seek legal advice than in previous research.[16] Thus although we consider this should be formally recognised as good practice in local authority guidelines a more pro-active approach would seem to be necessary. As a basic minimum social services departments need to provide simple written information on the importance of obtaining independent advice and support, what help is available, how to find a suitable lawyer if desired, and what it would cost. If this were to contain a list of practitioners experienced in family work this would remove the temptation (to which some social workers on their own admission succumbed) to 'forget' to mention lawyers with a reputation for making life difficult for social services.

Other developments in the provision of legal services,[17] such as franchising, also hold out possibilities for improving parental access to good independent and early legal advice. The particular skills needed to help parents in conflict with welfare agencies could spawn a new breed of para-legals. Organisations like the Family Rights Group might be funded to extend their coverage nationwide.

Fathers and other adult relatives

Attendance at meetings is only one aspect of the ideal of partnership which underpins the Act and as we have seen did little to make the parents interviewed in this research feel they had made a significant contribution to decision-making. For the most part, moreover, as previous research has also found[18] *parental* attendance means mothers. Both parents were invited to less than a quarter of case conferences which specifically recommended court action and fathers only to half this number. In contrast mothers received sole invitations to almost two-thirds. Mothers were also more likely to take up the invitation, having an acceptance rate of 76% compared to 67% of fathers.

In large part these figures reflect not just the perception that child care is a maternal responsibility[19] but the proportion of lone mothers in the study. However we also interviewed a small number of estranged and/or imprisoned fathers who were drawn in during court proceedings and were distressed that they had not been involved at an earlier stage. Some of the social workers concerned were also uncomfortable with what they acknowledged to be less than ideal practice. This deficiency is more likely to be exposed now since the Children Act requires that adults with an interest in the care of the child should be notified of the proceedings. If the social worker has not sought out the other parent or explored the potential of the extended family the Guardian ad Litem will almost certainly do so.

There were only three cases in which non-parent relatives were invited to the key case conference. This is in stark contrast to developments in New Zealand and Australia[20] where the extended family is not only consulted, but the primary decision-making responsibility rests with them rather than the agency. However, as we saw in the previous chapter, in most cases there was evidence that some contact had been made with relatives. The case of Michelle Symons was one of the few glaring exceptions.

* *

Michelle's paternal grandmother Avis had (reluctantly) had no contact with her for almost two years because of poor relations between the two families. However she had voiced her concern to social services about the care Michelle was receiving and asked that she be informed if official action ever proved necessary. The record of this interview lay buried in the first of many voluminous family files so that Avis only found out from neighbours that Michelle had been removed once court proceedings were underway. The fact that social services subsequently apologised was all too evidently of little comfort to Avis as she sat through hearing after hearing and heard the judge dismiss her application for residence or contact. The local authority obtained the Care Order they sought and planned to move swiftly to adoption. Leave to refuse all family contact was granted.

* *

Involving the wider kinship group is an area of work now receiving more attention,[21] and is a matter we hope to pursue in future research. Some of the practitioners interviewed in this study, however, were clearly doubtful about the whole idea:

> Sometimes I feel ambivalent about the requirement to consider. I would like to see it in a positive way, I have experience of quite a lot of grandparents looking after children in quite difficult situations informally and that's obviously better than care. But sometimes we've got such grotty families; you look at what they've done to their children. That's the rescue bit in you. In the past we could dismiss relatives we thought were unsuitable because of their track record; you can't do that now. How do you get the balance right?

Even without this degree of ambivalence, where family relationships are strained, when a parent has been striving to keep their difficulties a secret from the wider family or when a worker is still hoping to maintain the parent–child unit it can be difficult to judge whether or when to include relatives in decision-making. In Michelle's case it is doubtful whether the outcome would have been any different if Avis had been involved earlier. In others, however, particularly where the outcome was care with relatives, it is conceivable that the trauma of proceedings might have been avoided if kinship resources had been more fully explored.

Children's participation in decision-making

Taking account of the wishes and feelings of children is another key theme in the Act. It heads the list of matters to which the court must have regard in determining Section 31 applications[22] and is part of the local authority's duty to consult before taking any decision in respect of a child they are looking after or propose to look after.[23]

There was little evidence in this research of children being formally involved in decisions. Even those of secondary school age, for instance, were not invited to a pre-court case conference although their parents generally were. There were some signs that practice and attitudes were moving in the direction of greater participation: Area A for instance was running a pilot scheme evaluating children's conference attendance and a number of social work practitioners also expressed the need for the issue to be addressed more effectively. For the sample children, however, social workers were likely to be the main conduit by which their perspective was fed into the decision-making process pre-court.

Most of the case children of course were very young and many pre-verbal. Thus ascertaining wishes and feelings was a matter of observing their reactions to the adults around them and was scarcely differentiated in reports from assessing their best interests. At the other end of the spectrum many of the older children had already exercised a very potent influence on events in that they had initially drawn attention to their family situation, sometimes in very dramatic ways. Subsequently some of their parents would have been prepared to agree accommodation; it was the child's distrust of parental promises that prompted statutory action.

In the remaining cases only a few social workers told us they had not been able to get a sense of how the child saw things and many stressed how important a part of their role this was even though the child's perspective has to be evaluated against other factors. In one case where the oldest child was 7 the social worker told us:

> I've been aware of how the children felt from very early age; even before they were able to articulate: they've always had a close bond with their mother and wanted to stay with her. That has to be very important but it doesn't mean it has to determine the way the case is going. This family was very isolated from the rest of the neighbourhood; understandably that's all the children knew, they didn't want to be apart from it. It's understanding that but having to take different action. You have to safeguard what you think is best for them.

This order of priorities may have been clear in principle but the decision to take action in opposition to the child's wishes was sometimes particularly difficult, for Sammi Collins' social worker for instance:

> It was a very thin line. We were all very conscious of the risks at home but that had to be set against the distress he would have gone through if we removed him. When he was taken into care [before] he had no attachment to his family and was quite happy being with strangers. By these proceedings he was enjoying being with his family no matter what, he was happy with them.

Ben Smisson 'kept pleading not to be taken into care' prompting his social worker to take great pains to prepare him for the removal she increasingly saw as inevitable. Jenny Grayson's social worker felt unable to intervene until Jenny herself signalled that her home situation had become intolerable. When that eruption came, however, legal opinion was said to be distinctly pessimistic about the prospects of success. It is to the role of the legal department in decision-making that we now turn.

Local authority legal advice

Twenty-nine pre-court case conferences in our post-Act sample were attended by lawyers advising the local authority, an overall attendance rate of 54%, compared to 38% pre-Act. This rate varied considerably between the three authorities, however, (Figure 8.1) and actually fell in Area C, presumably as a result of the legal department's initial policy of not attending where parents are likely to be present. Lawyers elsewhere seemed to have come to terms with parental attendance and none reported difficulties in giving legal advice. They had, however, become more reluctant to take an active part in the general discussion, with many describing themselves as being 'more circumspect', 'less likely to ask questions', 'having to keep quiet'.

Figure 8.1 *Local authority lawyers' attendance at relevant case conference*

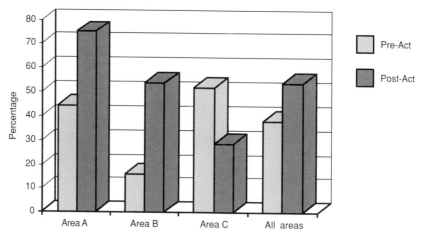

Both lawyers and social work practitioners regarded the solicitor's presence at case conferences as an important part of the service and regretted that it was not always possible. Lawyers attributed this variously to insufficient notice, inadequate resources and poor briefing which did not enable them to prioritise effectively. Where no one was able to attend and proceedings were being considered, all three legal departments said advice could be provided by means of a planning meeting, fax or telephone. What was striking, however, was that it was clearly inconceivable that a case might reach court under the Children Act without *some* form of consultation and that the legislation has operated to involve lawyers much more closely at the pre-court stage.

Legal departments have also, lawyers acknowledge, become 'more questioning', 'more challenging' 'more assertive' and in the view of social work practitioners, more 'influential'. This process of legal aggrandisement, certainly in the period covered by the research, generated new occasions for tension in an inter-professional relationship which has traditionally not been problem-free:[24]

> The solicitor's role needs to be much more acute now. It wasn't that any of the individuals before were *laissez faire*. But because the current situation is so different they need to be able to say to social services from time to time 'You haven't got a hope, you haven't got the grounds, you're concerned but you'll have to think about doing something else.' There have been times when some people have been disenchanted with that approach.

A number of factors contributed to this tension. As intermediaries between more testing legislation and practitioners forced to adapt to new ways, the element of 'shoot the messenger' should not be underestimated. Offering the client a realistic assessment of their chances of success is also a traditional part of any lawyer's role which may be misconstrued as an attempt to sway opinion – certainly there were cases where apparently incongruent accounts of events might be reconcilable in this way. The lawyer's role, however, is more complex when representing a corporate body.[25] Local authority lawyers may be instructed by particular social services personnel, but they act on behalf of the authority as a whole, whose interests they are charged with protecting. As such they may challenge those instructions more rigorously than they would a private client's. They also perceive that as local authority employees courts identify them with their client in a way they would never dream of doing with an independent lawyer representing a private individual. Thus their own reputation, as well as that of the authority as a whole, may be tarnished if an ill-founded case reaches court, with all that implies for future cases:

> The family proceedings court have a sort of belief that we are not going to advise that silly applications should be made; we've built up quite a solid reputation that if an application is made it's made for a good reason. We want to maintain that reputation. One of the reasons I was so unhappy about [a case which proceeded to court against advice] was that it could have thrown that sort of faith.

Linked with this is a view expressed by several social work practitioners that lawyers:

> only want to put cases before the court they are likely to win. They don't see the usefulness of putting things before the courts for direction, but that is useful.

This is a conceptualisation of the role of the court which lawyers recognise as more compatible with the pre-Act wardship jurisdiction and therefore no longer appropriate:

> There used to be this rush to court; it was the fact of actually getting the case into court . . . the feeling that the decision was passed to the court and if the court ordered that the child should go home then that was the court's responsibility. It's a big burden to carry.

Another source of conflict flows from the wider remit of the post-Act courts which are encouraged to look far more closely not only at what social services have already done but what they propose to do. In fulfilling their professional duty to advise on the strength of possible applications local authority lawyers have had to enter further into the social work arena than ever before. They thus risk overstepping a boundary which, according to some practitioners on each side of it, has become increasingly obscure:

> At times they're almost making social work decisions but backing it up by saying they're doing it from a legal perspective; the roles are becoming blurred; they're being critical of our decisions and recommendations. (Social worker)

> Before the Act the role was clearer, now it's more blurred, you have to have some knowledge of social work practice, what they can try, what resources they can put in, how things work. I'm prepared to question things more, especially in terms of looking at court action as a last resort, saying have you tried this, would it make a difference? (Local authority lawyer)

Some lawyers were clearly less tempted than others to stray. The pressure to do so could also vary, depending in part on the competence and confidence of the social worker and more importantly, their team manager. In Areas A and C in particular, there was frequent reference to social workers 'who don't only want legal advice, they want your suggestions' seeking to involve the lawyer in issues which should have been resolved with their team manager.

Formally, of course, the decision rests with social services. As one lawyer picturesquely put it: 'I'll swing from the chandeliers if they really want me to.' However the pressure it would take to make that happen was clearly something some social work practitioners felt less than confident about exercising:

> As a social worker when you ring the legal department for advice you have difficulty remembering that you are instructing them rather than the other way

around. Even as an experienced worker I have difficulty hanging on to that. If they say in my view you shouldn't do something I would have great difficulty saying sorry I'm overriding that.

Nor was this diffidence confined to basic grade social workers, one team manager ruefully conceding that 'perhaps we don't have the confidence to challenge as we should.' In one authority we were told there was an 'ongoing debate' about the legal department's approach:

Social services feel that our legal department are like any other solicitors – they should take instruction from us. But historically they don't here. They say they will only take instructions if they feel it will work in court but they are not going to represent us if they haven't got a good case. I can tell you of so many occasions when we have had this problem and it still hasn't been resolved. How can we force them?

This sense of social workers being intimidated by legal professionals is reminiscent of the early years of the guardian panels which saw social workers and lawyers jockeying for position in the novel tandem relationship the law bound them in.[26] Early anxieties that the established and powerful profession would take over, reducing guardians to lawyers' 'runners' have proved unfounded. Instead the two professions quickly learned to work together, combining different but mutually respected skills in a model of representation which is widely admired.[27] In earlier research evaluating the separate representation provisions[28] we noted with regret that the evident benefits of combining legal and social work skills in this way were not being realised as far as local authority representation was concerned. It is to be hoped that the new standards of professionalism the Children Act demands will create an environment in which this can become more of a reality.

When discussing the interpretation of Section 1(5) in the previous chapter, we commented on the particularly stringent and challenging approach of the whole legal department in Area A. Such careful screening undoubtedly led to a great deal of frustration and anxiety among social workers; on the other hand it was likely to ensure that really weak cases would be filtered out. In Area B, however, though the same type of complaint was made by a number of social workers, there was less evidence of a unified approach and some lawyers' description of their role suggested a more hands-off style. The downside of this was that some cases slipped through which would never have reached first base in Area A. The case of 2-year-old Samantha, to which we referred earlier, was the most extreme example of this.

Samantha was the youngest of Mandy's five children and the only one still at home. While there had been concerns about the standard of supervision in the home, to which a number of accidents had been attributed, the social worker felt things were improving. The older children were all in care under orders made in wardship proceedings. While in care they disclosed severe physical abuse by Samantha's father, who was by this time no longer in the household. A case conference was held principally to discuss plans for these children and almost incidentally, it seems, recommended that a Supervision Order should be sought on Samantha 'to gain a measure of control and ensure she is safe'. The justification for this action was the health visitor's information that Mandy had not been complying with the terms of a written agreement with regard to taking Samantha to clinic and ensuring appropriate medical treatment.

Although both the team manager and a local authority lawyer were at this conference the social worker was not and was flabbergasted to be told of the decision. In the ensuing weeks she tried on many occasions to voice her disquiet, but with some diffidence as a newly qualified worker with no experience of care proceedings under the Act. The team in which she worked was also so stretched that there were no supervision sessions when the issues might have been addressed, even though it was almost three months before the application was lodged with the court. Perhaps for this reason, perhaps because she simply assumed the accuracy of information given to the case conference, perhaps because she was not aware she needed to be chasing up the evidence, it was not until shortly before the proceedings that it became apparent that there was no basis to the case and it was withdrawn at the first hearing.

This case of course was a matter of considerable embarrassment to the local authority and it took courage for those concerned to discuss their individual contributions to the debacle. The most powerful image, however, was of practitioners so over-burdened with the incessant demands of their work that they were unable to find the time to discuss the case properly either within social services or with their legal advisors; too pressurised even to stand back and wonder why, if the case warranted legal action, a delay of three months was of no apparent concern.

The absence of effective legal scrutiny permitting ill-founded cases to reach court was a key criticism in the Cleveland Report[29] and one of the factors which prompted that Inquiry to suggest the establishment of an Office of Child Protection[30] which would, like the Crown Prosecution Service, decide whether cases should proceed. For most of the sample cases such an additional screening process would have been redundant in that local authority legal departments were operating a very tight if not absolutely fail-safe filter. Whether this will continue to be the case as arrangements for the provision of legal services within local authorities change remains to be seen and will need to be carefully watched.

Ironically, in the light of practice in the early years of the Act, such an agency might have its attractions for the quite opposite reason of providing a means by which cases causing serious concern could receive independent external scrutiny. On the evidence from this research, the need for such a mechanism cannot be said to be as yet proven, although it should be kept under review. Moreover the creation of a new agency to interpose between the local authority and the court still appears somewhat superfluous. Jurisdictions where the boundary between agency and court is less impermeable are in some respects enviable as the interest in the French system in particular attests.[31] The possibility of referring borderline cases to a judge rather than waiting until there is cast-iron legally admissable evidence would undoubtedly reduce the level of anxiety inherent in child protection work and increased by the Children Act. It is of note, indeed, that under previous legislation local authorities were encouraged to make use of wardship for just this purpose and the increasing popularity of the jurisdiction in part would seem to reflect an appreciation of this function. The Act, however, halted this development, requiring local authorities to apply for an order and to prove their case on the basis of legal evidence. Thus local authority and court are constructed as adversaries rather than as partners, and the task of the court is to assess whether the right of the state to intervene forcibly in family life has been established. While this remains the case social service departments will be left with the unenviable task of working with risk, not because that is felt to be in the interests of the child but because there is nothing else to be done.

On a more optimistic note, the research does suggest that in the early years of the Act there was a somewhat exaggerated perception of the *obstacles* to statutory intervention and that courts have generally been more liberal in their application of the criteria than was being anticipated. Local authority lawyers, who have often mediated this perception have, it appears, become more relaxed in their operation of the filter. For the moment, then, the way forward would seem to be in enhancing the capacity of social services departments to work with the legislation and thus to use, rather than to be dependent on, the expertise of their legal advisors.

The controlling role of the local authority

As the lead agency in child protection social services has always been extremely influential in terms of the overall management of a case.[32] The Act, however, has enhanced this position with respect to statutory intervention. They are now the only agency, apart from the NSPCC, authorised to bring care proceedings, a power the Act removes from the police and education departments. As one social worker rather bullishly put it, recalling a case where 'the police had been most insistent', 'now they can be as insistent as they like, it's our application'.

The differences between the old and new legislation, in particular the more stringent tests, were, a number of practitioners said, not always appreciated by other agencies:

> Cases have come up at child protection conferences where the network is saying we should be looking at taking legal action but legal are saying you've got the concerns but it's got to be a lot tighter, more specific.

In many cases, as we have seen, social services practitioners were equally dismayed about this approach. The interview data, however, also suggest that on occasion the tighter criteria provide both a useful means to force other professionals to firm up their evidence and to enable social services to resist external pressure to take court action where they feel this is inappropriate. Certainly there was evidence in several files of the frustration of both other agencies and relatives at what was perceived to be social services inaction. In the case of Colin and Antony Wyllie, for instance, the family aides were 'just about banging on the table saying nobody is listening to us'. Education and social services were at odds at several case conferences concerning Jenny Grayson and her grandparents were so desperate they considered bringing wardship proceedings. There were at least three cases, including that of Sam Philipps, where the police were distinctly unhappy with earlier decisions not to take court action.

Ben Smisson's file was littered with letters from health and education professionals urging action. There was also an earlier Section 37 referral[33] prompted by the concern of the court welfare officer acting in the matrimonial proceedings. The local authority had chosen not to apply for an order at that point, leaving both the welfare officer and the court impotent since the Children Act also removes the previous power of courts to make care and supervision orders on their own motion. In such circumstances the court can do nothing but 'look on helplessly and wring its hands with impotent concern'.[34]

Our interviews with the professional judiciary revealed considerable dissatisfaction with this emasculation of their previous powers and the Section 37 provisions, ranging, as these comments reflect, from concern to outright rejection:

> The interaction between Section 37 and Section 31 could usefully be looked at. There is a small minority of cases where there are serious concerns about children, you order a Section 37 report, those concerns aren't greatly allayed by the report but the local authority say they are not going to do anything about it. In that situation there's very little the court can do.

> Courts have got to have the power to say to the local authority whether you want to or not you will look after the child.

They thus add their voice to those academic and professional commentators[35] bewailing 'this gaping hole in the safety net afforded by Section 31'.[36] It would seem that the impact of this section of the Act is another matter meriting further investigation to establish whether this principally reflects regret for a vanished domain or a real diminution in the protection afforded to children.

Summary

The decision to initiate care proceedings was almost always taken in the context of interagency working, formalised in two-thirds of cases by a case conference. There was very little evidence of inter-professional dispute at this stage.

Case conference involvement in the decision to proceed was less likely in cases precipitated by a crisis, particularly those evoking compulsory emergency protection. The fraction of crisis cases with a pre-court case conference was lower post-Act than pre-Act.

Conferences were numerically dominated and chaired by social services staff although in two areas the chair did not have direct line management responsibility for the case. The size of the conference varied enormously though the average attendance was ten.

Children did not attend any of the pre-court case conferences and their views were usually communicated through others. Nor were members of the extended family generally present. In line with official policy, however, the majority of parents were invited and most attended. Women were more likely to attend than men. Ethnic minority families had the highest invitation rate but the lowest attendance suggesting greater difficulties in engaging this group in formal processes.

Parental exclusion from part of the conference was the norm in all areas. There was some evidence that on occasion conference members sought to use the opportunity for uninhibited discussion and also of the opposing danger, that issues were not adequately addressed because of the parents' presence. The skill of the conference chair in managing these dilemmas is crucial and additional training may be required.

Such training also needs to address the issue of the empowerment of parents in a professionally dominated and alien forum. Although most parents were glad of the opportunity to be present at the case conference they generally found the experience intimidating, paralysing and demeaning. Making participation a reality may depend on the presence of someone who can support parents and give them a voice. Attention should be given to how this might be done without turning case conferences into a quasi-judicial forum hijacked by lawyers.

The emphasis on managing cases outside the legal process makes it imperative that the broader issue of parents' access to sound independent advice and advocacy before the case reaches court is tackled. It is ironic that just at the point when parents have achieved the protection of due process within the legal system the court may have become a less important forum for decision-making. The potential contribution of lawyers and others as advocates, negotiators and mediators needs to be explored.

A higher percentage of case conferences were attended by local authority lawyers than under the previous legislation. The issue of the lawyer's position when parents are present had been a problem in only one area. Attendance was still not as high as both lawyers and their client authority would wish. Although lack of resources was a major reason for non-attendance, inefficient communication was also a contributory factor.

The gatekeeping role of the legal advisor to social services has been much strengthened by the new legislation. It has become inconceivable to lodge an application without consultation while legal departments have also become more challenging and influential. This has created new opportunities for tension in a relationship which has always been potentially difficult, as the changing nature of the task pulls lawyers further into the social work arena than ever before. The dangers of role confusion are exacerbated when social workers lack confidence in their own assessments and seek guidance from lawyers which should properly be provided by their team managers.

Legal scrutiny of local authority applications before they are lodged has resulted, for the most part, in an extremely stringent filtering process. Whilst this is not foolproof, the soundness of most of the applications passing through the filter post-Act provides no justification for instituting independent pre-court assessment, such as the Office of Child Protection suggested by the Cleveland Inquiry.

Such an agency has its attractions, however, as a referral point for borderline cases, a function which in other jurisdictions can be performed directly by the court. The need for such a mechanism is not proven although it should be kept under review. For the present, the way forward is seen rather in enhancing the capacity of social services departments to use, rather than to be dependent on, the opinion of their legal advisors.

NOTES

[1] The case conference, according to official guidance on interagency working 'symbolises the inter-agency nature of assessment, treatment and the management of child protection'. Home Office et al. (1991): *Working Together*. HMSO.

[2] Wingham G (1995): Choice or Change. *Child Care Forum*, Issue 5.

[3] Farmer E; Owen M (1995): *Child Protection Practice: Private Risks and Public Remedies – Decision-Making, Intervention and Outcome in Child Protection Work*. HMSO.

[4] Home Office et al. (1991): op. cit.

[5] Thoburn J et al. (1995): *Paternalism or Partnership? Family Participation in the Child Protection Process*. HMSO.

[6] Farmer and Owen (1995): op. cit.

[7] Farmer and Owen (1995): op. cit.; Freeman P; Hunt J (1998): *Parental Perspectives on Care Proceedings*. The Stationery Office.

[8] *Family Law*. June 1994, 343.

[9] Social Services Inspectorate (1995): *The Challenge of Partnership in Child Protection: A Practice Guide*. HMSO.

[10] See also Saves D (1996): Parental Participation in Case Conferences. *Child and Family Law Quarterly*, 8(1).

[11] *Working Together* (note 1) states: 'It may be that the parent or relative will feel more confident to attend if they are encouraged to bring a friend or supporter. . . . It will be incumbent on the chair to clarify the role of the additional person. The conference is not a tribunal to decide if abuse has taken place and legal representation is therefore not appropriate.'

[12] Farmer and Owen (1995): op. cit.

[13] Parton N (1991): *Governing the Family: Child Care, Child Protection and the State*. Macmillan; King M; Piper C (1990): *How the Law Thinks About Children*. Gower.

[14] Braye S; Preston-Shoot M (1992): Honourable Intentions: partnerships and written agreements in welfare legislation. *Journal of Social Welfare Law*, 511.

[15] Fish D (1995): Acting for Parents in Care Proceedings. *Family Law*, 414.

[16] Representation of the Child in the Civil Courts. Research Project 1985–90.

[17] Smith R (1995): Lawyers, Courts and Alternatives, in Smith R (ed.): *Shaping the Future: New Directions in Legal Services*. LAG.

[18] Farmer and Owen (1995): op. cit.

[19] Farmer and Owen (1995): op. cit.

[20] Ryburn M (1992): Family Group Conferences, in Thoburn J (ed.): *Participation in Practice: Involving Families in Child Protection*. University of East Anglia.

[21] Family Rights Group (1994): *Family Group Conferences*. FRG; Thomas N; Beckett C (1994): Are Children Still Waiting? *Adoption and Fostering*, 18(1).

[22] Section 1(3)(a).

[23] Section 22(4).

[24] Hildgendorf L (1980): *Social Workers and Solicitors in Child Care Cases*. Tavistock; Macleod A (1993): *Servicing Social Services*. HMSO.

[25] Macleod (1993): op. cit.

[26] Hunt J; Murch M (1989): *Speaking Out for Children*. Children's Society.

[27] Salgo L (1993): *Der Anwalt des Kindes: Die Vertretung von Kindern in zivilrechtlichen Kindesschutzverfahren – eine vergleichende Studie*. Bundesanzeiger.

[28] Hunt and Murch (1989): op. cit.; Murch et al. (1991): op. cit.

[29] DHSS (1988): *Report of the Inquiry into Child Abuse in Cleveland 1987*. Cm 412, HMSO.

[30] Lord Chancellor's Department (1988): *Improvements in the Arrangements for Care Proceedings*. LCD.

[31] Cooper A et al. (1995): *Positive Child Protection: A View from Abroad*. Russell House Publishing.

[32] Vernon J; Fruin D (1986): *In Care, A Study of Social Work Decision-making*. NCB.

[33] Section 37 of the Act states that 'Where, in any family proceedings in which a question arises with respect to the welfare of any child, it appears to the court that it may be appropriate for a Care or Supervision Order to be made with respect to him, the court may direct the appropriate authority to undertake an investigation of the child's circumstances'.

[34] Brasse G (1993): The Section 31 Monopoly. Nottinghamshire County Council v P Considered. *Family Law*, 691.

[35] White R et al. (1995): *The Children Act in Practice*. 2nd edition. Butterworths; Collins P (1994): Does the System Protect Children? *Family Law*, 686.

[36] Brasse (1993): op. cit.

9 Travelling together: participation, representation and continuity

Party status and participation

Party status

It is strange now to recall that it was not until 1988 that parents acquired automatic party status in care proceedings[1] and that until 1984[2] the only parties were the applicant and the child. Parents participated only because they were deemed to be acting on behalf of the child and if the child's lawyer considered their interests conflicted with his client's, parents could find themselves without a voice.[3] This injustice was partially remedied in 1984 by providing that where the *court* considered there to be a conflict, a separate representation order could be made, while in 1988 the element of discretion was removed. This remains the situation under the Children Act.

In contrast, in matrimonial and wardship cases it was *parents* who enjoyed full rights of participation while the children whose welfare was at issue were very rarely joined.[4] Thus by carrying over into the new unified jurisdiction the child's automatic party status the Act extends to all children involved in public law proceedings rights hitherto available only under the Children and Young Persons Act, a significant advance.

Although the Act does not preserve the special position grandparents attained in the dying years of the old legislation,[5] they, like anyone else 'interested in or affected by the proceedings'[6] may be joined with the leave of the court. Proceedings are based on the 'open-door' principle which was such a valued feature of wardship.[7] Practitioner reports that this has encouraged wider participation are confirmed by our sample cases, in 37 of which (45%) non-parent adults were either joined (30) or participated without being made parties,[8] a higher proportion than in pre-Act wardships (24%).

Proceedings still typically involve a parent (almost invariably the mother) and only one other adult, most frequently mother's partner. There were only 50 cases in which both birth parents were parties. A quarter of cases involved a single adult and only a fifth more than two. However there were also eight cases with four or more parties. One set of proceedings involved nine adults: mother, the fathers of the two children, two sets of paternal grandparents and an aunt and uncle. An even more complicated case resulted from the provision in the Act to consolidate all proceedings concerning children of the same family.

Since birth Clara (1) had been living in a foster home with her mother Jeanette. Jeanette has four other children: Susan (6) living with her paternal grandmother Mrs Bowers; Philip (5) and Julian (4) placed with prospective adopters and David (3) cared for by his paternal grandparents, the Jamesons, under the supervision of another local authority. Paternity of the three eldest children was disputed and whereas neither of the two putative fathers (Jon and Colin) seemed overly concerned, both grandmothers, Mrs Bowers and Mrs Jameson, were keen to claim a relationship with the children placed for adoption.

Care proceedings on Clara began after Mrs Jameson had applied for a residence order on David. Jeanette, who was applying for contact, Jon, Colin and the authority holding the supervision order were joined to proceedings. Adoption proceedings had also been started in respect of Philip and Julian and there were a number of pending contact applications concerning them by Jeanette and both grandmothers. These were all consolidated with Clara's proceedings to which was later added an application by Mrs Bowers for a residence order on Susan. Fifteen people in all were therefore parties in one or more actions in these consolidated proceedings: two local authorities, Jeanette, Jon and Colin, Mrs Bowers and Mr and Mrs Jameson, the prospective adopters and all the children.

In 31 cases at least one person was made a party after proceedings had started, including a third of the fathers taking part, seven being joined at the first hearing, five by the second and four later in the case. Fourteen sets of grandparents and eight aunts/uncles were among the other 27 parties joined late, 15 later than the second hearing. In view of the delays in proceedings associated with late applications local authorities need to make every effort to identify potential participants at an early stage. Sometimes, it is acknowledged, this may not be possible in the time available. The timing of interventions by the extended family may also be dictated by developments in the case with either the need or the opportunity not becoming apparent till proceedings are well advanced. For example, in one case where a girl had allegedly been physically abused by her stepfather, the local authority worked to rehabilitate the child first with both carers, then with the mother alone. Six months later, after this had failed, an aunt stepped forward to offer care.

However there were cases where more strenuous efforts to explore the family network might have resulted in earlier involvement, with consequent benefits to the legal process or to the way that process is experienced. Michelle Symons' grandmother Avis, for instance, was not the only relative to be left with a residue of bitterness. One of our angriest interviewees was a father in prison, speaking for a group who may be marginal to their children's lives but who are also particularly likely to be marginalised by the legal process.

Participation by adults

Data on the 30 cases we followed through the courts support the findings from the parental interviews[9] that most parents do make an effort to attend court hearings. Of the 196 *attendable*[10] hearings observed, 160 were attended by at least one parent, most commonly mothers. Fathers had a much poorer attendance rate (57% attending at least one hearing compared to all but one mother).

Of course neither formal rights of participation nor attendance equate with true participation and sadly it is clear both from our own interviews and research by the Family Rights Group[11] that in general parents feel just as disempowered, marginalised and to a large extent disregarded as they did before the Children Act.[12] The new emphasis on *partnership* with parents in child protection work does not appear to have impinged on the court process, an issue which needs to be addressed by policy-makers as well as practitioners. As we conclude elsewhere:[13]

> Whether as a result of the formality of the setting and the procedures, the adversarial process or the convoluted language, parents experienced proceedings as intimidating, disabling and depersonalising. What they would like to see is a more informal setting in which they could take part in a comprehensible discussion of their circumstances and speak directly to those who will be taking the decisions.

Children's attendance at court hearings

One of the more disconcerting practices in care proceedings under the old legislation was that of 'presenting' children to the magistrates. In previous research we used to watch appalled as whole sibling groups trooped into court and stood bemused before three total strangers who were searching for something friendly but neutral to say, watched by a courtroom full of people, most of whom were also unfamiliar. This 'barbaric'[14] practice, mercifully, appears to have ceased, the law no longer requiring children over 5 to attend unless their presence has been dispensed with.

Very few of the children in this sample took any direct part in proceedings. The majority of course were very young, but even among the 20 cases involving a child aged 9 or more there were only seven in which the child was present at any hearing, including three of the six cases involving teenagers. Nor did any of them meet privately with the judiciary in chambers although we observed occasional instances of this pre-Act[15] and it is still possible, though discouraged,[16] under the new regime. It is a feature of many cases involving older children, of course, that they are either at loggerheads with their parents or fearful of the consequences of the allegations they have made. Thus it would be understandable if, as happened in four cases, some baulked at the prospect of being with them in the courtroom. However, there were another four in which the child had asked to attend court but had either been dissuaded or denied attendance.

The research did not explore practitioners' views on children's attendance in court so we are unable to comment on the suggestion that it may be professionals rather than children who feel uncomfortable with their presence.[17] It does seem, however, to be an area in which practice is divergent. Judging from the comments of some social workers that 'he didn't ask and I didn't ask him' and 'I explained it to her; I don't think I offered her the opportunity; she never asked to come' (both children aged 10) the child may not even be consulted. There was also evidence that children had been dissuaded by their social worker, guardian, even solicitor and also of some differences on opinion among practitioners and courts. In one case the question of the child's attendance become a major focus of dispute.

. . . .

Marcus, almost 10 and described as 'very bright', wanted to be fully involved in proceedings. In view of his 'strongly expressed wishes' and to 'help to demystify the case and separate it from the concurrent criminal matter' the guardian agreed he should attend the first hearing. Social services, however, decided that in the absence of a court direction they were not required to produce him and he was not brought to court.

The matter was argued before the magistrates, the child's representatives taking the position that Marcus was of the requisite 'appropriate age and understanding' and that the local authority had not only let him down but pre-empted the court's right to decide whether he should attend. For their part social services argued that an application should have been made to the court, that attendance was not in Marcus's interests and asked for him to be excluded from subsequent hearings. The Bench concluded that the hearing should proceed but that Marcus should attend future hearings if he so wished.

Marcus accordingly came to the second hearing, again in the family proceedings court. As the guardian told us, 'He found it hard not to intervene in the proceedings . . . was bored and eventually left the courtroom.' Having asked to attend the third hearing he then changed his mind. When the case was subsequently transferred up to the county court the district judge made it very clear that in his view the child's presence was inappropriate.

● ●

The approach of this district judge finds support in some, if not all, subsequent judicial decisions. In Re C[18] for instance Waite J ruled that 'the presence of children should not be allowed to develop into settled practice', while in J v Lancs County Council[19] it was said that there would have to be exceptional circumstances for a 15-year-old to be present in court. In contrast in Re H, it was considered that to allow the 15-year-old subject to proceedings to be in court would ensure that he was better able to accept the court's decision.[20]

In general we doubt that many practitioners with experience of care cases would see the courts, as currently organised, providing a setting which is either appropriate for children or facilitates their participation. Indeed since our interviews with adult members of the family suggest it is often a hostile and disabling environment for the adults concerned this is scarcely surprising. Seven of the sets of parents we interviewed were also strongly against children attending, giving reasons such as their likely confusion, lack of understanding, boredom or distress and the effects on parents, such as being distracted, embarrassed or humiliated. In essence, these parents took the view that courtrooms were not suitable places for children when adults could be observed to be in conflict. Three of the six parents whose children had attended court were unhappy with this although the remainder were content and some of the parents whose children did not attend court felt they should have done so.

Unfortunately in this research we were not able to ascertain what the children themselves felt, another topic requiring investigation.[21] It may well be that most children would prefer to stay away. However if there are some children who would like to take part, or who would like to be able to put their views directly to the decision-makers, or perhaps simply to meet them, then it is not congruent with the spirit of the Children Act, nor with the UN Convention on the Rights of the Child, to which the UK is a signatory, to deny them those opportunities simply because it does not fit easily into the way the system is currently organised. This is a matter with which the courts will need to grapple more effectively. Pending change, however, most children will be dependent on the advocacy of others to protect their interests and advance their views.

Legal disability: Guardians ad Litem for children and adults

Children

Although children are parties to proceedings they normally have to exercise their rights through a Guardian ad Litem. Two systems for providing guardians existed prior to the Act: in wardship the Office of the Official Solicitor; in care proceedings local authority panels of Guardians ad Litem and Reporting Officers (GALRO). The two differed substantially in terms of organisation, professional qualifications and responsibilities.[22] Most significantly, while both had the dual role of protecting the welfare of the child *and* informing the court of the child's wishes and feelings, where these were in conflict and the child was deemed competent, the panel guardian was debarred from continuing to represent the child, the Official Solicitor was not. Thus in the Official Solicitor model the extent to which the child's views were advocated depended on the person charged with protecting their best interests.

The proportion of local authority wardship cases in which the Official Solicitor acted for children was very low (less than 10%)[23] and it was the local GALRO panels which were principally expected to meet the increased demand for representation resulting from the Act. The Official Solicitor remains a resource but one available only in the High Court and in 'exceptional circumstances'.[24] Moreover when he acts in Children Act proceedings, case law has now established the right of a competent child whose views conflict to instruct his own solicitor direct; the Official Solicitor can then be retained as an *amicus curiae*.[25] Thus the formal rights of children are further extended by the Act.

None of the sample cases was sufficiently exceptional to warrant the appointment of the Official Solicitor for the children who were all represented by panel guardians acting initially at least in conjunction with a lawyer. By the time the Children Act was implemented, social services departments and their legal advisors in Areas A and B were very familiar with the guardian's role, their juvenile courts having made appointments in virtually every care case under the old legislation.[26] For Area C, which brought most of their pre-Act cases in wardship, it was a relatively novel experience. This may help explain what appeared to us to be a greater degree of ambivalence, even open conflict, in this area, an echo of the early years of the guardian service nationwide and an amplification of the difficulties which still appear to exist to some degree in all areas. Though outside the remit of this project, it was clear that further work needs to be done by social services departments and the guardian panels to ensure that the inherent tensions in working relationships do not impede the progress of the case.

By the time the Children Bill was passing through Parliament the appalling delays which had dogged the guardian service in some parts of the country[27] had largely been dealt with. None the less the experience legitimised anxieties that backlogs would again develop as guardians were sought in an expanded range of proceedings[28] and appointed earlier in the case.[29]

The research shows that the intention of the Act to involve guardians at the earliest possible point has been realised to the extent that the majority of appointments (88%) were made before the first hearing and the rest at or shortly after that hearing. However whereas prior to the Act it was Area B which had the highest proportion of late appointments, post-Act it was Area C which had slipped behind, with one in four appointments being made at or after the first hearing, compared to less than one in ten elsewhere.[30] In the 27 first hearings we attended it was noticeable that whereas a guardian was present in nine out of ten cases in Area A and eight out of nine in Area B, in Area C the proportion was four out of eight. Difficulties in appointing guardians or in the guardian being able to start work were noted in seven cases in Area C. In one the court decided to defer appointment until it was clear the case was going to be contested. The guardian then only accepted the case on the basis that she could not start work on it immediately. Six weeks later she informed the court that because of unexpected delays in another case[31] she could not begin work for another month and asked that another guardian be sought.

In the course of working on files in the county court serving this area we also observed at first hand the frustration of staff as they rang guardian after guardian in an endeavour to persuade someone to take on a new case. On many occasions the carrot was offered that the guardian need not attend the first hearing if only they would take the case and get a solicitor instructed. Responsibility for allocating guardians in this area has now been transferred to the panel manager and the panel expanded and our most recent information indicates that the level of service has now been restored to something like its previously impressive level. It should also be noted that, throughout, the emphasis on the avoidance of prejudicial delay does mean that difficulties are addressed with a greater sense of urgency than was sometimes apparent pre-Act. In earlier research we noted a worrying level of resignation in some courts about ever-lengthening waiting lists.[32] Business committees attached to each care centre also provide, in theory at least, a mechanism through which such interagency problems can be addressed.

None the less it must be questioned whether the courts should be dependent for the provision of such an essential service on the resources of another agency; or whether it is reasonable to expect local authorities to fund a service over which they have no control. In these days of purchasers and providers one might argue that the service should at least be financed by the Lord Chancellor's Department or the Legal Aid Fund. More radically, given the persistence of doubts as to the independence of guardians whether actual (parents) or theoretical (practitioners and the judiciary) we continue to argue for a re-structuring of the service. At the time the Children Bill passed into law criticisms of the local authority link were deflected by the declaration that the future of the panels and that of the court welfare service were to be reviewed as part of the then government's *rolling programme*. Nothing as yet has materialised.[33] Yet the emergence of a distinct system of family justice,[34] heralded by the partial integration of the court system offers a new opportunity to revive at least the concept of a court-based welfare service, mooted over 20 years ago by the Finer Committee[35] and still worthy of consideration.

Adults

We commented earlier on the numbers of parents in the sample suffering from psychiatric illness or disorder. Several were in hospital at some point during proceedings and four mothers committed under the Mental Health Act 1983 were represented by the Official Solicitor. Assessment of legal competence in such cases, where the parent's condition seldom stays constant, can be difficult, as Laurie's case illustrates.

Plans to place Laurie with his mother in a residential placement never came to fruition and within a few months of the start of proceedings Gina's mental health significantly deteriorated. She was admitted to psychiatric hospital where she was detained for the remainder of proceedings.

In the few weeks before the final hearing Gina became more compliant with medication and on the first morning it was apparent that she was now quite lucid and capable of instructing. However her legal representatives, including the solicitor who had acted for her before the assessment of incompetence was made, were still representing the Official Solicitor, a distinction Gina found very difficult to grasp and even harder to accept. Counsel strove valiantly both to *present* Gina's view (that she was capable of looking after Laurie) and *represent* the Official Solicitor (whose instructions were not to contest the application for a care order followed by adoption). The judge made extraordinary efforts to ensure fairness. Moreover it is extremely unlikely that a different decision would have been reached had the situation been resolved and the resultant delay would have been prejudicial to Laurie. None the less the case left a lingering sense of injustice and fuelled Gina's already considerable sense of grievance.

Legal representation

Adults

It is now highly unusual for adult parties to participate in care proceedings without benefit of legal representation. In our post-Act cases only two non-parent partners and two other relatives did so, a representation rate of 97%. That is not to say that parties were represented throughout the case or that even when instructed lawyers necessarily attended all the hearings. Six mothers and six fathers were only represented for part of the proceedings (11 cases) as were six other adults. In eight cases we noted delay in parties seeking representation, six of which impeded the progress of proceedings. As suggested in Chapter 8, courts and social services departments, in consultation with local Law Societies, need to consider whether improvements could be made in the information available to families at an early stage which would reduce the incidence of late instructions. Simple explanatory leaflets issued along with the notices of proceedings, for example, would seem to be vital whilst a duty solicitor scheme for lawyers on the Children Panel might enable some non-contentious progress to be made on the case even when a parent turns up at court unrepresented.

The research also suggests that parents, even perhaps some lawyers, need to be better informed about the legal aid provisions. In care proceedings parents are now entitled to non-means, non-merit tested legal aid[36] thus the problems encountered in some of our earlier research[37] should be a thing of the past. However representatives of three mothers told the court of delays in obtaining legal aid which in at least one case necessitated an adjournment. In two cases the difficulty appeared to be linked with a residence application. One father understood from the solicitor he first consulted that he would not be eligible because he was employed, while a mother was apparently told she was ineligible because she was not opposing the proceedings.

Other adults who have leave to participate in proceedings are eligible for non-merit tested aid but still have their contribution means-tested.[38] Several practitioners, social workers as well as lawyers, raised this issue in interview and grandparents in two cases told us they were not represented because they could not afford the contribution. This situation seems anomalous and given the number of people likely to be involved, fairly petty. We would argue that if the court has recognised a legitimate interest by granting party status, legal aid should be granted on the same basis as to parents. Such a change might also encourage courts to be discriminating about the granting of party status in cases where, because separate interests are not involved, acting as a witness might be adequate. Although the study courts did not appear profligate, the extension of rights of participation and the high rate of representation inevitably increases the demands on a hard-pressed Legal Aid Fund and adds to the length of hearings.

Not all the 166 adult parties in the sample were separately represented. Grandparents or aunts and uncles were typically jointly represented and there were examples of other linkages, for example parent and new partner; grandparents and parent. One case involved seven adult parties but only three interests: mother and her parents, father and his parents, mother's cohabitee. There were only ten cases, however, where the birth parents shared a lawyer. In total 149 adult interests were legally represented with only 14 cases having more than two and two with more than three. Whilst actions involving large numbers of competing interests may well be more common under the Children Act, they are not yet commonplace.

Children

In general all the children in a case are assumed to have a common interest in proceedings and are represented by the same lawyer instructed by the same guardian. There were only three cases in the sample where the guardian and a competent child diverged. In two each was separately legally represented, as the Children Act for the first time made possible.[39] One of these resulted in the children in the family being represented by two different lawyers. In the third case the guardian was not represented.

In 70 cases the child's solicitor was appointed before the first hearing, with all the remainder for whom information was available being appointed at or shortly after that hearing. In our sample of observed cases there was only one case where the child was not legally represented at the first hearing.

The choice of legal representative

Children

Since the inception of the panels in 1984 guardians have been authorised to select and instruct the child's lawyer unless one has already been appointed or a competent child objects and this position was preserved in the Children Act.[40] In earlier research we found that the shortage of guardians made this a burning issue with guardians complaining of finding a solicitor in place whom they would not have chosen and with whom they might find it difficult to work and courts arguing it was vital the child had some representation as early as possible.[41] In this research we were aware of at least one case in each area where the solicitor was appointed before the guardian and the issue clearly remained very much alive, particularly for the over-stretched panel in Area C:

> It's vital to have a good child care solicitor. . . . I tend to use solicitors I already know and I only use ones I know are really good. . . . And I choose solicitors by areas so it's not as if I'm using the same one all the time. But building up a relationship with a new solicitor takes time. Although I got on very well with [the child's solicitor] I didn't feel that at the final hearing he totally reflected what I was saying on the question of contact. . . . The solicitors I normally work with would say exactly what I'm saying even if I'm going out on a limb.

Parents

Although not mandatory, guardians will almost always select a solicitor from the specialist panels established by the Law Society in the 1980s. While this may not be as reliable as some of our interviewees would wish in guaranteeing the quality of advocacy, it does stipulate conditions for entry and some indication of minimum levels of competence. Parents and other family members may be advised of the existence of this panel and, as recommended earlier, we think it is very important that they should be helped to obtain competent legal advice. At the moment, observation and parental interviews suggest, it is all rather random, and several parents reported wishing, in retrospect, that they had had a lawyer with greater expertise. They were not alone in suspecting that they were relatively poorly served; this was a persistent theme in practitioner interviews and reinforced by the judiciary:

> Those least well served tend to be adult family members whose solicitors might not be on the child care panel and who sometimes don't have the detailed knowledge of care cases. (District judge)

> Those who act for the parents, some of them are on the panel, some of them are SFLA [Solicitors' Family Law Association] members and some of them are completely at sea. (Magistrate)

As researchers with lengthy experience of public child care law we have been gratified to watch the development of the legislation from a situation where parents were not parties and had no entitlement to representation to one where they have full rights and state-funded representation. Formal rights are, however, meaningless if representation is poor. Slowly, perhaps, organisations like the Solicitors' Family Law Association may be able to improve standards. This, however, does nothing for the parents of today or tomorrow nor for the effective use of public funds. Like a number of other commentators[42] we are now in no doubt that this situation should not be allowed to continue. The time has come to establish basic standards of competence for all those practising in family law by establishing a family panel and restricting legal aid to panel members.

The local authority

Our three social services departments generally had no say in their choice of representative since at the time legal services were customarily provided inhouse. Views on the availability and quality of legal assistance tended to vary but in general social workers seemed to feel that the level of support could have been improved. Access to legal help was too often rationed, from the outset when a solicitor might not be able to attend a case conference where proceedings were contemplated to the final hearing when their assistance with preparing evidence or an opportunity for a conference with counsel might not be available. While workers struggling with resource problems themselves were not unsympathetic to the effects of high workloads they were none the less critical of delay or discontinuity:

> She didn't get things going. We had the review in October and decided nothing was happening and we had to go to court. It then took to January to get to court, the local authority solicitor kept saying she'd the file on her desk and it was making her feel guilty. I'd provided her with everything she'd asked for but she was overworked and this was a child who wasn't in any danger.

> The inconsistency was the major problem. We needed a lot of advice on this case; it was a very difficult case. We had different people picking it up all the time, and it would have been helpful to have had the same person all the way through. . . . If we got a different person, you see, they were saying something different and although everybody at the legal department knew a bit about the case they weren't obviously fully aware of it and had to really go into it, re-read it. . . . You felt you were retelling the story a lot of the time, and it was so difficult when we finally had the meetings with the barrister to put our case over to him, and I don't think that in the time that was available we were very successful in doing that.

When a legal department was able to provide a more substantial service this was unequivocally regarded by social workers as a great asset to their case preparation:

> It was extremely useful. I could ring them up and if I had any queries I would get a full and helpful response. Even if I changed my way of thinking they would make me stop and think about what I was doing. I felt sufficiently armed to go to court, safe, not alone.

Both positive and negative comments underline the need to keep under review the adequacy of the legal resources available to social services. The substantial cuts in legal services which have become evident in the course of our current follow-up research are much to be regretted.

On occasion private practitioners were called in to meet acute shortfalls in supply. Local authority contracts with such solicitors varied, with the fee-earner in some cases being used largely for advocacy with other support continuing to come from the legal department. Interviews suggest that in these circumstances the position and responsibilities of each lawyer need to be carefully delineated and explained to the social worker. The service offered by private firms also emerged as variable and in some cases did not appear to have been fully enough discussed with the contracting authority. If competitive tendering is to replace specialist in-house teams, local authorities will need to examine with some care what services are actually being offered to assess their comparability.

The use of counsel

In wardship cases prior to the Act all legally represented parties had the services of counsel since the first solicitors were granted rights of audience in the High Court only in December 1994. In care proceedings in the old juvenile court, however, it was usual for the case to be handled entirely by solicitors, with barristers only occasionally appearing for a parent or, when the legal department was particularly stretched, for the local authority. Counsel were least likely to act for children since one of the commitments lawyers on the Children Panel make is to strive to act in person.

Now that care proceedings can be heard at all levels of the court system the Bar is taking an increasing role. While barristers still acted most frequently for parents (16 of 29 cases) or local authorities (11) there were six cases in which the child's case was presented by counsel on at least one occasion. The proportion of cases in which counsel are engaged may also increase given judicial criticism[43] of the 'developing tendency of local authorities to use employed solicitors rather than specialist counsel'. Such a development, Thorpe J was reported as saying, was to be regretted because these staff had not the experience of contested children's cases which the Bar acquired during the years of wardship. Furthermore it was often difficult for them to advise the local authority during the litigation with the same detachment and strength. This reasoning, understandably, caused something of a furore, given the experience built up under the Children and Young Persons Act and the perceived slur on the professionalism of local authority lawyers. Equally, when the budgets of legal departments are limited, engaging counsel may have to be seen as an exceptional expense. Only one of the legal teams participating in the study included an in-house barrister.

Moreover although a barrister with special expertise in children's cases may be a joy to behold, the Bar has no equivalent of the Children Panel. We would wish to see this change. It could be argued, of course, that such a panel is less necessary since solicitors can exercise informed free choice on behalf of their clients and poor advocates will not be re-instructed. That is scant comfort for the families whose counsel is less than adequate. Though generally the standards we observed were good enough and in some cases outstandingly good, there were a few where we had occasion to criticise. In one case in particular the mother had an inexperienced solicitor and a poor counsel and the combination significantly affected the management, the duration and just possibly the outcome of the case, a point not lost on the instructing solicitor:

I regretted throughout using the counsel I did, he wasn't necessarily the right person for the job, he wasn't experienced enough. He was a last minute choice for the first interim and he sort of latched onto the case. I should have been harder and said I was going to move it elsewhere but I didn't and I felt terribly guilty about that.

The engagement of counsel can add to the amount of discontinuity in a case. In addition their approach was also perceived by a number of practitioners to introduce an unduly adversarial element increasingly out of step with the culture of care proceedings:

> Child care panel solicitors and good members of the Bar produce hearings which are very caring in tone, no raised voices or unnecessary cross-examination of vulnerable witnesses. When you get someone who comes in with a different attitude it shows up pretty quickly and puts everyone's backs up. (Guardian ad Litem)

For a parent, of course, as our interviews show,[44] a highly adversarial, point-taking barrister may be seen to be doing his all for his client. Indeed we have been present in court when a father who had no previous experience of care proceedings but was very familiar with the criminal justice system, sacked his barrister because she wasn't jumping up and down enough or being sufficiently aggressive. It can be no easy matter treading that tightrope between meeting the client's expectations and working within the usually much less adversarial atmosphere of the care court.

The introduction of concurrent jurisdiction meant that many guardians were having to work with counsel for the first time. Some still seemed rather wary, representing barristers as disempowering rather than enabling agents, particularly in the counsel-dominated culture of the higher courts. Again we were reminded of the early years of the panels when guardians and solicitors were circling each other warily and trying out effective ways of working together. We would therefore anticipate that in time, particularly as guardians become more at home in the higher courts and feel confident of their recognition by the judiciary, a similar process of accommodation and mutually satisfactory working practices will be achieved. This will presumably grow as the number of specialist child care barristers increases and might be accelerated if a specialist Bar were ever to be established. It may be necessary, however, for working with counsel to be a specific element in guardian training, perhaps as part of training in practice in the higher courts.

As a result of extended rights of representation, movement between levels of court and the greater involvement of the Bar, it is usual for a range of legal personnel to be present in court: solicitors, legal executives, clerks, counsel. There tends to be variety between the parties and between hearings. On average, however, the data from our observed hearings suggest that there will be between three and four legal personnel present at a first hearing and five at the final hearing, though certain more complex cases may accrue many more than this.

In retrospect we wished we had systematically recorded all the names so that we could have quantified the considerable discontinuity we observed, particularly among representatives for parents and the local authority. Such discontinuity is disconcerting for those represented; it also has implications for the effective management of the case as it moves through an increasingly complex system. As we demonstrate later, court hearings punctuate, rather than encapsulate, the decision-making process in care cases. Thus the professionals involved are best conceptualised as members of a 'small social organisation',[45] assembled to assist in a continuous process of problem or dispute resolution rather than merely offering differing perspectives for adjudication. Discontinuity within this matrix threatens the effectiveness of the process. While it is appreciated that total consistency of representation is unachievable and could produce delay, a greater degree of continuity should be the aim. Discontinuity, moreover, extends also to the judiciary hearing the case.

Judicial continuity

A degree of judicial discontinuity is inherent in a re-modelled court system which allows for transfers between different levels of court and encourages the division of responsibility in each. Potentially every case can be heard before at least seven different judicial personnel (that is three magistrates, Justices' Clerk, county and High Court judges, district judge), although fortunately none of our sample actually was.

Care cases, however, are also characteristically subject to multiple hearings, between six and seven being the average for the sample. In consequence, unless specific efforts are made to preserve continuity, which our observation indicates is unusual, even cases which are heard in a single forum and are not subject to divided responsibility are likely to be heard before a number of different adjudicators. The 15 sample cases of this type also had a lower mean number of attendable hearings than the sample overall and none was affected by lateral transfer, yet even in these most auspicious circumstances, perfect continuity of case handling was achieved in only two instances. The remainder were heard on average by nine or ten magistrates (rising to at least 18 in one case) or two or three judges/district judges, although only one case reached its theoretical maximum discontinuity rate.

In the sample as a whole at no judicial level was continuity of adjudication achieved in more than a third of cases. The cases of greatest moment, those requiring hearing by a High Court judge, were the least likely to be heard before the same judicial officer.[46] Indeed, over half the cases with more than one hearing at this level did not come before the same judge twice. Such total discontinuity was also experienced by two-fifths of cases at magistrates' courts level.[47] In addition, just over half the sample were vulnerable to discontinuity at more than one level, with the overall effect that twice as many members of the judiciary (116 magistrates, 26 district judges and 32 judges) were involved over and above the numbers made inevitable by structural factors.

Does discontinuity matter?

> You have to have, if you can possibly engineer it, continuity of tribunal.

> It doesn't particularly matter; in an ideal world maybe.

The extent of judicial discontinuity revealed in this research is rightly a matter of concern to those concerned with the administration of the courts.[48] As these quotes demonstrate, opinion among the judicial personnel we interviewed was very mixed, from those who were passionate about the issue and saw it as crucial to the effective operation of the court system, to those who saw it as largely irrelevant, with the general weight of opinion falling somewhere in the centre. Even among those who conceded the issue to have some importance opinion varied as to whether it was an unrealisable ideal not worth striving for or something which needed to be constantly sought and could often be achieved.

Very different practices were evident. One family proceedings court prioritised cases where there had been contested interims, trying to list the final hearing before the same Bench. In the same circumstances another had 'made a conscious decision not to have the same clerk or bench because it would look as if it was being pre-judged'. In one county court there was a policy among the district judges that 'once a case has started it comes back to the individual DJ [district judge] unless there is a good reason why it shouldn't'. In another 'because of the logistics we cannot allocate cases to us individually; you can have cases where all of us have given directions.'

Care cases now tend to involve high numbers of professional personnel, which, parents told us, can be an overwhelming experience. They may also find themselves in a different courtroom for each hearing and, if the case is transferred, in a different building, in a new forum with even more unfamiliar rules of behaviour. How much more disorientating then when even the people hearing the case change. Parents who kept the same judge/magistrates throughout were generally appreciative, commenting that it helped them to make sense of the decision-making process. Most of those who had experienced discontinuity were highly critical, seeing it as disruptive and time wasting. The mother who said: 'we swapped and changed all the time. It mattered because the story had to be told all again' expressed the resentment felt by several at the degree of re-capping involved. Parents were also anxious when a judge knew the case only from the documentation because 'reading it is not the same as hearing it', and equated discontinuity with potential or actual inconsistency. The fact that these criticisms were not related to case outcome suggests parents were making a fundamental criticism of the court system.

Discontinuity also has implications for the use of court time. Even if all those coming fresh to a case were to spend only ten minutes acquainting themselves with the salient facts about a case (a very conservative estimate given the typical volume of documentation), at a national level one could be talking about the squandering of around 3,000 hours of judicial time per year. In practice, of course, particularly at directions hearings in the higher courts, the judge hearing the case for the first time may come into court with no prior knowledge whatsoever, as we have also observed. It is then common to ask the legal representative for the local authority to provide a summary. For those already familiar with the case this is a waste of time and for parents a distressing repetition of painful events. Not infrequently, and particularly where counsel are engaged, that representative is also new to the case. Moreover, relying on the parties in this way scarcely reflects the managerial, inquisitorial court that was envisaged in the legislation.

Though the effect on parents and the duplication of effort were both mentioned in a number of judicial interviews it was the effect of discontinuity on the ability of the court to control a case which was most frequently cited. We shall return to this issue in Chapter 12. In the next chapter we turn to the new court structure set up by the Children Act, which, as we have seen, has vastly increased the potential for discontinuity within the system.

Summary

As a result of the 'open-door' philosophy of the Children Act proceedings now more frequently involve non-parental adults with an interest in the welfare of a child, typically members of the extended family. Abolition of grandparents' automatic rights to party status does not appear to have been detrimental. Late joinder, however, was a feature in over a third of cases and was associated with longer proceedings. More strenuous efforts by social services might have enabled some of these parties to participate from the outset and thus avoid delay.

Although the number of parties has increased, and is higher even than in wardship, cases with a large number of parties were still exceptional. A quarter involved only one adult respondent, typically the mother. Both birth parents were parties in only six in ten cases and even in these it was the mother who was most frequently present at court hearings.

Legislative reform has not improved the quality of the court experience for parents, who continue to report feeling disempowered, marginalised and disregarded. The court system is increasingly out of step with the current emphasis on concepts of partnership and participation within child protection social work and notions of parental responsibility enshrined in the Act. This issue needs to be addressed by the family justice system both as a matter of policy and practice.

Massive changes in the legal process would also be necessary if children are to participate directly in proceedings. This is extremely rare under the Act. Attendance at hearings even by older children is unusual; some children may not be consulted on the issue and others actively discouraged by practitioners or the judiciary. Research is needed into children's views on this issue.

Children enjoy greater formal rights under the new legislation than they did under wardship. The dominant mode of representation for children was via a lawyer on the Children Panel instructed by a guardian. Though new to the higher courts this system appears to have been accepted and standards generally deemed high although there are issues which need to be jointly addressed by guardians and the judiciary. Legal representation was almost invariably in place by the first hearing. However 12% of guardians had not been appointed by that stage and just under a quarter of observed first hearings did not have a guardian present. One of the guardian panels was clearly under-resourced and was subsequently expanded; elsewhere temporary pressures had to be relieved by the use of guardians from a neighbouring panel.

Although guardians do tend to be involved earlier in the case than under previous legislation it is vital that panel size continues to keep pace with demand.

The need for reform of the organisational and funding arrangements for the guardian panels remain. It is hoped that this is still on the agenda of the government's rolling programme of reform and that not much more time will elapse before this bears fruit in the form of a more appropriate structure. The greater integration of the courts under the Children Act makes a court-based welfare service, as suggested by the Finer Committee, a possible way forward.

Nearly all the adult family members participating in proceedings were legally represented at some stage in the case, though late instructions continued to cause delay. It is urged that this issue be addressed by courts and social services departments in conjunction with local Law Societies.

The introduction of non-means, non-merit tested legal aid has largely removed pre-existing financial barriers to representation as far as parents are concerned although there was some evidence of delays and poor advice. The court should take responsibility for advising parents of their entitlements. Greater problems remain for other family members. Where a relative has a legitimate and separate interest in proceedings it does not seem consistent with the principles of the Act that they should be denied legal representation on grounds of income. It is recommended that anyone granted party status in care proceedings should have the same rights to legal aid as parents.

The primary issue remains the uneven quality of representation available to adult family members. It is recommended that representation in care cases be restricted to solicitors and counsel who are recognised as competent in this field and that appropriate qualifying training be provided. In the meantime, courts should publicise the names of lawyers on the Children Panel.

There is also room for improvement in the accessibility, quality and continuity of legal advice available to social services. Legal services in all three areas were still largely provided in-house and all appeared to be severely stretched. The adequacy of the legal resources available to meet the increased demands of the Children Act needs to be kept under review.

Lawyers representing children commit themselves to retaining responsibility for the case throughout and, unless counsel is instructed, normally handle in-court advocacy. It is suggested, however, that guardians may need training in working with counsel and that this could be incorporated into training for working in the higher courts.

Discontinuity was a common feature of representation for parents and the local authority. Lack of familiarity with the case can reduce client confidence, waste court time and hamper effective case management. Consistency of representation should be the aim wherever possible.

A degree of judicial discontinuity is unavoidable in a system now based on concurrent jurisdiction and the division of judicial responsibility. Most cases also experienced a high degree of avoidable discontinuity. Judicial opinion on the need for and feasibility of continuity varied and very different court practices were evident. The majority of parents prefer consistency of tribunal and resent change.

The extent of discontinuity revealed in the research is known to be of concern to those responsible for judicial administration. It is therefore to be hoped that the matter is already being given close attention.

NOTES

[1] Children and Young Persons Amendment Act 1986, implemented 1 August 1988.

[2] Children Act 1975, Sections 64 and 65, incorporated in Sections 32 and 33 of the CYPA 1969 and implemented May 1984.

[3] Macleod A; Malos E (1984): *Representation of Children and Parents in Child Care Proceedings*. Socio-Legal Centre for Family Studies, University of Bristol.

[4] Masson J; Morton S (1989): The Use of Wardship by Local Authorities. *Modern Law Review*, November; Hunt J (1993): *Local Authority Wardships before the Children Act: The Baby or the Bathwater?* HMSO.

[5] Children and Young Persons Amendment Act 1986.

[6] Family Proceedings Court (Children Act) Rules 1989 Schedule 2(iii).

[7] Hunt (1993): op. cit.

[8] The adults most commonly joined to proceedings were grandparents, 22 of whom were parties in ten cases, while a further seven participated without being made parties and one was a party only as regards the children in a consolidated case. Twelve aunts or uncles were made parties in eight cases, with two aunts merely participating. The remaining 15 parties were an adult sibling (1), new partners of the parents (8) or grandparents (1) or non-related adults (5). Other non-party participators included other new partners of parents (2), family friends (2) and relatives or prospective adopters who were parties in consolidated proceedings (4).

[9] Freeman P; Hunt J (1998): *Parental Perspectives on Care Proceedings*. The Stationery Office.

[10] Excluding hearings for which the attendance of parties was excused.

[11] Lindley B (1995): *On the Receiving End*. Family Rights Group.

[12] Hunt J (unpublished): Parental Perspectives on Care Proceedings. Representation of the Child in the Civil Courts. Research Project working paper.

[13] Freeman and Hunt (1998): op. cit.

[14] Clark D (1995): Roundabouts and Swings – Recent Court Decisions about the Representation of Older Children. *GAL Panel News*, 7(4).

[15] Representation of the Child in the Civil Court. Research Project 1985–90.

[16] Re B v B (minors) (interviews and listing arrangements) ([1994] 2 FLR 489).

[17] Lyon C; de Cruz P (1993): *Child Abuse*. 2nd edition. Family Law.

[18] [1993] 1 FLR 832.

[19] *Children Act Advisory Committee Report* 1992–93. LCD.

[20] See also Lyon C M (1995): Representing Children, towards 2000 and beyond. *Representing Children*, 8(2).

[21] Since this report was completed the NSPCC has funded a study of children's views of their representation, which is relevant to this issue. Masson J; Oakley M (1997): Out of Hearing: the representation of children by Guardians ad Litem and solicitors in public proceedings. Research report. Faculty of Law, Warwick University.

[22] Murch M et al. (1991): *Representation of the Child in the Civil Courts: Summary and Recommendations to the Department of Health*. Socio-Legal Centre for Family Studies, University of Bristol.

[23] Hunt (1993): op. cit.; Masson (1989): op. cit.

[24] Harris P [the Official Solicitor] (1995): Representing Children. *Representing Children*, 8(2).

[25] Harris (1995) op. cit.; Re CT (A Minor) (Wardship: Representation) [1993] 2 FLR 278 and Re S (A Minor) (Independent Representation) [1993] 1 FLR 668.

[26] Our data on care proceedings initiated between 1989 and 1991 show a 96% appointment rate in Area A; 93% in Area B.

[27] Murch et al. (1991): op. cit.

[28] Principally applications for emergency protection, child assessment and secure accommodation orders.

[29] Under the old legislation it was common if not invariable practice to make an order appointing a guardian at the first hearing. Under the Children Act it is expected that the guardian will be appointed in time for the first hearing and an appointment can be made in an application for an Emergency Protection Order.

[30] In two of our observed cases it was necessary to appoint guardians from other panels in order to comply with the court's timetable.

[31] An example of the knock-on effect of prolonged proceedings (Chapter 13).

[32] Representation of the Child in the Civil Courts. Research Project, op. cit.

[33] Since this report was completed the new Labour government has issued a consultative document on the reorganisation of welfare services for the courts. DoH et al. (1998): *Support Services in Family Proceedings: Future Organisation of Court Welfare Services*. DoH.

[34] Murch M; Hooper D (1992): *The Family Justice System*. Family Law.

[35] The Report of the Committee on One Parent Families (1974): Cm 5629, HMSO.

[36] Legal Aid Act 1988 Section 15(3c) inserted by Legal Aid Act 1988 (Children Act 1989) Order 1991 SI 1924 art 2.

[37] Representation of the Child in the Civil Courts. Research Project, op. cit.

[38] As above, n. 35 art 2(b).

[39] Family Proceedings Court Rules r 11(3), Family Proceedings Rules r 4.11(3).

[40] (Family Proceedings Court (Children Act 1989) Rules 1991, r11(2)(a)).

[41] Representation of the Child in the Civil Courts. Research Project, op. cit.

[42] Dame Margaret Booth (1996): *Avoiding Delay in Children Act Cases*. LCD; Robertson I (1995): Comment. *Family Law*, 393.

[43] Re B (Local Authorities Representation) (1995) *The Times*, 19 May 1995. Since this report was completed the Lord Chancellor and the senior judges have taken a policy decision to restrict the right of audience of employed solicitors and specifically prohibiting local authority solicitors acting as advocates. *Law Society Gazette*, 5 March 1997.

[44] Freeman and Hunt (1996): op. cit.

[45] Murch and Hooper (1992): op. cit.

[46] Compare King's assertion that discontinuity of adjudication is a characteristic consequence of lay justice. King M; Piper C (1995): *How the Law Thinks About Children*. 2nd edition. Arena.

[47] In the Scottish hearings system, which similarly depends on lay adjudicators, it is required for at least one panel member to sit throughout. King and Piper (1995): op. cit.

[48] The material in this section is condensed from a paper commissioned by the Lord Chancellor's Department: Hunt J (1994): Judicial Continuity in Care Cases. Socio-Legal Centre for Family Studies, University of Bristol.

10 Where now?: concurrent jurisdiction and the transfer provisions

Integrating the court system

Concurrent jurisdiction

Prior to the Children Act the majority of child protection cases were dealt with under the Children and Young Persons Act 1969 and heard by lay justices in a juvenile court governed by procedures and rules of evidence specific to the magistrates' civil jurisdiction. A smaller but growing number of cases were brought in wardship where they were subject to the procedures and rules peculiar to the High Court and decided by legally qualified professional judges. The local authority could also seek orders in matrimonial proceedings, usually in the county court before a circuit judge, with a third set of rules and procedures.[1] Thus while all levels of court had some involvement in care work and there was an element of choice of initial forum, once that choice was made cases generally could only move between levels if there was an appeal or another type of application was initiated. In our pre-Act sample we found that such transfers added substantially to the overall length of proceedings.

Dissatisfaction with this fragmented framework had long fuelled demands for a more rational approach, from the 1974 Finer Report[2] to the Family Courts campaign. The Children Act reformers, self-consciously radical in so many ways, were not, however, that radical.[3] Attempts to insert provision for a Family Court as the Children Bill passed through Parliament were resisted with the argument that the primary purpose of the legislation was the reform of the substantive law.[4] Instead the Act sought to 'mobilise the courts' and 'make the best use of judicial resources'[5] by introducing a system of concurrent jurisdictions. The three levels of court were to remain discrete but all would have the same jurisdiction to hear care applications[6] and substantially the same remedies would be available in each. New Rules of Court were introduced to harmonise procedures throughout the system.[7]

At all levels cases were to be heard by more specialised adjudicators in dedicated courts. Lay magistrates were re-organised into family panels operating within a family proceedings court which would no longer deal with juvenile offenders, thus finally, as the Lord Chancellor put it: 'obliterating any criminal overtones'.[8] Cases requiring the expertise of a professional judge would be handled by nominated judges within a network of county court care centres and if necessary by the specialist judges of the High Court Family Division. Training in 'the philosophy of the Act and the new common procedures' gave substance to the government's claim that proceedings would be heard by magistrates and judges who had made a special study of family work.

Case allocation

Concurrent jurisdiction means that public law applications can now be heard in any of three fora. However it was laid down that in general they were to start in the family proceedings court[9] where it was expected the majority would remain.[10] Choice of level was not to be left to the parties but controlled by the Justices' Clerk using a set of defined, albeit fairly broad, criteria.[11] Refusal to transfer could be referred to a district judge.

The first two years of the Act saw a number of judicial pronouncements which in effect sought to reduce the discretionary element and ensure that more cases were transferred up. Cases where the estimated length of the hearing was likely to exceed two or three days, for instance, should be *considered* for transfer;[12] clerks must be *realistic* in establishing time estimates.[13] Cases involving non-accidental injury and the assessment of risk also 'asked a great deal of magistrates',[14] even though these were the very cases which they had been handling for years under the Children and Young Persons Act.

These encouragements to transfer were not well received in the lower courts although they could not be ignored. By 1994, such was the log-jam of cases in the higher courts that the Children Act Advisory Committee suggested that magistrates 'were capable of hearing straightforward cases lasting up to 4–5 days', where appropriate.[15] This pronouncement, though welcomed as signalling a reversal of the trend to move more and more cases up, also managed to offend sensibilities, since it could be perceived as flowing more from a realisation that the higher courts could not cope with the workload than a recognition of the value of the lay contribution.

Although the primary purpose of the transfer provisions was to ensure matching of court expertise to the complexity of the case it was recognised that vertical transfer might also be justified if it avoided undue delay. Another new stratagem with the same objective was the provision for 'lateral transfer' between courts at the same level; an attempt to maximise the use of resources by evening out demand. The implications of both these changes was that courts would have to overcome the isolation fostered by the previous structure and devise effective means for working together. A tall order indeed.

Lay justice

The Children Act settled, for the moment, the issue of whether lay magistrates should retain a role in children's cases. Indeed it was envisaged that the new family proceedings court would continue to handle the majority of cases. However the very fact that it was considered necessary to control transfer, rather than leaving it to the judgement of the parties, might be seen as reflecting a fear that, left to themselves, lawyers would opt for a professional judiciary, with all the cost implications that would entail. Research into the use of overlapping jurisdictions in private law[16] provided strong empirical evidence for this prediction.

Lay justice plays a greater part in the UK court system than any other in the Western world and the appropriateness of this reliance in children's cases, particularly child protection cases, has been called into question[17] by practitioners and legal theorists. While retaining the lay element the Act sought to improve performance, making the magistrates' court more specialist and bringing rules of evidence and procedures into line with those of the higher courts. Among the most significant changes were the introduction of statements and advance disclosure into a jurisdiction which had relied almost entirely on oral evidence. Magistrates were also to be required to produce reasons for their judgements, in stark contrast to previous policy which had discouraged them from amplifying their decisions in any way.

Practitioner perspectives on the changes

Concurrent jurisdiction

The introduction of concurrent jurisdiction was widely, though not uncritically, supported by all practitioner groups. Reservations were of three main types: (i) those who felt the family proceedings court jurisdiction had been unduly limited; (ii) those wishing to bypass the magistrates entirely and (iii) those arguing that the structures represented a poor substitute for a unified Family Court.

Previous research has demonstrated that, where family matters are concerned, solicitors tend to prefer the county court.[18] It was not therefore surprising that a third of those interviewed considered that magistrates should lose their care work. Among other practitioner groups fewer took this extreme view: 27% of team managers, for instance, 19% of guardians and only 14% of local authority solicitors. There was also variation between areas with solicitors in Area B being the least negative.

Reservations about the magistrates' jurisdiction clustered around four main issues:

♦ unduly long hearings, particularly the time taken for formulation of reasons, and the management of 'agreed' cases;

♦ the unpredictability of judgements between courts and Benches;

♦ judges' greater expertise, experience and confidence in controlling the court process; and

♦ the greater powers wielded by the higher courts.

These criticisms were encapsulated by one private practice solicitor:

> I think there is a real problem in not having professional judges. . . . I can see the logic of having a lay assessor but it seems very odd, these are enormously complicated cases which have very great impact, there's a lot of law. . . . I think it would be twice as quick and twice as economical and probably better decisions would be made in the end. It makes one anxious . . . when you have a case that involves risk because the temptation to play safe as a lay person is very great. And the (low) number of cases they see; they may have experience of everyday life but they haven't experience of everyday life of the kind they're dealing with. . . .

> The business of getting cases to work in the magistrates is terribly time consuming: in the sample case we had a directions hearing in the family proceedings court and I was there from 1.15 to 4.30. – If you'd been in (the county court) it would take 20 minutes. . . . The magistrates do not trust the advocates. . . . It's true as they say that they are not just a rubber stamp but the consequence of that is that you spend hours on something which should only take 10 minutes. My experience is that when there have been issues of substance they've dealt with it sensibly, the relationship between what is being dealt with and the time taken is quite reasonable. What is frustrating is when you've agreed an adjournment then having half to three-quarters of an hour while the magistrates sort out their reasons.

For many practitioners, however, it was a question of balancing the advantages and disadvantages of each jurisdiction. The family proceedings court was thus variously commended as a less formal setting, more local, offering greater continuity, more reliable timetabling, more efficient listing and above all speedier scheduling. Even those who in principle would prefer to see all cases heard in the higher courts, conceded that on occasion the point at which a case could be heard could be determinative.

Although there was some criticism of the restricted powers of the family proceedings court at the point the research was conducted (for example the inability to take undertakings or to appoint the Official Solicitor), in the main concerns centred on having a purely lay judiciary rather than on the powers or organisation of the court per se. Several practitioners thus commented favourably on the use of stipendiary magistrates:

> I think most lawyers prefer a legally qualified person to adjudicate whether alone or with the assistance of justices. I think it is nice to have two lay justices with a stipe, to strike a balance. I think lay justices do have a lot to offer simply because of their general experience but there are points of law that need addressing and I think it just does help if the chair is legally qualified. (Private solicitor)

> The stipendiary has a better control over his court and over the proceedings than the lay Bench. (Local authority solicitor)

Wider use of stipendiary magistrates, usually alongside lay justices, might therefore offer one way of dealing with the perceived drawbacks of the family proceedings court while retaining the acknowledged benefits of the jurisdiction. Other suggestions included improving the overall level of competence of the court clerks actually dealing with hearings, which, it was said, could be variable:

> I have had problems with clerks. . . . Mainly arising out of uncertainty, but the inability of the clerk has shone through and interfered in my view with justice because they now have a quasi judicial role. They therefore have considerable power, more than they ever did before and unless they are really knowledgeable about what they are doing they can really hinder justice. (Private solicitor)

> When you have justices on their own . . . you're very dependent on the clerk and I don't always think the clerk plays as important a role as they should. . . . And that's detrimental. (Private solicitor)

Such criticisms, and our own observation of variable levels of competence, suggest the need for more attention to be given to the training of court clerks to ensure more consistently acceptable practice.

The Justices' Clerks we interviewed were also conscious of the enhanced importance of their role in the new system and the vital place of training and support for magistrates. Indeed one clerk went further, arguing that Children Act work required a fully specialist Bench:

> Magistrates' work is so much bound up with criminal work. I think there are big issues around whether it stays with magistrates who do other work as well. I am not alone in this. There should be a specialist – it goes back to the three tier thing – whether this truly should be the Family Court System. Emphasising again the need for experience in family work. It needs excellent training and experience to ensure that expertise is maintained.

We too would question the assumption that the family Bench need to have or maintain experience in criminal work and support the need for continued training opportunities. The training pack produced by the Magistrates' Association[19] seems an excellent contribution to this process.

In judicial interviews we fed back, with trepidation, the finding that a third of solicitors would prefer magistrates to lose their care jurisdiction. Not unexpectedly there were some powerful reactions from magistrates, including comments that they could think of a third of solicitors who should not be practising in care cases! But such reactions came not only from the magistrates and their clerks. There was *some* support for the proposition among the professional judiciary on the grounds that it was inappropriate that 'enthusiastic part-time amateurs' should be handling cases of such moment. However several were even more outraged than the magistrates, describing the suggestion as 'ridiculous', 'nonsense', 'crazy'. Key themes were the value of the lay element, the quality of performance and in purely practical terms, the impact on the system:

> What a barmy view. Who the hell is going to do the work? How many judges are we going to need and who will pay for them and where would we find them? Our entire judicial system depends on the incredible contribution made by lay justices in all fields. It seems to me totally barmy, amazing. The Justices' response to the challenge of the Children Act has been very impressive, they have been very conscientious in training and the care they give to these cases is impressive. They really do take them seriously and try terribly hard, they try to get the right reasons and do the thing according to the book. Their reasons

are often most carefully assembled. I think they do absolutely marvellous work. I think they are the essential foundation on which our justice systems rest. If they were abolished by statute there would be a chaotic consequence.

Despite highlighting criticisms of the family proceedings court it is important to acknowledge that on balance the majority of interviewees accepted concurrent jurisdiction as far as it went, provided that cases were allocated appropriately. Thus the transfer criteria and their interpretation are critical.

The transfer criteria

The transfer criteria themselves proved broadly acceptable to the majority of informants, with few voices raised either against the concept of criteria or the ones chosen. The same cannot be said of attempts to constrain the discretion of the family proceedings court in their interpretation, which at best were seen to reflect judicial ignorance of magistrates' previous care work; at worst as evidence of contempt for the lay contribution and/or an attempt to snatch a larger share of what in the early years of the Act was a smaller cake. The so-called '3-day rule' in particular was seen to be arbitrary and, by family proceedings courts at least, related as much to the ebb and flow of court workloads as to the inherent needs of the case. In a fully integrated court system, of course, such a flexible system of workload management might be perceived quite positively. While the jurisdictions remain distinct it is, it seems, less acceptable.

Irrespective of any covert use, however, early judicial rulings suggest that the Family Division judges took the view that long cases were inappropriate for a lay judiciary, rather than simply difficult to accommodate. This was not generally supported in either our practitioner or judicial interviews:

> More work needs to be done on comparisons of length and complexity. There's a tendency to think the longer a case is listed for the more complex it is and I don't think that's necessarily so. I'm not on the whole in favour of rigid limits, each case depends on its own circumstances. If it isn't overly complex, and the FPC can sit on 3/4 consecutive days I see no reason in principle why they should not be able to. (District judge)

The advice that cases involving risk or unexplained injuries should be transferred was also questioned:

> Some of those cases are the easiest to decide upon because the danger is so clear, yet we are told we should send them up. Non-accidental injury. Most of the cases we had before the Act involved some degree of injury. . . . .

> Magistrates are quite capable of dealing with it. In many ways where there has
> been injury of that nature they are easier than some cases of neglect can be
> because it's easier to quantify the risk. (Justices' Clerk)

Transfers, some cynics suggested, were being requested for rather base reasons:

> You know if you go to the county court that they won't keep hearing
> contested interims whereas they will at the FPC. So if you feel you've got
> representatives for parents who are just going to make your life a misery
> with contested applications that's a very good reason for saying let's get
> it transferred. (Local authority solicitor)

> Of course the lawyers prefer the county court, they get higher fees for a start.
> (Judge)

Application of the criteria

It will be evident from the foregoing that the interpretation and use of the transfer provisions has been one of the areas of the Act which has taken a while to settle down. At the time of our practitioner interviews developments in case law, caseload and local practice had resulted in more cases being seen as transferable than at implementation. Nor, our interviews with the professional judiciary indicated, has this resulted in inappropriate transfer in more than a few cases. What did exercise a number of judges, however, was a suspicion that cases were still being kept down inappropriately and their experience that while a few cases were transferring too early, others were coming too late:

> Late transfer is still a serious problem. Magistrates are not spotting at an
> early stage or not having brought to their attention, cases that should be
> transferred. It is happening in a significant number of cases just before what
> should have been a final hearing.

Would it be more rational, therefore, if all cases were lodged in the county courts and then re-allocated as necessary? In principle we see a good deal of logic in this argument and all things being equal would have liked to recommend it. The majority of sample cases, as we shall see, ended up in the higher courts. Pragmatically, however, the most likely effect would be a further drop in the proportion of cases heard in the family proceedings court. Given the uncertainty which is characteristic of most care cases at the outset

(Chapter 7) and their mutability (Chapter 11) it might be considered incautious to make an early decision. Whatever the other merits of the argument, therefore, given that delay is primarily a problem in the higher courts (Chapter 13), this could not, at present, be advanced as a sensible strategy.

The transfer procedures

Although the parties can apply for a case to be transferred the decision about allocation lies with the court. We did not specifically ask practitioners whether they thought this was appropriate, or whether the family proceedings court should be the primary gatekeeper. The paucity of volunteered comment, however, suggests it was not a burning issue and is indicative of the fairly smooth operation of the procedures for vertical transfer in our study areas. Only five private solicitors reported any problems in the sample cases. Moreover where necessary, it seems, transfers have been effected with impressive despatch:

> Locally the practice is very effective. Just as an example, a second interim hearing came before the FPC at 10.30 in the morning and by 3 o'clock on the same day we were in the High Court, which I think is excellent. (Local authority solicitor)

Procedures in the research areas, however, may have been working rather more effectively than elsewhere.[20] A key factor in this has been the development of good working relationships and effective communication between court staff. The words of one clerk could easily speak for them all:

> Here we have a very good relationship with the county court. We built that up from before the Act; we had lots of meetings and so there has always been a very smooth transfer of actual case papers. There was one blip at first but we soon ironed that one out. Now as soon as anything is transferred it goes straight to the county court either immediately or within 24 hours. One court clerk rings down to the office and actually gets a transfer date. So everyone in court knows where it is going. For the interim hearing there is no delay. Also if we find we are dealing with a direction and it needs to go straight away into the county court for a hearing there and then we also arrange for them to contact the county court and we get to the stage where they actually go and interrupt the judges and the judge will say yes bring it across. So we have a very good relationship that works very well indeed on the transfers.

> It is vital they know who we are so then they know if we are ringing up saying we have got this case and we must have a hearing straight away, they will know that we wouldn't dream of bothering them unless it is an absolute

emergency. It is vital that you do get this local understanding and you make an effort to ensure that it is going smoothly.

Transfer to the High Court

So far we have concentrated on transfer from the magistrates' court to the county court. Under the Children Act cases can also be transferred from the county court to the High Court where:

> Having regard to the principle against delay . . . the county court considers that the proceedings are appropriate for determination in the High Court and that such transfer is in the child's best interests.[21]

Given such broad discretionary criteria and more importantly the fact that county courts already had their experience in wardship to draw on in determining the appropriate judicial level, it is perhaps not surprising that this aspect of the transfer provisions was not reported to be troublesome. Only a few points emerged from the interview material. The first was a plea from a Justices' Clerk that the family proceedings court should have the power to transfer directly to the High Court where it was evident this was necessary. The second a recognition that like the family proceedings court the county court has to take account of the impact of transfer on case duration: 'Sometimes you can't get a case before a High Court judge for six months and that may be a case for keeping it at county court level.'

A third constraint on transfer, a related point, was the availability of High Court judges on circuit, reported by one of our research areas:

> There are occasions when you say I would like to put this to a family division judge but I'm either struggling because there isn't one here or I have got to send the parties to London and I'm not going to do that so in most cases I would give it to a circuit judge.

If the case was really urgent and weighty, of course, use could be made of the system of 'fire brigade' judges, established for just this eventuality and reported to be working to good effect elsewhere:

> We don't send for them an awful lot so when we do on the whole they honour it. If we didn't have that the liaison judge would have to come down more often and for longer periods. And cases would have to wait until the next time he came. Whereas now we can find a time when all the witnesses can be available and then ask for a judge.

Vertical transfer in the sample cases

Incidence

Well over half the sample cases had their final hearings in the county or High Court (Table 10.1). This is considerably higher than the national average;[22] no doubt in part because the research was concentrating on child protection cases, which might be expected to present issues of gravity and complexity more frequently than other public law cases.

Table 10.1 *Location of final hearing*

	Area A %	Area B %	Area C %	All areas %
Family proceedings court	52	43	33	43
County court	34	47	42	41
High Court	14	10	25	16
(n=)	(29)	(30)	(24)	(83)

Vertical transfer was almost wholly upwards, with 39 (48%) of sample cases being transferred from the family proceedings court to the care centres. Only three cases were transferred from the High Court to a county court (one after an initial hearing discharging wardship) and none moved down to the family proceedings court.

Reasons for transfer

It was not part of our research brief to examine in detail the operation of the concurrent jurisdiction provisions. Thus the data on reasons for transfer are not as comprehensive as we might wish. However some information was available on 34 (87%) of the cases transferred from the family proceedings court. These show that by far the majority were transferred on the grounds of complexity, importance or gravity (25), although there was a smattering of other reasons: likely hearing length (7), consolidation (4), urgency (4), need to involve the Official Solicitor (4), unexplained non-accidental injury (2) and separate representation for the child and Guardian ad Litem (1).

It may be noted that only four of these cases included urgency among their grounds for transfer. Moreover neither in this intensive sample, nor in our extensive survey,[23] (where 9% of completed cases included expedition with gravity and complexity in their reasons for transfer) were there any vertical transfers solely on the grounds of the avoidance of delay. Given the listing problems in the higher courts throughout our research period (Chapter 13) this is scarcely surprising. The decision on transfer, therefore, was far more likely to involve balancing the prospect of delay against the gravity, importance or complexity of the case or estimated duration of the final hearing, as this lawyer complained:

> In some areas there is a very strong hidden agenda that the Justices' Clerks and the magistrates are fully aware that to transfer means transferring to a care centre where there is dreadful delay. The timetabling of a case because of delay should mean, how fast should this case go, this particular child's circumstances, it shouldn't mean such and such a care centre is bogged down or 50 miles away, because that means the child is actually deprived of having it heard at the right level. It's because of the system, not because of the case.

Actually setting a final hearing date before transfer is, of course, outwith the power of the transferring court, as the family proceedings court found to its cost in one of the sample cases:

> The FPC was reluctant to transfer because at that stage the guardian was saying this case should be heard as soon as possible. The Bench got the clerk to phone and get a date for the final hearing before sending the matter up. The clerk thought that was incorrect and when we went for the first directions hearing the DJ [district judge], who is normally the pleasantest person you can find, was furious, how could they set a final hearing in a court which hadn't even heard the case and made its own decision about time estimates and evidence and so on? (Local authority solicitor)

However, in line with guidance from the Lord Chancellor's Department, it was customary for enquiries to be made about the availability of hearing time when considering transfer. In the case of Michelle Symons the balance between the need for expedition and the gravity and complexity of the issues to be tried was one which exercised the court and the parties on several occasions.

• •

> On issuing proceedings the local authority's hope had been to rehabilitate Michelle and her siblings after a period of intensive work, ideally in a mother and baby home. Three months into the case this initial optimism had faded, assessment of Michelle revealed a highly damaging parent–child relationship and more severe developmental and health problems with the twins than had been realised. Claudette had continued to refuse a mother and baby placement.

Social services made plain their intention to seek Care Orders and long-term placement for all three. Claudette accepted that her relationship with Michelle was irretrievable and conceded the Care Order but contested the applications in respect of the twins. By this point both grandmothers and Michelle's father had been made parties and were seeking Residence or failing that, Contact Orders.

It was agreed that the complexity of the issues, the number of parties, and the estimated length of a fully contested final hearing clearly indicated transfer to the county court. However the earliest slot the listing officer could offer was ten weeks hence. It was therefore agreed to continue in the family proceedings court with the clerk maintaining close liaison with the county court and transferring the case if an earlier date became available. None did.

The family proceedings court made arrangements for the most experienced members of the Family Panel and the senior clerk to sit for the three days the case was expected to last. Unusually for this court the papers were made available to the magistrates the previous day. On the morning of the final hearing counsel acting for maternal grandmother, who was new to the case, backed up by counsel for mother, who was not, made a fresh application for transfer. This was opposed by the local authority and the guardian. Though accepting the case met the criteria, the magistrates considered it was outweighed by the delay principle and refused the application.

· ·

Generally, however, the issue of transfer does not appear to have been a matter of dispute, either between the parties or with the court. Although in all three areas there were cases where the question was deferred to a later hearing only two applications were refused. Both refusals were referred to the district judge. One was dismissed and continued to a two-day hearing with neither the length of the case nor the evidence apparently presenting any particular problem to the Bench. The second case was Michelle's, which went before the district judge two hours after the magistrates' decision, which was overruled. A hearing was 'virtually guaranteed' within eight weeks, a period which, unlike the magistrates, the judge deemed 'acceptable in view of the children's ages and circumstances'.

The timing of transfer

The late transfer of this case was disgraceful. First because of the implications for the children. Michelle was now known to be a severely deprived child. She had had two foster homes and would have to be moved to an adoptive family. Her existing placement was fragile. All three children would be difficult to place because of their special needs, particularly if the plan to place them together was to be realised. Having geared themselves up for the hearing both Claudette and her mother were distraught and uncomprehending. Avis, the paternal grandmother, was incensed because her earlier application for interim contact had been abandoned only on the understanding that the issue would be heard with the care application. Finally, there was the waste of time and resources. Nine legal representatives, the guardian, social worker, child psychiatrist and the witness from the family centre were all tied up for almost six hours. Nine other professionals were waiting at the end of a phone. All their timetables had to be rearranged at short notice. The court diary had been cleared for three days, the magistrates had set aside four days and the district judges' timetable was disrupted by having to hear the appeal and fit in a directions hearing and contested application for interim contact. Fortunately, although judicial interviews suggest this case is not unique, it was exceptional in our sample. As Table 10.2 shows more than half the transfers were made either prior to or at the first hearing.

Table 10.2 *The timing of allocation decisions*

	Area A	Area B	Area C	All areas
Before first hearing	50	0	12	19
At first hearing	21	47	38	36
Later	29	53	50	45
(n=)	(14)	(17)	(16)	(47)

There were differences in approach between the three study areas on the handling of early transfer applications. In Area A transfers were generally made at the outset without a hearing, the local authority and court clerk having developed sufficiently effective liaison to be able to categorise the case appropriately. Elsewhere the practice was to start the case in the family proceedings court, even where it was known that transfer was to be sought. As one solicitor acknowledged:

> Perhaps more could be done to speed things up at the outset. Often it's agreed by everyone who looks at the papers that a higher court should be dealing with it. Sometimes you can spend a whole day at the magistrates' court deciding that the matter should be transferred.

Nine cases did not transfer until a fourth or later hearing, for reasons which analysis reveals to be case-related. Seven were marked by paucity of information at the outset; usually because the family had not been long known and/or because proceedings had been precipitated by a crisis. Usually, too, these were cases where plans were not clear at the outset. Michelle's was one of the two remaining cases. The other also involved objectives which changed midstream and a proliferation of parties prompting transfer.

• •

Toni Morrell, aged 3, had been accommodated for two years. A succession of attempts to rehabilitate had failed and the local authority was seeking a Care Order followed by adoption. However, the investigation of the possibilities of placement within the wider family proved to have been inadequate. Paternal grandmother appeared at the first court hearing and offered to care. By the third hearing maternal grandparents were also involved and mother was contesting the adoption. The case was transferred and ended with Toni moving to her paternal grandparents as foster carers under a Care Order by consent.

• •

In Michelle's case late transfer clearly delayed proceedings though in the event only by five and a half weeks. Overall such cases did take longer than those transferred at the outset though not dramatically so, varying on average between an additional 16 days in Area B, 34 in Area C to 46 in Area A, with a mean of 18 days. Even transfer later than the first hearing seemed to have some impact, only one of these 21 cases completing in less than 20 weeks for example, compared to six of the 26 transferred earlier.

Fear of potential delay was said to be inflating the transfer rate:

> You often don't know if there is going to be disputed expert evidence until the time of the final hearing so you have a choice. You make a decision to transfer which may turn out to be wrong or you leave it until the evidence is in and then you have substantial delay. (Private solicitor)

Ironically, of course, transfer for such reasons makes the problem worse, clogging up the higher courts with cases which in the end could have been handled by the magistrates. Until we have a court system sufficiently well resourced to be responsive to the needs of cases as they develop, however, it is hard to see how to eradicate such ultimately self-defeating behaviour.

Lateral transfer

In sharp contrast to the heavy use of vertical transfer, lateral transfer was unusual in Areas A and B. Area C, however, fed into a large combined court system already accustomed to moving cases around to maximise the use of court resources. This practice continued post-Act, the location of any one hearing not determining the venue of subsequent hearings, which might revert to the previous court or any other. In general before the parties left the court the location of the next court hearing was settled. However on more than one occasion, because of other cases overrunning, parties, practitioners and researchers had to hop into taxis and speed across the city to another court with spare capacity. Although this is a flexible and efficient system, which undoubtedly helps to prevent unanticipated problems holding up cases, it is inevitably not without disadvantages and would be difficult to replicate elsewhere.

Only six other instances of (true) lateral transfer were noted. One case, for example, was transferred to a court 12 miles distant for a single hearing as the judge dealing with the matter was sitting there; in another the listing office had overlooked the scheduled hearing and failed to book a care judge. The case was heard on the listed day at a court 25 miles away. Two cases which came in on Emergency Protection Orders had their first hearing on the same day in other courts because of a temporary imbalance between demand and supply. They were then transferred back for the rest of the proceedings.

Moving a case outside the home area to another court, however, was not always seen to be an acceptable strategy. In one of the research areas the practice had therefore begun of bringing the judge to the case, a device which could usefully be considered elsewhere.

Experience of laterally transferred cases, though limited, was variable, with one solicitor's experience (confirmed by our own observation) leading him to describe lateral transfer as a 'disaster':

> We didn't object to any of the Interim Care Orders on the basis that mother could not offer anything that would have been acceptable at that stage. She had no fixed home and was in and out of psychiatric care and considerably addicted. She was very reasonable about that. And within the [local] system everyone knew what the situation was. Then we had the applications for interim contact . . . [and] it was transferred out to get a quicker hearing.

> When we got there . . . the justices started off by saying since there had been 'n' numbers of Interim Orders, there was nothing for them to decide. So we spent a considerable part of the time trying to convince them why we were there. They weren't prepared to listen, they had already made their minds up. If I had been sitting there as the client I'm sure I would have appreciated them as an offensive and rude tribunal who weren't interested in any semblance of justice but were very interested in getting this case out of court.

> What it provoked was a nasty hearing where points were taken. . . . It's convinced me that I will resist lateral transfer in future and if it does happen seek to define by exchange of letters exactly what is going on. . . . The [Bench] completely misunderstood why the case had been transferred and weren't prepared to be put right with an array of lawyers in front of them . . . even when we all agreed. They had made their minds up on reading the case papers and they made it clear. . . . It's what you don't want to sit in a court and see.

In general, however, the *possibility* of lateral transfer was regarded by practitioners as helpful even if relatively few appeared to have felt the need to use it. Ironically however, in the area which appeared to have a chronically, rather than temporarily over-burdened FPC, practitioners reported that lateral transfer or indeed finding a court to accept cases at all, was difficult to achieve. The onus, several local authority solicitors told us, was on the applicant rather than the court to establish which court had resources to deal with the case before filing the application:

> I'm still not happy with the issue of lateral transfer particularly at magistrates' court level, because the way it works at the moment, the responsibility of finding a court to take a case rests with me. If I trot along to my local magistrates and say 'I want to issue this case. It needs a hearing on such and such a day' and they turn round and say 'We can't do that day', I go round all the other courts doing it.

> The way I think it ought to work, and this is a question of where the resources are put (somebody, somewhere has to spend the time doing it), I should be entitled to lodge my application. The way it works at the moment, it isn't an actual transfer at all. It's not laterally transferred. We should lodge our application in our local court, it's our court, in our area. Then it's their responsibility to find the time in their own courts or if not to laterally transfer it. We are over a barrel. If they turn round and say 'go away' we can't spend the time arguing with them about whether it's right or not for us to go away because we have our client and the children to consider. We have to find somewhere to hear it. (Local authority solicitor)

Moreover, once the application was made or the case transferred to another court for a hearing, this local court was said to be reluctant to accept transfer back. On that specific issue court staff took a rather different view. However the difficulties in persuading other courts to help out were amply borne out and the cause of much frustration:

Other courts do not wish to take on work. They seem to think it is our work. We make the point that there is no jurisdiction in the Children Act and the only reason we are ever saying we cannot take the case is because we just haven't got any room or lists are full for that particular day. We say to the local authority if we cannot take the case it is up to you to ring round the area and find a court that can. Yet I would find I would be getting irate telephone calls from the other courts really being quite nasty about things. 'Why won't you take the case?' One particular court spent so long complaining that they could have dealt with it. There seems to be this thing that we are off-loading our work onto them because we don't want to do it. It is absolute rubbish because we have a huge workload. We hardly ever say we cannot take a case.

Similar experiences are documented in Dame Margaret Booth's report,[24] revealing a residual parochialism which the Act has not yet succeeded in eliminating. However the fact that these problems were not reported in two of the research areas suggests that the structural and attitudinal difficulties are not insuperable, although their persistence suggests the need to address them at least at circuit level.

Concurrent jurisdiction and the family court ideal

Speaking about the Children Bill while it was still before Parliament, the Lord Chancellor was uncharacteristically coy about the significance of such changes in relation to a Family Court:

So where will all this lead? I have heard the Children Bill described as a major step towards a 'Family Court'. I have heard it described as the end of the 'Family Court'. I have even heard it described as a ruse for avoiding a decision about a 'Family Court'. So which is it? The answer is that it is not a ruse.[25]

Other pronouncements perpetuated the ambiguity surrounding the government's intentions. During the Second Reading the Solicitor-General spoke of the Bill 'containing some constructive steps towards a . . . Family Court'.[26] By the Third Reading he was quoting the view of the President of the Family Division that the Bill 'in essence would set up a Family Court'.[27] Brenda Hoggett, one of the architects of the legislation, later described the process as the 'creation of a family court by stealth.'[28]

The need for further reform, Family Court campaigners were repeatedly assured as the Bill went through Parliament, would be kept under review as part of the then government's rolling programme of reform. As yet, however, nothing has emerged from the review process to suggest that any radical restructuring is contemplated in the immediate future. To what extent, then, does the new court *system* render further change unnecessary?

Despite a number of areas of difficulty it must be indisputable that the reformed system is a vast improvement on what went before. Cases can now be dealt with at the judicial level appropriate to their level of difficulty rather than being dependent on the legislative niche they happened to fit. The transfer procedures are working reasonably well. Pre-Act anxieties that the expertise of the Family Division would become difficult to access with the restrictions on wardship[29] have proved unfounded. The same basic remedies are available throughout the system and the same tests and principles have to be applied. Separate applications concerning the same family can now be consolidated. There is a more specialist and better trained judiciary. There are co-ordinating mechanisms at a local level tied in, for as long as the Children Act Advisory Committee continued, to a national structure. This is a colossal achievement.

Yet it would be difficult to argue that we have an integrated, let alone a unified system. Therein lies the frustration. The different courts may be treading parallel paths but it is not the same path. Keeping the lines of communication open in such circumstances is not easy. Indeed Dame Margaret Booth's research[30] suggests our three study areas were actually doing rather better in this respect than some elsewhere in the country and that worryingly, as the initial excitement of implementation has worn off, the component parts of the system are settling back into isolationism and putting up the shutters.

Clearly there are a number of ways this disappointing trend might be halted. The transformation of the Family Court Services Committees, for instance, into Family Court Fora, was intended to provide a more effective venue for the development of co-operation. A second round of Children Act training might help to inculcate a greater sense of common purpose. How much simpler it would all be, however, if there was a *single court*, with a single administration, dealing only with family matters. Such a development would also make it possible, as suggested in the last chapter, to reallocate responsibility for the Guardian ad Litem panels and to develop a specialist, rather than a more specialised judiciary, both professional and lay. It would further stimulate the development of a common culture, uniquely responsive to the distinctive needs of this form of law. Now that the Lord Chancellor's department is responsible both for the family proceedings courts as well as the higher courts, it is surely time to see whether further progress can be made on this front even if only to amalgamate local administration. Evolution rather than revolution may be the name of the game but stasis can lead to stagnation and regression.

Summary

The introduction of concurrent jurisdiction has proved broadly acceptable and had not given rise to major problems in the study areas. Transfer procedures were seen to be working well but were critically dependent on the establishment of good working relationships and effective communication between court staff.

The transfer criteria themselves were deemed appropriate. Their early interpretation in case law, encouraging higher rates of transfer, proved more contentious, generating concern over the diminishing experience base of the lay magistracy. There remained some concern among the judiciary that cases were being inappropriately retained in the lower courts or transferred too late. It is recommended that there should be regular meetings between the Justices' Clerk and the care centre to monitor this issue and the smooth operation of the transfer procedures.

There were sharp divisions of opinion both among practitioners and the professional judiciary over whether magistrates should continue to have jurisdiction in this area of law. Perceived deficiencies in the family proceedings court, however, also had to be set against its advantages, most notably speedier scheduling.

The role of the clerk handling the hearing was seen as crucial though standards were variable. It is recommended that training in hearing management is provided to produce greater consistency. Magistrates too need ongoing training, particularly assistance in the preparation of reasons. Consideration might be given to wider use of stipendiary magistrates to increase the flexibility of the FPC and enable lengthier and more complex cases to be heard.

More than half the research sample of child protection cases were heard in the county or High courts. Vertical transfer was almost wholly upwards and no cases were transferred down to the family proceedings court. About three-quarters of cases were transferred on grounds of complexity, importance or gravity. There were few disputes on the question of allocation. Decisions on transfer too often involved balancing the need for an appropriate forum against delay in the higher courts.

Just under half the transfers were made later than the first hearing though there were differences by area, with practice diverging on whether or not a case started with an attended hearing in the family proceedings court even if immediate upward transfer was envisaged. Late transfer added to duration but was usually related to lack of information at the start. Early transfer risked overloading the higher courts with cases which could have been handled by magistrates.

Lateral transfer was unusual though it was used to good effect to avoid delay in some cases. Most practitioners regarded the possibility of lateral transfer as helpful though few had experienced it. In one area it was reported that finding any court to take a case could be difficult and that the onus for this fell on the applicant authority. This is a matter which needs to be dealt with at circuit level. Moving a case outside the home area to another court is not always an acceptable strategy. The practice of bringing the judge to the case, which had been introduced in one area, could be given more general consideration.

Restructuring has not defused the argument for a family court despite the substantial improvements brought about by concurrent jurisdiction. Evidence that communication difficulties remain and that parts of the system are retreating into isolationism suggest that it is now time to reconsider the introduction of a fully fledged family court.

NOTES

[1] As pointed out in Chapter 6, these do not exhaust the routes to statutory care pre-Children Act, which included domestic proceedings in the magistrates' court and the administrative, non-court, parental rights resolution.

[2] Report of the Committee on One Parent Families (1974): Cm 5629, HMSO. See also e.g. Forward from Finer series, National Council for One Parent Families 1981.

[3] Murch M; Hooper D (1992) *The Family Justice System*. Family Law. According to Murch, it was seen as 'too costly and difficult'.

[4] HC Deb, Standing Committee B, 8 June 1989, Col 459.

[5] DoH (1989): *An Introduction to the Children Act 1989*. HMSO.

[6] Section 92(7).

[7] The Family Proceedings Courts (Children Act 1989) Rules 1991 SI 1395, Family Proceedings Rules 1991 SI 1247.

[8] Children Bill, Second Reading HOL 6 December 1988 Col 494.

[9] Section 92 and Schedule 2.

[10] The Family Proceedings Courts (Children Act 1989) Rules 1991 SI 1395, Family Proceedings Rules 1991 SI 1247 and Children (Allocation of Proceedings) Order 1991 SI 1677.

[11] Children (Allocation of Proceedings) Order 1991 SI 1677 provides that proceedings may be transferred to the county court if this is in the child's interests. When deciding this, the court must consider first the presumption against delay, second whether the proceedings are exceptionally grave, important or complex for one or more of the following reasons:

(i)   complicated, sensitive or conflicting evidence about the risk involved to the child's physical or moral well-being or about other matters;

(ii) the number of persons involved or interested;

(iii) conflict with the law of another jurisdiction;

(iv) some novel or difficult point of law which could affect the outcome of the proceedings; or

(v)   some question of general public interest.

[12] Re H (A Minor) (Care Proceedings) [1992] 2 FCR 330.

[13] L v Berkshire CC [1992] 1 FCR 481 and Re L (A Minor) (Removal from Jurisdiction) [1993] 1 FCR 325.

[14] S v Oxfordshire CC [1993] 1 FLR 452.

[15] *Children Act Advisory Committee Annual Report* 1993–94. LCD.

[16] Murch M et al. (1987): *The Overlapping Jurisdiction of Magistrates' Courts and County Courts*. Socio-Legal Centre for Family Studies, University of Bristol.

[17] King M; Piper C (1995): *How the Law Thinks about Children*. 2nd edition. Arena; Ackroyd W (1994): The Nature of Proceedings, the Family Court and the Selection of the Judiciary. *Family Law*, 89; Bissett-Johnson A (1995): Scottish Office White Paper: Scotland's Children – Proposals for Child Care Policy and Law: a critical analysis. *Journal of Social Welfare and Family Law*, 17(1).

[18] Murch et al. (1987): op. cit.

[19] Ball C; Berkeley-Hill B (1994): *The Welfare of the Child: Assessing Evidence in Children Cases*. The Magistrates' Association.

[20] Dame Margaret Booth (1996): *Avoiding Delay in Children Act Cases*. LCD.

[21] Children (Allocation of Proceedings Order) 1991 SI 1677.

[22] Thirty-nine per cent of all care cases completing between July and December 1994 were heard in the higher courts. *Children Act Advisory Committee Annual Report* 1993–94. LCD.

[23] Thomas C; Hunt J (1996): *The Care Workloads of the Civil Courts under the Children Act*. Report to DoH. Centre for Socio-Legal Studies, University of Bristol.

[24] Booth (1996): op. cit.

[25] Lord Mackay of Clashfern (1989): Joseph Jackson Memorial Lecture: Perceptions of the Children Bill and Beyond. *New Law Journal*, 505.

[26] Children Bill, 2nd Reading, 27 April 1989, *Hansard* 1182.

[27] Children Bill, 3rd Reading, 23 October 1989, *Hansard* 545.

[28] Hoggett B (1992): Ten Years of Family Law Reform. Paper delivered at the Annual Conference of the Socio-Legal Studies Association, April 1992. Reported in the *SLSA Newsletter*, Winter 1992.

[29] Hunt J (1993): *Local Authority Wardships before the Children Act: The Baby or the Bathwater?* HMSO.

[30] Booth (1996): op. cit.

11 *(Re)drawing the map: experts, assessments and change*

A more enquiring court

> The courts have an independent duty to do what is best for the child. To discharge that duty often they will have to take an active part in proceedings rather than simply acting as umpires between the contending parties.[1]

The English legal system is based on an adversarial model in which disputing parties are pitted against each other. It is up to the applicant to prove his case; rules of evidence protect the interests of the respondent; the court acts as a referee.

Children's cases, long governed by the principle of the paramountcy of the child's interests, do not fit comfortably into this tradition. For at least two decades arguments as to whether such proceedings were essentially inquisitorial or adversarial have periodically surfaced[2] and several different models have co-existed. Wardship proceedings, as part of the inherent jurisdiction of the High Court, were based on the doctrine of *parens patriae* and hence inquisitorial. The court therefore was not restricted to evidence presented by the parties but could order other enquiries to be made. Matrimonial proceedings operated as adversarial disputes between parties mitigated by the power to order a welfare report. Care proceedings were constructed on a juvenile justice model, with the child as defendant. An inquisitorial element was, however, introduced into proceedings by the advent of the panel guardian, who is not only the child's representative but an independent reporting officer to the court.

The Children Act did not itself resolve, unequivocally, the issue of whether care cases are now inquisitorial or adversarial. Proceedings still have the structure and the trappings of an adversarial process. Indeed it could be argued these have been strengthened – by the provisions extending party status, for example, and the guardian's right to independent legal representation. Countering these, however, is what appears to be a growing culture which emphasises the centrality of the child's interests, not simply for the court but for all those concerned in the case.[3] This trend is reflected in the Solicitor's

Family Law Association's professional code of practice.[4] Most significant, however, have been decisions relating to reports from experts instructed on behalf of parents which do not support their position. In Re D and M,[5] for instance, it was stated that:

> Our system of civil justice has become more open. Judges have had to become more interventionist . . . it is of particular importance to note that in the Family Division, care proceedings do not have an essentially adversarial character.

Similarly in Oxfordshire CC v M [1994],[6] Sir Stephen Brown ruled that:

> Children's cases are to be regarded as being in a special category. In these circumstances, the court has power to override legal professional privilege in relation to experts' reports when it gives leave to parties to obtain them. Relevant information should be made available to the court in order that it can arrive at a conclusion which is in the overriding interests of the welfare of the child.

Even more radically in Re R,[7] Thorpe J stated:

> For my part I would wish to see case law go yet further and make it plain that the legal representative in possession of such material relevant to determination contrary to the interests of their client, not only are unable to resist disclosure by reliance on legal professional privilege, but have a positive duty to disclose it to the other parties and to the court. . . . Indeed, if parties initiate or are joined in proceedings, with or without leave, and within those proceedings seek to establish rights or to exercise responsibilities in relation to a child whose future is the issue for the court's determination, it should be understood that they too owe a duty to the court to make full and frank disclosure of any material in their possession relevant to that determination.

These and other reinforcing judgements[8] serve to wrest children's proceedings further and further away from the adversarial tradition and nearer to a model in which proceedings become an enquiry into the child's interests. In this model the Guardian ad Litem is pivotal.

The Guardian ad Litem

> Courts are encouraged to make use of the Guardian ad Litem in local authority cases to ensure that the case and the options for action are fully explored.[9]

By the time of the Children Act the Guardian ad Litem service had already become not only an established but a highly esteemed part of care proceedings. Our interviews with magistrates in previous research[10] suggested that while the guardian's role as representative of the child was not overlooked, it was the function of independent investigator and informant which was particularly valued. Under the new law the guardian, who retains wide-ranging investigative responsibilities,[11] remains the primary means through which the court can exercise its inquisitorial role.[12]

Though well established in the lower courts with their primarily lay judiciary, panel guardians were an innovation for the legally trained judiciary in the higher courts, whose principal prior experience would either be of court welfare officers, or, more rarely, of the Official Solicitor. It is evident from the interview material that in the early years after implementation many guardians were acutely conscious of the need to prove themselves anew in this less familiar and as some would see it, more testing forum. It is equally evident that they have done so most convincingly. Almost without exception the judges, district judges, Justices' Clerks and magistrates we spoke to praised the general very high standard of reports and their unique value to the judicial process, although the occasional critical comment indicates that the service cannot afford to be complacent.

The issue of who to include in inquiries is a matter for individual judgement but the file data confirm the general perception (also reported in previous research)[13] that these are almost always extremely thorough and extensive. Indeed there were a few complaints to the effect that some guardians tended to 'over-egg the pudding' as well as a good many comments about the length of some reports.

On average guardians consulted between eight and nine professional sources per case (with 38 having ten or more) and between four and five lay sources. The lay sources were typically the case children, their parents and parents' current partners, but guardians also consulted 22 friends/neighbours and 123 members of the extended family, principally grandparents (68) and aunts and uncles (39). While the court usually had direct access to the parents' views through their own evidence the guardian's report was often the only *independent* source of information on the wider family perspective. The views of all other family members, adults and children alike, were more often recorded in the guardian's report than in their own statements. Only 24 grandparents, for instance, and 34 other relatives actually filed evidence. Guardians also recorded information from over a hundred professionals who did not provide statements. The views of foster carers, teachers, probation officers and nurses were as, or more likely to be represented to the court through the guardian's report than through their own depositions.

It seems, from the comments of a number of guardians, that thorough as enquiries were perceived to be already, the effect of the Children Act has been to extend their scope even further. The guardian is expected, for example, to be able to advise the court on the existence of anyone with an interest in the child who should be informed of proceedings.[14] This, plus the general principle that children should be cared for within their kinship network wherever possible, requires an investigation of the extended family. They are also expected to be able to advise the court on the various options available and to comment on the local authority care plan.

In general, the Children Act has enhanced the guardian's ability to carry out these enquiries. It establishes, for instance, the right to examine and copy local authority and voluntary agency records and to adduce them as evidence.[15] While we are not aware of any evidence that guardians had encountered more than sporadic resistance to their inquiries from welfare agencies hitherto, the new Rules put the matter beyond doubt. None of the guardians interviewed in this research reported being actively obstructed in their enquiries by professionals although social workers do still vary in their availability, defensiveness, or readiness to keep the guardian informed of developments. However, several guardians also commented on a changing atmosphere in their relationships with local authorities, characterised by a more open and co-operative approach:

> Previously I had so many battles . . . in even setting up contact and being present. None of that has happened since. There is very ready access to documents, there's no bar or difficulty about photocopying – apart from one particular team manager who will strictly do it himself and see what I have. I'm not only invited to case conferences nowadays, but to reviews quite often. Not always, not all teams do that but it's helpful. That has spread to a much more co-operative kind of case.

The investigative task has also been facilitated by earlier appointment and the provision of written information. In the past it was not uncommon for guardians to receive only the barest details from the court.[16] Now from the date of appointment a summary of the issues and relationships involved should be available on the application form, usually fleshed out by a full written statement. The process of subsequent enquiry is also eased by written statements from most of the significant people in the case.

The volume of evidence commonly submitted, however, also complicates and can slow down enquiries, while in Area B particularly, though not exclusively, regular difficulties were reported with the service of evidence, a very practical issue which one cannot help thinking should have been resolved:

> In the FPC I will get papers from the court, I will generally get sent from legal services and often the solicitor will send paperwork, so often I can end up with three. In the county court, I don't seem to get anything from anybody and I have to chase up. There is confusion who is responsible. It can mean delay for writing your report or that you go and see a parent and have not read a statement. . . . The Panel believe that responsibility lies with the court; the issue in particular here is the cost of photocopying. Who pays? The Panel refuse to pay.

Guardians in all areas, however, reported frustrations about other parties, particularly local authorities, not meeting deadlines for the submission of evidence (Chapter 12) so that their reports had to be drafted and sometimes submitted before they had sight of an important document. This could particularly be a problem for guardians working from home without the assistance of modern technology. Again, although the long-term solution lies with professional practice, the obvious practical remedy is to ensure that all guardians are equipped with, and trained in using, word processors. This might also result in the production of less verbose reports.

Recognition that schedules tend to slip means that guardians have to play a little safe, with a consequent impact on the overall timetable:

> When the timetable is drawn up social services are given three weeks for their statements then parents are given two weeks to reply. . . . Then guardians want to see the statements before completing the report. If you ask for a week and the statements come in later you're actually putting yourself in quite a difficult position. So you then ask for a reasonable time, say ten days, and you've stretched the timetable quite a bit.

Generally, of course, statements will not contain any bombshells and though the receipt of reports was evidently still not as good as it might be, there was a broad consensus that:

> It's a vast improvement on the old way where you'd turn up on the day of the hearing and be handed various reports which sometimes contained things completely different from what people had said in private.

Practitioner perspectives on the use of experts

In the role of welfare reporter the Guardian ad Litem is not limited to collating and assessing information but is also expected to be able to advise the court as a professional social worker. In this sense the guardian is recognised as an expert and is permitted to give opinion evidence. He or she may however, be required by the court to arrange for other expert evidence and as representative of one of the parties he or she can do this as of right. Guardians have been urged to 'recognise the limits of their expertise'[17] and strongly criticised for failing to do so.[18]

Research focusing specifically on the use of experts in care proceedings has been part of the Department of Health's programme of Children Act studies.[19] This should illuminate an aspect of the court process about which there is little information but a great deal of official concern. Our interviews with guardians strongly indicated that they are much more likely to consider involving an expert than they were pre-Act and that many are aware of instructing experts more frequently. A number of reasons were suggested for this development:

- the increasing complexity of cases;

- guardians now handling cases that would have been dealt with in wardship;

- a perception that the higher courts are used to and expect experts and are reluctant to rely on the guardian's expertise;

- the guardian's own uncertainty operating in the higher courts, an expert thus being seen as bolstering the case for the child;

- a response to the use of experts by other parties; and

- an expectation that other parties will instruct experts, therefore a wish to ensure that the right expert is instructed.

It was also abundantly clear, however, that it is not only guardians who are conscious of turning to experts more frequently themselves and of the increasing use of experts by others:

It's the fashion. I don't know why. I don't know if it's the Act or just the flavour of the month. You've got an expert in the guardian but everyone is finding they have to have joint instructions for psychiatrists, psychologists and so on. I suspect I'm as guilty as the next person for suggesting it. . . . Everybody is getting on the bandwagon and it's just snowballing away. (Private practice lawyer)

It was notable that while in all professional groups there was some acknowledgement of personally contributing to this trend, there was also a strong sense that somehow it was a reaction to what others were doing, almost to something in the air. Practitioners might often present themselves as somewhat reluctant participators but many were none the less rather fatalistic about being swept along by the tide.

The process begins, it was suggested, in the local authority, even before proceedings are decided on:

> Social workers tend to rush off to psychiatrists because they are completely de-skilled. They have insufficient supervision and management to feel equipped to take these decisions and so they look to someone outside to make a decision for them. . . . It's highly unsatisfactory. (Local authority lawyer)

Once court action becomes likely, as predicted by several commentators[20] an expert may be brought in to ensure the evidence can meet the more stringent grounds, withstand the more rigorous scrutiny of the court, including perhaps, experts instructed by other parties, and compensate for the fact that: 'People don't consider social work assessments are good enough. There is a basic distrust in some cases in what social workers have done' (local authority lawyer).

Even social workers who feel secure in their own assessment and have a weight of experience to validate it, may lack confidence in demonstrating expertise[21] and may not make the most effective witnesses. Many will have had little experience of the court process and very often, it was said, were 'not prepared properly for giving evidence'.

For all these reasons a case may arrive in court with one or more experts already attached. From that point on, it was said 'the case tends to mushroom'. The lawyer acting for the parents may want an expert, 'in response to the local authority doing it', because 'getting an expert is the best way to contest evidence of abuse', particularly 'if you can see a chink', because 'to understand what others are saying and argue against them in their own language you need an expert' or because: 'proceedings are so adversarial, lawyers, perhaps rightly, take the view that their client is entitled to have an expert.'

As lawyers acting for parents become more specialist and experienced, our interviewees suggested, they have also become more aware of the complexities of care cases, recognising the need for specialist input and extending their knowledge of the available resources. Instructing an expert is therefore seen as part of 'doing a better job', the result of being: 'a lot more concerned to investigate backgrounds and causes and to see whether there is anything whereas perhaps before . . .'

If the local authority has an expert and the parent's solicitor is asking for an expert the pressure is then on the child's representatives to join in. As one children's lawyer put it: 'If someone calls a psychiatrist and you haven't got one then you're up a gum tree; the more other parties get experts involved the more we feel we have to.'

Children's lawyers, however, like the guardians whose views we reported earlier, may also contribute to this process 'as part of being more proactive for the child', because 'guardians are frequently saying let's get an expert in' or because courts, particularly the higher courts, are believed to place more value on psychiatric than social work opinion, even when that is contributed by a guardian:

> The courts want [experts]. They do not consider the guardian to be an expert, that's the bottom line. In the higher courts more so, especially the High Court because they're used to the Official Solicitor. So if you don't want to have your case undermined, just chucked to one side because you've got no one there of importance, you get them in.

The expectation that one or more parties may ask for experts, even if they have not already done so, or the anxiety that the need may arise in the course of the case also led, it was suggested to the prophylactic instruction of experts:

> If I think other parties are going to want an expert witness then I will try and get in the driving seat so I can influence who it is. (Guardian)

> You have to suggest it early on in case you need it. (Solicitor)

Alongside all this jockeying for position in a potentially adversarial contest, however, there were also hints of some deeper anxieties, 'the desperation to get it right'; the complexity of the issues, the stakes being played for. Given such a quest for certainty the increased reliance on experts by practitioners operating within a changing and uncertain legal environment is entirely understandable. Over time, as familiarity and confidence increases, demand might settle at a more appropriate level.

Certain issues, however, need to be addressed. Guardians' perceptions, for instance, that their expertise is less highly, rather than merely differently, regarded, by the professional judiciary, have to be tested and explored. Guardians may well, as has been suggested,[22] be more reluctant to instruct an expert than the Official Solicitor. The fact that this comparison was even drawn, however, is revealing, since the case officers in the Official Solicitor's department are civil servants, with no child welfare expertise, who manage their responsibilities to the child through the co-ordination of the evidence of others.

It is also important to tackle the issue of social work expertise and its presentation in court. Reference has already been made in earlier chapters to the need for social workers to become more skilled and confident in the application of the threshold criteria and to organise their evidence more cogently and analytically. However since all cases can potentially end in a contested hearing with oral evidence and cross-examination, it is also necessary for social workers to be able to operate effectively within the court-room. Some social workers love court, relish the opportunity to give aggress-ive barristers as good as they get, have lots of experience and are impressive witnesses. Many, however, are as apprehensive as their clients and almost as unfamiliar with the court system. Care proceedings, particularly under the Children Act, are not a regular part of a social worker's professional experi-ence. However in court they will be expected to behave as if they were.

Although some training in court craft is now likely to be part of pre-qualification training, a considerable time may elapse before it can be put into practice. Regular updating is probably not cost-effective, and it would be more useful if self-teaching materials, such as videos or computer pro-grammes, were made available and could be accessed at the point of need. These could help to ensure not only that inexperienced social workers are familiar with courtroom layouts, procedures and etiquette, but enable them to think about their evidence and anticipate the questions which might be asked. Some team managers perform this role; others, it would appear, do not and perhaps cannot. Local authority solicitors probably do not have the time and could be accused of coaching. Supplementary ways of enhancing profes-sionalism are needed.

Experts and assessments in the sample cases

Who is an expert?

At least 605 professionals submitted written evidence in the sample cases in addition to the Guardians ad Litem; an average of between seven and eight per case (Chapter 15). While many of these (for example health visitors, GPs, nursery staff and teachers) may be regarded as having *expertise* they are not what is normally envisaged by the word *expert*. Typically they will have been routinely involved with the child before proceedings commenced as part of the services available to the general population. Psychiatrists, paediatricians and psychologists (of whom 139 provided evidence) provide more specialised services and tend to be the professionals most frequently called upon to provide *expert* reports unless there is a particular issue, involving, for instance, the interpretation of medical findings, when a range of other specialists may be consulted. In the analysis which follows these groups are defined as *psycho-medical experts*. In between these two categories are a range of other professionals with specialist functions in the case, for instance agencies undertaking assessments of the family. Unless otherwise specified, the term *expert* should be understood to imply this less restrictive definition.

Local authority expert evidence

The use of experts prior to proceedings

Practitioner perceptions that the process of expert accretion often begins before the case arrives in court are confirmed by the case data: 42 of our 83 post-Act applications were supported with reports prepared by experts already involved prior even to any events precipitating proceedings.

The chances of a case already having an expert varies with the extent and nature of prior local authority involvement. Almost three in five of the already active cases had expert reports, the proportion rising to more than four in five where the family had been in a supervised setting and even higher where the children had experienced both supervision and separation. Duration of involvement also had an effect: just over a quarter of those which had been worked on for between one and three months had expert reports, compared to half of those with between four and six months' work and over two-thirds of those with more than this. While psycho-medical involvement was less frequent the pattern was the same: three-fifths of cases which had been continuously worked with for more than six months, for example, had accrued such expertise.

The care application relating to one of these long-term families was bolstered with reports from no fewer than six prior expert sources, including two separate family assessments. This, however, was exceptional: 23 (55%) of the cases with at least one established expert had no more than this and only five had more than two, the mean being 1.7. The proportion of cases with more than one prior psycho-medical expert was even lower with more than two-thirds having only one. Four of the six experts in the case cited above were psycho-medical personnel; however this was the only case to boast more than two.

Local authority experts involved as the result of events precipitating proceedings

A total of 71 experts, 43 of them psycho-medical, provided evidence in 42 cases on the basis of their prior acquaintance with the family. As described in Chapter 5, however, 38 of the sample cases arrived in court as the result of a precipitating crisis while a further six erupted into crisis before the first hearing. Just under half these events resulted in new expert evidence (from 25 sources, all psycho-medical), becoming available to the local authority. These were typically reports on injuries.

Only three cases involved more than one source. It was also unusual for a case which already had an expert on board to ship another at this point, this occurring in only three cases. Thus while these new experts inflated the total number to 96, these were spread over 60 cases, a mean of 1.6 per case. While 40% of cases (24) now had more than one expert, only 12% (7) had more than two. The 68 psycho-medical experts now involved were similarly spread over a large number of cases (50), with only 15 cases (three in ten) having more than one and two more than two.

Local authority experts introduced in the course of proceedings

By the first hearing therefore, almost three-quarters of the sample applications already had supporting expert evidence, and three in five psycho-medical evidence. In the course of proceedings half the 22 hitherto expert-free cases acquired at least one, and five more than one. Experts in such cases might be regarded as having a *compensatory* function. Strikingly, however, nearly half of the 60 cases with experts already attached also acquired more in the course of proceedings.[23] Of the 66 new sources of expert evidence brought into the sample cases 45 were in cases where such evidence already existed and thus might be categorised as *supplementary*. Supplementary psycho-medical evidence was also furnished by the local authority in 22 of the 50 cases with existing evidence of this type, and complementary in 13 of the 32 cases previously without. Thirty of these 61 new sources were instructed in cases where there was expert psycho-medical opinion already.

As a result of these processes only 19 applications were not buttressed with some form of psycho-medical expertise, the remainder generating evidence from 119 sources, a mean of 1.9 per case (Table 11.1). Evidence was also provided from 43 other experts so that only 11 cases had no expert opinion at all on behalf of the local authority, the rest averaging 2.3 per case (Table 11.2).

Table 11.1 *Local authority psycho-medical experts*

	Area A	Area B	Area C	All areas
Cases with psycho-medical expert				
Number	24	22	17	63
%	83	76	71	77
Number of experts	40	41	38	119
Mean	1.7	1.9	2.2	1.9
Number of experts per case				
1 only	12	13	4	29
2	9	3	8	20
3 or more	3	6	5	14

Table 11.2 *Local authority experts*

	Area A	Area B	Area C	All areas
Cases with any expert				
Number	24	28	19	71
%	83	97	79	87
Number of experts	49	64	49	162
Mean	2.0	2.3	2.6	2.3
Number of experts per case				
1 only	7	14	2	23
2	11	5	10	26
3 or more	6	9	7	22

Variation by area

As Table 11.3 reveals, the proportion of cases involving local authority expert evidence was high in all the research areas but varied from 79% in Area C to 97% in Area B. Similarly there was some variation in the point at which experts first entered the case in each area. Area A, for instance, had by far the highest proportion of cases with experts already involved; Area B of experts brought into the case at a point of crisis. Such differences echo variations in the life histories of the cases (Chapter 4). Thus Area A had not only a high proportion of active cases but, on average, a longer period of social work involvement per case. Area B had the highest proportion of cases reaching court as the result of a crisis (Chapter 5). Area C had the lowest proportion of active cases and more cases arising out of a crisis than Area A but fewer than Area B.

These different profiles help to explain why at the point of entering the court system more cases in Areas A and B already had experts on board. Other factors, such as the incidence of parental mental health problems or variations in the pattern of local resources, rather than differential practices in the use of expert opinion, also go a long way to explain the apparent higher use of psycho-medical experts in Area A prior to proceedings.

Area C had the highest proportion of cases where experts were brought in for the local authority during proceedings. This, however, was not simply a matter of compensating for the lack of previous experts in inactive cases since, as we have already shown such experts were primarily being brought into already expertised cases. Why this should have been felt to be necessary is the question to which we now turn.

Table 11.3 *Expert opinion for the local authority: summary data*

	Area A		Area B		Area C		All areas	
	No.	%	No.	%	No.	%	No.	%
Any expert								
Expert brought in:								
prior to precipitating events	18	62	14	48	10	42	42	51
at precipitating event	6	21	9	31	6	25	21	26
during proceedings	12	41	14	48	14	58	40	49
Total with experts	24	83	28	97	19	79	71	87
Psycho-medical expert								
Expert brought in:								
prior to precipitating events	16	55	7	24	8	33	31	38
at precipitating event	6	21	9	31	6	25	21	26
during proceedings	10	35	12	41	13	54	35	43
Total with experts	24	83	22	76	17	71	63	77

Gilding the lily?

Notwithstanding these variations, the fact that a substantial proportion of applications accumulated new expert evidence for the local authority in the course of proceedings might be considered to beg the question: should not social services have had its evidence sewn up more tightly from the start?

In some cases, of course, this was not for want of trying; due to parental resistance it was only possible to conduct a medical or psychiatric assessment of some children once legal authority to do so was conferred by the court. In other cases it only became apparent that there was a problem requiring expert opinion once the children were away from home.

More significant, however, is the fact that at the point most cases came to court the local authority's long-term intentions were far from clear, indeed were often expressed as being dependent on subsequent developments (Chapter 7). Experts were introduced into 32 of these *contingent* cases in the course of proceedings, almost three in five, rising to more than three-quarters of those previously inactive. In contrast it was comparatively unusual for the local authority to instruct an expert during proceedings in cases where they came to court with a firm objective (8 of 27), particularly when an expert was already involved. Such figures suggest that the local authority's purpose in introducing new expert opinion during proceedings was not so much the forensic one of boosting the evidence, as a developmental one, relating to the ongoing processes of decision-making and case management, of what is to be done, rather than what has happened.

This was particularly evident in the 17 cases which involved a specialist assessment of parenting during proceedings. The majority of these had been worked with for a comparatively short period (11 less than three months) and in all but two initial objectives were not firm. One of these exceptions, both of which were forced on the local authority by changes in the case, was that of Zara Butler.

● ●

Zara was only a few days old when the local authority applied for an Interim Care Order, clearly stating their intention to move to a full Care Order and thence to adoption. Sandra opposed the application, stated she had separated permanently from Phil and asked to be placed with Zara in a mother and baby home. She was supported in this by her psychiatrist, a specialist in learning difficulties, to whom she had been referred by the local authority for counselling on the loss of her other children and the proposed removal of her expected baby.

The guardian also opposed the local authority and the application was refused, the judge clearly indicating that there ought to be a test of parenting of this child. Subsequent evidence was then submitted by social services on the assessment at the mother and baby home and by two paediatricians on Zara's development and the mother–child interaction.

● ●

The most frequent reason, however, for the local authority to consult experts previously unfamiliar with the case, was some form of assessment of the child (32 experts in 16 cases).

Evidence relating to the child's physical, emotional and psychological condition is, of course, highly relevant to the decision the court has to make. Where the case turns on the child's development such evidence may be needed to establish the threshold conditions and it will certainly be relevant to the question of which order to make. Thus there will always be a forensic element and information obtained as the result of such examinations can have considerable probative value. Indeed in two cases it actually revealed hitherto unsuspected abuse. Few of the new child-focused assessments undertaken at the behest of the local authority, however, seem to have been instigated *primarily* for forensic purposes and none with the purpose of establishing whether any alleged abuse had taken place. Indeed had court proceedings not been underway we would judge that most of these assessments would have been felt to be desirable anyway in order that the process of welfare decision-making might move on. Whether parental permission or the resources to undertake them would have been forthcoming without the imperative of the court process is another matter.

On the whole the cases in which the local authority arranged assessments of the children were not the same ones as those where there were also assessments of the family; only four cases overlapped in this way. In the ten remaining cases in which the local authority submitted evidence from new experts six involved psychiatric reports on a parent's current mental health, a reflection of the high incidence of psychiatric problems in this sample.

Joint instructions

In addition to the 162 experts giving evidence for local authority applications, it is also presumed that the local authority will have had some input into the selection and instruction of those experts who were jointly instructed. Although this has increasingly been urged as a matter of good practice, at the point at which this research was conducted it was not a common occurrence in any of our court areas. Even the area with the highest incidence (A) had only five cases with joint instructions, compared to two in B and none at all in C. Four of these instructions concerned an assessment of parenting, three an assessment of the child. All were undertaken by psycho-medical experts. None involved an expert giving a second opinion on the conclusions of another expert from the same discipline already involved in the case, thus all could be regarded as enhancing rather than complicating the information base available to the court.

Experts instructed by the Guardian ad Litem

One of the purposes of joint instructions is to ensure that the expert approaches the case from a neutral and objective perspective. An alternative way of achieving the same end is for the Guardian ad Litem to instruct. Again this was by no means a frequent practice in our research areas, occurring in only nine cases, four of them in Area A. All of the ten experts involved were psycho-medical practitioners, eight reporting on the child, one on the parent and one providing a second opinion on the evidence of alleged sexual abuse. This last case was the only one in which the guardian's expert was called upon to comment on the conclusions of another expert. Again, therefore, we found the expert being brought in with the objective of extending the information pool rather than stirring up the waters.

Experts instructed by parents or other adult family members

Forty-one experts (38 of them psycho-medical), were instructed by parents or, in two cases, other family members seeking care of the child. These were concentrated in 23 cases, a rate of less than one in three, which scarcely indicates that the use of experts to counter social services' case is a near universal practice. Analysis of the particular reports commissioned, moreover, further questions this perception. In only four cases were experts instructed to give a second opinion on evidence of abuse. By far the commonest function was to advise on the past, current and likely future functioning of parents with specific impediments to parenting (15 cases, 22 reports). This reflects the prevalence of parents struggling with psychiatric illnesses, drug or alcohol addiction or a degree of learning disability. Only nine of these experts appear to have been brought in solely for the purpose of the legal proceedings.

A further five experts (four cases) provided assessments of parenting capacity where there was no known disability. In one of these, the parent's expert appears to have been instructed to give a second opinion on the adverse conclusions of the psychiatrist who had been jointly instructed. This was, however, the only case where this occurred. Moreover there were only five cases where the expert advising on parental functioning was giving a second opinion on the assessment made by another expert, no matter by whom they had been instructed.

Too few experts?

Only ten of our 83 cases therefore involved experts second guessing other experts on behalf of parents. In total parents had only 41 experts of their own and a part share in a further seven, to pit against the 172 marshalled by the other parties and the 300 or more other professionals giving evidence for the local authority. In well over half the sample cases parents had no experts of their own at all.

It was abundantly clear from our interviews with parents that they perceived there to be far too many experts for the other side, a persistent theme being their sense of being 'outgunned' by social services, even 'stitched up' by colluding professionals. Those few parents who had engaged an expert (10) generally felt grateful for any supportive evidence they gave, counteracting the generally negative picture being presented. However they were also of the opinion that such evidence was ignored or devalued by the court. Thus we cannot say that there was any great demand for more experts, even among parents who had previously been unaware that this was a possibility.

Indeed judging from the effect of those experts who were instructed for parents it would be hard to make any great play for more despite the great imbalance in power the current rate of use suggests. All the experts called in to provide a second opinion on whether abuse had occurred, for instance, concluded that the evidence was sound. Similarly, of the 11 experts who might be regarded as very broadly giving a second opinion on the case, only four differed from the local authority assessment, and only two substantially so. One at most may have had an impact on the outcome, and even then we would judge that the recommendation of the guardian had more impact in setting the case onto a different track.

Too many experts?

The issue engaging the Children Act Advisory Committee, however, has been that there are too many experts.[24] Our judicial interviews show that this concern is widely seen as valid. Practitioner concern about the use and mis-use of experts also prompted the establishment of a working party, the Expert Witness Group, on the topic. So much smoke, the old adage would suggest, indicates something at least is smouldering. The data presented, however, indicate that, at the time this research was undertaken, it had not yet become a blaze, at least not in these particular areas. The view expressed by the Expert Witness Group that 'multiple experts . . . appear to be commonplace in child care cases'[25] is perhaps somewhat alarmist, at least as far as the aver-age case is concerned.

The data certainly substantiate practitioner perceptions that it is now excep-tional for a care case to get through the court process *without* an expert: only three of our sample cases managed this. They also confirm the penetration of the legal domain by psycho-medical expertise, such experts being involved in 72 of the sample cases. However, of the 79 cases which had at least one expert, 29% (23) had no more than this and only a quarter (20) had more than three (Table 11.4). Less than a fifth had more than three psycho-med-ical experts and over a third no more than one. High numbers of experts were the *exception*, not the rule, in all our study areas.

It will already have become clear from the preceding sections that a high pro-portion of these experts were already involved in the case before the legal process was set in train and that many of the remainder were brought in by the local authority. Even experts instructed by other parties were rarely offer-ing a second opinion on the local authority expert evidence and even more rarely disagreeing with it. Thus it would appear that in most cases the accu-mulation of expert evidence was complementary rather than supplementary or adversarial.

It was also found that although 33 proceedings involved some form of expert assessment of the child these were usually complementary rather than sup-plementary. Where more than one expert was involved these were typically bringing different types of expertise to bear. Again this suggests a process of extending the court's information base rather than testing the evidence. Moreover all the second opinion assessments were paper only.

Even if a child is not directly abused by multiple examinations, however, there may be indirect damage through delayed decisions. The use of experts, particu-

Table 11.4 *Experts by area*

	Area A No.	Area A %	Area B No.	Area B %	Area C No.	Area C %	All areas No.	All areas %
Cases with expert								
one only	7	26	12	41	4	17	23	29
2 - 3	14	52	9	31	13	57	36	46
more than 3	6	22	8	28	6	26	20	25
Mean	2.8		2.9		2.8		2.8	
Median	2.0		2.0		2.0		2.0	
Maximum	8		12		7		12	
(n=)	(27)		(29)		(23)		(79)	
Cases with psycho-medical expert								
one only	10	37	11	46	5	24	26	36
2 - 3	12	44	8	33	12	57	32	44
more than 3	5	19	5	21	4	19	14	19
Mean	2.4		2.5		2.5		2.5	
Median	2.0		2.0		2.0		2.0	
Maximum	7		10		6		1.0	
(n=)	(27)		(24)		(21)		(72)	

larly those brought in during proceedings, was found to be associated with longer cases (Chapter 13). The legal process, too, has to bear costs over and above the expert's fees: in delay, in court time, in more complex interparty liaison. These system costs have to be weighed against the value of the particular opinion sought. More generally, since experts, we were repeatedly told by practitioners, are a scarce resource, spreading them thinly may not be the most efficient use of resources. Thus even where the commissioning of an expert report may not have any negative effects on the child in question, by tying up an expert, and therefore making him or her less available, that action may have a serious adverse effect on another child, because of the resultant delay.

This prompts the question: to what extent is all this expert advice really necessary? Years ago, so we were told, experts were a rarity in care cases, now it seems proceedings cannot be managed without them. It is of interest that in the past similar arguments were made about guardians, whose position in care proceedings now seems unassailable. It seems unthinkable that we shall reach the point at which expert opinion in every care case is established as a matter of public policy. Rather the message emanating from the centre is of the need to pull back from the brink and for courts to wrest control of the decision from the parties, to be much more robust in their questioning of the need for an expert, and to establish the precise contribution the expert is expected to make to the decision-making process.[26]

This all seems eminently sensible, provided it is not used to constrain the use of experts for solely resource reasons. Such a level of control was certainly not notably in evidence in the sample cases although there were individual examples of close questioning or of late requests for experts being refused in the magistrates' court as well as the higher courts.

Judicial interviews, however, suggest that in the intervening period, and particularly following the strongly worded advice from the Children Act Advisory Committee and members of the judiciary, such practices may have become more general. One of the questions put to interviewees was whether concern about the increasing use of expert evidence was justified. By far the majority of the replies indicated that this was the case. Interviewees also strongly supported the notion that it was the court's responsibility to exercise control, with some indicating that well-established practices meant that the problem had long been manageable, others that they were now adopting a more robust approach:

> We were sometime ago being – not led by the nose but – we were being told well we need this that or the other expert because we don't know what the problem is or what would be thrown up. A lot of it used to be a question of: 'Well we are all a bit in the dark about this the experts will enlighten us – we are not quite sure who we want or what we want or why.' We have cottoned on to that. Especially when we see the huge sums that they have claimed for saying little or nothing. We now look much much more closely at requests for experts and no one is allowed to go to experts without our authority. Our philosophy is that the fewer people pulling and pushing and prodding and taking up the child's time the better. We are looking for the appointment of a senior expert rather than one by every party.

To implement such an approach, which cuts across the tradition of legal practitioners making their own judgements and of the partisan use of experts, has clearly not been plain sailing:

> We try to tighten it up here. Unless the case is exceptional we only have one expert, jointly instructed. [Practitioners] did jib to begin with, one or two of them who tend to be a bit partisan. Then they were sent away to do a joint

letter of instruction because they said that was a problem and now they've come right round. Now they've got a joint letter they can live with one expert.

Partly it is, as one district judge put it:

> a question of education. Now the profession is more aware that experts, while not being frowned on, are being looked at in a different way. When I'm talking to solicitors I beg them to look at CVs. I beg them to talk to an expert whom everyone is prepared to pick. I beg them to ask before they instruct them, have you got the time to do this, how long is it going to take, what are you going to charge, when is your report likely to come in, have you done this sort of thing before? There's no reason why they shouldn't ask those sort of questions.

However, he went on:

> Not many people do. They come to court saying we're thinking of instructing an expert psychiatrist. Are you? Who? Well a name has been given to us and it could be so and so. I say I'm sorry, you come back next week when you've spoken to him and established that he's quite comfortable with your instructions, at least with the ethos of what's going on, that you can afford him, he can do it quickly and it all fits in with the timetable. If you can't then I'm sorry to say you're not going to have him. I think you have to be quite brutal because there is no alternative. I can't pretend that makes me particularly popular.

Also unpopular may be the complaint by several district judges that their efforts to prevent the uncontrolled use of experts were unavailing when cases came up from the family proceedings court with leave already granted. From our interviews with magistrates and Justices' Clerks we would anticipate this perception would not be shared: Clerks in particular felt they were careful to question the need for experts. We are not able to resolve this from our sample data. One might speculate, however, that since magistrates do not have to manage the consequences of giving leave for a multiplicity of experts (since such cases are likely to be transferred) they may be less motivated to resist practitioner demands and consciousness of their lay status may make them less confident in doing so. As one district judge suggested: 'Justices are far more willing to accede to a request from a powerful advocate than we are.' A comment from a magistrate suggests an additional factor:

> Our whole background, attitude and training as magistrates is to be fair, to hear the arguments and not to block them. It is very difficult to resist the

application for a psychiatric report or whatever when clearly the more information you have, the more likely people will feel that they have had a fair hearing.

Magistrates, however, are not unique in linking the unrestricted use of experts with the desire to ensure justice is seen to be done. One district judge, who acknowledged that practice was changing, told us:

It's difficult to control [the use of experts] as against the need to allow a parent, who is in danger of having his or her child removed, to conduct the case as his/her legal advisor considers appropriate. The inclination is always for the court to bend over backwards to enable a parent to present their case in as unrestricted a manner as possible.

The issue of expert evidence thus embodies some difficult questions about the nature of care proceedings while developments in this area give perhaps the clearest indication of the move towards less adversarial, more co-operative and more consensual practice. The preferred approach is to be a single expert instructed either jointly or by the guardian. Where this is not possible, experts are to meet and identify areas of agreement and dispute. Experts instructed by parents are to remember their duty to be objective and the dangers of producing *tendentious* reports.[27] Such developments, sensible as they may be seen by many, might be seen by others to herald trial by expert and as reducing the capacity of parents to defend the integrity of their family against the child welfare bureaucracy. Opinion among our lawyer interviewees, for example, was sharply divided as to the practical as well as theoretical merits of the Oxfordshire[28] decision, with a number arguing that its effect would be to discourage them from seeking expert opinion. The possibility that a backlash effect will halt this apparently inexorable move towards the non-adversarial use of experts therefore cannot be entirely discounted.

As yet, it appears that the investigatory role of the court has been restricted to agreeing or refusing the requests of the parties for leave to instruct experts. There were no instances in our sample of the initiative coming from the court. Moreover, unlike in criminal cases, where a defendant can be ordered to submit to a psychiatric examination, for example, or to comply with a direction for assessment or treatment, in Children Act cases such matters entirely depend on parental consent, to the frustration of some practitioners. Since such constraints are not universal in child protection proceedings in other jurisdictions it is conceivable that there may be increasing demand for UK law to move in this direction.

Despite the attention which it has attracted, the use of experts is only one aspect of a broad process of assessment, welfare input and local authority decision-making taking place alongside the court process which can change the configuration of the case. Moreover the act of entering the legal process does not put the case into suspended animation: the life of the family goes on, indeed it may go on at an exaggerated pace as the result of court action. New services may be offered or the attitude of parents towards services they have previously rejected shift. Fresh information may come to light or old information be re-interpreted. In the next section we examine some of the changes in our sample cases during the time they were before the court.

A moving target: the fluidity of care cases

Changes in family composition

In one of the post-Act cases a mother believed to be dead re-appeared; in another the man whom everyone had treated as the father turned out not to be. Though these are the most extreme examples, many cases were marked by some degree of change in family membership or relationships. Eighteen couples separated or reconciled at some point during proceedings; ten did both. At least eight formed new relationships, two of whom married. Five babies were born. Three mothers, previously primary carers, disappeared and five parents who had no role in the child's life at the start of proceedings reappeared. Several adults went to prison and one died. Thirty-five cases were affected by one or more of these eventualities.

Such changes in adult relationships and household composition have to be incorporated into thinking about the child's future care. In this respect there is a tendency to think simplistically of the departure of an alleged abuser making it safe for a child to live with one parent. None of the sample cases was as straightforward as this. Although 13 involved the severance of relationships between a parent and a partner perceived as the primary risk, usually the situation was far from black and white, requiring an assessment of the remaining risk or the capacity of the non-abusing parent to cope on their own. Moreover parental resolve was not always maintained; several relationships broke and re-formed, or were carried on covertly. Thus the decision-making process is complicated by the need to assess the permanence as well as the implications of relationship change. The consistency of Sandra's determination to break with Phil was one of the key issues in the thinking around Zara's future.

The court having refused social services' application Sandra was allowed to take Zara home under an Interim Supervision Order, reinforced by an order prohibiting her allowing Phil contact with the child, pending availability of a mother and baby home placement. After a month at home with intensive support, Sandra and Zara moved to the home in April. The Prohibited Steps Order was not renewed and Phil was allowed to visit. A month later, Sandra requested that he might join her and Zara in the placement. With some misgivings, this was agreed.

This period was acknowledged to be a difficult time for the family. Not only were they under close supervision but there was an adoption hearing for two older children and Sandra was discovered to be pregnant again. The parents' relationship was under obvious strain and after a series of rows culminated in a violent argument, Phil was asked to leave. Sandra subsequently left the home on several occasions to find him, leaving Zara behind. The local authority terminated the placement, obtained an Interim Care Order and placed Zara in foster care.

At a hearing in October, Sandra was firm that her relationship with Phil was over, despite circumstantial evidence that they were still in contact. The judge accepted the guardian's proposals for gradual rehabilitation. By the spring, a year after the start of proceedings, Zara was living with Sandra and her new brother with the help of respite care and other support. Phil was again firmly on the scene.

Changes in family circumstances

Shifting family constellations are, however, only one aspect of change. The configuration of the case may also be affected by improvement or deterioration in a parent's physical or mental health (9 cases) One parent died in the course of proceedings; three attempted suicide; some went into psychiatric hospital and others came out; a few did both. One mother responded dramatically well to new medication following a re-diagnosis of manic depression rather than schizophrenia and in consequence rehabilitation became a possibility. Gina became severely ill and was eventually sectioned under the Mental Health Act; plans to place her and baby Laurie together in a mother and baby home were dropped. Jenny Grayson's removal drove her mother over the edge; she was admitted to psychiatric hospital from court and remained hospitalised throughout proceedings. Moreover, as we found in the previous section, changes were not necessarily unidirectional or evenly sustained.

● ●

Mr and Mrs Cooper suffer from chronic recurrent psychiatric illnesses and in the months leading to proceedings were each in a downward spiral, generating acute concern for the physical and emotional welfare of Michael (6) and his sister Elizabeth (3). Matters eventually came to a head when Mrs Cooper was committed to hospital. Mr Cooper, who was acutely distressed by this, initially agreed to the children being accommodated but then changed his mind. The children were removed by the police. Mr Cooper was also sectioned a week later after he first admitted himself to, then discharged himself from, hospital.

Both parents were considered by their psychiatrists to be so ill that there was no contact with the children for eight weeks. Mr Cooper, against expectations, then made a fairly rapid recovery and his order was allowed to expire although he remained in hospital voluntarily. Mrs Cooper's condition proved rather more resistant and she was placed on a six-month treatment order. A course of ECT (electoconvulsive therapy) then produced what appeared to be a dramatic recovery and she began to spend time at home. The section was discharged after two months, prematurely as it turned out because she relapsed and was readmitted to hospital. Although she was then again released after further treatment and the plan was to rehabilitate the children, the local authority, with the support of the guardian, decided to seek a Care Order. At what was to have been the substantive hearing Mr and Mrs Cooper opposed the application and the case was adjourned for two months while rehabilitation was started. By the time of the final hearing the children were at home although Mrs Cooper was still not considered fully well and there were again doubts as to whether she was compliant with medication.

● ●

The deterioration in Gina's mental health was triggered in part by Matt's imprisonment. Another case was thrown into crisis when the mother's violent ex-partner was released from prison and she fled. Parallel legal proceedings could also impact on families and case management: in a quarter of cases one of the adults concerned in the case was involved in criminal proceedings not directly relevant to proceedings while in a fifth of cases there were either outstanding criminal proceedings for ill-treatment or civil proceedings relating to other children in the family.

New information

Changes in family composition or circumstances may affect the evaluation of risk or plans for the child's future. Information coming to light in the course of proceedings can have a similar effect.

• •

Mr and Mrs Francombe had been known to the welfare services ever since the birth of their first child, Siobhan, now 4, although because of parental non-co-operation and local authority staff shortages there had been continuous social work involvement only for a few months prior to proceedings.

Mrs Francombe is partially sighted and was thought to have a degree of learning difficulty. Her husband experienced personality changes as the result of head injuries several years ago and at the time proceedings were brought was terminally ill. The family lived in very poor housing with no hot water and no inside sanitation but had persistently refused offers of help. Siobhan and her brother Karl (3) attended nursery where staff reported continual concerns about their low weight, inadequate clothing, lack of concentration and developmental lag. Siobhan was also displaying a range of unusual behaviours and it was felt she might need special education. The family had been subject to a number of child protection investigations related to a series of small but odd injuries to Siobhan, not all of which were accepted as accidental. In the course of one of these it was discovered that the parents were in the habit of keeping the child in bed at night by tying her down.

Two months before proceedings both children were placed on the Child Protection Register under the categories of neglect and emotional abuse, Siobhan being also registered under physical abuse. Two voluntary contracts were drawn up but when these failed to engage the parents' co-operation, court action was taken and assessments begun under conditions attached to Interim Residence and Supervision Orders. These initial assessments appeared to support a picture of a family under severe stress and a mother whose efforts to care for her family had been impeded by her own handicaps and her husband's domineering ways.

A month later, after further injuries to Siobhan, both children were removed and only a few weeks later Mr Francombe died. The local authority then began rehabilitation, and the children moved to be with their mother in a residential placement. Siobhan's behaviour, however, proved too much for her mother to cope with and she was moved to a specialist therapeutic placement. Here she began to disclose regular and horrific physical, emotional and sexual abuse.

Though denying the allegations of sexual abuse Mrs Francombe admitted gross physical abuse and acknowledged her own part in this. By this time it had also been concluded that she was unable to parent Karl either and Care Orders were sought for both children.

· ·

There were several other cases where the instigation of proceedings opened up similar cans of worms. In one case for example, the local authority brought proceedings after older children alleged sexual abuse. Subsequent investigation also revealed an incredible history of suspicious injuries to the younger children. Because the parents had used different hospitals no one had put the picture together, with the result that the children had been subject to persistent abuse for years.

Parental attitudes

The majority of care cases reach court because it has not been possible for social services and parents to reach a mutually acceptable accommodation which will protect the children from future harm. The shock of proceedings, however, several practitioners told us, can 'bring people up short and make them realise that unless things work out they could lose their children' (guardian). In one case, for instance, where the mother eventually sought treatment for alcoholism the guardian wrote:

> Mother has talked to me about the state of shock she was in when her daughter was removed. Her life experience is that she has never known any children who have been removed into care and her family has never been involved with social workers and she had not realised that it was possible for them to so easily remove a child from parental care. This realisation and that she was responsible has shocked her into sobriety. It has been enough to convince her that she must ensure that the situation never gets as bad again.

In all, attitudinal changes, either in parental readiness to co-operate or willingness to accept specific treatment, were noted in 25 cases (30%). Not all were sustained, of course, some did not even make first base and others came too late in the day. Claudette Symons, for instance, only reconciled herself to a mother and baby home at the point when social services had decided that was no longer a viable option. Yet others were counteracted by developments. One mother, for instance, who had assaulted the previous social worker, seemed to have established a much better relationship with her replacement, stimulating hopes for rehabilitation. The situation, however, had to be re-assessed yet again when the couple were arrested and it was revealed that they were involved in substantial criminal activity to fund their previously unsuspected heroin addiction and were likely to receive custodial sentences.

If the instigation of proceedings is going to have a shock effect it would, of course, make the court process much simpler if change occurred right at the beginning of proceedings and was sustained. Unfortunately however, things are rarely so convenient. In a few cases parents only seemed to see the abyss when they were about to fall into it. Sometimes, as with Claudette, it was by then too late. A few others, however, were successful in persuading the court to agree to a last-minute reprieve.

- -

The local authority's expectations that the institution of proceedings would stimulate Joanne Phillips into changing her behaviour and undertaking treatment for her drinking proved unfounded. After a number of incidents over the next four months Sam and his siblings were removed by the police two weeks prior to what should have been the final hearing. At that hearing the local authority, supported by the guardian, applied for a Care Order. Joanne's solicitor, however, succeeded in obtaining an adjournment to allow her to obtain treatment. Regular reports were provided to the court by the therapeutic unit to which Joanne was admitted and the local authority application was finally heard ten months later.

- -

Alternative carers

Finally, decisions have to take account of possible alternative carers emerging in the course of proceedings. This occurred in 35 of the sample cases. Again, of course, some of these possibilities were more serious than others; some evaporated relatively quickly, others were investigated and proved unsuitable; yet others resulted in alternative arrangements being made. Some were straightforward and acceptable both to the local authority and the parent; others were hard fought and involved several contending parties. Some emerged as soon as proceedings were underway, others not until it was apparent that the local authority was not planning rehabilitation.

A month after Christopher O'Brien was returned home he wandered into the police station late at night, to be followed a little later by his grandmother, who was supposed to be baby-sitting. According to the police, Vera was drunk, so was Christopher's aunt, the only other person in the house. Christopher was taken into police protection again and proceedings begun.

At the outset the local authority hoped that this would galvanise Tara into getting the help she so obviously needed and at first this seemed to be the effect: she referred herself to an alcohol treatment unit and co-operated with the regime. Gradually, however, her attendance fell away. Similarly she agreed to see a psychiatrist for assessment but didn't start the therapeutic programme recommended. An expert assessment of Christopher's needs and Tara's capacity to meet those needs in the foreseeable future was pessimistic. Social services, supported by the guardian, sought a Care Order with a plan to give Tara a period of six months to effect some change, after which an adoptive placement would be sought.

Vera had already offered to care for Christopher during proceedings, but had not felt able to offer him a permanent home. Now that it was clear that her grandson might be lost to the family altogether, however, she decided to seek care. By this time the final hearing was imminent. The hearing was adjourned and another assessment carried out, this time of Vera's capacity to care. Two months later, the court granted her a Residence Order.

While few cases involved such a dramatic reversal as this one, any change has the potential to throw a case off-balance. We estimate there were no more than 12 cases which did not involve some degree of change, whether this was essentially only turbulence, which was of no more than nuisance value, or a significant development which affected the shape of the case.

It should now be evident that any notion that care proceedings are a matter of processing cases through a machine or that the key task is the preparation of the case for trial is grossly misconceived. Rather a care case resembles a flotilla of vessels of varying degrees of sophistication and sea-worthiness, ploughing its uncertain way through choppy and largely uncharted waters, where the eventual destination is only vaguely known and where the passengers and crew keep changing. The Children Act, of course, is quite clear that the task of steering this motley convoy safely into the right harbour, and in the shortest possible time, belongs to the court, assisted by the Guardian ad Litem. In the next chapter we look more closely at the navigational process.

Summary

Judicial interviews indicate that the guardian's role as the principal independent advisor to the court has been well accepted in the higher courts and guardians themselves were generally highly regarded. The only major criticism was the length of some reports.

Certain aspects of the new legislation have made the process of the guardian's investigation easier, particularly early appointment and written evidence. However the scope of enquiries has become more extensive while the process can be slowed down by the volume of evidence, late production of evidence and confusion over the distribution of documents.

There was a broad consensus that guardians were more likely to seek expert advice than hitherto. The suggestion that this may be partly a response to the expert-based culture of the higher courts is a matter which needs to be addressed in discussions between local panels and the judiciary.

Other practitioner groups testified to a developing culture in which there was increased reliance on expert evidence. A certain circularity was apparent, lawyers wanting experts to balance those put up by social services, the local authority seeking expert advice in anticipation of experts being instructed by the other parties. A need to strengthen the expertise of social workers and to enhance skills in the presentation of evidence was identified.

Although it was exceptional for cases not to have any expert witnesses only a quarter of the sample cases had more than three. The vast majority of experts were giving evidence on behalf of the local authority, more than half of whom were already involved in the case prior to the case reaching court. Less than a third of cases involved experts instructed solely on behalf of parents of whom only a quarter were giving a second opinion on the case and only one in 20 a second opinion on alleged abuse.

The increasing use of experts has serious implications for the duration and cost of proceedings. The use of joint instruction wherever possible and a robust questioning of the need for expert opinion will help to minimise unnecessary proliferation. Such practices were relatively unusual at the time the research was conducted although there was some evidence of subsequent change.

However the data suggest the primary issue is not the adversarial bolstering of opposing positions. In most cases the accumulation of expert evidence was complementary rather than supplementary or adversarial, extending rather than duplicating or complicating the information available to the court. It thus principally reflects the need for certainty and fairness in the determination of complex and vitally important issues.

The expertisation of proceedings is only one aspect of a broad process of investigation, assessment, development and change taking place alongside the legal process. Care cases are characteristically fluid. In the course of proceedings there were changes in family membership, household composition, circumstances and attitudes; new information coming to light; new potential carers within the family coming forward. The majority of cases (85%) were affected by one or more of these factors, any of which could necessitate a re-assessment of the situation and significantly alter the position of all the parties.

NOTES

1 DoH (1989): *An Introduction to the Children Act 1989*. HMSO.

2 Humberside Cc v DPR [1977] 1 WLR 1252; R v Birmingham Juvenile Court, ex-parte G and others (minors) [1989] 2 FLR 454; R v Hampshire CC, ex-parte K and K [1990] 2 WLR 649.

3 Cobley C (1995): *Child Abuse and the Law*. Cavendish Publishing Limited.

4 SLFA (1994).

5 Re D and M (minors) (1993) 18 BMLR 71.

6 1 FCR 753.

7 Re R (Minor) (Legal Professional Privilege) (Disclosure of Material) [1994] 1 FCR 225.

8 E.g. Re DH (A Minor) (Care Proceedings: Evidence and Orders) [1994] 2 FCR 3.

9 DoH (1989): op. cit.

10 Hunt J; Murch M (1989) *Speaking Out for Children*. The Children's Society.

11 R11(9)(a)–(c).

12 The Honourable Mr Justice Wall (1995): The Use or Misuse of Experts: a judicial perspective. Paper given at NAGALRO conference. 29 March 1995.

13 Murch M et al. (1991): *Representation of the Child in the Civil Courts: Summary and Recommendations to the Department of Health*. Socio-Legal Centre for Family Studies, University of Bristol; Hunt and Murch (1989): op. cit.

14 Family Proceedings Courts (Children Act 1989) Rules 1991 r1(6)(c).

15 Section 42.

16 Hunt J (1986): The Role and Practice of the Guardian ad Litem. Report to DoH (unpublished).

17 Wall (1995): op. cit.

18 B v B (Child Abuse: Contact) [1994] 2 FLR 713.

19 Brophy J (forthcoming): Guardians ad Litem, experts and care proceedings. The Stationery Office.

20 Cretney S (1990): Defining the Limits of State Intervention: the child and the courts, in Freestone D (ed.): *Children and the Law*. Hull University Press.

[21] Bell M; Daly R (1992): Social Workers and Solicitors: working together? *Family Law*, 257.

[22] Wall (1995): op. cit.

[23] This figure excludes fresh reports from experts with some previous acquaintance with the case, which were submitted in 35% of all cases.

[24] *Children Act Advisory Committee Annual Report* 1993–94. LCD.

[25] Newsline. *Family Law*, May 1994.

[26] Re AB (Child Abuse: Expert Witnesses) [1995] 1 FLR 181; *Children Act Advisory Committee Annual Report* 1993–94.

[27] Re AB (Child Abuse: Expert Witnesses) [1995] 1 FLR 181.

[28] Re D and M (minors) (1993) 18 BMLR 71.

12 *Controlling the pace*

The duties and powers of the court

> A court hearing an application for an order . . . shall . . . draw up a timetable
> with a view to disposing of the application without delay.[1]

No formal limits were set for the duration of proceedings. However following the much publicised statements of key members of the judiciary involved
in implementation a target of 12 weeks became common currency.[2] It was, for
example, the presumptive time-scale used in a pre-Act timetabling experi-
ment[3] and in guidance on workload management issued to managers of the
guardian panels.[4] The court, the Act goes on to stipulate, shall also:

> give such directions as it considers appropriate for the purpose of ensuring,
> as far as is reasonably practicable, that that timetable is adhered to.

Giving the court both the responsibility for case progress and powers to
enable that responsibility to be effected, is 'something of a novelty' in English
law,[5] which has traditionally left such matters to the parties.[6] Little detailed
guidance was provided nor was the issue of sanctions against parties for non-
compliance addressed.[7] Thus, although a certain amount of initial training
was provided, in the early years of the Act's operation the courts were largely
left to tackle these new duties as best they could.

As the Act has bedded down, however, and particularly as it has become evident that case throughput is falling a long way short of the 12-week target,
there has been a stream of pronouncements and practice directions aimed at
encouraging and assisting courts to control, monitor and expedite case
progress. Directions have dealt, for instance, with the instruction of experts,[8]
the preparation of trial bundles,[9] time estimates[10] and directions hearings.[11]
Very detailed standard directions forms have been issued and revised. The
Children Act Advisory Committee devoted considerable space to the issue in
its 1993–94 report. Subsequently a Practice Direction issued by the President
of the Family Division[12] identified elements of good practice including setting limits to the duration of submissions and oral evidence; defining issues,

meetings of experts to agree areas of dispute and pre-trial reviews. Moreover, it stated: 'Failure by practitioners to conduct cases economically will be visited by appropriate orders for costs, including wasted costs orders.'

Such guidance, our judicial interviews revealed, has generally proved very welcome. The concept of the managerial court has also become more familiar throughout the civil justice system as Lord Justice Woolf's review[13] has progressed. For most of our research period, however, the courts were still trying to make their accommodation with a changing culture. In the next sections we look at the effect of these changes on the sample cases.

Drawing up the timetable

Scheduling the final hearing

The point at which the final hearing was listed

As Table 12.1 shows, less than a quarter of cases were set down for hearing on their first appearance before the court. Given that issues relating to case progress are intended to be sorted out primarily at a separate directions hearing, this is not particularly surprising. More notable is the finding that only just over half the sample were timetabled by the end of the second hearing, while nearly two-thirds were left for four weeks or more (Table 12.2). The mean interval between the date the case was first heard and the listing date was just over eight weeks.[14] Indeed by 12 weeks a fifth of the sample had still not been listed for final hearing. Ironically, although in each of our study areas the listing point under the Act was many weeks earlier than in pre-Act wardships, it was still later than had been the case under the Children and Young Persons Act, varying from a few days in Area A to over three weeks in Area C.

Table 12.1 *Hearing at which full hearing listed*

	Area A %	Area B %	Area C %	All areas %
Hearing 1	45	11	8	22
Hearing 2	35	25	25	28
Hearing 3	10	21	25	19
Hearing 4	7	11	17	11
Hearing 5	0	4	8	4
Hearing 6+	3	28	17	16
(n=)	*(29)*	*(28)*	*(24)*	*(81)*

Table 12.2 *Interval between first hearing and listing date*

	Area A %	Area B %	Area C %	All areas %
Hearing listed within				
2 weeks	48	14	13	26
4 weeks	62	18	25	36
8 weeks	79	47	54	61
12 weeks	93	61	83	79
20 weeks	100	93	100	98
(n=)	*(29)*	*(28)*	*(24)*	*(81)*

The point at which cases were commonly first scheduled varied between the three areas. In A 45% (13) were set down at the first hearing and only 21% (6) later than the second. In contrast only three (11%) of Area B's cases and two (8%) of C's were listed at the first hearing and around two-thirds in each were scheduled later than hearing two. Similarly 48% of cases in A (14) were first set down within two weeks of the first hearing and 62% (18) within four weeks. By this time only around a third of cases in the other two areas had been listed. Forty-six per cent of cases in Area C (11) and 54% (15) in Area B were not set down until eight weeks or more had elapsed.

Early scheduling was more in evidence in Areas B and C in the second year of the Act though paradoxically the reverse was true in Area A, which perhaps indicates a growing congruence of practice. None the less even in year 2 between 44% and 75% of all cases remained unscheduled at four weeks and between 22% and 42% at eight weeks. Given the stress laid on early timetabling why should this have been so?

> Usually the local authority bend over backwards to give mother a chance to prove her ability to parent the child. The best assessments take three months. At the end it will either have succeeded, in which case there will be an uncontested application for a supervision order, or it will have failed, in which case there will be a heavily contested application for a care order. So how do you timetable at the beginning of the three months? Do you allow a week – in which case nothing else can be put in, a waste of a valuable resource, or do you wait and see how the assessment is going and then if you need a week you're three months further down the queue. (District judge)

The capacity of the court to map out a case's progress depends in no small measure on how clearly its destination can be foreseen at the outset. Putting it crudely, if you want to know how to get somewhere and how long it will take, it helps enormously to know where you are going. As Figure 12.1 shows, cases in which the local authority's long-term objective was clear tended to be scheduled earlier than those in which the outcome was seen as contingent on developments during proceedings. In Year 2, for instance, two-thirds of cases in which the objective was long-term substitute care were set down for final hearing within four weeks compared to one-third of those with contingent objectives. Since we know that the eventual objective was clear in only around a third of the sample cases overall (Chapter 7) and that this was actually a lower proportion than in the pre-Act sample, the courts are perhaps to be congratulated that they managed to set cases down as early as they did.

Figure 12.1 *Weeks to listing date (cumulative)*

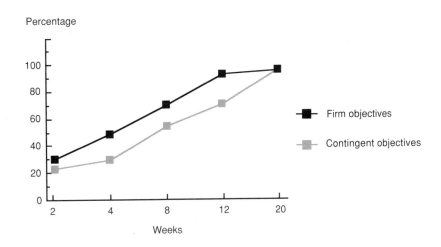

Although the proportion of cases with firm objectives is eerily the same as the proportion which were listed early the association is by no means perfect. There were previously inactive cases, for instance, in which the final hearing was listed at the first hearing when very little was known about the family and cases which were not listed even though a great deal was known about the past and the local authority's objectives were clear. Thus other factors were coming into play.

Transfer, or the likelihood of transfer, of course, was one such factor. Though the family proceedings court often enquired about dates for final hearings before sending a case up it was rare for a date to be actually reserved at this point. *Delays* in appointing guardians were particularly relevant in Area C; courts were normally reluctant to timetable without having some idea of when the guardian's report could be available, though again it did happen in a few cases. *Non-attendance* or non-representation of parents was another factor. Finally even when the local authority's intentions may have been plain at the point they lodged their application, by the time of the first hearing the family situation may have changed. In one case, for example, it only came to light on the morning of the hearing that the parents had separated. The court therefore yielded to the view expressed by all the parties, especially the guardian, that it would be premature to list at this point.

In most cases, therefore, there were reasons why very early timetabling was not seen to be possible, it was not simply going by the board. That said, we did not consider that these reasons were always sufficient. In the case cited above, for instance, the parental separation admittedly re-configured the case. However we do not accept that this should have made it impossible to timetable. Even if an assessment needed to be made of the permanency of the separation and whether this would enable the child to return home and under what legal protection if any, it should have been possible to gauge how long this would take and fix at least a provisional timetable.

In this case it was the court which was pressing for the timetable to be set and the parties who successfully resisted. In others it was the parties who were pressing for early scheduling and the court which was resistant, while in a few we were perturbed by the apparent lack of urgency displayed by both the parties and the court at this stage.

• •

Jamie Harris (aged 18 months) had been accommodated at the request of his parents, Andy and Frances, since he was 4 months old. There was regular contact with both parents, who seemed quite content with the arrangements, but no progress had been made on rehabilitation. Thus reluctantly (and painfully slowly) social services concluded they had to resolve the situation by seeking the power to make long-term arrangements, although in the hope that such action would jolt Andy and Frances out of their apparent apathy.

The case was listed for a first directions appointment at 9.30 am. Waiting outside court all the professionals expressed commendable concern about the need for a speedy resolution to the case. The local authority solicitor, indeed, considered that social services were vulnerable to criticism for letting matters go on for so long.

By 9.30 everyone was present except for Frances and the solicitor Andy had asked to represent him. Another case was listed before the same clerk and went in first. Due to the illness of another clerk, however, there was also a long list of other matters which had to be dealt with and as time went on and neither Andy's solicitor nor Frances turned up the clerk started on this list. Eventually it was accepted that Frances was not going to arrive and it was established that there had been a misunderstanding between Andy and his solicitor and he would not be able to turn up either. By this time, however, the court had started hearing a lengthy case and the social worker had had to leave to give evidence in another court. It was agreed with the clerk that written directions should be drafted by the lawyers and approved by the magistrates and that everyone could leave. These directions included leave to commission a psychiatric report (the psychiatrist being as yet unidentified and no directions given in relation to filing the report). A new directions hearing was listed for six weeks hence.

· ·

In these unfortunate circumstances there is no way this case could have been timetabled on this first occasion. What we found surprising, however, was that the court was prepared to adjourn the case for six weeks. At the very least we would have thought the guardian, who was to commission the psychiatric report, should have been required to inform the court whether this had been arranged and how long the chosen expert would require. As far as we are aware there was no such understanding.

The target time-frame

Given a flexible and not over-burdened court schedule, there is no reason why cases which are not set down for final hearing early should take any longer than those which are. If, for instance, a court were in a position to offer a three day hearing within a month, listing could be left until eight weeks had elapsed when the time estimate for the hearing might be clear and the case would still be completed within the 12-week target originally envisaged. Not surprisingly, however, given that the current court system meets neither of these prerequisites, we found that the earlier a case was scheduled the more likely it was that the target date would fall within the presumptive time-frame. Thus 14 of the 21 cases which were timetabled within two weeks were scheduled to be completed within 12 weeks and 20 within 16. Even a couple of weeks delay, however, sharply reduced these proportions: of the eight cases timetabled between two and four weeks from the start of the case only one was scheduled to complete within 12 weeks (13%) and 6 (75%) within 16. By eight weeks the proportion hoping to complete within 16 weeks had dropped to 55% (27 of 49) and by 12 weeks to 13% (2 of 16).

Area A was the only authority in which early scheduling was customary. As Table 12.3 indicates, it was also the only area working to a relatively short presumptive time-frame. In this area, 52% of cases were originally listed to be heard within 12 weeks of the first hearing and 72% within 16. In contrast 50% of cases in Area B and 62% of those in C had initial time-frames exceeding 20 weeks, with only 14% and 4% respectively falling within the 12-week period. Moreover we found that irrespective of the point at which the case was first set down, the interval between that date and the target completion date was shortest in Area A (9 weeks) compared to 11 in Area B and 16 in Area C.

Table 12.3 *Interval between first hearing and listed date*

	Area A %	Area B %	Area C %	All areas %
Within 12 weeks	52	14	4	24
Within 16 weeks	72	39	33	48
Within 20 weeks	83	50	38	57
(n=)	*(29)*	*(28)*	*(24)*	*(81)*

The impact of court schedules on the target time-frame

In listing a case for final hearing two principal factors are relevant: when the case will be ready for hearing and when a suitable slot can be made available in the court timetable which key practitioners, essential witnesses and legal representatives can attend.

It was sometimes impossible to gauge, on the basis of documentary evidence alone, how these factors had impacted on an individual case. Even when the researcher was present in court, but not necessarily privy to all the discussions between the parties, or between the parties and court staff, the reason for setting a particular time-frame 'was sometimes obscure. However of the 62 cases in which the first schedule meant the case would exceed 12 weeks, there were 34 in which there was some relevant information. In over a third of these (13) *lack of court time* was the principal determining factor. Only one or two cases in Areas A and B were known to have been held up in this way; but in Area C there were seven (of 11). The lawyer acting for the child in one such case was so incensed he not only raised the matter with the court and with the researchers but wrote to the Court Service Secretariat to complain:

> I have read your charter and as a member of the Children's Panel I wish to draw your attention to the appalling delays in hearing Children Act cases. I have been recently instructed on behalf of (X). All parties would be ready within the 3-month timetable. However the only available dates [at the FPC] for a 3-day case are nearly 4 months [later]. This not only leaves the child in limbo and uncertain about the future but increases the suffering of [mother]. . . . All the professionals and lay people I work with try to minimise the suffering which is necessarily part of proceedings. I am horrified at the way the ideals of the Act are being frustrated by delays. Please draw this to the attention of the necessary authority to attempt to make other courts available to speed up the listing of cases.

The general tenor of this letter was reflected in many of the practitioner interviews we conducted in this area, most of whom identified lack of court time, particularly in the higher courts, as one of the main reasons for overly lengthy proceedings (see Chapter 13). Moreover it was clear from our later judicial interviews that while the problem had been alleviated to some extent as the result of the provision of additional courtrooms and an increased complement of judges, it had not been overcome:

> It's pressure of business and not enough judges. The wait for final hearings is still unacceptable. They may have been brought down but they're still significant. At the moment for a 3–4-day case even if it were ready we couldn't provide a slot in under 4 months.

Although the imbalance between supply and demand would seem to be most severe in Area C, it was not simply a local problem. Indeed the interview material would suggest that the case data under-represent the problems elsewhere. In Area B for instance, we were told:

> There's a problem of finding judges, just having judge time. The judges here are under enormous pressure, they're under-resourced. Particularly when they're moved off from time to time to other courts.

In Area A there was a suggestion that ensuring judicial time was available for care cases was being achieved at the expense of other parts of the court's workload.

Time estimates

In order to list the court needs a reasonably realistic estimate of the duration of the final hearing. Indeed on a number of occasions it was the inability of practitioners to provide this with any degree of confidence which meant that listing was deferred. This was particularly the case in Area C. Gauging how long a case will take before all the evidence is in and before the parties' positions are clear is a very inexact science. As Table 12.4 shows, initial estimates were *accurate in fewer* than three out of every ten cases. For cases listed within four weeks of the first hearing the accuracy rate was as low as one in five rising to no more than two in five for those listed even as late as over 16 weeks.

Table 12.4 *Accuracy of initial time estimates*

	Area A		Area B		Area C		All areas	
	No.	%	No.	%	No.	%	No.	%
Accurate	6	21	14	50	3	13	23	29
Over-estimate	16	55	10	36	19	83	45	56
Under-estimate	7	24	4	14	1	4	12	15
(n=)	(29)		(28)		(23)		(80)	

The fact that, on the basis of an inaccurate initial estimate, cases are booked in for an inappropriate, usually excessive, amount of court time, does not mean, necessarily, that they remain so, although there were some glaring examples of this. As the case proceeds, and its shape becomes clearer, time estimates are frequently readjusted. This is known to have occurred at least once in 35 cases and was commonest in Area A (17) as one might expect, given their practice of early scheduling. None the less since it is on their initial estimate that cases get into the court timetable the effect is that the lists can become unnecessarily clogged for months ahead.

The imbalance between court workload and court time was particularly a problem in Area C. Thus it has to be a matter of concern that this area had an especially low accuracy rate, just over one in ten and that while all three areas tended to over-, rather than under-estimate, this was particularly marked in C. Six cases in this area, for example, were initially estimated to last for five days or more; only one of them did so, while each of the three cases listed for ten days was completed well within this time.

As a result of increasing delays and a high proportion of cases going short, the county court in this area had, cautiously and with some trepidation, returned to the practice of over-listing. So far, we were told, there had been no disasters, probably because there was a sufficient complement of judges to list cases 'back to back'. Elsewhere, such a practice carries a greater risk of final hearings having to be deferred. This risk should be minimised by careful monitoring of the progress of the case. Moreover the availability of lateral transfer and, in High Court cases, the 'fire brigade' judges do provide a safety net of sorts. If the practice of over-listing provisional bookings for final hearings were to be generally returned to, however, which the prevalence of over-estimating the duration of hearings might suggest would be logical, additional safety measures would probably be necessary, such as a pool of deputy or roving county court judges, who could be deployed as and when necessary.

Rescheduling the final hearing

Rescheduling rates

Our pre-Act research revealed that rescheduling final hearings was a fairly common feature of child protection proceedings, although the rate varied by area and type of proceedings. In care proceedings in the juvenile court, for instance, 36% of final hearings (rising to 44% in Area A) did not take place on the date first listed, while 52% of wardship cases were re-listed (rising to 80% in Area B). Therefore although just over a third of the post-Act cases did not make their first listed date, this represents an improvement both over-all and specifically in terms of care proceedings.

Area A had the highest rescheduling rate pre-Act and continued to do so post-Act.[15] Moreover nine of its cases were rescheduled more than once compared to only one or two cases elsewhere. This is not entirely explained by the practice of earlier timetabling. Between them the other areas had seven cases which were listed within the first two weeks; of which six were heard on schedule. Only three of 14 comparative cases in Area A did not have to be relisted. Rather the data tend to suggest that since very early scheduling was unusual in Areas B and C it tended to be used only for the more straight-forward cases which could be relied upon (insofar as this can be said of any care case) not to go off the rails. In contrast, early timetabling in A, being standard practice, was less discriminating and consequently more likely to be disrupted by unforeseen circumstances. It should also be remembered that Area A also tended to set a tighter timetable than the other two areas, which thus allowed less leeway in which any unforeseen developments could be accommodated.

Reasons for rescheduling

Analysis of the 29 sample cases in which adequate information was available revealed that the need for rescheduling arose from one or more of eight different reasons: administrative error (1); late reports from the guardian (1) or other experts (2); non-availability of witnesses (2); late transfer (5); upward revision of time estimates (5); uncertainty or disputes over the care plan (4) and above all the need for assessments (11), particularly new assessments in the light of changing circumstances. Thus it appears it is the *mutability* of care cases which most typically sabotages the timetable. As one judge put it:

> I don't think [timetabling] has worked as it was intended to by statute. I don't think the theory of the draftsmen ever realised that the raw material is human lives and whatever may be the pace of the court the pace of human lives may be more leisurely. Suddenly up pops an uncle and the local authority had better do a 12-week assessment – or mother goes missing or overdoses or whatever and the whole process is aborted for that.

Abortive final hearings

The word rescheduling might be taken to imply a degree of forward planning and this would often be appropriate. However 14 cases had to be re-timetabled because what was expected to be the final hearing did not result in case resolution. We have already referred in earlier chapters to such events in a number of cases: Michelle Symons, where an application for transfer was made on the day the case was expected to proceed; Christopher O'Brien, where having heard two days of evidence the court accepted the need to assess his grandmother as a potential carer and adjourned for a further three months; Sam Phillips, whose mother was able to persuade the court that this time she really did intend to tackle her alcoholism and to allow her time to prove it. Zara Butler's case, however, which was re-listed no fewer than four times, had the dubious distinction of having three *final* hearings.

● ●

At the first hearing, it may be recalled, the court indicated that there should be an assessment of Sandra's ability to parent this latest child. Despite the changes this necessitated in the case plan a final hearing date 11 weeks ahead was set. This was the first slot available for what was estimated to be a three-day case. By this time Zara would be 3 months.

After a month of intensive supervision at home, Zara and Sandra moved into a mother and baby home. Phil's contact was increasing. To allow time to monitor the situation it was agreed to defer the hearing, the judge directing that: 'as soon as people are ready to make a sensible guess at the final hearing, contact listing', in itself scarcely the 'hands-on' approach envisaged by the Act.

The date eventually set was four months later than the original date, with the time estimate subsequently increased to four days. By this point Zara would be over seven months. Phil joined Sandra and Zara in the mother and baby home and for a time it seemed that the family could be kept together. By the time of the revised date, however, Phil had been asked to leave, Sandra's placement had broken down and Zara was in a foster home. The local authority's position was that every effort had been made to support Zara in her family and a full Care Order should now be made, with a view to adoption, their original plan.

Sandra wanted Zara home and was supported by the guardian. At this point Phil was out of the picture. Evidence was heard over four days at the end of which the judge declined to make a final order although he accepted the threshold criteria were met. A third final hearing date was set six weeks ahead, with a time estimate of $1^1/_2$ days. After hearing one day of evidence the judge again declined to make a final order. Among other uncertainties, Phil was again involved and was seeking contact; the judge wished this to be assessed.

Another final hearing was set for 11 weeks later. Zara was now 11 months old. She also had a new sibling, unfortunately born that very day. Proceedings were adjourned for a further two months. This time the hearing went through to completion. The local authority abandoned its care application and accepted a supervision order. Zara had now passed her first birthday.

● ●

The impact of rescheduling on case duration

The impact of rescheduling was considerable, adding on average between 13 weeks (Area C) and 18 weeks (Area B) to proceedings. However, ironically, the differences in duration between cases which did and did not meet the original timetable was smallest in A, the area with the highest rescheduling rate. Moreover the mean duration of all cases there was around 20 weeks. This is actually shorter, by about two weeks, even than cases in the other areas which managed to keep to schedule. Similarly, though, cases in A which did not keep to schedule were substantially longer than those in the same area which did; they were only about a week longer than cases in the other areas which were not rescheduled.

Is it better then to schedule early, perhaps on the basis of very little information and accept a case may need to be re-listed; or wait until the picture is clearer and set a timetable which has a greater prospect of being adhered to?

On balance, the weight of the evidence is *not* in favour of very early listing. In courts which can be fairly flexible about their lists, such as the family proceeding court in Area A, there is no particular need to set the final hearing immediately in order to get into the queue. By delaying listing until the parameters of a case were clearer, thus cutting its rescheduling rate, Area A might have been able to reduce its overall durations. (Of the cases which were not listed until between four to eight weeks after the first hearing, four out of five kept to schedule.) In the other areas, court lists were very much more clogged. Being very discriminating about early listing produced in these courts a very low rescheduling rate, a strategy which would appear to be entirely sensible in such straitened circumstances.

Interim hearings

Scheduling interim hearings

Timetabling was not simply intended to be a matter of fixing the final hearing but of mapping out the points along the way: specifying when evidence should be filed and arranging any other hearings deemed to be necessary. At the point they listed the final hearing in the sample cases the courts did indeed generally set such comprehensive timetables. Examination of the 29 cases which were scheduled within four weeks of the first hearing, for instance, showed that detailed directions were given about evidence in all but seven cases and hearings fixed right through to the final hearing in all but two. As we have seen, however, the majority of cases were not scheduled at the beginning, therefore timetabling was most frequently done in stages. Thus before the final hearing was set it would be more usual to timetable ahead only to the extent of fixing one or two further hearings ahead.

In itself this represents a greater degree of forward planning than was usually evident in wardship. In care proceedings under previous legislation, our previous research would suggest, it was customary to fix at least the date for the next hearing before the case left the courtroom. Necessarily so, indeed, since most cases involved Interim Care Orders, which had to be renewed every 28 days. In wardship cases, however, where there was no time limit on Interim Orders, and proceedings tended to proceed at a far more leisurely pace, it was not unusual for the direction to be given 'case to be listed on the first open date after . . .'.[16] Sometimes that could be some considerable time away.

Children Act Rules require a return date to be set at each hearing[17] and the research data demonstrate that this was almost always done, usually while everyone was still in court. While this could sometimes produce irritating hiatuses in a hearing it was accepted by practitioners as an important means of ensuring the case did not drift, particularly since, as we shall see later, fewer cases were subject to the automatic discipline of interim care orders.[18] Indeed according to one of the judges we interviewed: 'The greatest cause of improvement is the requirement that a case should never be adjourned without another date being fixed.'

From the drift occurring in the few cases where this was not done (amounting to a hiatus of ten weeks in the worst case) and knowledge of pre-Act wardships we would heartily concur with this assessment.

When final hearing dates were rescheduled, of course, any hearings which had already been set to bridge the period between the listing date and the anticipated end date also had to be readjusted. This, plus other unanticipated developments, (for example transfer, illness, conflicting demands on judicial time, unavailability or non-service of evidence) meant that in just over a third of cases at least one interim hearing had to be rescheduled. Taken as a percentage of relevant hearings, the rescheduling rate works out at around one in ten, slightly higher than that noted pre-Act even in wardship and matrimonial proceedings (6–8%) and much higher than in pre-Act care proceedings (1%).

Spacing of interim hearings

Court control under present arrangements is still largely exercised through court hearings. Thus the frequency and the timing of hearings is relevant as an indicator of the court's opportunity to monitor progress.

A number of factors potentially affect the timing of interim hearings. Most important is probably whether or not there are any Interim Care or Supervision Orders in force. The Act allowed a first Interim Order to be made for a maximum eight weeks, double that permissible under the Children and Young Persons Act 1969. Thereafter, orders have to come back for renewal every 28 days. This structure reflects the initial faith in a 12-week time-scale. Thus, the thinking seemed to be, the case would essentially be assembled within the first eight weeks, during which time recall would serve little purpose, waste valuable court time and perhaps give another opportunity for contest. Then the court would check that all was going to plan, make any necessary adjustments and the second four-week order would carry the case to completion.

In practice, since few cases have been able to fit this presumptive time-frame, most cases which are subject to interim care or supervision throughout have had many more than two orders. Thus, as time has gone on, increasing use has been made of the provision, new to care proceedings, whereby renewal may be made without appearance where the circumstances are unchanged provided that, in the family proceedings court at least, the court is notified in writing of the consent of all parties.[19] More than half the sample had at least one order renewed by this means, and almost a third more than one. Indeed a small number of cases, in which everyone was agreed that a period of assessment or monitoring was required, were dealt with by a whole series of such orders.

These two legislative changes mean that, in theory, cases need to appear before the court less frequently than would have been the case under the Children and Young Persons Act 1969. On the other hand, the introduction of the directions hearing,[20] an innovation in care proceedings though a familiar feature of proceedings in the higher courts, potentially has the opposite effect. While directions can be given by the judge or bench taking an interim hearing, the Act also allows them to be made by a single justice, or, most significantly, a Justices' Clerk at a separate hearing.

Thus there can be two distinct strands running through care proceedings, one dealing with substantive matters, the other with process issues. These strands may remain distinct throughout, they may be run in tandem or, typically, they may at times run together and at others separately. Hence while some hearings are clearly substantive and others clearly directions, some hearings may be both. In non-observed cases the court documentation alone did not always allow us to differentiate.

The mean number of *attendable* hearings in our sample cases was between five and six. Over two-thirds of cases had between four and eight such hearings with under a fifth having three or fewer and just over a tenth having nine or more. Areas A and B both had cases with 14 hearings; the maximum in Area C being 11. Without the provision to renew orders by post, however, between one and two hearings on average would have been added to each case, the proportion with three or fewer dropping to around a tenth, those with nine or more rising to over two-fifths. In Area C an additional five cases would have needed to go before the court on nine or more occasions while in Area B one case would have appeared 25 rather than 14 times.

The *number* of interim hearings, of course, reflects in large part the duration of the case. A more useful measure, as far as the issue of court control is concerned, is therefore the *frequency* of hearings. Huge variation was apparent between individual cases in this respect, from every 17 days to every nine weeks. However, on average, cases came back to court for an attendable hearing every 33 days, rather more frequently than this in Area A (every 29 days), less frequently in C (34) and B (35) This is much less frequent than found in pre-Act care proceedings, where the mean interval between hearings was 24 days, but it is considerably more frequent than was customary in wardship (72).

Whatever their frequency in a case overall, hearings tended to be unevenly distributed, clustering towards the beginning of proceedings. Thus within the first eight weeks three in five cases had three or more attendable hearings, with a mean interval of 20 days between each appearance. Moreover this frequency was not simply a matter of inserting directions hearings between the first hearing and the hearing eight weeks later to renew any interim orders. Only six cases (10% of relevant cases) had initial interim care or supervision orders made for the maximum permitted period, the average being 33 days.[21] Indeed in over a fifth of cases the initial order was made for less than 28 days, the maximum permissible under the old Children and Young Persons Act legislation.

At the other end of the proceedings we understand from judicial interviews that pre-trial reviews held within the last few weeks before the final hearing are increasingly becoming standard practice, as urged by the Children Act Advisory Committee.[22] At the time the sample cases went through the courts, however, this was fairly unusual, only four cases being specifically listed in this way, all in Area A. It is true that over three-quarters passed within the court's purview for the penultimate time within four weeks of completion and a third within two weeks. However in many instances this involved only an automatic review of interim orders rather than an occasion when all the parties and their representatives were assembled to satisfy the court that the case was ready for hearing. Usually, moreover, the guardian's report would not be available by this point and certainly not a paginated bundle of evidence, as stipulated by the Committee; nor, generally, would the hearing be taken by the trial judge/Bench.

From the evidence in this study we would strongly recommend that pre-trial hearings become a standard part of all cases still contested, not simply those cases which are listed for five days or more.[23] Had all the sample cases been subject to such scrutiny it seems likely that in at least some, such as Michelle's, the fact that the final hearing was likely to prove abortive would have become apparent, enabling court time to be released for other cases and sparing the family a good deal of anguish.

The submission of evidence

The pace at which cases can progress through the legal system depends in no small measure on the evidence being submitted. Thus controlling the point at which written statements and reports are filed, as well as whether they should be filed at all, was envisaged as a vital weapon in the court's armoury. As far as care proceedings are concerned it represents another innovation, since under the Children and Young Persons Act 1969 most evidence was oral, there was no obligation on any party to disclose in advance, and it was not unusual for reports to be unseen by other parties until the day of the hearing.[24] While such practices were certainly unjust and might on occasion produce delays, on the whole they allowed for the relatively swift disposal of cases. In wardship and matrimonial proceedings, however, where advance disclosure of the predominantly written evidence was customary, time had to be allowed for the preparation, swearing and exchange of affidavits and, as was common practice, the submission of further affidavits in response. Submission dates were usually quite generous, on average about 28 days, so that when filing was sequential, considerable periods of time could elapse.[25]

Our research into pre-Act wardships, both in this project and in the 1993 *Local Authority Wardships* study,[26] shows that it was comparatively unusual for leave to be given to file evidence unaccompanied by a filing date (around a fifth in both studies) although about two-fifths of cases had at least one direction which was not time-constrained. The data from the post-Act sample show that this aspect of proceedings has been further tightened up: in three-quarters of cases all directions regarding evidence were time constrained while less than one in ten of all such directions were not subject to time limits.

Compliance rates have also improved though perhaps not as much as might have been hoped. In the pre-Act wardship sample almost half (49%) the filing directions were not complied with and all such directions were complied with in only one in ten cases. Post-Act the non-compliance rate has dropped to 39% although the number of cases in which all filing dates were met remains disappointingly small (11, 13%). These proportions were broadly similar across all three areas. Fortunately much of the late evidence was late only by days and its effect was usually to penalise the other parties by reducing their opportunity to consider the latest statement rather than to delay the court process by rendering the hearing ineffective. None the less, there were at least six sample hearings which were ineffective or had to be adjourned due to non-submission of evidence and, as we shall see in Chapter 13, many more cases where problems in gathering evidence unduly prolonged the court process.

Who were the culprits? Of the 183 late submissions for which we have details 98 (53%) were from 'professional' sources and 85 (32%) from the families concerned. As parents and other relatives put in far less evidence than the professionals involved (218 statements as against 904) this represents a far higher proportion of late submissions by the parents (45% as against 11%) and confirms practitioner comments about the difficulties parents and hence those working with and representing them had in working within the confines of court schedules. Two-thirds of late 'professional' evidence (65) was from local authority social workers and a quarter from psycho-medical sources (24). This meant that about one in five social work statements were late and one in ten psycho-medical reports. Reasons included 'administrative error'; sickness, leave or changes in employment; parental 'confusion', and solicitors not having received directions from their agents or the court. By far the commonest reason given for late family evidence was difficulty in obtaining instructions.

The Guardian ad Litem's report

Guardians are constrained by the court's timetable as much as other court users. The Rules give them a new duty to file a full report at least seven days before the final hearing although in a majority of the sample cases the court also made a specific direction. On the whole the guardians in the study areas met court deadlines and when they did fail had good reasons. Thirteen final guardian reports (16%) were not submitted by their required date. These were spread evenly between the court areas. In some of these cases we know the reasons for delay: in at least two cases, extensions were requested by the guardian due to late receipt of expert evidence, in another delay in receipt of the social worker's statement. Another guardian had her recommendations ready for the pre-trial review though the full report was not ready for another two days. The mean delay was 4.4 days, with a range of one to ten days. There was no case where the guardian's report was not available for a scheduled final hearing nor where such a hearing was deferred because of late submission.

Time-limits were also set by the court for the filing of 23 interim reports from the guardian and for 12 supplementary reports. About a third of these are known not to have been met but again information seems to have been available in time for the relevant hearings. Some guardians made a practice of filing further interim reports without any court direction to bring the court up to date at hearings.

The data thus indicate that the guardian panels in these areas have generally been able to maintain their pre-Act standards of timeliness. Since in all care cases guardians now perform the welfare reporting role taken in pre-Act wardships by the court welfare officer or occasionally the Official Solicitor this too can be seen as an overall improvement. In most of our pre-Act cases it was customary for the final hearing date to be determined by the point at which the welfare report could be ready while in those for which a filing date was set it was exceptional for that date to be met.

Court control and the prevention of drift

Judicial perspectives

The rationale behind requiring the court to exercise greater control over case progress was that this would help to eliminate drift and thus reduce unwanted delay. We were therefore concerned to discover how this strategy was rated by those responsible for implementing it.

First of all, was court control seen to be necessary? The answer to this, unequivocally, was yes, with several respondents commenting on the inherent vulnerability of these cases to entropy:

> I think the Woolf proposals may be going too far for ordinary cases but as far as family matters are concerned it's extremely important for the judge to keep tabs on the case. Delay is very easy to achieve, you've got to concentrate constantly.

> We are erecting the scaffolding around a case for it to go to a final tribunal and unless we've bolted everything very firmly into its appropriate place the whole edifice is going to collapse or at least creak very badly.

Those with experience of pre-Act wardships also admitted that though the High Court might have had similar powers of control as are now bestowed upon all courts they were exercised rather loosely:

> The court had the power and the responsibility but it wasn't identified.
> I suppose the word is discipline which has been promoted by this regime which wasn't the case before.

Given this change in the climate of litigation have the mechanisms established under the Act proved helpful? On the whole again the answer was yes. Are they sufficient? Are they effective? Here views were rather more mixed.

A great deal, it seems, depends on how robust the individual judge or clerk is prepared to be. Temperamentally, the interviews suggested, the exercise of control over a case comes more naturally to some people than others. This was borne out in our court observation where we noted considerable differences in the extent of control and the balance of power between the court and practitioners. Having a reputation among legal practitioners as a tough judge or magistrate may not make one the most popular person on the circuit but it greatly facilitates the exercise of authority. As one judge put it:

> As long as you have strong interventionist judges then you can accommodate what I call the outside difficulties, e.g. the expert who doesn't give his report in due time. It's calling people to account, saying why isn't it ready? When is it going to be ready? Or substituting someone else.

Court control, such comments suggest, can be an effective strategy. Thus opportunities to share ideas of good practice are vital. However, as Dame Margaret Booth pointed out, while training in case management and control is essential 'it is not always on offer.'[27]

Other, less personalised, enabling factors were also identified, among them *judicial continuity*. As we commented at the end of Chapter 9, although there was a range of views about the importance of this, the balance of opinion was very much that discontinuity reduces the capacity of the court to maintain ongoing control, leaving too much latitude to the parties to manipulate the situation. One district judge who felt particularly strongly on the issue told us:

> I would like things allocated to specific judges then you could really run things which was the intention, they're court-led proceedings. Then if someone comes along and says we want to explore this avenue you would hopefully have read and understood why that would be appropriate and why it would not. You wouldn't be reliant on the advocate and what they're telling you. . . . If you're growing up with it you would be formulating your views on what needs to be pursued and if you had an application you could quite easily say why do you need that, I don't think it's necessary, and I'm not going to give you leave. There is a tendency to try and argue something before one judge, find it fails then next time you can try again and perhaps it will succeed. That has the effect not only of increasing the costs of the whole thing but of perhaps knocking it off its line. It's very easy to go off at a tangent and then find you're up a blind alley and you have to come all the way back.

The degree to which continuity was an objective of local practice, however, indeed whether it was seen as being in any measure achievable, varied considerably, in part reflecting local organisational differences. In one area, for instance, cases were commonly reserved to particular judges and district judges, indeed one judge who was particularly convinced of the importance of continuity regularly arranged to fit in hearings on *his* cases even when he was sitting elsewhere. Elsewhere reserving cases was explicitly discouraged by the court administration because it reduced overall flexibility.

However this issue might be resolved in the future, a degree of discontinuity may be unavoidable. Exercising control in those circumstances, therefore, several interviewees were convinced, depends on being on top of the case. Ideally, this entails being able to read the papers in advance of directions hearings as well as final hearings. This is a requirement in the magistrates' court.[28] Some of the professional judiciary also told us they made great efforts to do this and a few that they normally managed it.

In reality, given the demands on judicial time, the size and disorder of some court files makes this an objective more likely to be honoured in the breach than the observance. Indeed, outrageous as this may seem to a lay person, even before final hearings, most judges told us, they can often only get the gist of a case and have to rely on opening statements, seizing opportunities to read crucial documents later. Getting to grips with every case before a 30 minutes directions hearing, particularly if you haven't seen the case before and may not see it again, is not, many would say, a practical proposition. Ensuring that those handling interim hearings do have adequate reading time is, of course, an obvious solution. Failing that, we would agree that, as one district judge urged, keeping a meticulous file log is a very practicable second best:

> The only way I can keep up to speed is to keep a file log. When I look at that I know exactly where I am. . . . When I'm making notes I'm reporting to myself; I don't even put down the directions, they go on a separate sheet, I put down why I'm doing it, what activity I expect to happen at the next appointment. . . . It only has to be a few lines on each topic. And if we're having experts coming in I say why, and if we're having an assessment again I put down what we are seeking to address in the assessment.

> Those diary sheets are abused or overlooked and in my view they are far more important than people realise. It produces a continuity in the mind of the tribunal which is absolutely crucial because if a case is going to lose direction it certainly isn't going to be helped by the helmsman being completely at sea. And of course if I'm on leave or called away unexpectedly another judge picking it up is going to say what on earth is going on here if that is blank. If I've filled it out at least he can see where I think the case is going and if I've had it more than once he can see what I've done each time.

In this area there was a particularly strong sense of group identity among the district judges. More generally, working as a team, communicating with each other, feeling confident in the approach of other members of the team (a theme which emerged very strongly among the district judges interviewed) helped to maintain continuity of management even when continuity of adjudication could not be achieved. Good communication with the trial judges was also seen as crucial, though sadly not always achieved, so that the decisions made at directions hearings would result in an acceptable case package.

Implementation of all these suggestions would help to ensure that the court is able to keep control of a case through the decisions made at interim hearings. Though this is vital, a number of interviewees had also come to appreciate that this was not enough – control also had to be exercised effectively *between* hearings rather than, as often at present, 'once a file is shut and the case goes back to the filing cabinet we don't see it until the next hearing'. Thus one district judge told us:

> I would like to see the court being in a position to have someone whose responsibility it is to keep a diary on a daily basis, of what should have been filed today and if it isn't filed by 4 p.m., tomorrow morning the phone starts ringing to see why not. It may be there is another way but I have got a bee in my bonnet about this.

In one of the family proceedings courts, the Justices' Clerk was exploring how this might be done:

> [That's] one of the things we are looking at at the moment, the question of policing directions, having a comprehensive check before hearings to see whether directions are complied with and then for there to be chase up procedures. In some of the smaller FPCs that is managed because of the number of cases. We are looking at whether we can do that.

The combination of the episodic[29] approach to care cases and judicial discontinuity undermines the principle of court control. In addition to the suggestions already made we would therefore recommend that the feasibility of allocating each case to an individual case officer should be investigated. This person, who would need to be a designated court clerk or district judge, would retain oversight of the case throughout, ensure compliance with court directions and deal with any issues arising between hearings. It would be vital for the case officer to have adequate administrative support. One judge who had managed to put a system of case monitoring into operation and was convinced of its value, stressed that this was the key issue:

I instituted a mechanism for very crude monitoring. When an order was made that a report should be prepared within a certain time someone checks that it's filed. Come the 25th May, whatever, the guardian should have given a report, and it's not there. You list it before the judge, say by the 30th, to have an explanation as to why not. Or the consultant psychiatrist or any other discipline, you find if they have to come along and explain why they defaulted, it doesn't happen again and you keep to the timetable.

That involved part-time use of a clerk, whose services I obtained because I streamlined the system whereby orders were drafted, I got counsel to do all that. So it meant that court staff weren't doing it and they were released to do other things. But I found the saving was appropriated by the LCD [Lord Chancellor's Department]. We do not get the support we need for this type of case.

Moreover administrative support, others urged, is not just a matter of bodies on the ground but being able to rely on the expertise developed through the accumulation of experience in family work:

I had a paper recently on listing. It was brilliant but my heart sinks; it talks of keeping a listing officer in post for a minimum of 3 months; we're managing it here for 3 years. Every time you change a listing officer it's chaos. . . . We had a very very bad patch . . . when we had a listing officer who didn't understand the priority of children's cases. . . . In the end the court's administrator came to my rescue and now [X and Y] are doing it. They talk to the people in the magistrates' court, they get to know the case, when they ring me up about a particular case they are able to tell me a bit about it and I remember.

The general thrust of judicial opinion, then, would seem to be that the mechanisms for exercising court control are helpful and a considerable improvement on what went before. They can be made more effective where the person charged with exercising that control is confident in exerting his authority, is well-informed about the progress of the case to date and there are well-supported systems in place to check on progress between hearings.

What also emerged very strongly, however, was that the manageability of the court's task is significantly affected by how practitioners approach theirs. Sound pre-hearing preparation by individual practitioners, good advance discussion between the sides and timely liaison with the court, all facilitating factors, unfortunately cannot always be relied on:

What more needs to be done? Far and away advocates negotiating with their clients, speaking to their clients and their witnesses and generally doing what they should have done prior to the hearing.

They don't seem to have given any thought before they get to court what they will be asking the court to do and they haven't corresponded with each other either. It's unlike any other form of civil litigation, they just don't seem to communicate. I've said on many occasions there are things like telephones and fax machines or you could even write a letter.

Alongside these critical comments, however, a number of judicial interviews gave some grounds for optimism not only that there is also good practice, particularly among specialist lawyers, but that attitudes are changing as a result of the Act:

It's the advocates for the parties who are more aware of the delay principle as well. In wardship the court may have been concerned that these things shouldn't go to sleep but now delay is looked upon as something very bad and everyone knows they have to get on at a great rate of knots.

In the next section we look at what practitioners had to say on these issues.

Court control: the practitioner response

It took some time for practitioners to get used to the idea that the court had a management role but that's more recognised and accepted now. (Judge)

Practitioner interviews revealed general support for the principle of court control and for timetabling and directions hearings as the mechanisms through which this should be exercised. The frequent use of words such as *focus, concentrate, discipline, structure* reflects what appears to be a near consensus that the new framework does offer a means of keeping both courts and practitioners 'on their toes' and preventing cases 'going to sleep'. The odd cavalier comment, such as 'if you're not ready what is the court going to do but shout' was all the more shocking because of its rarity. There was a much greater spread of opinion, however, as to whether courts were actually exercising control, whether things were being tightened up or slackening, old ways being overcome or slipped back into. A few comments demonstrate the range of opinion encountered:

I think we've all slid back into our old ways, everyone is firmly back in control of that one, the court has given up. I think they did initially take it seriously but when everyone says we're not ready they say well . . .

Locally there is immense respect for time limits.

> They haven't been exercising control until recently. People don't stick to timetables.

The commonest response was that the courts were making an effort but the material suggested the picture was very patchy, with variation in each area between court levels and individuals. In none of the research areas was there general agreement that the courts at all levels were exerting themselves equally, with a number of practitioners specifically commenting on differences between the family proceedings court and the higher courts, although there was no common view as to which was more likely to exercise effective control. Many practitioners, echoing judicial opinion and our own observations, also commented on the importance of the individual and their experiences of different approaches:

> If you've got a good clerk who can grapple with the case things can progress quite speedily. If you haven't unfortunately no.

> It depends on the person in charge. Some district judges are more laid back than others.

The interviews also reflected different perceptions of the appropriateness of the control exercised. Here there were more suggestions that the level of court at which the case was heard was important, with several practitioners commenting that the higher courts were more able to tailor the approach to the case, the magistrates doing it more 'by the book'. The family proceedings court in one area in particular were said to have been somewhat over-zealous in the early days:

> The magistrates went too far to start with . . . it took a lot of effort to persuade them that the delay principle was not a tablet of stone and that the timetable should fit the case.

Again, however, opinion was not unanimous:

> If you are before a district judge he will be less likely to listen to what you have agreed, he will have his own opinion and he will tell you what he wants whereas with the magistrates everything has been sorted out before you go in; you've agreed and that's what you get. It does mean that with the DJ you sometimes get a timetable you don't want and which is unrealistic. You then have to go back at the end of the time and explain you've done your best. I find that is easier than arguing at the time because once they've made their mind up they're not going to change.

Thus we might infer that the acceptability of the principle of court control is linked to *how* that control is exercised, particularly whether timetables are set in consultation with practitioners taking due account of the needs of the individual case. A court which unilaterally and consistently set unrealistic timetables would be likely to provoke token compliance if not outright resistance.

In exercising their managerial function, then, the courts have to operate a fine discretion so that realism does not slide into slackness, consultation into abdication of responsibility or getting a firm grip on a case become oppressive and counter-productive.

As commented earlier, the weight of practitioner opinion would seem to be that on the whole the courts in our study areas had been trying, even if to varying degrees, to discharge their managerial responsibilities. How successful have those efforts been?

> My daughter, when she is at home during her vacation, is wonderful at preparing a chart of the way she will do her work on holiday. She does it extremely neatly and extremely tidily and with coloured patterns all round it and plans it all out and nothing really comes of it. I think, sometimes, it's the same with timetabling . . . the actual overall effect on the way the case is run isn't greatly different. (Private practice solicitor)

Again, there was a great deal of variation among respondents but, the answer seems to be, on balance more successful than not. Timetables are broadly rather than meticulously kept to and may have to be re-adjusted but are not normally completely flouted. Evidence rarely comes in on the day it is due, but will be days rather than weeks late. Moreover, many practitioners emphasised, timekeeping is a good deal better than it used to be in wardship:

> Dates in directions are often missed, there's no doubt about that, reports and statements are frequently filed late but the fact that there is a discipline of a timetable is good otherwise things would come even later. I remember one particular wardship. . . . Every time there was a hearing a motorcycle courier would arrive at 3 p.m. with a massive affidavit and the hearing would be adjourned for months. We would file an affidavit and the same thing would happen next time. That doesn't happen now. Days late is common now, weeks occasionally but often if there is slippage there is good reason.

Moreover, this lawyer went on, 'people know they have to justify it'. Several other practitioners, however, saw the problem arising precisely because tardiness was not challenged:

I have a client who nothing in this world will convince if the court says a particular date it's got to be then. Life is done at his pace. But I haven't had any difficulty if it's late, I just send it in. You know the people in the court are too busy and without any reference to dates they won't pick it up.

People are a bit naughty about producing their statements, not to the extent that it becomes a problem . . . I haven't had hearings wasted because a statement isn't there. But there is a bit of a slippage. The court doesn't do anything about it; you don't get bollocked for being late; that's why they're late.

Such comments suggest that were the expectation of being called to account to apply to all courts in every case the problem of slippage might be more effectively dealt with.

The case management role of the Guardian ad Litem

In care proceedings under the Children and Young Persons Act 1969 the Guardian ad Litem already had a dual role: representative of the child and reporting officer to the court. The Children Act adds a third dimension: guardians are now expected to advise the court on matters relating to case management, including timetabling.[30]

Interviews with lawyers revealed that this new aspect to the role was not perceived to have had a significant impact. Although as usual there were some notable exceptions (and one panel in particular seemed to be rather more active in this respect) for the most part, responses were along the lines of: 'I've not seen the guardian particularly take the upper hand in timetabling and certainly not over the others involved.'

Some told us they had not even been aware of the new expectations while others had a vague memory but were not conscious of very much happening in practice. Even in talking to the guardians themselves there was little sense that they had embraced their new responsibilities with gusto.

In the interval between our interviews with practitioners and those with the judiciary the Social Services Inspectorate organised a series of regional conferences devoted to case management.[31] If these have had any widespread impact it was not, however, apparent. At all levels of court and in all areas the responses hardly varied: 'I'm not aware of it', 'It isn't happening', 'I haven't noticed that'.

Typically this was not voiced as a criticism. Indeed, even those who would like to see the guardians taking a more active part were often at pains to express their appreciation of the difficulty of the task or the quality of the service otherwise offered. Most interviewees, however, perhaps particularly in the higher courts, saw case management as the court's responsibility, into which the guardian would have an input, but often no more than anyone else. There were thus two recurrent themes, first that case management by the guardian was unnecessary because it *was* being done by the court; second that it was inappropriate because it *ought* to be done by the court. Such doubts about the necessity and legitimacy of the guardian having a special responsibility for case management echo those voiced in our earlier interviews with practitioners. There, however, the emphasis was less on the primacy of the court's role than on the contribution of the other participants:

> I wouldn't have thought that was exclusively a guardian's role. I don't get the sense that the guardian is there cracking the whip. It's more the clerk and generally everyone has in mind no delay if possible. (Lawyer)

> Everyone is aware of delay. Sometimes I find myself arguing about it but mostly the avoidance of delay has just become part of the thinking so guardians haven't had to take a leading role. (Guardian)

In addition a number of lawyers, including some who regularly worked with guardians, were dubious that the role was appropriate or manageable:

> It's asking too much to expect the guardian to do the work and police the case at the same time.

> It's not appropriate for them, they need to stand apart.

Among both lawyers and the judiciary, however, there were a few voices regretting that guardians were not the linchpins the Act envisaged them being:

> The guardian's role doesn't appear to be very pro-active. I think it ought to be. I would like to see them undertake a more positive and pre-emptive role in directions appointments. At the moment they are a participant and tend to comment on case strategies rather than making suggestions of their own. It is all a commentary rather than a leadership role. Bearing in mind that the child is the most important person in the case they ought to adopt a more pro-active and leading role. They should state right at the start of a directions appointment and indeed before, so that all parties know: we expect this and why and if you don't like it you can tell the judge. (District judge)

As noted in an earlier chapter, guardians are new players in the lawyer-dominated higher courts. Issues of status, power, perhaps even gender, may well have affected both the guardians, inhibiting the vigorous exercise of their new responsibilities, and the courts, in not actively encouraging such a development. Certainly a number of lawyers as well as guardians suggested that the role did not carry the same kudos as it did in the magistrates' court. It is important to note, therefore, that guardian case management seemed to be no more in evidence in the family proceedings court, where, we were told, for example: 'I haven't noticed any difference to be honest' and 'They're not doing it as much as we hoped they would.'

If this idea is to be persisted with, therefore, it would seem, more needs to be done, and not only in terms of assisting guardians themselves to work on this aspect of their role. Were guardians to become part of a court-based service this element in their role might become more acceptable and practicable. Indeed one might even envisage them becoming part of a case management team. Pending this, the creation of a single referral point in the person of a case officer, as suggested earlier, could help to build closer and more effective partnership between the individual guardian and the court.

However the clear message to emerge from both sets of interviews is that effective management of a care case has to be a *collaborative* effort. If ever there was an area where joint training is required, this is surely it. For maximum effect we would recommend that this should take place at a local level but with considerable non-local input.

Summary

The Act gave the court the duty and power to set and monitor a timetable for the case. Early timetabling was encouraged. In practice very early through timetabling proved to be unusual in the sample cases and was common practice in only one area.

The rescheduling rate was lower than in pre-Act cases, even in care proceedings. The earlier the timetable was set the more likely it was to be subsequently revised. This reflects the uncertainty surrounding most of the cases coming to the care courts and their mutability. Cases listed four and eight weeks after the start were more likely to keep to timetable though one in five still had to be rescheduled.

The practice which most nearly meshes with the needs of care cases would be to fix a moderately early provisional and comprehensive through timetable, adjusting as necessary. Unfortunately court lists, particularly in the higher courts, are generally too over-burdened to make this a practicable proposition at present. Lack of court time, rather than the needs of the case, too often determined the pace of proceedings, sabotaging the intentions of the Act.

The requirement that a case should not leave court until a return date was set was almost always complied with and was reported to be highly effective in preventing drift. However the time limits on Interim Care and Supervision Orders were not found to provide an appropriate time-frame for most cases.

Pre-trial reviews were not a regular feature of the sample proceedings although there was evidence that recently they have become more common. The research supports the recommendations of the Children Act Advisory Committee that they should become a routine part of contested proceedings.

Greater control was exercised over the timetabling of evidence post-Act than was apparent in pre-Act wardships and compliance rates have also improved. Parental evidence was the most commonly late submission though tardy social work statements could present a problem for guardians completing their reports.

Court control of the pace of proceedings was intended to be the key strategy in the prevention of delay. The principle was widely welcomed by the judiciary and generally accepted by practitioners. The mechanisms established for the exercise of control were seen as appropriate. Interviews revealed, however, that implementation of the strategy was patchy, with inconsistency between and within courts in the firmness and appropriateness of the control exercised. It is clear that the judiciary need assistance to hone their case management skills.

Judicial discontinuity seriously undermines the concept of court control. The negative effects of unavoidable discontinuity would be somewhat mitigated if there were sufficient time for reading the case papers before a hearing, if comprehensive notes of previous decisions were kept and if there were good liaison within the judicial team. It is further recommended that the feasibility of allocating each case to a case officer should be investigated. This officer, a court clerk or district judge, would retain oversight of the case throughout, ensure compliance with court directions and deal with any issues arising between hearings.

It is vital that the judiciary are supported by an efficient and properly resourced court administration, whose staff are allowed to remain long enough to become skilled and command practitioners' respect.

The guardian's case management role has not developed to the extent anticipated with some confusion evident as to its meaning and opinion divided as to its appropriateness or feasibility. Joint training for guardians, court clerks and district judges might enable this particular strategy to move forward.

It was evident that the effectiveness of court control depends critically on practitioners, both individually and jointly, playing their part. Deficiencies were reported in case preparation, inter-party communication and liaison with the court. A more hands-on approach by the court should effect some change. The expectation of being called to account may be a more effective sanction than is commonly thought. Practitioners also need to incorporate the goal of efficient case management into their practice and strive to develop ways of working which are more appropriately collaborative without being collusive. The need for joint training was glaringly apparent.

NOTES

[1] Children Act 1989 Section 32(1) re S31 and Section 11(1) re S8 applications.

[2] *Children Act Advisory Committee Annual Report* 1991–92. LCD.

[3] Plotnikoff J (1992): *The Timetabling of Care Proceedings before the Children Act*. HMSO.

[4] DoH (1992): *Manual of Management for GALRO Panel Managers*. HMSO.

[5] Law Commission Report No. 172, para 4.57.

[6] E.g. compare Davis's description of ancillary relief. Davis G (1994): Simple Quarrels. *Family Law*, 323.

[7] Lord Elwyn Jones (HL Deb, 20 Dec 1988, Vol. 502, Col. 1253) proposed a clause stating that the court had power to commit for contempt anyone not adhering to the timetable. This was rejected on the grounds that the courts have that power anyway and there was no desire to give prominence to powers of punishment. White R et al. (1995): *The Children Act in Practice*. 2nd edition. Butterworths.

[8] Re G (Children's Cases: Instruction of Experts) [1994] 2 FCR 106.

[9] The Honourable Mr Justice Wall: B v B (Practice Judgement) [1994] 1 FCR 805.

[10] Re MD and TD (Children's Cases: Time Estimates) [1994] 2 FCR 94.

[11] B v B 1994 1 FCR 811.

[12] Case Management [1995] 1 All ER 586.

[13] Lord Justice Woolf (1996): *Access to Justice*. HMSO.

[14] In the extensive study, with its much larger sample, the mean interval between the first hearing and the listing point was also eight weeks. Thomas C; Hunt J (1996): *The Care Workloads of the Civil Courts under the Children Act*. Centre for Socio-Legal Studies, University of Bristol.

[15] The extensive survey (Thomas and Hunt (1996): op. cit) confirms variation between areas in the extent of rescheduling. However while Area C still had the lowest rate (35%), Area B was highest (48%), Area A being intermediate (42%). Since this intensive study covers only child protection applications, while the extensive study includes a wider range, it is possible that Area B was differentiating between the types of case.

[16] Hunt J (1993): *Local Authority Wardships before the Children Act: The Baby or the Bathwater?* HMSO.

[17] FPC (CA1989) Rules 1991 r15(5); FPR 1991 r4.15(2).

[18] Brasse G (1994): A Tightly Run Procedure? Interim Care Orders under strain. *Family Law*, 261.

[19] r28 Family Proceedings Courts (Children Act 1989) Rules 1991 SI 1395 and r4.14(7) Family Proceedings Rules 1991 SI 2067.

[20] r14 FPCR; r4 FPR.

[21] The extensive survey (Thomas and Hunt (1996): op. cit.) confirms that few first orders were made for the maximum duration though the proportion was slightly higher (15%) and their mean durations longer (4.8 weeks).

[22] In its 1993–94 report the Committee advised that there should always be a final directions hearing approximately two weeks before the substantive hearing. This should be conducted by the judge or clerk who will preside. The guardian's report, chronology and paginated bundle should be available at the hearing which should be attended by all relevant parties and their advocates.

[23] Practice Direction: Case Management [1995] 1 All ER 586.

[24] In the course of the Representation of the Child in the Civil Courts Research Project, the research team observed several hundred hearings in ten juvenile courts, 1985–86 (Murch et al. 1991).

[25] Hunt (1993): op. cit.

[26] Hunt (1993): op. cit.

[27] Dame Margaret Booth (1996): *Avoiding Delay in Children Act Cases*. LCD .

[28] FPC (CA 1989), r 21(3). See also S v Merton London Borough [1994] 1 FCR 186 and M v C (Children Orders: Reasons) [1993] 2 FLR 584.

[29] King M (1995): Law's Healing of Children's Hearings: the paradox moves north. *Journal of Social Policy*, 24(3).

[30] Family Proceedings Courts (Children Act 1989) Rules 1991, r11.

[31] Reported in: *Practice in Progress 1994: the A-Z of Case Management*. Irchin.

13 Roadblocks and diversions: the phenomenon of delay

Delay prior to the Children Act: the need for Section 1(2)

Recognising the problem

> In any proceedings in which any question with respect to the upbringing of a child arises, the court shall have regard to the principle that any delay in determining the question is likely to prejudice the welfare of the child.[1]

Delay in the legal process has a long if dishonourable history in the UK, as anyone familiar with the novels of Dickens will be aware. It is, however, only relatively recently that the issue has become a focus for public policy concerns and the extent to which delay has become endemic properly appreciated.[2]

Before the Children Act there were no nationally collected data on the duration of children's cases. A number of research studies,[3] however, suggested that delay was pervasive across a wide range of proceedings and in care proceedings the evidence began to mount. A study for the Child Care Law Review, for instance, revealed that between 1983 and 1985 there was a growth in the use of successive Interim Care Orders.[4] Other research showed that over the period 1983–86 certain types of proceedings, particularly those involving the abuse or neglect of children under 5, had become substantially longer[5] and a follow-up study showed a further slowing down over the next three years.[6] Events in Cleveland not only revealed how the juvenile court had seized up dramatically, but showed the chronic delays existing even before the crisis occurred.[7]

The adverse effect of prolonged legal proceedings has been a recurring theme both in official reports[8] and in the literature on delay. For children involved in public law proceedings it was seen to be particularly detrimental. The *Review of Child Care Law*,[9] for instance, stressed the unsettling effects of prolonged uncertainty and the likelihood that the child would be subject to a series of short-term placements. The Law Commission[10] underlined the difference between a child's and an adult's sense of time. Lynch and Roberts, in their follow-up study of abused and neglected children, discovered that children who did well were less likely to have experienced protracted proceedings.[11] Our own research into representation in care proceedings uncovered several cases where it was evident that delay had compounded the child's or the family's difficulties.[12] The principle that delay is damaging to children was also underpinned by a venerable body of literature on attachment and separation,[13] plus more recent studies on the uncertainties of local authority care,[14] the withering of family links the longer children remain in care[15] and the diminishing likelihood of their return home as the weeks pass.[16]

Research into the causes of delay suggested a complex interplay of multiple factors both within and outside the court's control,[17] which might be variously susceptible to specific remedial strategies. Studies both here and in the United States, however, also highlighted the significance of the local legal culture in shaping attitudes to delay and expectations of normative pace.[18] Thus it was argued there was a need not only to devise remedies for particular ills but to create a climate inimical to delay.[19] Expressing their concern right at the start of the process which was eventually to produce the Children Act, the House of Commons Social Services Committee concluded that:

> What would help most would be a more widespread recognition of the evils attendant on uncertainty and a sense of urgency from all involved.[20]

Section 1(2), therefore symbolises official recognition not only that delay *was* a problem but that an important part of the solution lay in ensuring that courts and practitioners became more *delay conscious*, thus creating a climate in which the law's delays were no longer tolerated. The concept of the managerial court was to give concrete effect to this strategy. As the Law Commission put it:

> The most effective practical action which can be taken to remedy matters is to place a clear obligation upon the court to oversee the progress of the case.[21]

'For the first time', the Minister of State for Health confidently pronounced, 'there will be a means of ensuring that children's cases are dealt with expeditiously.'[22]

Much of this chapter will be concerned with examining how effective the Act has been in preventing delay. We look first, however, at the enormity of the task which all those concerned with the operation of public child care law were, for the first time, officially set.

The slowing down of legal processes

'A system with a huge inherent potential for dislocation, disorder and drift. A process being increasingly and apparently inexorably slowed down by the operation of a number of powerful forces'. Such was our conclusion as the result of many years involvement with public law cases prior to the Act.[23]

First there was the *nature* of the cases coming before the courts and the *process* by which they arrived there. The life circumstances of the families involved were usually characterised by a high degree of turbulence. Most proceedings were precipitated by a crisis and increasingly preceded by a Place of Safety Order, often of very short duration, giving little time for either the family or the agency to take stock. Thus many cases arrived in court in a volatile, contentious and raw state. For social services, as well as for the court, decision-making was contingent on developments *during* the case rather than simply preceding it, and the legal process was all too often thrown off course, as legal and welfare professionals had to react to unforeseen events. The speed with which many cases proceeded from precipitating crisis to a court hearing meant that families would almost certainly be in a state of shock in which it was understandable that some failed to instruct solicitors until proceedings were well advanced. Even where the progress towards court was more measured, a major determinant in the local authority's decision to seek compulsory powers would usually be the level of parental co-operation. Wielding the big stick by instituting proceedings very often would not dramatically alter this attitude.

Then there was the increasing *complexity* of the cases. As our understanding of the ways adults can mistreat children has expanded,[24] from battered babies and dirty houses to emotional and sexual abuse, Munchausen's Syndrome by Proxy, organised and ritual abuse, so the evidential requirements have become more complex and subtle. Moreover child protection cases, which tend to absorb the greatest number of court hours, have come to constitute an ever larger proportion of the courts' care workload.

Third, throughout the 1980s local authorities and courts were operating in a climate of considerable public ambivalence about the appropriate conditions for state intervention. There was serious questioning of the state's ability to provide a better alternative to unsatisfactory parental care or to provide the considerable resources needed to try to sustain the child in the community. In this context, local authorities were encouraged to bring their uncertainties to the courts, particularly, but not exclusively, the wardship courts and the legal process was used increasingly not simply to adjudicate, but to nurse, cudgel or cajole a case towards a resolution of the welfare as well as the legal issues. Such changes in the role of the lower courts, resulting in cases being held in the legal process for longer than might previously have been thought either necessary or desirable, may not have been entirely unrelated to the increasingly central role of the Guardian ad Litem.

Fourth, there had been an explosion in the amount of *information* the courts were able to call on in order to make well founded decisions. More and more sophisticated, and usually lengthy, techniques of assessment had developed and it had become increasingly common for the legal process to await the outcome of such interventions. Interventions, moreover, which could be suggested by the representatives of an increasing number of parties. The decade preceding the Children Act also saw dramatic changes in the availability and effectiveness of *representation* for both children and their families. As the court process became more equitable so, it would seem, it became longer.

It also became vastly more complex and *professionalised*. As the essentially inter-disciplinary nature of the joint task was increasingly acknowledged, more and more cogs were added to the machinery, each cog itself part of other, usually larger systems, each with its own set of concerns and priorities, to which the needs of the family justice system may have been fairly marginal. None of these systems, nor the justice system itself, had much capacity to absorb acute, or even prolonged changes in demand. Complex, interdependent, tightly resourced systems, without strong overall co-ordination, are easily disrupted. One defective cog and the whole apparatus can seize up. The larger the system, the more likely that is to happen.

As a result of these underlying trends it was clear that minimising delay after the Children Act would be a formidable and problematic task. Problematic because it could involve some robust balancing of the potential impact of delay on the child against the court's need for information, or the parties' right to treatment which not only *was* fair but was *experienced* as fair. Formidable because of the very messy and disruptive reality of the cases whose progress through the legal system somehow has to be brought under control but which are always threatening to drift out of control.

Pre-Act, however, it seemed the task was being addressed, if at all, inconsistently and not very effectively across the country. Courts were not generally aware of their own speed of throughput nor how that compared with others. Local norms of what was an acceptable level of delay had developed.[25] Professional systems themselves, either by action or inaction, seemed to be exacerbating drift. No one appeared to have either the responsibility or the power to manage the process. 'A problem with so many causes it was never dealt with' and 'an intractable culture of delay and drift affecting social agencies and courts alike': these were some of the depressing conclusions practitioners themselves voiced about pre-Act practice.[26]

Pre-Act delay in the study areas

Interviews with guardians, team managers and lawyers suggested that Areas B and C very much reflected this picture. Asked 'was the avoidance of delay a principle which needed emphasising in your area?' around nine in ten informants in these areas considered it was. Typical comments included: 'there were huge delays in the juvenile court'; 'there were a lot of unnecessary adjournments', and 'there were tremendous delays in getting matters listed, especially in wardship'. In contrast, the most frequent comments in Area A were to the effect that: 'we had quite a good record in getting cases through here'. Less than a third of respondents here thought there was any problem and even these tended to qualify this in some way, for example that it was 'only the county court', or 'some wardships'.

Pre-Act data for the three authorities confirm these perceptions, as Table 13.1 illustrates, with Area A completing each type of proceeding substantially faster than the other areas. Our extensive study of court workloads[27] also shows that in the two years preceding the Act the mean duration of proceedings in the magistrates' court in Area A was ten weeks compared to 21 weeks in C and 22 weeks in B.

Table 13.1 *Mean duration of pre-Act proceedings (weeks)*

	Area A	Area B	Area C
Care proceedings	11	26	21
Wardship	25	61	45
Matrimonial	21	—	—
More than one type	42	51	95
All types	19	35	44
(n=)	*(41)*	*(36)*	*(27)*

The impact of the Children Act

Exacerbating the problem

As described in the previous chapter, the Act gave courts and practitioners more appropriate tools to deal with the difficult task of reducing delay. At the same time it also, potentially, made that task harder. Only 12 of the lawyers and guardians we interviewed, for example, did not mention at least one aspect of practice under the Act contributing to longer proceedings. For instance:

The process of preparing each case for hearing is more thorough because of:

♦ the more stringent and testing threshold conditions;

♦ the wider range of options to be explored; and

♦ the greater complexity of cases.

In consequence the guardian's enquiries have to be more thorough and wide-ranging, assessments are likely to be requested to ensure everything possible has been tried, and experts instructed to ensure the court has the best available information.

The production of evidence is more time-consuming because:

♦ it is written rather than oral and tends to be sequential;

♦ more information is required by the court;

♦ local authority evidence is more detailed, uses more sources, uses more experts; and

♦ evidence in response is more detailed.

Hearings tend to be longer because:

♦ judges are unable to read the greater volume of evidence in advance;

♦ there are more witnesses, especially expert witnesses;

♦ there are more issues to be argued about;

- cross-examination is more probing as the result of advance disclosure;

- there are more legally represented participants; and

- (in the FPC) magistrates are required to give reasons for their decisions.

There are more hearings because of:

- the introduction of directions appointments; and

- the separation of directions and interim hearings.

Finally the introduction of concurrent jurisdiction and judicial pronouncements on the transfer criteria means that cases which might previously have been heard in the magistrates court moved into a jurisdiction which traditionally operated at a slower pace.

The following specimen response from a local authority solicitor encapsulates practitioner opinion:

> [The cases] all take longer. People need 3–4 weeks to lodge statements. There are more experts. The hearings all take longer. That's about people taking it much more seriously. Here in the local authority we can remember when you'd go down to court and you'd have six files that were all really thin; you knew vaguely the names of your witnesses and you knew a bit about the case but you didn't have anything written down. You'd turn up at court and grab the social worker and you'd be writing things down. You'd go into court and present the case and hope to God your witness said what they'd told you outside the court door. Then the other side didn't have any statements so they had to cross-examine on the hoof which meant their cross examination was shorter. The whole thing was concertinaed. Now there's this huge body of information that flies around being faxed to people; huge 20-page statements. If you're acting for the guardian or the parent you can go into great depth but it all takes much longer.

Changing the culture

Despite this consensus that the Act increases the potential for lengthy proceedings the research data do indicate that its anti-delay philosophy has managed to penetrate quite deeply into professional cultures. In 47 of the sample cases, for example, there was evidence of attempts to speed up the legal process.

The Guardian ad Litem/child's solicitor were responsible for ten of the 16 instances of chivvying other parties or the court. Local authority activity was less evident but there were at least seven occasions when it was clear that specific action had been taken to secure evidence speedily, for example by making urgent referrals for assessments or arranging provisional appointments with experts prior to court leave.

There were 29 instances of *court* action to expedite proceedings recorded, 11 of which were known to be at the instigation of one or more of the parties. Examples were noted at all levels of court and in all areas, although in Area B the higher courts appeared to be most active, while in the other areas it was the family proceedings court. Intervention included attempts to circumvent listing problems in the court as well as to chivvy others.

· ·

Timmy (2) became subject to proceedings following severe physical injury in circumstances which never became clear. After six months, during which both his mother and then his father had been separately assessed, the parties indicated they would be ready to proceed in six weeks and that a three-day slot would be required for a contested hearing. Protests were made when the first available date was three months away and the judge undertook to see if anything could be done. Ten days later notices were served bringing the date forward by a month.

· ·

Practitioner interviews also suggest a generally positive if patchy picture with two-thirds considering that delay was taken seriously now by courts and practitioners and almost a quarter that it was in part. Only one in ten thought the principle was being ignored or mere lip-service being paid. Not unexpectedly the most frequent response in Area A was that delay was generally taken seriously pre-Act and continued to be. Area B displayed a more dramatic contrast, many practitioners describing a pre-Act culture where there was 'drift', 'lack of focus', 'lack of structure' and 'delay was accepted as a way of life'. The position in Area C was rather more ambiguous, generating a number of disturbing comments about the initial impetus to change fading away as the cases stacked up in the courts:

It's in danger of being taken a lot less seriously than when the Act came in. That's because people see delay as inevitable because of lack of court time. Sometimes people try to expedite things to compensate for the court's delays but generally 2–3 years in people have realised there isn't much they can do short of providing the court with more resources.

Nowhere was the cultural shift complete, with criticisms of tardiness being made about individual members of all professional groups, particularly perhaps psycho-medical experts and lawyers representing parents, indicating there remains scope for improvement. The overwhelming theme, however, was that while those who have to operate within the system have become very delay conscious, their efforts are not sufficiently supported by an adequately resourced infrastructure, whether this is the local authority, the health services or the court system itself. As a result, despite the best efforts of those concerned, proceedings were still lasting longer than they should. The problem of drift may have been substantially addressed, that of delay has not.

The duration of proceedings under the Act

On the basis of our pre-Act research into the duration of care proceedings we reached the rather pessimistic conclusion that:

> If the final hearing should normally be held within 12 weeks from the initial hearing then truly a revolution in approach will have to be achieved with the coming of the new Act. [28]

Despite initial reports to the contrary[29] such a revolution has not generally taken place. The 'continuing problem of delay' it has been said 'can only be described as a dark cloud';[30] 'delays are building up again to unacceptable levels';[31] 'we now know that some cases take far too long to reach a conclusion'.[32] The average duration of Section 31 proceedings completing in March 1994 was 22 weeks in the family proceedings court, 37 weeks in the county court and 44 weeks in the High Court.[33] All those figures represent a deterioration from the same period the previous year.

Our sample cases reflect this larger picture, only around one in ten completing within 12 weeks[34] (Figure 13.1). Indeed 38 took more than twice as long as the hoped for norm, 12 took three times the time and five cases took four times. The mean duration of proceedings was just over 25 weeks.[35]

The figures, moreover, suggest a slight lengthening of proceedings over the research period. Mean duration, for example, rose from just over 24 weeks in Year 1 to almost 26 in Year 2 while the proportion of cases completing in 12 weeks dropped from 15% to 7%. By Year 2 only 35% of cases were going through the court process within 20 weeks, compared to 46% in Year 1, although the proportion of cases taking more than 26 weeks had fallen slightly (from 41% to 37%) (Table 13.2).

Figure 13.1 *Duration of post-Act proceedings*

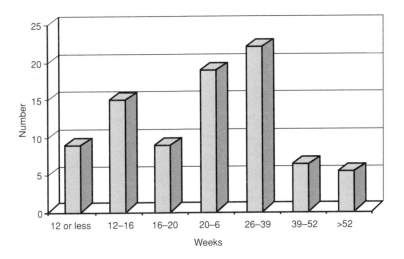

Table 13.2 *Duration of proceedings by area and year*

	Area A		Area B		Area C		All areas	
	No.	%	No.	%	No.	%	No.	%
Completing within								
12 weeks								
Year 1	3	27	3	19	0	0	6	15
Year 2	3	17	0	0	0	0	3	7
Both years	6	21	3	10	0	0	9	11
20 weeks								
Year 1	8	73	6	38	4	33	18	46
Year 2	8	44	4	31	3	25	15	35
Both years	16	49	10	30	7	29	33	40
26 weeks								
Year 1	10	91	9	56	4	33	23	59
Year 2	13	72	7	53	7	58	27	63
Both years	23	79	16	55	11	46	50	61

Variation by area

Area A, which tended to set the fastest pace for proceedings, achieved the speediest rate of throughput, with a mean of just over 20 weeks (compared to

27 weeks in B and 28 weeks in C). Even here, however, only one in five cases completed within 12 weeks while in C not a single case did so. Furthermore over the two years there appeared to be quite a dramatic lengthening of proceedings in Area A, the mean rising from under 17 weeks in Year 1 to almost 23 weeks in Year 2, and the proportion taking 26 weeks or less dropping from almost three-quarters to under half. The other two areas showed much smaller differences between the study years. It should also be noted however that while the proportion of cases requiring more than six months to complete increased in Areas A and B it actually fell in Area C.

Comparison with the pre-Act position

Are child protection proceedings in general longer, shorter or much the same under the Children Act? In the absence of national data on the duration of all the various types of relevant proceedings under previous legislation this, unfortunately, is an unanswerable question. Indeed, even were such data available, pre- and post-Act proceedings are not strictly comparable. Apart from differences in the legal process itself the cases differ in certain important respects, as shown in earlier chapters. The data presented in this section therefore need to be read with these caveats in mind.

Our extensive survey suggests that applications for care and supervision orders take about four weeks longer under the Children Act than under the Children and Young Persons Act 1969.[36] The data from this much smaller child protection sample also reflect this change, although the mean difference is slightly greater, at five weeks. The figures for the three areas are also broadly comparable across the two samples, with the mean duration remaining about the same in Area B but increasing in the other areas by between six and eight weeks.

Children Act proceedings fare better in comparison with pre-Act wardships. In five areas surveyed in our earlier research for example,[37] wardship cases were taking an average of 53 weeks, even longer than in Masson's[38] wardship study (38), while the mean duration of the small sample of wardship cases brought by the three areas participating in this project was 42 weeks. Against those figures the 31-week mean for the sample cases with their final hearing in the higher courts (the nearest equivalent) seems positively speedy. Moreover, cases remaining in the family proceedings court completed on average within 18 weeks, which was actually two weeks faster than care proceedings in the old juvenile court. Thus it would be unduly gloomy to conclude that no progress has been made even if it is far less than had been hoped.

Factors affecting the duration of the sample cases under the Children Act

In a later section we shall examine the specific issue of delay. Delay, however, is a value-laden term carrying connotations of unreasonable length and direct causal connections not always easy to establish. In this section, therefore, we explore the associations between an objective variable (length of proceedings), case characteristics and legal process.

The nature of the cases

Most discussions of delay tend to focus on the legal process. Our previous research, however, suggested that the pace of proceedings might also be affected by characteristics of the cases themselves or the process by which they reached court.

The pre-Act data revealed a striking contrast in speed of throughput between the magistrates' court in Area A and that in Area B.[39] The mean duration of care proceedings in A for example was 11 weeks, that in B 26 weeks. In Area A 68% of cases completed within 12 weeks, and all were completed within 26. By this point 66% of B's cases were still outstanding. Detailed comparison of the cases coming before each court revealed that in Court B, cases were *less* likely to :

 ♦ be preceded by a continuous period of welfare involvement;

 ♦ follow a multi-disciplinary case conference;

 ♦ have a clear objective identified at the outset; and

 ♦ record legal advice having been sought before proceedings were instituted.

This profile suggested that cases in Area B were less well 'worked up' in both legal and welfare terms than those coming before the faster court, with the result that more time was required before they were sufficiently 'ready' for adjudication. Cases in this area were also more likely to:

 ♦ arise out of a crisis;

 ♦ begin with a Place of Safety Order; and

 ♦ be followed by an Interim Care Order.

While this more rapid-response, intrusive and controlling approach may well have been entirely justified by the circumstances of the cases, we thought it conceivable that it set a tone which then persisted throughout proceedings. Cases in this area seem to have been more contentious: they were more likely to have contested interim hearings, to remain disputed to the end, to have hearings lasting over several days and to have a high number of professional witnesses.

In exploring the continuing problem of delay under the Children Act, we therefore examined a number of possible associations between case profile and duration. None of the inherent characteristics of the case families showed any appreciable or consistent relationship with duration, nor did the nature of the significant harm alleged or associated concerns about the family. Certain aspects of the families' interaction with welfare agencies seemed, *prima facie*, to be more promising. It appeared, for instance, that cases which were precipitated by a crisis, or started with compulsory emergency protection were likely to be shorter than those which did not, in contrast to our pre-Act data. The effect of these factors remained when previously inactive cases were discounted, although the differences were less marked.

Many of the remaining factors, however, seemed to be pointing in one direction. Cases based on the 'is suffering' ground, for instance, seemed to be shorter than those based on risk. So also did those where there had been previous proceedings on the case children, where they were currently on the Child Protection Register, where there were five or more factors causing concern or where welfare intervention had not been confined to in-home services. When only active cases were considered the relevance of these factors seemed to be greater. It might be considered that all these factors lend weight to the local authority's case, perhaps rendering it less open to time-absorbing challenge.

Finally duration seemed to be associated with the clarity of the local authority's objectives in initiating proceedings (Chapter 7). Cases in which the objective was long-term substitute care were speedier than all other cases. Once again, given what we know about these cases again one might hypothesise that they were less vulnerable to being thrown off course. When previously inactive cases are excluded this factor becomes statistically significant (at $p < 0.05$).

None of the other factors is statistically significant. Thus while they are interesting pointers to the way case differences may affect length they are not a full explanation. It might be tempting, none the less, to conclude that one remedy would be for social services to tighten up their planning before bringing cases to court. As seen earlier, uncertainty about the direction of the case was a primary reason for the court's inability to timetable early in the proceedings and later scheduling was associated with lengthy cases. However, it will also be apparent from the data presented in Chapter 7 that although some improvements could probably be made in this respect the scope is not that great. Moreover, certainty of objectives was very often only achieved at the cost of deferring court action to the overall detriment of the child's welfare. Such a general strategy therefore might be neither feasible nor constructive.

Variation by area

Variation in rate of throughput between Area A and the other study areas has already been noted. The difference only just falls short of statistical significance when the three courts are treated separately and becomes significant when the data for courts in Areas B and C are amalgamated. The critical question then is: is this a consequence of the cases going into the respective courts or a reflection of court process?

To illuminate this issue we compared the time taken to complete cases sharing a common characteristic. On every dimension available, relating either to the characteristics of the families or their welfare and legal histories, cases proceeded fastest through the courts in Area A. In most instances the difference amounted to several weeks.

Given the possible distorting effect of Area A cases we were interested to see whether the data for Areas B and C alone would reveal any further associations between pace and the nature of the cases entering the courts. However, none emerged. Therefore although a larger data set might be able to generate more subtle associations we are forced to the conclusion that the major influences on the pace of proceedings stem not from the nature of the case itself or the way it has been handled prior to court action but from what happens *once it enters the court system*.

The court process

We pursued a similar mode of analysis in an attempt to identify factors relating to the court process which might have an impact on duration. The only ones to prove statistically significant in explaining variance were related to experts and the level at which the final hearing was heard.

Experts

The total number of experts, the total number of local authority experts, the number of experts brought in in the course of proceedings and the number of experts instructed by parents were all found to be statistically significant in explaining case duration. Thus, unequivocally, addressing the use of expert evidence is one of the keys to shortening proceedings. Such a strategy, however, as Chapter 11 indicates, is far from straightforward, since experts can impact on duration in a number of quite different ways: through the time taken for a family to complete an assessment, for instance, or the time waiting for a place, or the time taken to find an expert to give a second opinion.

Clearly there is scope for more careful questioning of the need for a particular expert, for joint instructions and for greater precision in the instructions given. Representatives need to come to court better informed about the availability of their preferred expert and, where that expert is not available, be prepared to look for a substitute. Such consistent good practice would undoubtedly have an effect. Tackling the expert-based culture of the higher courts and the hierarchy of expertise which positions guardians below psychiatrists and social workers below guardians also needs to be addressed so that an objective assessment of added value can be made in each case.

None the less expert opinion will continue to have a valid role in care cases and even if the demand is reduced by the measures suggested the supply may still be insufficient in some areas. The extent and nature of the resource shortfall and the appropriate remedies need to be evaluated at a local level. Authorities seem to vary, for instance, in the availability of local resources and their readiness to fund external assessments. There will always be a tension within care cases between the need for speedy decision-making and the need for a good basis of information for those decisions. Resource difficulties unreasonably exacerbate that tension.

Court level

The impact of court level on case duration is also undeniable (Table 13.3). The mean duration of cases with their final hearing in the family proceedings court was 18 weeks, while those completing in the county court took 30 weeks. Seventy-five per cent of the FPC cases were in the first quartile of cases to complete and only 5% in the fourth. In contrast only 10% of county court cases were in the first quartile and 60% in the fourth. Differences between the county and High Court were much less marked and somewhat contradictory. They are also based on fewer cases and of course many will have had directions hearings at county court level so the basis for differentiation is less reliable. The crucial difference clearly, however, is whether the case leaves the family proceedings court. Once it does so the whole process is likely to slow down.

Table 13.3 *Duration by court level (weeks)*

	Area A		Area B		Area C	
Court level						
Family proceedings court	17	(16)	20	(12)	18	(9)
County court	28	(8)	29	(14)	33	(8)
High Court	18	(5)	45	(3)	36	(7)
County or High Court	24	(13)	32	(17)	34	(15)

Sorting out which is the more important factor, experts or court level, is of course difficult, complicated as it is by the fact that the number of experts in a case and potential conflict of expert opinion tends to be used as a measure of complexity warranting transfer up. Indeed it was the only characteristic of our cases which was found to be statistically related to transfer. There were only two cases in the sample, for instance, which had three or more experts but remained in the magistrates' court. However, tests comparing the 68 cases which had fewer than three experts across the three tiers showed that the level at which the case was heard remained statistically significant ($p = 0.0007$): the family proceedings court disposed of such cases on average within 19 weeks, the higher courts took nine weeks longer. The critical factor was again whether the case remained in the family proceedings court, somewhat surprisingly such cases having their final hearing in the High Court finished almost two weeks earlier than those completing in the county court.

Logically, therefore, reducing rates of vertical transfer should reduce durations. Judicial backtracking on this issue, particularly the length of hearings considered suitable for the magistrates' courts, is likely in itself to lead to fewer cases being transferred. It would be entirely unreasonable, of course, if cases which required professional adjudication were denied justice because of the need to even out pressure on an overloaded system. Equally it is counterproductive if cases are transferred before the need has been shown, merely to pre-empt delays arising from later transfer by getting into the queue early.

Variation by area

In an earlier section we explored but rejected the hypothesis that variation in pace between the three areas might be a function of differences in the cases themselves. Similarly we compared the three areas across a range of court-related variables. This revealed a rather less clear cut picture: generally cases still seemed to proceed rather faster in Area A than in either of the other two courts whatever the measure chosen but there were differences in detail. Moreover while cases in this area were quickest at each court level the differences were sometimes small and as far as the magistrates and county court were concerned, not statistically significant. The key factor seemed to be differences in the transfer rate. As noted in Chapter 10 Area A had the highest proportion of cases remaining in the family proceedings court and Area C the lowest.

So far we have dealt with the neutral question of what factors are associated with longer proceedings. Length of course is not the same thing as delay, although from the child's point of view the distinction may be immaterial. In the next section we turn to a more value-laden issue, what causes delay?

Practitioner explanations for delay

Lawyers, guardians and team managers were asked what they had found to be the main sources of delay in proceedings under the Act. This was deliberately framed as an open-ended question to prevent our hypotheses influencing the responses. Accordingly, although there was a remarkable consensus on the primary factors, a good many others were mentioned:

- shortage of guardians (7) or late appointment (1);
- number of parties (5) and late joinder (1);
- cases being more complex (4);
- more thorough preparation (4);
- courts hanging on to cases (4);
- judges and magistrates reserving cases to themselves (4);
- changes in the case (3);
- over-long hearings (3);
- lack of preparation by the local authority (3);
- late evidence (3);
- late requests for assessments (2);

- issues not defined early enough (2);

- legal aid for experts (2);

- parents not instructing solicitors (1);

- sequential evidence (1);

- 'laid back' social workers (1);

- local authority administration (1);

- concurrent criminal proceedings (1); and

- the adversarial culture of the higher courts (1).

Had respondents been asked specifically whether such factors caused delay there would probably be a high level of agreement. Indeed many echo comments made about the ways in which the Children Act has increased the potential for delay and all are consistent with our own observations. They would probably remain eclipsed, however, by what practitioners overwhelmingly identified as the key problems, namely: assessments (26); experts (41) and above all: lack of court time (74). Over and over again, accompanied with varying degrees of cynicism, resignation, despair, anger and resentment we heard essentially the same diagnosis:

> All these discussion about delay relate to court time. Yes of course the question of delay had to be addressed but they should have done that by providing more court time. If they're not going to do that they may as well not open their mouths. That's probably not absolutely the answer and in some cases there clearly was unacceptable delay due to lack of organisation on the part of the local authority and lack of push on the part of parents' solicitors. And maybe those sorts of delay have been reduced by the Act. But every day what we face is the problem of not being able to get cases heard because there is no court time and that is the great frustration.

Few would argue that lack of court time and insufficient resources in the health and social services to enable expert reports to be provided and assessments carried out expeditiously amount to the type of delay the Children Act sought to avoid. Both practitioners and members of the judiciary, however, were at pains to stress that delay was not always an evil, that there were circumstances when prolonging proceedings might be in the children's interests. In examining the sources of delay in the sample cases it is therefore also necessary to explore the issue of when delay might not be delay, in other words when is it justifiable to prolong proceedings?

Acceptable and unacceptable delay

The reasonable processes of preparing a case for trial

Taken to its logical conclusion the principle enacted in Section 1(2) that any delay is likely to prejudice the welfare of the child could produce a system in which decisions were made at a single hearing immediately an issue requiring adjudication arose. Such an approach, which would be unlikely to result in sound or just decision-making, would clearly be untenable. Thus right from the start the legislation embodies a fundamental tension between the need for speed and the need for enough time to allow for the reasonable processes of case preparation.

What is deemed reasonable, however, has radically changed over the years. Social workers and local authority lawyers with long memories will recall a time when a Fit Person Order, the precursor to care orders, was obtained simply on presentation of oral evidence and a Social Enquiry Report. It would be rare to have more than one or two hearings, neither the parent nor the child would be represented and it would be most unusual to have any 'expert' evidence.

With the advent of guardians it became accepted, reluctantly in some quarters[40] that it was reasonable to allow a period of at least six weeks for enquiries and that this was justified in terms of due process and well-informed decision-making. The same arguments legitimise the elongation of proceedings since the Children Act as a result of the introduction of written evidence and advance disclosure and the requirement that the guardian's report be submitted at least seven days before the final hearing. None of our interviewees, even those who identified such factors as adding to the length of proceedings, suggested that we should return to the system pertaining in the mid-1980s when most of the evidence was oral, all parties were entitled to keep their cards close to their chest and it was not unusual for parents to see the guardian's report for the first time on the morning of the hearing.[41]

Of the 82 sample cases, there were only 16 (20%) which appeared to have no other sources of delay except those which would be accepted as the reasonable processes of preparing the case for trial.

The true proportion, however, is probably lower than this since sources of delay may not be comprehensively recorded. The more complete information available on 28 observed cases revealed that only one in each area was not subject to any other delay (11%). Their average duration varied between six weeks in Area A, 14 weeks in B and 17 weeks in C.

Planned and purposeful delay

Though commonplace, the involvement of experts in care proceedings in addition to the social worker and the guardian has not quite become a routine and therefore unchallenged, part of the normal trial process. Nor has the practice of conducting assessments in the course of proceedings or of deferring the final hearing until a parent has completed a treatment programme. The issue of whether the benefits outweigh the costs is therefore very much alive – a balancing exercise which has to be carried out in each case. Many practitioners expressed concern that in the early days, particularly in the magistrates' court, the delay principle was being interpreted too rigidly so that cases were being rushed through inappropriately and requests for what they saw as legitimate adjournments refused.

Case law has now established that Section 1(2) should not be interpreted to mean that delay is always detrimental. The case of Robert Barnes is one example of the 'planned and purposeful delay' which may be considered beneficial and therefore acceptable:[42]

• •

Welfare agencies had been anxious even before Robert's birth about the capacity of his mother, Doreen, to care. Although Robert was her first child she had been largely responsible for her partner's son, 4-year-old William, who was already on the Child Protection Register for neglect. The social worker's efforts to persuade Doreen to go into a mother and baby home had, however, proved unavailing. When Robert was born premature and handicapped professional anxiety about his safety if he went home increased. Doreen's visits to the hospital, moreover, had been extremely erratic and by the time Robert was ready for discharge, at 3 months, there appeared to be no mother–child bond while Robert's father, Jack, appeared to take no interest at all. Doreen still maintained she wanted to care but since she was not prepared to agree accommodation, the situation reached stalemate. Accordingly the local authority brought proceedings.

By the time of the first hearing Doreen's attitude seemed to have changed, largely as a result of the efforts of her solicitor and it was agreed that the aim would be to seek a placement in a mother and baby home to be preceded by a period of intensive work in Robert's foster placement to strengthen the mother–child relationship and develop Doreen's skills in caring for Robert's special needs. By the next hearing everything seemed to be going quite well and the final hearing was set for 11 weeks ahead by which time Robert and Doreen should have been in the mother and baby home for several weeks.

● ●

Planned and purposeful delay was noted in half the sample cases. Their mean duration was 29 weeks compared to 21 weeks where no such delay was noted. However there were only eight cases (10%) where this was the sole source of delay. Their mean duration was slightly shorter, 25 weeks.

In the observed sample the proportion of cases involving such delays was higher (19, 68%). The difference in the average rates however was very similar, at around seven weeks. Only two cases, lasting 20 weeks on average, had no other source of delay (7%).

Changes in case configuration

As demonstrated in Chapter 11, care cases rarely stand still and changes in family circumstances can alter the whole shape of the case. Any resultant delay may be reactive rather than planned but could still be regarded as purposeful.

● ●

Ian Morse was made subject to proceedings after a period of accommodation in a foster home and the failure of attempts to use the placement to develop his mother's parenting skills. Like Robert Barnes, Ian had special needs arising from congenital difficulties – though far less severe and not likely to cause permanent disability. Unlike Doreen, his mother Brigid was willing to go into a mother and baby home but the placement had been suspended after she admitted causing bruises to Ian's face. Although the plan was for the placement to be resumed after a programme of gradual re-introduction this did not work out.

Brigid, who has slight learning difficulties, was 17 when she became pregnant and concealed this until a few weeks before Ian's premature birth. Her parents initially rejected her completely, although they later relented to the extent of offering weekend stays. Although contacted on several occasions by the social worker they were not prepared to provide more either at the point Ian was accommodated nor when social services moved towards court action. Indeed Mr Morse expressed the view that Brigid would never be able to cope with Ian even with support and two days before the first hearing was endorsing the plans for adoption, even though by this time he had allowed Brigid herself to return home. Mrs Morse was more supportive of Brigid and hopeful that she would be able to care but did not envisage playing more than a normal grandparenting role.

The final hearing was set eight weeks ahead. Four weeks later Mr and Mrs Morse told social services they were prepared to offer a home to Brigid and Ian. The final hearing was adjourned by consent in order that the plan might be assessed and if appropriate phased rehabilitation attempted. Over the next few months Brigid took increasing responsibility for the care of Ian who began to spend more and more time in the Morse household, eventually moving there full time. The final order, by which this became a 'permanent' arrangement by consent, was made four months later.

● ●

Delay for similar reasons occurred in 25 (30%) of the sample cases. Their mean duration was 31 weeks, compared to 23 weeks where there was no such delay. The two cases which had no other sources of delay lasted on average 24 weeks.

The proportion was only slightly higher in the observed sample (9, 32%) although the difference in duration was greater (9 weeks). No cases were delayed for only this reason.

Resource difficulties

In an ideal world a court weighing up the need for planned and purposeful delay in the light of Section 1(2) would only have to consider the disadvantages of not having an assessment, for example, and the detrimental effects on the child of the time this would take. In reality, sadly, the court often has to take into account how long it will take for the assessment to even start. In the most dramatic example of this, a case involving Munchausen's Syndrome by Proxy, an initial assessment had concluded placement in a specialist treatment unit was necessary. Proceedings were held up while social services and the health authority argued over funding – not surprisingly since the cost was £15,000 per month. The matter was only resolved following judicial review and the intervention of the Secretary of State. Other examples of funding delays or problems in getting an expert report could be cited.

Similar choices have increasingly had to be made about choice of forum. The avoidance of delay is one of the criteria for vertical transfer. Ironically, however, because of pressures on the higher courts the operation of the delay principle can mean that cases which are held to need professional adjudication are not transferred. The case just described, surely complex enough to warrant transfer, was heard throughout in the family proceedings court, mother's solicitor 'making noises' but agreeing not to proceed with an application because it would delay the case even further. In the next case, however, transfer was agreed, in the event unnecessarily, precisely in order to limit any later hold-ups.

●　●

Care proceedings were brought on Michaela (5) and Robin (3), principally because of emotional abuse. At the first hearing the case was transferred to the county court because of the likely numbers of experts involved and possible conflict: social services would be submitting evidence from two previous assessments and representatives for the children and their mother indicated they would probably be seeking leave to instruct experts. The magistrates accepted the argument that: 'there is such a backlog in the county court that the sooner we get into the list the better.' The county court accepted the same argument for fixing the date of the final hearing which was expected to last five days. The first available date was 20 weeks ahead, at least six weeks longer than the maximum the parties considered they needed to be ready.

●　●

Twenty-two cases (27%) were known to have been delayed because of resource difficulties in some form. Their average duration was 33 weeks, 11 weeks longer than those where this factor was absent. The four which appeared to have no other source of delay lasted on average a week longer.

The observed sample suggests that resource difficulties were in reality more prevalent (13=46%) and their impact on case duration more marked (34 compared to 20 weeks). The mean duration of the three cases which had no other discernible source of delay was 37 weeks.

Family non-co-operation with the legal process

Most families reach court not only because of the allegations of significant harm, but because they and the welfare agencies have not been able to work effectively together to address the concerns. It would be surprising then if their relationship with the legal process was all plain sailing. Delays can arise from parents deferring legal representation or not working effectively with the representative, missing appointments with the guardian or social worker, not co-operating with assessments, not turning up at court, or, as in the following example, showing a total disregard for the authority of the law.

Fourteen-year-old Mary was taken into police protection after she and two older siblings ran away from home and were found sleeping rough. Although their allegations of physical and emotional abuse aroused considerable concern about the well being of the two children remaining at home (Ruth (12) and Peter (10)) the local authority did not seek removal, but applied for a Prohibited Steps Order preventing the children being taken abroad, as their parents apparently planned. While the application was being heard, however, Ruth and Peter were already on their way, not being returned to this country for another two weeks, during which a Recovery Order was issued and care proceedings started on all three younger children.

On their return the children were placed in a foster home from which Peter was again abducted. In view of Peter's apparent compliance with his parents' action, on return he was placed in a separate placement from which he was later returned home under an Interim Supervision Order bolstered with a condition of residence and parental undertakings. Despite these, just prior to the final hearing Peter and his mother again disappeared and the inherent jurisdiction was invoked to secure his return. Care Orders were made in respect of Ruth and Mary, but Peter's case was not heard for another four weeks.

The only case in which parental non-co-operation was the sole source of delay lasted for a mere 12 weeks. Such delay however was a factor in 22 (27%) of the sample cases. These lasted on average 27 weeks, compared to 24 weeks where no such delay was noted.

None of the cases in the observed sample was delayed solely for this reason although it was evident in 11 (39%). Their mean duration was 29 weeks, five weeks longer than other cases.

Disruption

Parental non-co-operation might be regarded as one particular form of disruption to the legal process. A range of other disruptions were noted in 33 cases (40%). Included in this category are, for example, delays arising from hearings which were ineffective or adjourned part-heard, problems arising from the non-availability of witnesses, administrative mix-ups or delays either in the court or local authority systems and difficulties associated with the work of the guardian.

The mean duration of cases affected by such disruptions was 26 weeks (compared to 24 of those without). Seven cases had no other source of delay, their mean duration was 18 weeks.

Of the observed sample 54% (15) were affected by some form of disruption. Somewhat bizarrely their mean duration was *less* than cases where this factor was absent (25 compared to 28 weeks). The one case experiencing delay arising solely from disruption lasted for a mere nine weeks.

The explanation for such paradoxical findings may lie in the fact that although disruptions can occur in any case, those which are running to a particularly tight timetable are most likely to result in delay. In contrast more extended schedules can accommodate even a whole series of hiccups.

Concurrent proceedings

Finally there is delay arising from parallel proceedings, whether these be criminal prosecutions for child abuse or other offences or civil proceedings relating to other children in the family.

The seven cases (9%) in which such delay was noted lasted an average of 28 weeks, three weeks longer than other cases. The two cases held up for this reason alone lasted for 19 weeks.

In the observed sample four cases (14%) were delayed because of concurrent proceedings, but lasted a mere week longer, at 28 weeks, than others. None experienced delay arising only from this source.

Delay: a multifactorial problem

Most cases, then, are affected by more than one form of delay. Indeed, as Table 13.4 shows, although no case was so unfortunate as to experience all six types, over a third of our observed sample suffered four or more.

Moreover each category is made up of several factors. In all specific delays were linked to 39 separate causes. Excluding cases where no delay was evident, the mean number of factors in our observed sample was four, with 15 cases having at least this number, rising to a maximum of 11. The mean varied from three in Area C and four in A to six in Area B. Higher numbers of factors were linked with longer cases but the association was not perfect and fell just short of statistical significance (Figure 13.2).

Table 13.4 *Duration by number of types of delay*

Number of types	Cases No.	%	Duration (weeks)
Whole sample			
0	16	20	17
1	22	27	24
2	22	27	26
3	8	10	32
4	10	12	31
5	4	5	34
Observed sample			
0	3	11	13
1	6	21	27
2	5	18	24
3	4	14	24
4	7	25	32
5	3	11	33

Figure 13.2 *Number of factors causing delay by case duration*

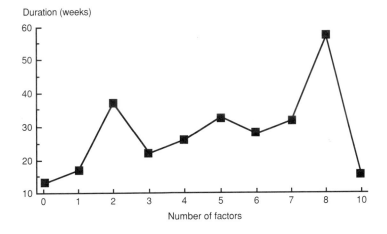

What this reflects is that the impact of each individual delay was not equivalent, varying from a matter of days to several months. The same factor might also have a very different effect depending on the case or the area. Lack of court time, for instance, had very different ramifications when relating to the family proceedings court in Area A where one would be talking about a matter of weeks than when it related to the High Court in Area C which could involve delays of many months. Overall only two individual delay factors proved statistically significant in explaining difference in case duration: delay caused by new parties being joined to the case and delay caused by lack of court time.

Factors were only counted as *causing* delay when a direct link could be established. We did however also record whether factors responsible for delay in some cases existed in others: for example was there a specialist assessment of parenting, was there evidence of parental non-co-operation, of ineffective hearings and so on. A count of such *potential* delay factors in the observed cases reveals an astonishing 13 per case, varying only slightly from precisely that in Area A to nearer 14 elsewhere. It is conceivable, of course, that such factors may have caused delay in more cases than could be positively identified by the researchers. Another possible interpretation is that the courts were doing extremely well to steer cases through this morass of potential delay. Neither of these explanations can be discounted and as indicated earlier in our discussion 'changing the culture' there is certainly evidence of the latter.

In many cases, however, where the pace of proceedings was determined by the operation of one powerful factor, usually court lists or an assessment, unless other factors disrupted that timetable they would not have been counted as a source of delay overall even though they may have affected the timing of various interim procedures. This is of great relevance to future strategies to reduce delay because it means that even if the major causes of delay were dealt with the problem would not entirely disappear, as secondary factors would then assume a new significance, if with rather less impact.

Moreover, whatever the reason for lengthy proceedings, the longer the case, the more court hearings it will require and the more resources it will consume. Therefore even though the overwhelming cause of delay would seem to be an insufficiency of court time, attention to any of the other factors would, indirectly, render this problem less severe. The need for expedition also has to be seen not only in the context of the individual case but in terms of the impact on the system as a whole and the welfare of other children. Thus leave given for an expert report in one case, whilst not damaging to the child concerned, may indirectly cause another case to be delayed because the deferral of a final hearing takes up another slot on the court list or hampers the ability of the guardian to start work on another case. Thus *constructive* delay in one case may be the cause of *detrimental* delay in another.

At the same time as there is a need to look globally at the overall system and the interaction of its constituent parts it is also clear that local systems operate very differently. The factors which *can* cause delay are probably universal. Whether they do, and what their impact is, will vary according to local circumstances. Thus it is vital that each area develops systems to monitor the progress of cases, identify the factors slowing them down and develop locally-supported strategies to remedy them. Family Court Business Committees are the obvious umbrella structure within which such systems could be developed, perhaps by setting up a small working group with a specific brief. It would be a cost-effective use of public funds to provide a small resource, as a pump-priming exercise, to facilitate some pilot projects. Alternatively, one of the charitable trusts with an interest in the development of the family justice system might be persuaded to assist.

The maximisation of scarce resources

From the range of data presented in this chapter it will be apparent that although myriad factors can slow down the legal process major blockages have developed as the result of two critical factors: *shortage of court time*, especially in the higher courts, and *shortage of resources for assessments*. We thus have no hesitation in supporting calls for better resourcing.[43] However we are also pessimistic that any substantial increase in resources will be forthcoming. It is with a certain reluctance, therefore, that we turn to explore alternative options, to see whether existing resources within the court system could be deployed more effectively and/or the demand on straitened resources be reduced. In doing so we should emphasise that our research brief was not to conduct an efficiency study of the family justice system; nor have we done so. What follows is therefore based on data which may be partial and were collected for other purposes.

The use of hearing time

Direct observation of hearings was a key element in the research, yielding data not otherwise available. One of the more surprising incidental findings related to the way *hearing* time was actually spent.

The calculations used were based on the time participants are required to be at court. They thus exclude lunch breaks and other released time; the interval between the time participants arrive and the listed time (which is often spent in discussion and negotiation) and the period after the hearing ends, which is commonly spent in further discussion. They therefore considerably underestimate the demands on practitioner time generated by each court hearing. Even so only *half* the time practitioners have to be at court is spent with the court engaged in full session; indeed in Area C it was as low as 41%.

Waiting time

'Hanging around at court' was a persistent theme raised by our practitioner and family interviewees and a glance at Figure 13.3 shows they have some justification. Of all the time they are *required* to be at court an astonishing 35% was spent waiting for the hearing to start. Over the course of the observed cases an average of 5 hours 21 minutes per case was spent in this way, easily the equivalent of a typical court day.

Figure 13.3 *Court hearings: allocation of attendance time*

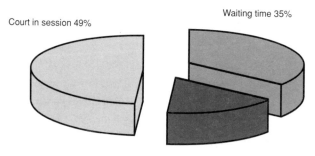

Court in session 49%

Waiting time 35%

Internal adjournments 16%

The large numbers of professional personnel likely to be involved in proceedings, moreover, mean that this waiting period has to be multiplied many times to give a true picture of the potential waste involved. Each hearing day we observed was attended on average by between six and seven practitioners. By multiplying the actual waiting time per hearing day by the number of practitioners present it was found that on average waiting time per day swallowed up $5^{1}/_{4}$ hours of practitioner time. Over the course of proceedings this worked out at 35 hours 38 minutes per case, a *full working week*.

Late starts almost always mean wasted time for someone: court, parties or practitioners. Apart from the distress this can cause parents and the cost it represents to the public purse,[44] human resources are, as we have seen, at a premium in this system. Every hour a guardian, for instance, spends waiting to go into court increases the amount of time each case absorbs, reduces his or her capacity to take on other cases and restricts his or her availability for other court hearings. Moreover, since the guardian is probably the one person in whose absence the final hearing will not take place, it is entirely possible that waiting time at one hearing in case X may mean that proceedings in case Y are unduly prolonged. This means more interim hearings and therefore more court time.

In addition to the direct loss of time which late starts involve there can be an indirect loss because of unpredictability. We found there was a great deal of variation both between and within cases. A case might be lucky enough to get in on almost every occasion more or less on time. In one case in Area B for instance, over the course of six hearings waiting was never longer than 20 minutes, adding up to only 40 minutes overall. In contrast, in another case in Area A, with the same number of hearings, there was no occasion on which the wait was for less than 20 minutes and three on which it was for more than two hours, adding up to an outrageous 9 hours 20 minutes or 41% of the time required to be spent at court. In consequence even if a case is listed for a half-hour directions hearing in the early morning it may be impossible for practitioners to plan the rest of the working day with any confidence, another potential waste of scarce resources. Again this is likely to have the severest impact on guardians.

The severity and prevalence of the problem did however vary a good deal between the three areas and the different levels of court. Area B seemed to be rather more successful overall in its listing arrangements than either of the other areas with a mean total waiting time per case of 2 hours 37 minutes and a maximum of only $3^{1}/_{2}$; a period which some of our other cases put in on a single occasion. In Area B 52% of hearing days started within ten minutes of their listed time compared to only 31% in Area C and a paltry 15% in Area A. At the other end of the scale it was rare for cases to hang around for more than two hours before going into court in Area B, but this happened in almost a quarter of cases in Area C. Overall it appeared that the higher courts were generally able to get their cases started most promptly. In Area C, where the differences were most marked, almost 60% of hearings in the higher courts started within ten minutes of their appointed time and 80% within 30 minutes. Comparative figures for the family proceedings court were 3% and 19%.

There may, of course, be all sorts of reasons for these differences. Magistrates' courts, for instance, typically hear most first hearings and emergency applications, which undoubtedly make the task of managing the day's list more difficult. The reasons for late starts lie as much with practitioners and their clients as with the court. However the fact that some courts manage to start more punctually than others does suggest that the problem is not intractable. Creating a climate in which a prompt start is the norm, as was the case in some courts, is clearly an important part of the solution. Courts need to audit the amount of waiting time and devise strategies for its reduction. Again action research projects in a few areas might show how the issue might be most effectively addressed.

Waiting time is not necessarily wasted time; we acknowledge there are occasions when it can be used productively and may even shorten the hearing. At the moment, however, it is very much a question of serendipity: cases *happening* to start late and everybody *happening* to be there on time to enable fruitful discussions to take place. Indeed sometimes it appears as if practitioners rely on late starts in order to do this. If the case is called punctually they have to ask for time, which can then have an impact on the rest of the list. Inappropriate as it would seem to be in care cases, the traditional legal culture of 'last-minutism' still holds sway, as this advice to guardians indicates:

> Quite frequently solicitors and counsel come to life half an hour before the starting time and new ideas are put up for consideration. So be there early.[45]

The same arguments, moreover, that unplanned non-purposeful delay can turn out to serve a constructive purpose, have not been allowed to undermine the operation of the delay principle and we see no reason why it should legitimise excessive waiting time. The disciplined and planned use of time has to be the criterion. Practitioners should be expected to be ready to proceed at the appointed time and to make whatever adjustments to their practice are necessary to enable them to do so. This might require lawyers for parents to ensure their client is there on time and all lawyers to obtain up to date instructions before the morning of the hearing, communicate with the representatives of the other parties and exchange statements in advance. If the court corridor is still considered to be the indispensable forum for negotiation, then time should be set aside so that all parties are present by arrangement rather than happenstance. If practitioners are to be required to put their house in better order, however, they have the right to expect the court to do the same. For example, it would not be unreasonable to expect that arrangements will be made to hear emergency applications which do not eat into allocated hearing time and that the judge/magistrates will have done whatever preparation is considered necessary by the listed time, and not expect practitioners to wait while they do so.

Time in court

Once started a hearing cannot be guaranteed to proceed without interruptions. There are unexpected hiatuses, for example for instructions to be taken or for the parties to hammer out an agreement. Such hiatuses may shorten the case. The same cannot be said of adjournments to enable the judge to read the papers.

Fifteen professionals (six lawyers; the guardian, two social workers, a team manager, four other witnesses and a community care team manager) were at court for the first day of a three-day final hearing. The hearing started 95 minutes late because another case had been slotted in. When the case got on, just before lunch, the judge announced he had not read the papers but would hear the opening submission. When the hearing resumed (late) after lunch we were in court for 14 minutes before the judge adjourned the case for the day to spend the afternoon reading the papers. In total 77 minutes were spent in court out of an expected hearing day of around five hours and seven of those were spent re-arranging the remaining hearing days.

While this may be an efficient use of the judge's time it is an incredibly wasteful use of practitioners'. The reason for this practice, we were told, lies in the number of cases which settle at the door of the court. Thus the solution may lie in devising systems to maximise the opportunities for earlier settlement. At the very least, however, if this practice is to be allowed to persist, practitioners and parties need to be informed in advance. In the case cited above social services had clearly come to court expecting to proceed and had assembled their first witnesses. Not only was their time wasted but the schedules of all those expecting to give evidence on subsequent days were thrown into confusion.

The principal scheduled interruption in the family proceedings court is occasioned by the Bench rising to consider their decision and, since the Children Act, to formulate their reasons. The time magistrates take to prepare reasons was a frequent topic of practitioner complaint. We attended 39 hearings at which reasons were required. Retirements ending in their production lasted on average for 47 minutes and represented 11% of net hearing time. It was usually impossible for us as researchers, of course, to differentiate between the time taken for the magistrates to reach a decision and that taken to produce reasons for that decision because the two processes were usually run together and we did not retire with the Bench. However from the frequency with which magistrates referred to these new duties, apologising for the time taken, it would seem reasonable to infer that the formulation of reasons has added substantially to the duration of retirements.

Interviews with magistrates and Justices' Clerks do suggest that the requirement to give reasons is helpful as part of the process of thinking through a case. Moreover, prior to the Act magistrates were discouraged from saying anything other than announcing their decision.[46] Consequently many hearings, as we can attest, ended with an abruptness and a coldness that must have been distressing for parents. However our parental interviews suggest that when reasons are read out now most parents are too anxious and upset to hear very much at all. What they would prefer is an opportunity to go through a copy of the reasons afterwards with someone who can also explain what the decision means.

We would therefore question whether the time spent waiting for reasons to be prepared is the most productive use of everybody's time and suggest that dispatch of a copy of the order accompanied by reasons would be more satisfactory. It seems particularly wasteful in cases where orders are agreed by all the parties and therefore the likelihood of the bench disagreeing is extremely remote, again a source of vociferous criticism by practitioners. That is not to say that the Bench should automatically accede to lawyers' agreements; merely that if all that is at issue is the form of words there are better uses for everybody's precious time. In one memorable case, for example, we noted it took the Bench 1 hour 12 minutes to produce reasons for an uncontested care order.

Given that magistrates' courts appear, in general, to be coping rather better with their workload than the higher courts, saving time in this way might be regarded as irrelevant to the main issue. As against this we would again argue the need to look at the overall system and the knock-on effects of wasting practitioner time. Moreover, if one solution to the resource difficulties in the higher courts is seen to be a lower transfer rate, one might expect time in the family proceedings court to become more at a premium.

Internal adjournments took up a quarter of what one might term net hearing time (that is exclusive of waiting and other released time). The formal processes of submissions, evidence and judgement accounted for just over half. Surprisingly little oral evidence was taken. More than three-quarters of all hearings and almost half of final hearings had none at all, while evidence lasting in total for more than 15 minutes was heard in only 21% of initial hearings, 32% of final hearings and 4% of other hearings (Figure 13.4).

It might seem therefore that there is little scope for savings in court time here. However one of the themes to emerge from the interview data was a degree of surprise that written evidence has not reduced the amount of oral evidence as much as had been anticipated: as we observed in a number of our sample cases, lengthy evidence in chief continued to be given. The developing prac-

Figure 13.4 *The use of in-court time*

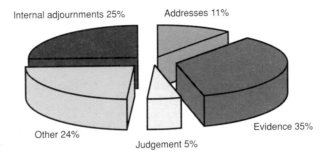

Internal adjournments 25%   Addresses 11%

Other 24%   Judgement 5%   Evidence 35%

tice of allowing statements to stand as evidence in chief, as recommended by the Children Act Advisory Committee[47] and directed by the President[48] could therefore result in clawing back some time with little ill effect provided that, as many of the judges we interviewed urged, witnesses can still be fed a few warm-up questions by their own side to settle them down before being proffered for questioning.

Similarly, cross-examination was widely reported to be more rigorous as the result of advance disclosure and, given the higher number of represented parties, can be a very lengthy process. Some advocates are more efficient than others at probing the opposition's case – a point which emerged in a number of judicial interviews – while closing addresses can sometimes be extremely long-winded. This tends to be the case particularly when the case being advanced is pretty hopeless. One can sympathise with an advocate who knows he cannot win but needs to demonstrate to the client that he has made his best effort. We also know from interviews with parents that even if they have lost their children it helps to feel that they have fought for them. Clearly there are times when judges are prepared to be patient with repetitive cross-examination and rambling addresses for this reason. Equally, however, judges vary in their readiness to control the advocates. As a result, as listing officers are all too well aware, a case which might take X days before Judge A, is likely to take X + Y days before Judge B, while magistrates seem reluctant to cut evidence or addresses short at all.

Thus attention to the respective skills of advocacy and hearing management might bring long-term benefits in the form of tighter hearings. In the short term, practices such as setting time limits for both cross-examination and addresses might help to concentrate minds, as would a requirement for representatives to submit written arguments in advance.[49] We saw this used most purposefully in a case which, it became apparent at the pre-trial review, was likely to overrun its allotted time, and it would seem to have a more general application, as others have recognised.[50]

The research also supports the need for the directions given by Mr Justice Wall[51] on the preparation of trial bundles. The time wasted in a hearing because of badly prepared documentation (missing papers or pages, unnumbered, illegible or undated documents) may only add up to minutes rather than hours but it tends to disrupt proceedings and create a unhelpful sense of disorganisation. Responsibility for assembling the trial bundles is traditionally the applicant's, although some local authority lawyers might argue it should properly be the court's. Given the pressure legal departments are working under and in some cases the shortage of clerical support it is understandable, if not acceptable, that mistakes are made.

Since the evidence in care cases tends to come in intermittently, the current mode of preparing bundles seems illogical and wasteful of time and money. We would therefore endorse the suggestion[52] that there should be a running bundle, each legal representative, and the court, being responsible for keeping their own copies in good order. (The requirement for court staff to compile such a bundle as the evidence comes in, rather than just shoving everything in an increasingly large and chaotic file as happens in some cases, would also be of inestimable advantage to the judiciary taking directions hearings.) All that would be necessary at the end therefore, would be for the local authority to distribute to the other representatives and the court a final list of documents and the order in which they should be arranged.

Eventually, presumably, the legal system will come to terms with the modern world and start distributing information electronically. Perhaps too, the ultimate consequence of the increasing quantities of written evidence and its more efficient preparation and presentation will further diminish the traditional significance of oral evidence and the *day in court* and bring procedures closer to those in other jurisdictions which appear to rely primarily on written depositions and the court dossier.[53]

Effective management of the substantive hearing, of course, does not begin when the parties enter the courtroom. In one sense everything that has happened up to that point is a preparation for this occasion. If a case has been allowed to ramble and acquire extraneous parties and witnesses then it would require a miracle worker not a trial manager to get it into some sort of order at this point. As we indicated in Chapter 12, the routine use of pre-trial reviews seems an efficient use of court time. We would also concur with the view of the Children Act Advisory Committee that, to be effective, all the advocates who will handle the final hearing need to attend and all the evidence should be available, particularly any expert evidence. Ideally the guardian should also be present and if at all possible the hearing should be taken by the judge or the clerk who will officiate at the final hearing.

If these criteria are met then the pre-trial review would help to ensure not only that everything is in place for the substantive hearing but that the issues are clarified, particularly any disputes between experts, the evidence bearing on those issues and the witnesses who will have something pertinent to say about them identified, and the time estimate refined. Moreover, since a well-prepared pre-trial review becomes a dummy run for the final hearing, and parents would normally be expected to be present, it seems likely that a number of cases might even settle at this point, releasing court and practitioner time sufficiently far ahead to be usefully re-deployed.

Better preparation by both advocates and judiciary should equally improve the effectiveness of interim hearings. There may also be scope for saving time by reducing the *number* of such hearings.

Number of hearings

The study areas varied in their arrangements for the transfer of cases from the family proceedings court (Chapter 10). Savings could be made by streamlining the arrangements everywhere, so that where possible the decision was taken administratively by a clerk rather than at a hearing before the Bench. We would also argue that the agreed joinder of new parties should be made by the clerk, magistrates being called upon only to adjudicate on any dispute.

Another prime candidate for such reduction would be the renewal of agreed interim orders, where again different practices were evident. In one court, for example, the local authority was required to attend, wasting perhaps only a few minutes of court time but, given the travel involved, perhaps two hours of the lawyers'. This was an added burden for a particularly hard-pressed legal department which had difficulty providing legal advice to case conferences, liaising with social workers and on occasion organising evidence in advance. In another area positive confirmation that the order was agreed, signed by all the lawyers, had to be sent to the court, involving a great flurry of last-minute activity. Sometimes it was the researchers' inquiry as to whether the order was being renewed under Rule 28/4 that initiated this while in a few non-observed cases it had clearly gone unnoticed that no application had been submitted and the order had expired. A third variant was to give a direction for automatic renewal unless application was made for a contested hearing. This would seem to be the most sensible approach, provided that the court can allocate time to hear a contested application where necessary.

The time limits on interim care and supervision orders could also be re-considered, indeed whether there need be any mandatory limit at all. The initial eight-week provision is of little use when hearings cluster towards the beginning of proceedings and the four-week restriction on further orders is unduly constraining, this being the point when things are likely to be hanging fire waiting for the outcome of assessments. Therefore either courts could be given greater flexibility as to when they use the longer order, or initial orders could be made for the duration of the case unless any of the parties wishes to bring the matter back for reconsideration.

Such a change, of course, like the use of 'roll-overs',[54] has its dangers, principally that the court will not be aware if the case drifts. However there is no reason why this cannot be guarded against through directions appointments. Indeed we would argue that these, rather than interim hearings, should now constitute the primary mechanism for case management. If our suggestions for increasing court control between hearings, particularly case allocation, were adopted, the risk would be minimised.

Where there is to be a contested interim, however, then directions should be given on the same occasion; a common source of complaint in one area being the practice of separating substantive and directions hearings so that practitioners might have to be in court one week for an interim hearing before the magistrates and again the next week for a directions hearing before the clerk.

Directions hearings themselves have now become an essential part of the mechanics of care cases and are widely perceived to be invaluable in facilitating court control (Chapter 12). However there were those who considered that appointments were sometimes made routinely, without sufficient regard to their value at that point in the case and that where no directions at all were needed, or all the directions were agreed, matters could be handled without a fully attended hearing. One representative, for instance, instead of all, could report to the court. We would suggest that this should be the child's solicitor.

Some directions, it was further submitted, could be adequately dealt with by letter or telephone. Technology, particularly telephone conferencing, could transform the courtroom-based culture of the legal process, as ambitious experiments in other jurisdictions are demonstrating.[55] Indeed there are indications that even some UK practitioners are beginning to exploit the possibilities.[56]

Over half the interim hearings in our observed cases lasted for 30 minutes or less. Cutting out one of these shorter hearings per case would save several hours of practitioner time and nationally would add up to several hundred *days* of court time per year. On the basis that each of our observed cases took an average of almost 10 hours *hearing* time this might enable the system to accommodate another 200 cases per year and thus reduce waiting lists.

Contested interim hearings now tend to last for at least a day. Some practitioners were anxious that in an attempt to reduce demands on the court it might become more difficult to obtain more than one contested interim and we share their concern that this would not be in the interests of justice. However, there was also a view that contested interims often only became necessary because proceedings were dragging on, creating a vicious circle in which because court time was scarce there were more contested hearings which absorbed even more time, exacerbating the problem.

The allocation of judicial resources

In the first few years of the Act it has been the higher courts which have suffered most severely from the imbalance between supply and demand. As far as the avoidance of delay alone is concerned, therefore, logic demands that wherever possible cases should be heard in the family proceedings court and not transferred unnecessarily.

A degree of tension between the family proceedings court and the care centre is probably inherent in a divided structure, in itself an argument for integration. Where good working relationships can be developed, however, it should be possible to reach a mutually acceptable interpretation of the criteria which could take account of particular local circumstances and changing workloads. More extensive use of specialist stipendiary magistrates, as suggested in an earlier chapter, would strengthen the capacity of the lower courts to handle more difficult or lengthy cases. For cases which do need to be heard at the care centre consideration should be given to enhancing still further the jurisdiction of the district judges in order to relieve the burden on the designated judges. Again, establishing sound working relationships between the district judges and the designated judges would be essential to ensure compatibility of approach.

Where these measures are insufficient to relieve pressures then, as the Act envisaged, resources may need to be sought elsewhere. Lateral transfer has not so far proved a very popular option, partly because it requires the case to travel. While this is undoubtedly convenient for the judge it is wasteful of other professional resources and public funds. In the only research area to make much use of external resources the judge now travelled to the case, a very successful arrangement, if less satisfactory than increasing the pitiful complement of local judges would have been. This arrangement also makes it feasible for the search to extend beyond neighbouring courts which may be equally over-burdened. If there is sufficient spare capacity in the system as a whole, extending this approach would even out local imbalances. Given the widespread complaints about court resources reported elsewhere,[57] however, its main value is likely to be as a temporary means of relieving bottlenecks.

Many members of the judiciary who are qualified to handle care cases, of course, are only engaged on that work for part of their time. Circuit judges hear criminal as well as private family law cases. District judges are primarily occupied with ancillary relief and other civil matters. This is clearly a difficult issue, involving questions about the status of family law within the judicial system and both the willingness and the capacity of the judiciary to keep to a staple diet of family work. The effect on other children's cases of the priority given to public law cases also has to be borne in mind (although developments such as the Child Support Act and the Family Law Act 1996 may in time make this less of an issue). A more specialist judiciary, however, would also facilitate the development of skills in hearing and case management which have already been identified as critical in keeping cases to time.

Consideration needs to be given to whether the system, which tends to suffer from peaks and troughs in demand, needs a cadre of *locum* judges. Such systems exist in both education and health while in the legal system there is already provision for urgent cases to be heard by deputy High Court judges during the long judicial vacation, (a tradition which, some interviewees suggested, was, like the standard 10am to 4pm court day,[58] an unjustifiable anachronism whose reduction would itself increase the amount of judicial time available).

The limits of court involvement

Until a court is in a position to dispose of a case, legal proceedings go on. The time taken to reach such a position will vary, which is why the Act does not set a figure for maximum duration. However there is also variation in the point at which courts consider they *are* in that position. Pre-Act, for instance, cases heard in care proceedings in Area B were far more likely than those in A to be kept within the court process until the welfare disposition was clear.

Thus assessments tended to be carried out during proceedings and rehabilitation monitored under an Interim Care Order. In Area A, however, assessments and rehabilitation might start but the final order would not normally await their outcome. This we considered was an important part of the explanation for the speedier proceedings in this area.

This difference was still discernible post-Act with several examples of cases being disposed of by the family proceedings court in Area A at a point when there was still considerable uncertainty about the future: whether the child would go to a relative or a stranger placement for instance; whether parental treatment for alcoholism would enable the child to be rehabilitated; whether an apparent change in parental attitudes would be maintained so that the child could be protected without an order. In both the other areas we feel fairly confident in predicting the court would have remained involved for longer.

We also suspect, however, that had these cases been transferred to the county court in Area A they would not have been expected to leave the legal process so rapidly. One of the most contentious issues to arise over implementation of the new legislation has been that of the proper boundaries between the court's and the local authority's jurisdiction. Under wardship, for instance, which was the professional judiciary's principal previous contact with public law children's cases, all important decisions had to be referred to the court, even after a child was committed to local authority care. Under the Children and Young Persons Act, the (magistrates') court's involvement terminated with the final order.

As we shall see in Chapter 15, there has been considerable dissatisfaction with this aspect of the Act, resulting in various attempts to circumvent legislative intent by keeping the court and perhaps more particularly the guardian, involved. Thus cases have been kept going with successive Interim Care Orders while rehabilitation has been tried, or care orders have been accompanied with time-limited Contact Orders so that progress can be monitored. Since these strategies have been repeatedly criticised by the Court of Appeal[59] the judiciary may have to abandon their resistance to this aspect of the Act and leave the field to the Children Act reformers. Equally it is possible that for as long as there is no power to add conditions to a Care Order or to bring back cases for review ways will be sought to keep the most worrying cases before the court until the welfare as well as the legal issues have, as far as is possible, been resolved. Thus paradoxically, the determination to separate the judicial and executive spheres reflected in the Act may be actually deferring the point at which that separation takes place.

Reducing the use of the courts

The suggestions so far have been aimed at redressing the imbalance between supply and demand once cases are within the court system. Is there also scope for reducing the volume of cases reaching court?

Given what has been said in earlier chapters about the damage done by delay in invoking the legal process, and the generally tight filter operating in the early years of the Act the potential for further diversion from the court system at the point the local authority considers this is necessary would not appear to be great. However the fact that cases such as Samantha's and Josie's ever got to court indicates that the screening process was not yet fail-safe. In other cases, longer Emergency Protection Orders, as recommended in Chapter 5, might allow some crises to subside or be resolved by voluntary agreements. Harnessing the resources of the extended family more effectively, whether or not this involves the use of family group conferences, is another possibility.

Many cases, however, get to court because social services and the parents have not been able to work together. Some of these might yet be diverted from the compulsory route if strategies were developed for unlocking or circumventing these blocked relationships. Sometimes this might be as simple as changing the social worker or bringing in another worker for the parents. In others it might require the involvement of another agency, particularly where parents have accumulated a great deal of resentment against social services, perhaps because of what has happened to previous children. Empowering parents via earlier access to advocacy might, paradoxically, reduce conflict. It is even possible that some form of alternative dispute resolution, which is transforming private law, would be useful. Some such initiatives, such as that at the Tavistock Clinic, are already under way.

Ultimately, we would argue, the volume of cases reaching court is largely a function of the effectiveness of policies to meet family need. Thus eventually, outlay on one part of the system – preventative services, which are comparatively cheap – should reduce demand in another – the legal system, which is hideously expensive. Finally it might be questioned whether it is sensible that all care applications, which as we have seen are enormously varied, are processed in the same way with the full panoply of due process. We consider this question further in our final chapter.

Summary

Section 1(2) of the Children Act attempts to inculcate a sense of urgency into all those dealing with children's cases. The need for such an imperative was recognised as necessary by practitioners and the judiciary in both the research areas where delay was a serious problem pre-Act and in all three as a valuable principle.

Pre-Act research revealed how problematic and formidable the reduction of delay was likely to be. Interviews confirmed that in some respects the new legislation has also made the task even more difficult. It was concluded, however, that the emphasis on avoiding delay has been remarkably, if not totally, successful in effecting culture change.

The thrust of practitioner responses, however, was that while those within the system had become very delay conscious, their efforts were not supported by adequately resourced infrastructures in local authorities, health services or the courts. Drift may be less in evidence, the problem of delay remains.

Only one in ten of the sample cases completed within the original 12-week target. Over a third took more than six months with the longest case lasting for 78 weeks. Speed of throughput varied by area and court level. Care proceedings take longer under the Children Act than under the Children and Young Persons Act 1969 although all court levels seem to have improved their level of performance, cases completing in the family proceedings court slightly more quickly than pre-Act care proceedings and those heard in the higher courts substantially more quickly than wardships.

No association was discovered between the characteristics of the cases and their duration. Certain aspects of the families' interaction with welfare agencies did appear to have an impact, suggesting that the firmer the case can be made before it comes to court the more quickly it will proceed through the legal process. As a strategy for reducing overall delay this was argued to be of limited value, since such certainty was usually achieved at the cost of pre-court delay. It was concluded that the court process itself was the major influence on the pace of proceedings, particularly the use of experts and the level of court at which the case was finally heard.

Practitioners identified a range of factors causing delay under the Act but the primary causes were held to be assessments, experts and lack of court time, particularly in the higher courts. The case data confirmed that delay is a multifactorial problem and that most cases experienced more than one form of delay. Longer cases tended to have more sources of delay. Delay caused by the joinder of new parties or lack of court time were statistically related to variation in duration. Factors identified as causing delay were categorised and their impact on case duration assessed. Resource difficulties affected almost half the cases and their impact was most marked of all.

The effective operation of local systems, it is argued, is key to the eradication of delay. Funding to develop mechanisms to monitor delay at a local level is urged as a cost-effective strategy to address the problem. It is recommended that for this purpose a small working group be established in each care centre, accountable to the Business Committee.

The research wholeheartedly supports practitioners in their call for better resourcing of the system. Recognising, however, that there is unlikely to be a massive injection of funds in the foreseeable future it begins to address the issue of the maximisation of scarce resources.

A number of suggestions were made for reducing the length of hearings. Waiting time is of particular concern. There is a need for courts to audit the amount of time spent waiting for cases to start, to identify the reasons for this and devise strategies for ensuring cases start promptly.

The research endorses recommendations about limiting evidence in chief, better preparation of trial bundles and requiring the issues and arguments to be set out in writing in advance. Hearings might proceed more expeditiously if all lawyers were well prepared, knowledgeable about child care law and had developed skills in economical advocacy. Time limits on cross-examination could be usefully considered. Social workers need more training in giving evidence and the judiciary in hearing management. Wherever possible the judge/Bench taking the final hearing should run the pre-trial review and should have read at least the key evidence in advance. Hearings in the family proceedings court might be shortened if magistrates had more training in the formulation of reasons or these were produced subsequent to the hearing. The value to the parents of listening to their delivery was questioned.

Suggestions were also made for reducing the number of hearings. Agreed transfer, joinder of parties, renewal of Interim Care Orders and some directions might be dealt with without appearance; modern technology could permit some directions to be dealt with by telephone conferencing. The value of directions hearings in bringing the parties together and keeping practitioners up to the mark is fully recognised. It is argued, however, that the culture of last-minutism is inappropriate in children's cases and needs to be changed. Continuity of management by the court should minimise the risk that this will increase drift.

Reallocation of judicial resources would also help to relieve blockages. Generally less pressurised lists in the lower courts are a powerful argument for reversing the trend towards higher rates of vertical transfer. Greater use of stipendiaries might increase the flexibility of the family proceedings court. Consideration should be given to enhancing the jurisdiction of the district judges and to increasing the proportion of their time spent on care cases. Bringing the judiciary to the case might be a more effective means of evening out workloads than lateral transfer. Developing a cadre of locum judges would prevent cases piling up and relieve particularly acute pressure points.

The impact of purposeful delay on the overall system, however legitimate the individual circumstances, needs to be taken into account. The boundaries the Act establishes between the judicial and the executive domains, which should curtail the duration of court involvement, may be prolonging it. Redrawing these boundaries, paradoxically, might encourage courts to bow out more quickly.

Suggestions are also made for reducing the intake of cases, including alternative mechanisms for resolving disputes. It is questioned whether it is appropriate that the full spectrum of cases currently reaching the care courts are dealt with by the same complicated and resource-intensive process.

NOTES

[1] Children Act 1989 s1(2).

[2] See for example: *Civil Justice Review* (1988): Cm 3944, HMSO; Home Office (1989): *Scrutiny of Administrative Arrangements in Magistrates' Courts.* HMSO; Lord Chancellor's Department (1986): *Interdepartmental Review of Family and Domestic Jurisdictions.* LCD.

[3] Frankenburg C; Tarling R (1983): Time taken to deal with juveniles in criminal proceedings. Research Planning Paper 18. Home Office; Law Commission (1988): *Family Law Review of Child Law: Guardianship and Custody*; Masson J; Morton S (1989): The Use of Wardship by Local Authorities. *Modern Law Review,* November; Murch M et al. (1993): *Pathways to Adoption.* HMSO.

[4] Farmer E; Parker R (1985): *A Study of Interim Care Orders.* School of Applied Social Studies, University of Bristol.

[5] Murch M; Mills E (1987): *The Length of Care Proceedings.* Socio-Legal Centre for Family Studies, University of Bristol.

[6] Between 1983 and 1986 the average length of a sample of applications for care and supervision orders brought on the grounds of ill-treatment was nine weeks. By 1986–89 this had risen to 17 weeks. 15% took more than 32 weeks. Thomas C et al. (1993): *The Duration of Care Proceedings: A Replication Study.* HMSO.

[7] DHSS (1988): *Report of the Inquiry into Child Abuse in Cleveland 1987.* Cm 412, HMSO.

[8] See for example the *Civil Justice Review* (1988): op. cit.

[9] DHSS (1985): *Review of Child Care Law: Report to Ministers of an Interdepartmental Working Party*. HMSO.

[10] Law Commission (1988): op. cit.

[11] Lynch M A; Roberts J (1982): *Consequences of Child Abuse*. Academic Press.

[12] Representation of the Child in the Civil Courts. Research Project 1985–90.

[13] See for example Bowlby J (1971): *Attachment and Loss*. Penguin; Douglas J (1970): Broken Families and Child Behaviour. *Journal of the Royal College of Physicians*; Rutter M (1972): *Maternal Deprivation Re-assessed*. Penguin; Wolkind S; Rutter M (1973): Children Who have been in Care – an epidemiological study. *Journal of Child Psychology and Psychiatry*, 14.

[14] Summarised in Rowe J (1985): *Social Work Decisions in Child Care – Recent Research Findings and their Implications*. HMSO.

[15] Millham S et al. (1985): *Lost in Care*. Gower.

[16] Aldgate J (1980): Identification of Factors Influencing Children's Stay in Care, in Triseliotis J (ed.): *New Developments in Foster Care and Adoption*. Routledge and Kegan Paul.

[17] E.g. Report of the Home Office's Working Group on Magistrates' Courts (1982).

[18] Murch and Mills (1987): op. cit.

[19] Church T W Jr (1979): Civil Case Delay in State Trial Courts. *Justice System Journal*.

[20] House of Commons (1984): *Second Report of the All-Party Parliamentary Select Committee on Social Services* (Session 1983–84): Children in Care (The Short Report). HMSO.

[21] Law Commission (1988): op. cit.

[22] House of Commons 23 May 1989.

[23] Hunt J (1992): The Problem of Delay. Unpublished conference paper.

[24] A process described by Dingwall as *diagnostic inflation*. Dingwall R et al. (1983): *The Protection of Children*. Basil Blackwell.

[25] Murch and Mills (1987): op. cit.

[26] Murch M; Thomas C (1992): *Feedback from Family Court Business Committees*. Socio-Legal Centre for Family Studies, University of Bristol.

[27] Thomas C; Hunt J (1996): *The Care Workloads of the Civil Courts under the Children Act*. Centre for Socio-Legal Studies, University of Bristol.

[28] Thomas et al. (1993): op. cit.

[29] *Children Act Advisory Committee Report* 1991–92; DoH (1992) *Children Act Report*. HMSO.

[30] Mrs Justice Bracewell (1995): Comment. *Family Law*, February.

[31] Rupert Hughes, Assistant Secretary, Community Services Division, DoH: *Children Act News*, February 1995.

[32] Mrs Justice Hale (1995): Foreword, in White R et al. *The Children Act in Practice*. Butterworths.

[33] *Children Act Advisory Committee Annual Report* 1993–94.

[34] Figures exclude the case which was withdrawn at the first hearing.

[35] This is only a few days longer than the mean duration of all the Section 31 cases covered in our extensive survey (Thomas and Hunt (1996): op. cit.).

[36] Thomas and Hunt (1996): op. cit.

[37] Hunt (1993): *Local Authority Wardships before the Children Act: The Baby or the Bathwater?* HMSO.

[38] Masson and Morton (1989): op. cit.

[39] Pre-Act Area C brought too few cases under the CYPA 69 for a useful comparison to be made.

[40] Representation of the Child in the Civil Courts. Research Project, op. cit.

[41] op. cit.

[42] C v Solihull Metropolitan Borough Council [1993] 1 FLR 290 at 304. Re B (A Minor) (Contact) (Interim Order) [1994] 2 FLR 269.

[43] Mr Justice Singer, for instance, is reported to have been particularly uncompromising on this issue, stating that even if all other delays were eradicated, if cases which were going to settle settled earlier, and if hearings were curtailed, there were not enough judges to cater for children and their families. A 33-week wait to hear a 4–5-day case in London called for action. The human and physical resources to deal with the volume of work did not exist: 'If nothing is done we risk being over the edge of an abyss' More Judges. *Family Law*, November 1994, 604.

[44] Each practitioner would only have to be earning on average £25 an hour for the cost of waiting time to come to almost £1,000 per case. Given the number of care applications per year nationally the cost runs into several million pounds.

[45] His Honour Judge McCarraher. Conference Report: Practice in Progress, June 1994. Irchin.

[46] London Borough of Brent (1985): *A Child in Trust: Report of the Panel of Inquiry into the Circumstances Surrounding the Death of Jasmine Beckford*. London Borough of Brent.

[47] *Annual Report* 1993–94.

[48] Practice Direction: Case Management [1995] 1 All ER586.

[49] Practice Direction: op. cit., 49.

[50] *Children Act Advisory Committee Annual Report* 1993–94.

[51] B v B (Practice Judgement) [1994] 1 FCR 805.

[52] Burrows D (1995): *Family Law*, 38.

[53] King M; Piper C (1995): *How the Law Thinks About Children*. 2nd edition. Arena.

[54] Brasse G (1994): A Tightly Run Procedure? Interim Care Orders under Strain. *Family Law*, 261.

[55] Purcell T (1995): Technology's Role in Access to Legal Services and Legal Information, in Smith R (ed.): *Shaping the Future: New Directions in Legal Services*. Legal Action Group.

[56] *Bristol Law Society Newsletter*, December 1995.

[57] Dame Margaret Booth (1996): *Avoiding Delay in Children Act Cases*. LCD.

[58] It should be noted that in one of our care centres the judiciary regularly started hearing cases much earlier than this which enabled them to slot in urgent applications without compromising the day's list.

[59] E.g. Re J (Minors (Care Plan)) [1994] FLR 253 and Re CN (A Minor) (Care Orders) [1992] 2 FCR 401.

14 Staging posts: Interim Orders; interim hearings

Extending choice

Until the court is in a position to dispose of a case, which as we have seen may not be for some considerable time, it may adjourn or make one or more of a range of Interim Orders. Although under the Children and Young Persons Act 1969 the choice was limited to an Interim Care Order or nothing, more varied and flexible disposals were available in wardship and in matrimonial proceedings.

The new *menu* of orders introduced by the Children Act 1989 brought the management of the interim period nearer to the wardship model and was intended to make case handling more accountable to the court and more responsive to the needs of the individual situation. Interim contact can for the first time be controlled; Interim Supervision Orders made and, since these are *family proceedings* within the meaning of the Act, a range of private law orders (Residence, Contact, Prohibited Steps and Specific Issue) are also available and can be used on a time-limited basis. The legislation thus provides for a spectrum of control pending the final decision. As one solicitor put it:

> It is like a washing machine with twenty cycles, you can be creative, we don't automatically go to court and say you have got to accept an Interim Care Order, we do try and negotiate.

In principle, this aspect of the Act was widely welcomed by the practitioners interviewed. Though the menu has, to a certain extent, fallen short of expectations, for the most part practitioner criticism has focused on final orders and will therefore be dealt with in Chapter 15. We concentrate in this chapter on the application of the menu at the interim stage in the sample cases: is the potential of the 20 cycles being fully exploited or is it that, as another practitioner put it, simply extending the same image:

> You have thousands of programmes but at the end of the day you have two or three that are your favourites and I think that is what is happening really, there isn't a huge variety.

Application of the menu in the sample cases

Changing choices: initial and subsequent orders

Almost three-quarters of the sample cases began with a public law order, typically an Interim Care Order (Figure 14.1). Protection via Section 8 orders alone at this stage was fairly unusual, although there were a further four cases where they were used in addition to Interim Supervision Orders. The second most common outcome of the initial hearing, however, was an adjournment without any order at all. For the most part in such cases social services were in agreement with this. The majority involved children who had already been accommodated for some considerable time (11) and whose parents were prepared to continue on this basis. There were also two cases of children removed in a crisis but subsequently accommodated. There were only three cases where children remained in parental care without any public law protection. Although proceedings had eventually been brought on the Phillips children, for instance, the intention was for them to remain at home while further attempts were made to work with the family situation.

Figure 14.1 *Initial orders (n=82)*

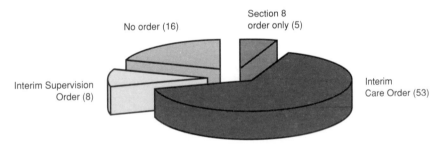

There were, however, four cases in which the local authority's application was thwarted at the outset, of which three followed opposition from the guardian: Zara Butler, where the court made a Prohibited Steps Order preventing her removal from hospital rather than the Interim Care Order sought; James Pallister, who went to live with his aunt under a Residence Order; Sammi Collins who stayed at home without any order. In one remarkable case, however, although the application was strongly supported by the guardian the court took the view that insufficient evidence had been presented, to the amazement of all concerned, including the researchers. Subsequent analysis showed that this case had the highest number of factors causing concern (Chapter 6) in the whole sample.

Zara was subsequently made subject to an Interim Care Order and in the course of proceedings *different* orders were made in almost a quarter of the sample cases (19). Eight cases which started without any public law order subsequently attracted Interim Care Orders. The initiation of proceedings, for instance, did not have the desired effect on Joanne Phillips; she continued to drink to excess and the children were removed under police protection and Interim Care Orders made. Another set of children came into care after placement with their grandmother broke down. In other cases parental consent to continuing accommodation was withdrawn or the local authority decided it needed to control contact. Only one of the cases which began with no order at all moved to an intermediate position with protection via private law orders: Jamie Harris moving out of accommodation to live with his father and stepmother under an Interim Residence Order.

In contrast 11 cases moved down the legal tariff, either to no public law order at all or to an Interim Supervision Order from an Interim Care Order. Jenny Grayson, for example, moved to live with her grandparents under an Interim Residence Order after her mother agreed to in-patient psychiatric treatment. Children in two other cases similarly moved to relatives and one to a separated parent. Ahmed Khan and his mother were rapidly rehabilitated under an Interim Supervision Order following a short period in a psychiatric unit. Four other cases also involved rehabilitation and a fifth a reduction of the legal protection considered necessary on a child who had been placed, from the start, with her mother in a residential unit. The eleventh case, which concerned the Wyllie children, was rather different in that an Interim Supervision Order was allowed to expire after they were accommodated under threat of an Emergency Protection Order.

Despite this evidence of change in a proportion of cases, typically the initial order set the pattern for the rest of the proceedings. Forty-three cases starting with Interim Care Orders and seven with Interim Supervision Orders had such orders throughout. Cases without any public law order in the first instance were the most subject to change (two of five).

Comparative incidence

Thus, as Figure 14.2 reveals, Interim Care Orders remain by far the most widely used order, at least one being made in almost three in four cases. In comparison the use of alternative orders was relatively uncommon with only Interim Supervision and Residence Orders approaching a frequency of one in five.

Figure 14.2 *The use of Interim Orders (cases with at least one such order)*

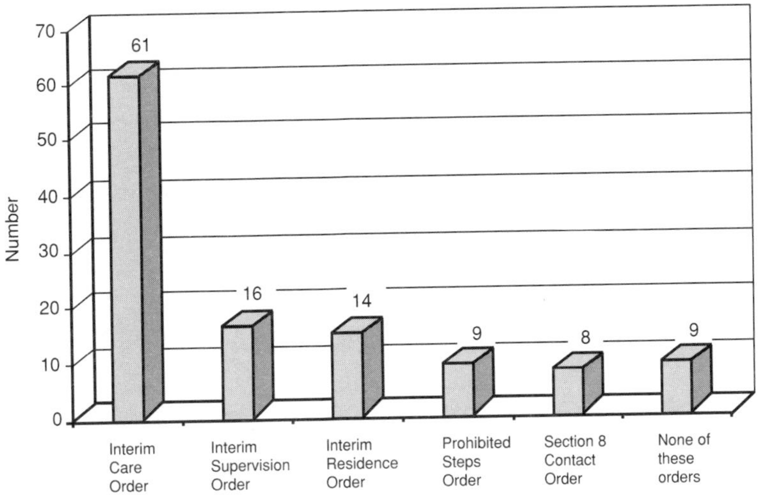

Variation by area

Table 14.1, which shows the number of cases per area in which at least one order of each type was made, reveals a good deal of variation between the three areas. Area A used public law orders in many fewer cases than the other two and in cases which did attract such orders used Interim Supervision Orders more often. It also had more cases where no order was used at all. Area C, in contrast, had by far the highest rate of use of public law orders, used Interim Supervision Orders very infrequently and private law orders scarcely at all. There was only one case in this area where no order was made, baby Laurie being accommodated throughout.

Table 14.1 *Interim Orders: variation by area*

	Area A		Area B		Area C	
	No.	%	No.	%	No.	%
Interim Care Order	17	59	22	76	22	92
Interim Supervision Order	7	24	6	21	3	8
Interim Care Order or Interim Supervision Order	20	69	26	90	23	96
Interim Residence Order	6	21	6	21	2	8
Prohibited Steps Order	5	17	3	10	1	1
Section 8 Contact Order	2	8	5	17	1	1
No order	6	21	2	7	1	1
(n=)		(29)		(29)		(24)

Comparison with the pre-Act position

Valid comparison of the pre- and post-Act use of interim orders is difficult, of course, in view of the differences in the available options and the types of proceedings. Moreover it is another instance where interacting and/or countervailing factors produce rather unexpected results. Disconcertingly, for instance, as far as Interim Care Orders are concerned the aggregated figures for the whole sample would suggest the Act has had minimal effect, the proportion of cases in which such orders were made being almost exactly the same in both periods (Figure 14.3) while the fraction in which such orders were made throughout was only slightly smaller (Figure 14.4).

Figure 14.3 *Interim Care Orders before and after the Children Act*

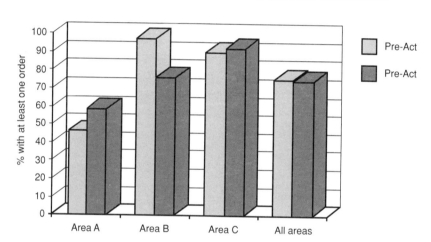

Figure 14.4 *Interim Care Orders throughout: a pre- and post-Act comparison*

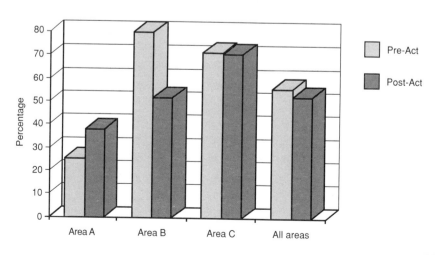

Analysis of the data by area reveals a more varied, but confusing picture. Area B shows a very substantial decrease in the use of Interim Care Orders on both measures; Area C is virtually unchanged and Area A actually shows an increase. Only in comparison with pre-Act care proceedings was there a reduction in all three areas in the proportion of cases with any Interim Care Order, while in comparison with wardship cases Areas A and C both show an increase.

Area A's figures are particularly puzzling, given the lower use of public law orders compared to the other two areas which was apparent both pre- and post-Act. In previous chapters, however, we have commented on the particularly rigorous screening process in this area (Chapter 8), the higher overall significance rating of the cases brought (Chapter 6) and the longer period of social work involvement pre-proceedings (Chapter 4). We would therefore hypothesise that although Area A *was* trying to operate in the spirit of the Act in the sense of questioning the need for Interim Orders, indeed we would judge was doing so more markedly than the other two areas, the nature of the cases the local authority was bringing to court post-Act made the use of compulsion during proceedings much harder to avoid.

The new orders

Interim Supervision Orders

Almost half of the children on Interim Care Orders in our pre-Act sample were at home, the orders providing protection and local authority access not otherwise available save in wardship. It was hoped that the power to make Interim Supervision Orders would help prevent such anomalies and thus 'lower the tariff'.[1]

In the Children Act sample there were 16 cases where Interim Supervision Orders were made. The majority of these related to children at home with their mothers (six families where children were at home throughout proceedings; three where they were returned home after a period in care; two where an initial period at home under an Interim Supervision Order was not sustained and Interim Care Orders or accommodation had to be used). In Zara's case and one other, the period of supervision covered a stay at a mother and baby home. Only five orders protected placements with relatives, each combined with an Interim Residence Order.

We found no evidence that the addition of interim supervision to the courts' arsenal has operated to increase the use of compulsion. If the pre-Act legislation had still been in force we calculate that Interim Care Orders would have been made in at least 14 of these cases. Further evidence of tariff reduction comes from a number of cases in which the order was not in accord with the local authority's application, of which Zara's case was one of the more obvious examples. Social services also sought Interim Care Orders on Joseph and Molly, even though they had already been returned to their mother. This was contested and the court made an Interim Supervision Order plus a Residence Order with a condition of residence in a bail hostel.

Time-limited Residence Orders

Residence Orders were made in the course of 14 cases. In half of these instances orders were made to members of the extended family, typically maternal grandparents or aunts. In six cases, however, they were made in favour of one parent and in one, briefly, to both in order that conditions might be attached. Orders were normally only in force for part of the proceedings, preceded (7) or followed (3) by other arrangements, usually an Interim Care Order. Two of the four cases where Residence Orders continued throughout were made in the face of opposition from the local authority which was seeking interim care.

In all but three cases additional orders were made in support. The Act stipulates that when a court makes an Interim Residence Order in Section 31 proceedings it shall also make an Interim Supervision Order unless the child's welfare can be 'satisfactorily safeguarded' without.[2] Unlike a final order an Interim Order can be made on the court's own motion. Not surprisingly therefore, Interim Supervision Orders were made in the majority of cases (10). Four of these were made in conjunction with Prohibited Steps Orders. In the case of 3-year-old Sophie Farrow, the Residence Order was buttressed with just about every order and direction possible.

• •

Proceedings began very inauspiciously with Joe arrested, Lisa missing and Sophie whisked into police protection. For a time it seemed that nothing was changing, Lisa and Joe continued to drink to excess and their relationship remained as volatile as ever; neither seemed to acknowledge the effect this had on their parenting. The social worker was unable to secure placement in an alcohol treatment unit. Therefore although Sophie failed to settle in care and her behaviour seriously regressed both social services and the wider family considered that early rehabilitation was too risky.

The guardian, however, took the view that care presented a greater risk and successfully opposed renewal of the Interim Care Order. Sophie returned home protected by an Interim Residence Order to Lisa, an Interim Supervision Order, and a Prohibited Steps Order preventing Lisa from leaving Sophie in Joe's sole care and from leaving her with anyone else without the permission of the local authority. Furthermore these orders were made on parental undertakings that Joe would make himself available for meetings with the social worker and Lisa would:

- continue to attend the alcohol recovery project and participate in such programmes of assessment or treatment as may be required;

- admit the social worker and any other specified persons to her flat including visits made without prior notice; and

- enrol Sophie at a playgroup.

Conditions as to parental contact and social services access were also attached to the Residence Order made in respect of James Pallister in order to allay in some measure the local authority's anxieties about the placement with his aunt without a public law order.

Prohibited Steps Orders

Prohibited Steps Orders were made in nine cases, mainly to control contact between the child and an alleged perpetrator, a usage subsequently disallowed by the decision in Nottinghamshire CC v P.[3] Orders were also used to prevent the child being removed from a specified place (hospital or foster home), being taken abroad or moved to another school, while in Sophie's case, as noted above, the aspect of parental responsibility being controlled was the freedom to choose with whom to entrust the care of the child. In one of the sample cases a Prohibited Steps Order had also been sought as an alternative to an Emergency Protection Order, to prevent the children being removed from the country.

The Nottinghamshire decision, it appears, aborted the developing practice of using Prohibited Steps Order imaginatively and flexibly, not only in the specific ways dealt with in the decision but more broadly. Only one of the orders in the study post-dated the decision (by a month) and it was not renewed. As we shall see in the next chapter, it is one of the developments in case law which practitioners most regret.

Section 8 Contact

The primary use of Prohibited Steps Orders in the sample cases was to control contact where the child was not in local authority care. Until the Nottinghamshire decision the general understanding, encouraged, it must be said, by official guidance on the matter,[4] was that a Contact Order only related to positive contact and could therefore not be used to limit or prevent contact. This undoubtedly helps to explain the low use of Section 8 Contact Orders in the sample cases, most of which pre-dated the Nottinghamshire judgement.

Over half the sample cases (46) included children who were not in local authority care for at least a part of the proceedings. However it appears that for the most part contact was negotiated by informal means apart from the use of Prohibited Steps Orders for this purpose. Contact orders were made in only seven cases. In two of these the child was with one parent with orders governing contact with the other parent, in three with a relative with orders relating to parental contact.

There were also three odd cases where Contact Orders were made in relation to accommodated children. Colin and Antony Wyllie, it may be recalled, were accommodated in the course of proceedings. A key element in obtaining Grace's agreement, which enabled social services to withdraw their renewed application for an Interim Care Order, was that she should have contact with each son three times a week. This was framed in the form of an order, though the section of the legislation being used was not specified.

Section 34 Contact

The new Section 34 Contact Orders, on the other hand, regulating contact with children on Interim Care Orders, were very frequently used, being made in 36 cases (53% of relevant cases).

Under the Act the local authority must allow *reasonable* contact. This in itself was perceived as a vast improvement on the previous position under the Children and Young Persons Act, and according to a number of practitioners, such as this guardian, has had considerable impact on practice:

> I think contact is one of the big issues that has improved in the Children Act.
> At the interim stage that often wasn't addressed in any formal manner. It was
> a bit haphazard. Now social workers are much better at arranging contact
> immediately or putting it in writing making sure that the parents are aware
> so that they have got an opportunity to question.

If social services wish to impose restrictions they must apply for a Contact Order. Conversely parents or other relatives who are not prepared to trust or are dissatisfied with the local authority's interpretation of 'reasonable' may seek orders limiting the department's discretion. As one guardian put it:

> I think very often parents feel that they are getting something as of right in situations which are very critical of them and really, demoralising for them. Somehow, to be granted an order can be a very positive thing to work with.

Parental interviews also indicate that a number preferred orders because of their mistrust of social services. However the sample cases indicate that the primary use of Interim Contact Orders was as a *control* on parental contact. Where there were not thought to be dangers inherent in contact no order was made, though once an order had been made it might be continued as part of a phased relaxation of controls. This was not unnoticed by the parents interviewed, who reported problems with most aspects of contact and particularly with intrusive supervision.[5] In all but one case an order at some stage involved either supervision of parental contact or contact only at the discretion of the local authority. However even though orders were typically being used to constrain contact there were only four orders denying contact altogether, all directed at fathers.

There were no parallels to Section 34 orders in the Children and Young Persons Act. Comparison with Interim Access Orders in wardship shows that the proportion of Interim Orders regulating contact has fallen from 80% to 43%. However, the majority of those earlier orders were for 'reasonable access', a category now rendered superfluous. The only orders in the current study expressed as 'reasonable contact' related to Interim Contact Orders with supervisory conditions.

Placement under Interim Care Orders

As indicated earlier, Interim Care Orders remain the most frequently used order. The effect of an order, however, merely allows the local authority to exercise parental responsibility; it does not determine where the child shall be placed. Thus such children may be living in vastly different circumstances: with one or both parents at home or in a residential unit, with members of their extended families, or in non-related foster placements and children's homes.

All these arrangements were found in the sample. Comparison with the pre-Act cases, however, (Figure 14.5) shows that a higher proportion of post-Act

Figure 14.5 *Placements under Interim Care Orders*

Pre-Act

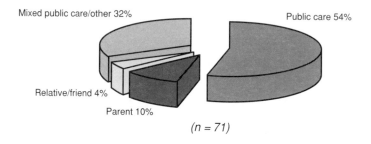

Mixed public care/other 32%

Public care 54%

Relative/friend 4%

Parent 10%

(n = 71)

Post-Act

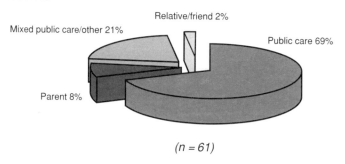

Relative/friend 2%

Mixed public care/other 21%

Public care 69%

Parent 8%

(n = 61)

orders were used *only* while the children were in public placements. None of the post-Act orders was used to protect children who remained at home throughout proceedings; those who stayed with the parent who had previously had care (5) were all in supervised placements. Mixed regimes typically involved a period of foster care followed by phased rehabilitation to the previous carer (4), to the other parent (2) or to relatives (4). Only one case moved in the opposite direction, the children coming into foster care as the result of a placement in a residential unit, which had been covered by an Interim Care Order, breaking down. There were no cases in the sample where the court attempted to direct placement under an Interim Care Order, a practice which has been declared unlawful.[6] Under wardship, of course, a placement had to be authorised by the court.

Accommodation

In the same way that an Interim Care Order does not necessarily mean the child is in the physical care of the local authority, the absence of such an order may not mean the child is at home. One of the new features of care proceedings under the Children Act is the use of accommodation as a means of interim protection.

Twenty-one of the sample proceedings were brought on children who were already accommodated prior to any events leading to proceedings. These arrangements were continued for a period in nine cases and throughout the child's stay in care in six cases. Accommodation was also used as a holding operation pending the initiation of proceedings in a further five cases, two of which continued throughout. Another three children were accommodated in the course of proceedings. In total then there were 14 cases in which accommodation was used as an interim measure and ten in which the child's entire stay in care during proceedings was on this basis. The practice was a particular feature of cases in Area A where one in every three index children cared for outside their family network was accommodated at least for a time, compared to one in four in Area B and one in ten in Area C.

As discussed in Chapter 4, accommodation as a means of avoiding care proceedings was often initiated or sustained under duress. This was even more clearly the case during proceedings where the threat of an Interim Care Order or an Emergency Protection Order was usually explicit. Indeed in one case a Prohibited Steps Order was used to prevent removal. While such practices are again a distortion of the theory of accommodation, at least within the legal process parents have some protections and there may be advantages to them in avoiding formal measures of compulsion as long as possible. Interviews with parents reveal that most considered Interim Care Orders to be heavy-handed and that the authority of the court and the likely consequences if they reneged on agreements was a sufficient disincentive even if they were tempted. As we conclude elsewhere, therefore:

> The use of parental undertakings might be one way of ensuring the security of a placement while giving parents the sense that they are partners in a contractual, rather than coercive, arrangement. The instrumental value of at least formal co-operation is a lesson that by this stage often seems to have gone home and there was some sign of the softening of attitudes. Thus there may be an opportunity, however slight, for beginning to develop a more constructive partnership.[7]

As far as most parents and children are concerned, however, the most important issues during proceedings are less likely to be the legal orders made than whether they were separated and for how long, and if so, what arrangements were made for contact. It is to these matters that we now turn.

Arrangements for the child's care and contact

Separation

As described in Chapter 4, proceedings in the sample cases were in the main brought in respect of children living with at least one parent, usually at home, occasionally in some form of supervised placement. Just over a quarter were living apart while nine had so far not experienced parental care. By the time of the first hearing (Chapter 5), however, although 22 were still with one parent, only 11 were in what would be their normal domicile. Moreover two-thirds were not only separated from either parent but placed outside the family network altogether. In the course of proceedings children in a further eight cases were separated from their previous primary carers.

In all there were only 14 index children who did not spend a period apart from their parent(s) at some point during proceedings and four of these had been briefly separated during the crisis which precipitated proceedings. These periods of separation were usually of some considerable length, the median duration being 22 weeks. Only ten were for less than three months while 25 were for more than six months. Moreover many of these children were already separated prior to proceedings. Some had been removed at a point of crisis, others had been accommodated and we have already reported (Chapter 4) our concern about the lengthy period of limbo to which these children had been exposed. If these factors are taken into account the periods of separation considerably increase, to a median of 29 weeks. Sixty (of 68) children were separated for at least three months and 40 for six or more.

Care proceedings mainly concern young children whose capacity to sustain relationships over periods of separation is different from that of adults. Thus the duration of separation is of especial importance where it is planned to return the child to former carers. We found (Table 14.2) that the median period of separation in such cases was 24 weeks, ranging from a minimum of five (a young baby) to a maximum of 88 (2-year-old Jamie Harris). There were only three cases where the children were returned home within three months. On a more positive note, however, it was found that on average these children experienced shorter periods of separation than any other group.

Children destined for substitute care outside their families of origin, for example, had on average been separated for about five weeks longer than those returning. A number of lawyers acting for their parents considered this had been helpful, allowing their clients to come to terms with the inevitable. Conceivably one might also see some benefit to the children if it frees them

Table 14.2 *Duration of total separation by plans for the child*

	Mean	Median	Minimum	Maximum	(n=)
Return to both/sole parent	25	26	5	56	(12)
Return to one parent only	33	24	14	88	(6)
Return to any former carer	28	24	5	88	(18)
Kinship care	42	32	10	125	(11)
Long-term substitute care	33	30	6	67	(39)

to make new relationships with future permanent carers. Sadly we suspect that for many children this would not be the case and that the interim period becomes an apparently interminable period of uncertainty, during which they may form relationships with short-term carers, which subsequently have, in their turn, to be severed.

Eleven separated index children, however, were neither returning to one or both parents nor going into long-term public care but were to live with relatives. Indeed five had already moved into such kinship placements before the end of proceedings while two were there from the point emergency action was taken. Thus, although on average the period of separation from their parents by the end of proceedings was the longest of all (median 32 weeks, mean 42, to a maximum of 125), the period spent outside their family network was marginally less alarming (mean 33 weeks).

Placements

Around half the sample (42) were cared for within their family networks for at least part of proceedings. The majority (64), however, had to cope with a period of non-related care. For the most part this involved foster care although nine index children spent a period in residential care (seven of them in Area B) and two, both from Area B, remained in such a placement throughout.

Children accommodated prior to proceedings generally remained in the same placement, only two of the 21 changing. Those entering public care as the result of a crisis are much more vulnerable to placement change – in an emergency social workers are thankful to get any placement and cannot afford to be too choosy. Children may then have to be moved on within a short time. In all, 40 index children were fortunate enough to remain in the same placement throughout their stay in public care. A minority, however, had to adjust to two (18 cases), three (5) or even, in one unfortunate case, four placements.

One of the factors which may help children to adjust to unfamiliar surroundings is the presence of a sibling.[8] The majority of the sample cases, of course, involved only one child, whilst in others the children did not all require non-familial care at the same time, if at all. Some children were initially placed together and then separated as it became apparent their needs were incompatible. In all seven sibling groups were split up at some stage during their stay in public care, in four because of the lack of a suitable placement. Two of these, which involved families of four and five children, remained split into groupings throughout; the other two, involving pairs of siblings, were reunited, although in one case not until after the guardian had made a formal complaint to social services management.

The separation of siblings was among the complaints made about placement in our interviews with parents. Other situational criticism included undesirable influences from older children, distance from home, disruption through moving school and neighbourhoods and culturally inappropriate placements. However, although the majority of parents could not recall having being consulted about the choice of placement, and many argued that the children could have safely remained at home throughout proceedings, we were surprised to find a high level of satisfaction with the quality of care provided. Given that these were parents whose own standards of care were usually being called into question one might have expected them to be hypercritical of the foster carers. This was not the case, a huge tribute to the foster parents concerned.

Even when a foster home was recognised to be providing a positive experience, however, visiting a child in such circumstances remained, for most parents, an acutely distressing experience.

Contact

Face-to-face contact between at least one parent and child was permitted in all the sample cases, usually throughout proceedings. There were only a few cases where all contact was suspended for a period: Mr and Mrs Cooper, for instance, were initially judged by their respective psychiatrists to be too ill to see the children and Nasreen's contact was terminated prior to the final hearing. There appeared to be only one case where neither parent took up the opportunity of contact at all.

Most parents, however, were dissatisfied with some aspect of contact. Supervised contact, in particular, was universally resented and disliked.

While recognising that there are circumstances where supervised contact is a vital safeguard, enabling a parent to have contact which might otherwise be deemed too great a risk, we do question whether it is over-used. Using supervision to assess parent–child interaction is of questionable value given the artificiality of the situation and if it puts already strained relationships under pressure may be counter-productive.

Accordingly we would argue for more satisfactory contact arrangements to be negotiated, perhaps using contact centres, even videos or one way screens where necessary. The current arrangements are not only clearly not meeting the needs of parents, they can also put them at a disadvantage in the court proceedings since the quality of contact, based on observation of contact sessions, is often a significant factor in decision-making.

Interim hearings

Multiple interim hearings are common in care cases. Information from the observed sample suggests that most are relatively short. Even initial hearings tended to be over in less than two hours (Table 14.3) whilst subsequent hearings took up, on average, only half that time (Table 14.4). Of course there are always the exceptions: one initial hearing in Area A, for instance, lasted for over eight hours and one interim for nearly 16. At the other end of the scale were interim hearings which were over in a matter of minutes and even initial hearings taking much less than half an hour. Clearly whether the hearing is considering substantive or procedural issues has a bearing on duration, as does whether and to what extent the hearing is contested.

Table 14.3 *The length of initial hearings*

	Area A	Area B	Area C	All areas
Mean	1h 32m	1h 57m	1h 53m	1h 45m
Minimum	0h 14m	1h 15m	0h 18m	0h 14m
Maximum	8h 21m	3h 23m	4h 25m	8h 21m
1 hour or less	7	0	2	9
2 hours or more	10	1	2	4
(n =)	*(10)*	*(6)*	*(8)*	*(24)*

Table 14.4 *The length of interim hearings*

	Area A	Area B	Area C	All areas
Mean	1h 23m	0h 33m	0h 54m	0h 58m
Minimum	0h 03m	0h 04m	0h 04m	0h 03m
Maximum	15h 52m	1h 40m	5h 01m	15h 52m
% 30 minutes or less	58	64	49	56
(n=)	(38)	(33)	(41)	(112)

Interim contests

Interim hearings are not intended to be a dress rehearsal for the substantive hearing[9] although in proceedings under the Children and Young Persons Act parents' lawyers often sought to use them in this way.[10] Without the current provisions for advance disclosure and largely oral proceedings, contesting an application for an Interim Care Order could be the only way to get sight of the evidence. Interviews with practitioners in the current study suggest that now that parents' lawyers are not kept in the dark in this way this strategy is no longer so regularly employed. As one lawyer told us:

> Having to produce written evidence may produce delay but that is outweighed by the advantages; you tend to have fewer contested hearings. . . . You're not faced with a completely unknown quantity so you have an opportunity to advise the client and get a considered answer to the allegations. In the past you would get to court and not know what was going to come out. You tended to allow the first interim to go ahead on a contested basis simply to find out what the case was whereas perhaps now you would reserve your position.

Case documentation alone was not always sufficiently detailed for us to gauge whether a particular hearing had been contested. However of the 359 attendable hearings for which adequate data were available, one in five involved some degree of contest while 40 of the sample cases were known to have had at least one contested hearing. These ranged from those which were 'fully' contested, involving witness evidence and cross-examination on both sides, to the majority in which parties pursued their opposition by seeking to influence the process and interim handling of the case, perhaps with the assistance of one witness. There were also several examples of cases in which contest was averted by door of the court agreements: at interim as at final hearings, parties were often ready to make concessions when the weight of the opposing evidence became clear.

Information on the contested issues was most reliable for the 30 observed cases. Twenty-six contested hearings were noted, distributed between 14 cases (though three of these were intended to be final hearings). The most likely occasion for contest was in response to local authority applications for Interim Care Orders (eight cases at nine hearings). At two further hearings in one of these cases there was agreement on the Interim Care Order but dispute as to whether this should be used for rehabilitation. Contact was the most disputed interim issue (five cases, six hearings). The remaining contests (nine in six cases) related to procedural issues – transfer up to the county court (four in two cases), filing evidence (three in two cases), whether the child might attend hearings (1) and adjournment of the final hearing (1).

If substantive issues were going to be contested at the interim stage, this was normally at the initial hearing or (two cases) the hearing at which a particular application was first made. It was rare for the same issue to be contested on a subsequent occasion, whichever party had lost. However six cases did involve more than one contested hearing (with a maximum of five) while in the non-observed sample we were aware of a few cases, albeit a tiny minority, in which every possible issue seemed to be the occasion for courtroom battles.

Decisions in the observed contests were balanced fairly equally between those in favour of parents (8) and social services (9), although in disputes over interim contact the latter were successful in every case. Of the four cases where Interim Care Orders were contested but not made, Interim Supervision Orders were made in two and undertakings accepted in another.

Contests at an interim stage were not a good predictor of what would happen at the final hearing: only half the cases with contested interims ended in a disputed final hearing. Similarly, as we shall see in the next section, Interim Orders were not an infallible guide to case outcome.

Interim and final orders

In the pre-Act sample it was found that the probability of a case ending in a Care Order was strongly associated with the use of Interim Care Orders. In all three areas cases managed without an Interim Care Order were very unlikely to end in a Care Order (3, 13%) while the proportion rose to 28% (5) for those with a mixed regime of Interim Care Orders and adjournments and 68% (36) for those with Interim Care Orders throughout.

Post-Act this association no longer held. Cases with Interim Care Orders throughout were still the most likely to end in a Care Order (35, 76%), indeed the proportions had increased in Areas A and C though they had fallen in B. However more cases without Interim Care Orders also ended in a Care Order (7, 33%) while in Areas A and C such cases were more likely to end this way than those with a varied regime. The use of accommodation as an alternative to interim care is undoubtedly the main explanations for this. Colin and Antony Wyllie, for instance, accommodated in the course of proceedings, were eventually made subject to Care Orders, so too was Gina's son Laurie, accommodated from the start, as well as a number of other children accommodated prior to proceedings.

Even the last interim order made in a case was not a reliable indicator of the final outcome. Ten of the 41 cases with an Interim Care Order up to the final hearing did not end in a care order. Two of the six cases with only Section 8 orders ended with other dispositions, seven of the 14 Interim Supervision Orders and most discrepant of all, nine of the 11 cases without any Interim Order. In the next chapter we look more closely at the processes through which these decision were reached.

Summary

The new legislation provides a range of orders through which the child can be protected pending the final court decision. Though perceived as somewhat less flexible than the wardship jurisdiction, on which the provisions were essentially modelled, there was little evidence that the orders available had proved insufficient and the changes were broadly welcomed.

Almost three-quarters of cases began with a public law order, usually an Interim Care Order. Initial protection by means of Section 8 orders alone was rare. In one case in five no order at all was made at this stage, usually because the children were accommodated. There were only three cases where the children remained in parental care without legal protection. The local authority obtained the initial legal outcome they sought at the outset in all but five cases, in four of which the parents had the backing of the guardian.

Typically the initial order set the pattern for the rest of the proceedings. However there were changes in almost a quarter of cases, subsequent hearings resulting in cases moving both up and down the tariff, as circumstances changed.

Interim Care Orders remained the most widely used order with alternative disposals comparatively rare. Use of orders was not uniform across the sample: Area A used fewer public law orders than the other areas, used Interim Supervision Orders more often and had more cases with no order. Area C, in contrast, had the highest use of public law orders, used Interim Supervision Orders infrequently and had only one case with no order. The use of undertakings as an alternative to Interim Care Orders, which many parent would prefer, should be explored.

Comparison of pre- and post-Act use of interim orders is not straightforward in view of the legislative changes and variation between the three study areas. Compared to proceedings under the Children and Young Persons Act, however, Interim Care Orders were made in a smaller proportion of cases and in two of the research areas fewer cases were subject to Interim Care Orders throughout. Interim Care Orders were used less frequently post-Act to protect children not in the physical care of the local authority.

Interim Supervision Orders were made in one case in five. It was concluded that such orders have operated to lower the tariff, primarily by replacing the protection of children at home under Interim Care Orders. A quarter of Interim Supervision Orders were used to support placement with relatives under an Interim Residence Order.

Interim Residence Orders were made in 14 cases, half to members of the extended family, most of the rest to a separated parent. Orders were normally in force for only part of proceedings, either preceded by or followed by other arrangements, and in all but three cases other orders were made in support.

Prohibited Steps Orders (one in ten cases) were mainly used to control contact between the child and an alleged abuser, a usage subsequently disallowed by the Court of Appeal in a decision which was widely regarded by practitioners as impeding the imaginative use of the new legislation to protect the child in a less draconian way.

For the most part contact with children not in local authority care was negotiated informally. Section 34 Contact Orders, however, were made in over half the relevant cases, almost always to allow the local authority to regulate or supervise contact. Orders permitting the denial of contact were rare.

Accommodation during proceedings is a feature of post-Act practice most evident in Area A where one in three index children cared for outside the family network was accommodated at least for a time. This use of accommodation, which was even more clearly initiated or sustained under duress than arrangements made prior to proceedings, remains a distortion of the concept. The protections provided within the legal process, however, are substantially greater.

Seven out of ten index children were separated from their parent(s) for at least part of proceedings. Although a few were returned relatively swiftly most spent many weeks or months apart, usually placed outside their family network. For those already accommodated prior to proceedings the duration of separation was considerably longer.

Children returning to live with former carers had usually endured the shortest period of separation although only three returned within three months. Those destined for long-term substitute care had on average been separated for five weeks longer. Those who were to be cared for within their extended families had usually endured the longest separations of all.

Half the index children were cared for within their family networks at some point during proceedings. Three-quarters, however, spent a period in public care, usually in a foster home, though in Area B a quarter were placed in residential accommodation at least for a time. The majority of placements were stable, children coming into care as the result of a crisis being most vulnerable to change. However four out of ten children had to adjust to more than one placement and one in ten to more than two. The separation of siblings was relatively uncommon and was due in only four cases to non-availability of placements. Keeping family groups together, however, did sometimes necessitate using residential care for quite young children.

Parents reported a high level of satisfaction with the quality of care provided by foster carers although they had rarely been consulted about the placement. Visiting a child in a foster placement, however, was an acutely distressing experience.

Direct contact with at least one parent was permitted in all the sample cases, usually throughout proceedings. The majority of parents were dissatisfied with some aspect of contact, supervision being universally disliked. It is recommended that the need for supervision is rigorously assessed and that where unavoidable more satisfactory arrangements are explored.

The sample cases typically appeared before the court six or seven times before reaching a final hearing. Most of these interim hearings were relatively short and only one in five was contested, although half the cases had at least one contested hearing. Challenges were normally in relation to the first application for an Interim Care Order or contact. It was rare for the same issue to be contested again. Disputes were resolved almost equally in favour of the local authority and parents except that in those involving contact the local authority was always successful.

Contest at an interim hearing was not a good predictor of contest at the final hearing. Nor were the orders made at interim hearings an infallible guide to case outcome.

NOTES

1 Hunt J; Macleod A (1993): *Child Protection Proceedings before the Children Act: A Case for Change?* Report to DoH (unpublished).

2 Section 38(2).

3 Nottinghamshire CC v P [1993] 3 All ER 815.

4 DoH (1991): *The Children Act 1989 Guidance and Regulations. Volume 1: Court Orders.* HMSO.

5 Freeman P; Hunt J (1998): *Parental Perspectives on Care Proceedings.* The Stationery Office.

6 Re L (Minor) Court of Appeal, 22 May 1995.

7 Freeman and Hunt (1998): op. cit.

8 Wedge P; Mantle G (1991): *Sibling Groups and Social Work.* Avebury.

9 Re W (A Minor) CA 1994.

10 Representation of the Child in the Civil Courts. Research Project 1985–90.

15 Journey's end: the substantive hearing

The menu of orders

The Children Act both fetters and extends the order-making powers of the court, on the one hand removing powers to make Care or Supervision Orders in the absence of an application (Chapter 8), on the other increasing the range of disposals. The explicit intent was to confer on all the care courts much, though not all, of the flexibility of wardship.

Under the Children and Young Persons Act 1969 five options were available once the statutory tests had been satisfied, although in practice only the Care or Supervision Order was commonly used.[1] The Children Act repeals the power to order a parent to enter into a recognisance, accepting the argument that:

> If a parent fails to exercise proper care or control the proper response seems to us to be further care proceedings and we cannot see what, apart from further eroding the relationships between the parents and the child and local authorities, exacting what amounts to a fine from the parents would itself achieve.[2]

In contrast, though similarly little used, hospital and guardianship orders under the mental health legislation were left as an option. The discretion to make no order at all not only remains but is given more vigorous expression in Section 1(5) (see Chapter 7).

Care and Supervision Orders remain the most important public law disposals. Care Orders follow the Children and Young Persons Act model, conferring decision-making powers on the local authority, rather than the wardship model, where important decisions had to be referred back to the court, thus endorsing the principle that:

> Courts should make long-term decisions impinging directly on the rights and duties of children or their parents, and that the local authority or other welfare

agency should make decisions on matters which, though they may be of equal or greater importance, are not susceptible to clear and unambiguous resolution.[3]

Contact issues, it was accepted, have features of both types and thus all the care courts are now able to make Contact Orders alongside Care Orders. The Act also followed the Review in rejecting the Select Committee's recommendation that Care Orders be time-limited and subject to court review.

The Select Committee had also been concerned about the scant use of Supervision Orders and perceptions of their ineffectiveness. The Act therefore takes up the recommendation, endorsed by the Child Care Law Review, that these orders should be strengthened by conferring new powers to impose conditions on parents rather than, as hitherto, only on the children. The Review considered the option of giving the court a wide discretion in this matter, appreciating 'the advantage of being able to tailor each order to the individual needs of the particular case'. However in view of 'the risk that [the courts] will impose requirements which local authorities have neither the facilities nor the resources to meet' it opted for limiting choice to a specific list of requirements (to be contained in secondary legislation where they could be adapted over time), otherwise retaining the supervisor's powers to give other directions. This is the position in the Act. At the same time as giving Supervision Orders more teeth, however, the new law also reduces their initial duration from three years to one and makes it impossible to vary the order to a Care Order without re-proving the Section 31 criteria,[4] changes which might be regarded as making the new Supervision Order a less attractive option.

Alongside a Supervision Order, or as an alternative to a Care Order, a court hearing a Section 31 application can also select from the range of Section 8 orders, whether or not a formal application has been made. Thus it can rule that the child shall reside with a parent or any other individual; make directions as to contact and determine particular issues related to the exercise of parental responsibility by making a Prohibited Steps or Specific Issue Order. If it considers no public law order is necessary but the family would benefit from social work help, it can, with the family's consent, make a Family Assistance Order.

Thus the new *menu* of orders alters and considerably extends the range of disposals previously available to the old juvenile courts. It does not however, allow all the flexibility which had been cited as one of the main advantages of the wardship jurisdiction.[5] In the next section we consider how these changes were viewed by those practising within the new framework.

À la carte or table d'hôte: perspectives on the available options

> I think the orders offer social services, families and children various methods of protection, with different degrees of protection from us. I just think there is an order appropriate for each family and circumstances. (Social worker, Area A)

> I don't think the menu offers a particularly wide range of dishes. . . . We thought it was going to give us the flexibility to do everything but it seems it doesn't. (Social worker, Area A)

> There's a lot of scope for alternatives . . . there is much more flexibility within the system that people aren't using. (Solicitor, Area C)

> The High Court seems to dish out decisions which make the Children Act less and less flexible. (Solicitor, Area C)

A fragmented and confusing picture emerged in responses to our question: is the menu of orders available in care proceedings under the Children Act sufficiently comprehensive and flexible? As the above comments suggest, no consensus could be discerned within any professional group or study area let alone across the interview data as a whole. There were those who extolled the menu's flexibility and others who described it as a straitjacket; those who were just waking up to the possibilities and others who saw choice being eroded; those who had nothing but praise and others whose expectations had been dashed. Three broad propositions, however, would probably be generally accepted:

- the range of orders is an improvement on those previously available under the Children and Young Persons Act even if it does not quite provide the flexibility of wardship;

- it offers increased scope for ingenuity in matching remedies to needs if not the tailor-made packages which appeared to be promised; and

- it covers most situations adequately if not every situation perfectly.

The availability of private law orders in public law proceedings was, without a doubt, the most widely appreciated reform, seen as offering a less intrusive way of dealing with family problems, encouraging the search for alternatives to state care and allowing the issue to be resolved within the same set of proceedings. Also mentioned as among the positive benefits of the new legislation, though far less frequently, were the power to control contact after a Care Order, to impose conditions on adults under a Supervision Order and, by one or two people only, the option of seeking an order of No Order as an alternative to withdrawal.

Three principal themes emerged among the suggestions for further improvements:

- the desire to constrain local authority discretion in the operation of a Care Order;

- the diminishing value of Supervision Orders; and

- restrictions on access to private law orders.

The global Care Order

One recommendation which got no further than the Child Care Law Review was the Select Committee's recommendation that Care Orders should initially be limited to three years, the local authority being then required to come back to court for the order to be confirmed or discharged. While applauding the Committee's concern over evidence that children could drift in care the Review considered that:

> Such a scheme would risk the court facing cases where even though the care provided had been unsatisfactory, especially as regards long-term planning, there was no alternative but to order that the child should remain indefinitely in care.

Accordingly, it concluded: 'the idea of a review without powers to direct how the child is to be treated in future is unrealistic.' Since the boundaries between the judicial and executive domains had already been defined in a way which precluded courts having such powers, a line was drawn under the debate.

As far as practitioners were concerned, however, the issue was far from closed. Unease with the extent of the powers allocated to the local authority under a Care Order was a dominant theme in the interview material. It was the most frequent and most emphasised reservation in all groups and indeed for many respondents it was the sole aspect of the court's order-making powers under the Children Act they chose to criticise, expressed in comments such as:

> There are not a lot of problems other than the Care Order.

> It's pretty well covered other than the need to review the Care Order.

> Care Orders, that's the big hole.

As one might expect, members of the professional judiciary were among the most vocal critics of the new regime. Almost all regretted the loss of court control previously enjoyed, theoretically at least, in wardship. As one judge put it: 'that's the thing about wardship which really sticks in the gullet'. However disquiet was also voiced by a majority of lawyers and guardians and by some members of all other professional groups. Such widespread and, among family justice practitioners, substantial rejection of one of the fundamental principles of the new Act was fuelled in the main by pragmatic, rather than ideological, reasoning: less than 100% confidence in local authority services and decision-making. Though voiced in terms which reflected anything from outright distrust to a sympathetic recognition of the constraints under which departments may be operating, the same themes were constantly reiterated:

> I am deeply unhappy with the fact that having determined there is significant harm and that parents cannot act either alone or with the local authority the court then has to say over to you chaps. In a perfect world that would be wholly satisfactory. But we know, I'm afraid, that resources being what they are and team management being what it is and human beings being what they are and the frailties of local authority budgets that errors occur. Social workers are not assigned to cases, families do get cut adrift, wrong decisions are made, decisions are made without proper input. (District judge)

Thus we consider it would be a mistake to view calls for some form of continuing court involvement as simply reflecting a reluctance finally to let wardship go, or to adjust to a shift in the balance of power between the court and the local authority. For the most part practitioners are concerned about the practicalities and their attitudes are moulded by their experiences. If this aspect of change is proving, as it seems to be, one of the hardest to adjust to, then it seems likely that the flaw is in the Act itself.

If that were to be the case it is scarcely surprising since the fundamental issue is nothing less than what is the appropriate role for the court in child protection cases. The previous legislation offered a whole range of models, from a form of appeal against administrative decisions (parental rights and access cases) through settling the limits of state intervention (care proceedings) to control of all important decisions concerning a child's upbringing (wardship). None of these was seen to be entirely satisfactory and none was adopted *in toto*.

Even among those most critical of the Children Act model there were few who wished to restore the entire wardship scheme. As one judge put it:

> The mere fact that a child is a ward of court shouldn't require the local
> authority to expend the resource of swearing affidavits and appearing before
> a district judge just because the child needs grommets.

It was also recognised that though theoretically wardship allowed the court 'to exercise a benign control until the child reached 18', the reality, as Masson[6] demonstrated, might be rather different:

> I don't think effectively the High Court did review or control in any substantial
> way. I think the idea that . . . the benevolent court was sitting there keeping a
> permanent eye was pretty elusive. The court never looked at anything unless it
> was prompted to do so and even then it wasn't sure what it was looking at.
> (District judge)

Few respondents, therefore, seemed to be calling for total ongoing court control. Nor did most interviewees wish control to be exercised as a matter of routine in every case. Rather, it seemed, what was being sought was an effective *mechanism* which allowed the court to place *some* constraints on the implementation of a Care Order in *some* cases for a *limited* period. Suggestions as to how this might be achieved included:

- extending the Guardian ad Litem's involvement with an option to return to court;

- requiring return to court if it was proposed to deviate significantly from the care plan;

- requiring social services to submit a progress report after a specified period;

- allowing conditions to be placed on Care Orders: for example regarding the child's placement, or the services to be provided by the local authority;

- giving the court discretion to bring the case back for review; and

- allowing the court to make a provisional order for a limited period.

All of these options have their peculiar advantages and disadvantages, as many of their proponents acknowledged. Court review, for instance, which seemed to be the most favoured, would present considerable logistical problems; add to the burden on courts and professional services, most seriously perhaps the guardian panels; risk prolonging the period when the child is in limbo, giving parents unrealistic hopes for overturning the court's decision and returning to the worst wardship scenario where the litigation process comes to dominate a child's growing up. None the less the very clear message from those whose working lives are spent within the family justice system is that while these issues have to be tackled they do not add up to a convincing rebuttal of the argument for revising the boundaries so recently established by the Act.

The tension between the statutory framework and those operating within it has also been reflected in practice by the use of what practitioners described as 'devices' and 'strategies' to keep the case within the legal process. One lawyer, for instance, told us:

> I was in a case recently where everyone agreed there should be a Care Order but the local authority wanted it to make plans for adoption whereas the mother wanted rehabilitation though she recognised it could only be done under a Care Order. Either way the court is going to make a Care Order. What we had to do was to get the judge to adjourn for three months on the basis of constructive delay while rehabilitation was tried out. We worked him round Re C a bit. . . . If he'd just made a Care Order and had no power to direct the local authority, the next time [the case] would have come back would be when the local authority applied to terminate contact or perhaps free for adoption. By which time it would be too far down the road for rehabilitation.

In one of the sample cases both the guardian and the mother accepted the need for a Care Order despite their unease about the plan to move the child from her foster home where, after 11 months, she was well settled. At what was expected to be the final hearing the court made an Interim Care Order instead. The local authority successfully appealed and a Care Order was subsequently made.

This verdict is in accord with the general attitude of the Court of Appeal to such prolonging tactics and other attempts to control the implementation of a Care Order.[7] It remains to be seen, however, whether practitioners and courts will resign themselves to the reality that active resistance is precluded and if so, whether the new regime will eventually secure a greater measure of support. Alternatively will the issue remain a running sore, with on occasion collusion between courts and like-minded practitioners allowing the intentions of the legislation to be sabotaged? This was clearly still happening even after the significant decisions in case law had been reported, as one local authority lawyer explained:

> There's a real problem with Interim Care Orders. Our court is using them in a wardship kind of way so the matter can be brought back before the court even

> though there's been fairly strict guidance that that shouldn't be done. . . .
> They're going through all kinds of contortions to allow that to happen. I'm
> a bit unhappy with that because it makes a bit of a mockery of what we're
> meant to be doing; I'm a bit of a purist and I think either we're Children Act
> or we're not.

It is recognised that there are difficulties in devising any scheme which would meet the demand for an effective mechanism allowing the implementation of some care orders to be constrained. The research supports the view of other commentators, however, that the current position is unsatisfactory[8] and that while day-to-day decisions have to be left to the local authority, more fundamental decisions should not. We do not consider that the question of whether a child on a Care Order should live with his parents or in state care, for example, can possibly be construed as a day-to-day issue.

The power bestowed by a Care Order, moreover, seems strangely out of tune with other elements in the Act. In public law the local authority's power has been circumscribed through the introduction of Section 34 Contact Orders, for instance, and shorter renewable Supervision Orders,[9] while during the currency of proceedings almost every aspect of the case is under court scrutiny. In private law the emphasis has shifted away from the issue of the right to make decisions to the resolution of the practical issues, in particular the question of where and with whom a child shall live. Only with respect to Care Orders, one of the most draconian disposals available to the court, is the power handed over to one of the parties to the action. We would strongly recommend, therefore, that the whole issue be reconsidered.[10]

Supervision Orders: not worth the paper they are written on?

Dissatisfaction also extended to the Supervision Order. A few practitioners, it is true, had found the facility to impose conditions on adults valuable and in one area there were more favourable comments. For the most part, however, interviews suggest that despite the intention to strengthen them, Supervision Orders are now of even *less* use than they were under previous legislation. Their value, it was said, had always been limited because they depended on parental co-operation and there were no sanctions against breach. The Children Act, however, was perceived to create new disadvantages: the same tougher statutory criteria as for a Care Order means that local authorities are less likely to apply, the short duration of the initial order is unrealistic given the problems that bring most families to the care court; and if there is any doubt that the order will be effective the requirement to prove the grounds afresh to obtain a Care Order acts as a powerful incentive to seek a Care Order in the first place. Perhaps most influential of all, however, is the perception that the voluntaristic orientation of the Act makes Supervision Orders almost superfluous. Thus we were told:

- the less serious cases for which Supervision Orders were previously appropriate are no longer reaching court;

- cases tend to have been worked with for longer before court action has been taken so the possibilities for co-operative working have usually been exhausted; and

- even where they have not, an order can only be effective if there is co-operation and if that is forthcoming a written agreement may be just as satisfactory, in which case Section 1(5) would be difficult to overcome.

Thus whether seen as ineffective or merely irrelevant it seems clear that the remodelled Supervision Order has proved a disappointment. It may not, as yet, have fallen into the same desuetude as the now defunct parental recognisance. It had some apologists among all professional groups and even among the most disparaging of critics there was acknowledgement that there were some circumstances in which an order could be of use: a shot across the bows to which some parents might respond, for example, or a means of increasing the chances of resources being made available.

The ingenuity with which such orders had been deployed by a few practitioners suggests that with more extensive experience and further guidance on their appropriate use, they might become more widely appreciated. It did appear to us that some practitioners were a little vague on the powers which a Supervision Order conferred, what conditions could be attached and by whom and that different practices were operating. One guardian, who did not usually work in the study area, told us she was:

> trying to get it absolutely straight about the directions that can be given with a Supervision Order; there seems to be a difference of opinion. The understanding [in my home area], after some disagreement between solicitors and guardians, is that it's not for the guardian to recommend what directions can be given; they can comment on what directions they think would be helpful but the directions are to be given by the supervisors not the court. . . . [So] to my knowledge there have been no supervision orders where specific directions have been attached. But I went on a training day recently where that was certainly not the understanding or the experience of how guardians or the courts are working.

Bearing out this perception we have the enthusiasm of another guardian who had found:

> conditions very useful, I've used them several times. For example in one case I'm asking for an order with very specific conditions: that the child be medically examined, that mother will notify the local authority of any substantial changes in circumstances like someone moving permanently into the household; that she will co-operate with nursery care, child-minding, etc. Social services and I discussed what we each thought the conditions should be and I think I was more stringent than they were, I felt it was important we had those conditions. Under the old Act I would have been obliged to ask for a Care Order.

A lawyer in the same area, however, complained that:

> I have a case at the moment where mother has a history of unsuitable partners and what we would like is for her to notify the local authority if the composition of the household changes. We can't do that under a Supervision Order.

Similarly a social worker told us:

> We have had recent legal guidance to say we can have very flexible conditions attached to Supervision Orders. That is very helpful and if I've understood it properly it includes orders in respect of a parent as well, so a parent could be directed to attend a clinic for alcohol counselling, for example.

On the other hand, another lawyer argued that:

> We need something to give the local authority additional express powers to give directions to adults. Directions with Supervision Orders are primarily addressed to managing the child. It is hard, for example, to get a mother to attend psychiatric treatment.

Some clarification, therefore, would seem to be of benefit.

None the less it does appear that the Supervision Order as currently constructed is a relatively feeble tool[11] and that if it is to continue to have relevance as a disposal further consideration needs to be given to making it more robust. Practitioner suggestions to this end included:

♦ the option of longer orders reviewable after a specified period;

♦ sanctions for breach of conditions;

- powers to direct the adult with care to undertake a specified course of treatment; and

- abolition of the requirement to re-prove the threshold criteria in order to convert to a Care Order.

It is recommended that guidelines should be issued clarifying the powers available under Supervision Orders and that practitioners are given opportunities to explore their potential. It is also recommended that further consideration be given to making the order itself more robust and useful.

Who may dine at the table?

The third major theme concerned not so much what orders are now available as who may use them. We have already reported disquiet among the professional judiciary at the loss of their previous power to make Care and Supervision Orders on their own motion and the diminished powers of district judges. We also encountered practitioner irritation that while in most respects the Act provides, as promised, 'a consistent set of legal remedies . . . available in all courts and all proceedings'[12] there remained some remedies – injunctions, enforceable undertakings and penal notices – for which it was necessary to go to a higher court. Above all, however, it was the restrictions on the use of Prohibited Steps Orders which generated the greatest volume of criticism.

The decision in Nottinghamshire County Council v P[13] was still fresh at the beginning of the interview programme, thus local authority lawyers in particular were still reeling from that bombshell. In this case the Court of Appeal ruled that a Prohibited Steps Order could not be used to oust a father accused of sexual abuse nor prevent his contact with his children. It thus closed off what had seemed to offer to local authorities a much needed means of protecting children without removal and without the use of more draconian orders. The strength of the reaction to the decision is evidenced in such typical comments as:

It was working extremely well until Nottingham; that really put a spanner in the works.

I think it was a great pity Nottingham was interpreted in the way it was. It's perfectly apparent to all of us that the Children Act was meant to allow for a flexible approach and avoid care proceedings when other orders would do.

Apart from its specific import the Nottinghamshire decision also threw into relief the whole issue of the public–private division in the new legislation. It demonstrated that 'there is no statutory link between the private and public law parts of the 1989 Act',[14] a comment which, as Parry points out: 'came as a surprise to those who thought that the Act was about the harmonisation, if not the fusion, of public and private law'.[15]

Prohibited Steps Orders could not be used for the purpose sought because their effect, the court determined,[16] would be the same as making a Residence and Contact Order and they were specifically out of bounds to local authorities. To do otherwise, the argument goes, would be to open up a back door route to state intervention without first satisfying the statutory tests. Theoretically that is no doubt correct. However in practice it means that there are situations where the only options available to the local authority are equally unsatisfactory, as one local authority lawyer explained:

> There are situations where the obvious answer is a certain package which needs supporting by court order because it's integral to its working. The individuals concerned may not be in a position to make applications but there's a clear need for the children's benefit for orders of that nature to be made. We then come into the situation where in order to achieve that objective private individuals are told by the social worker 'really you ought to apply for these' and they either do or they don't. If they don't social services either do nothing and leave it or there's the whole panoply of care proceedings.

Where individuals are reluctant to apply should social services have the power to do so on their behalf? Some practitioners opposed this on the grounds of efficacy, rather than legitimacy, while others were less dismissive, as these responses from private practice solicitors demonstrate:

> Either you have a parent who is behaving properly and is capable of excluding the other parent or you have one you can't trust and therefore the child is at risk of significant harm.

> Having talked to a lot of women where allegations have been made [about their partner] the disbelief and the horror of it are so problematic that getting them to go off and get an injunction is very hard, it would be better for the court to be making that decision, for someone else to do it for them.

Although the 1996 Family Law Act now allows courts to exclude an alleged perpetrator from the home this is only in the course of care or emergency protection proceedings. Nor does this fully answer the problems of restricting contact with suspected abusers.[17] Case law, as has been pointed out, is also confusing[18] in an area where it is vital that local authorities should be clear about whether a child can be protected by a non-abusing parent, a course of action the Act itself implicitly encourages.[19]

It is urged that further consideration should be given to this whole issue, not only in terms of the protections that can be sought by private individuals but the powers which should be made available to local authorities. If controlling contact with an alleged abuser, whether a parent or not, is deemed sufficient to enable a child to remain at home without the need for a Care or Supervision Order then it seems quite contrary to the intention of the Act, to minimise state intervention in family life, that this should not be possible. It is unfortunately not possible to judge from our data how many care applications such a change might avert, since at the time local authorities were making decisions on the basis of the pre-Nottinghamshire model. However, the intensity of feelings demonstrated by the interview material suggest that such cases might not be particularly rare.

It would, of course, be necessary to ensure that even such lesser interventions are warranted, probably by satisfying a version of the threshold test. The precedent for such variants already exists. The test for an Interim Care Order, for instance, is not as strong as for a full Care Order, the court merely has to be satisfied that there are 'reasonable grounds for believing' that the criteria are met. For a Child Assessment Order the test is 'reasonable cause to suspect'[20] the child is suffering or likely to suffer significant harm and for an Emergency Protection Order 'reasonable cause to believe'.[21]

Compared to the passions aroused by the prohibited steps issue, frustration at the local authority's inability to apply for Residence Orders on behalf of others was much more muted. Again, however, the main criticism was the failure of the law to recognise the practical and emotional hurdles facing private applicants. Relatives who could not afford the legal costs, for instance, or who did not wish to jeopardise their relationship with a parent by taking the initiative, although they were perfectly willing to provide a home for a child who would otherwise go into public care. Thus the criticism was not that local authorities were disbarred from obtaining Residence Orders themselves, which would again circumvent the statutory criteria, but that complicated manoeuvring was necessary in order to get them made to other people. Local authorities might see themselves being forced to institute care proceedings, for instance, when there was no intention to seek a Care or Supervision Order and then relying on the other parties, particularly the guardian, to suggest the court make an order of its own motion. The transparent use of such a strategy was strongly criticised in court in the (sample) case of Louise Milsom. It is to the use of the menu in the sample cases that we now turn.

The disposition of the parties in the sample cases

The local authority primary application: continuity and change

At the point of initiating proceedings, as we explored in Chapter 7, the local authority's long-term objective was clear in only a minority of cases; in most the eventual outcome was seen to be contingent on subsequent developments. After anything up to 18 months under the microscope of the legal process, the sample cases reached journey's end, the substantive hearing. By this stage the majority had crystallised to the extent that social services were clear whether they were still applying for a public law order and if so which and for what purposes. Table 15.1 sets out the legal orders being applied for using the framework devised in Chapter 7 to categorise objectives and Table 15.2, the plans for the child if the application was successful.

Original objective long-term substitute care (20 cases)

Twenty cases were originally brought in order to arrange long-term substitute care. Usually this was to be outside the family, thus requiring a Care Order, though there was one possibility of kinship care (the Tomlinson children) and Louise Milsom was expected to remain with her grandparents. Final hearings took place between nine and 57 weeks later (median 17). By then social services were only seeking a Supervision Order on Louise to accompany a package of Section 8 orders. Members of the extended family were also caring for the children in four other cases. In only one of these five was no public law order being sought: two placements, including the Tomlinsons, were to be protected by Care Orders, two by Supervision Orders. Ian Morse was to live with his mother and grandparents under a Conditional Residence Order. Of the rest only Zara Butler was to stay with her parents, under a Supervision Order.

There were only two cases in which plans no longer included a public law order. However, either in terms of the legal order being applied for (5) or the plans for the child (6), by the time of the final hearing intentions had changed in seven cases, and in Zara's were diametrically opposed.

Table 15.1 *Final local authority application by initial objective*

	Care Order	Supervision Order	No public law order
Original objective – firm			
Long-term substitute care	15	3	2
Supervision within family	2	4	2
Original objective contingent			
New-born	6	1	0
Inactive cases	6	4	3
Active < 3m	9	0	5
Active > 3m	13	2	6

Table 15.2 *Local authority plan by initial objective*

	Long-term substitute care	Placement with relatives	Placement with one parent only	Placement with both/sole parent
Firm objective				
Long-term substitute care	13	5	1	1
Supervision within family	2	0	1	5
Contingent objective				
New-born	5	0	0	2
Previously inactive	4	2	1	6
Active < 3m	5	2	4	3
Active > 3m	10	3	3	5

Original objective supervision within the family (8 cases)

The degree of change was even more marked in this small group of cases which lasted between zero and 63 weeks (median 20). The case in respect of one child (Samantha) was withdrawn at the first hearing because of lack of evidence and in another at the last, because the perpetrator had been committed to prison. In both the intention was to continue voluntary supervision. In two cases the children were destined for long-term substitute care under Care Orders, one because the hoped-for change in mother's attitude had not occurred, while the child thrived dramatically in foster care; in the second because during proceedings new information came to light about previously unsuspected serious abuse.

There were only four cases where the application at the final hearing still envisaged statutory supervision within the family. Moreover in two of these there had been a point earlier in proceedings where things might have been very different. Long-term care for the Phillips children, for instance, was only averted at the last minute when Joanne's solicitor persuaded the court to give her one last chance.

Contingent objectives: new-born babies (7 cases)

Zara, it will be recalled, was the only child to be removed at birth without any intention to rehabilitate. In all the rest there was to be a period of assessment although in some cases there was clearly a degree of pessimism about the prospects of success. By the final hearing (between 14 and 37 weeks later, median 25) it was intended that only two children would remain with their parent(s). One, who had already gone home, was to be monitored under a Supervision Order, another (baby Julia, see below) who was still in a residential unit with her mother, was to be subject to a Care Order while the assessment was completed and rehabilitation to the community hopefully achieved.

All the rest were to be placed for adoption. Care Orders were therefore sought as the first stage in this process. Nasreen, sadly, was unable to convince even her own experts that she would not present an unacceptable risk to her baby's safety. The guardian, who at the outset of the case inclined to the view that social services were being precipitate, changed her opinion entirely. Gina never did get into a residential placement with Laurie and her mental health seriously deteriorated. One of the cases with the poorest initial prognosis, however, confounded everyone's expectations.

* *

Carmen was heavily pregnant and sleeping rough when she returned to the area where two years previously her first baby, Thomas, had been removed. Her circumstances were unchanged; she had had no antenatal care and there was great concern that this child would also be born unattended, particularly since she was uncontactable until she turned up at hospital three days before Julia was born. An Emergency Protection Order was then taken, following the recommendation of a pre-birth case conference and in the light of Carmen's threats to call on her friends to snatch the baby and smash up the hospital.

Legal advice was very strongly that the court would require a period of assessment of Carmen's care of this baby. However her previous stay in a mother and baby home had been so spectacularly unsuccessful that the staff were not prepared to consider readmission without assessment in a psychiatric unit, for which there was a three-month waiting list. Julia was placed in foster care. Carmen suffered from short-term memory loss, which meant she was unable to remember whether she had fed Julia, but refused to have neurological investigations. Finally her relationship with the social worker (who had also dealt with Thomas) was so soured that a change was clearly necessary. Unfortunately, even at this obviously critical time, the case could not be immediately re-allocated.

In spite of this terrible start, by dint of diligent string-pulling by some very assiduous professionals and Carmen's determination, what seemed a near inevitable slide to long-term care was averted. Carmen and Julia were reunited in a psychiatric unit five weeks later, moving to the mother and baby home after three weeks. They remained together throughout proceedings and though their stay was not problem-free things appeared to be moving in the right direction. The new social worker established a more constructive relationship and apart from continuing to refuse medical tests Carmen co-operated with the helping services. The local authority, supported by the guardian, applied for a Care Order, the plan being that after a further three months mother and child would be rehoused in the community.

Contingent objectives: previously inactive cases (13 cases)

Unlike this last group of cases in which parents were usually trying to shake off their past reputations, there was a group of families who were not already being worked with and usually so little was known that proceedings had to include a period of investigation as well as assessment. At the end of this process, which lasted between six and 40 weeks (median 20), public law orders were no longer being sought in only three cases. In each the children were returning or remaining with parents, one on a Residence Order with conditions, two on an order of No Order. One of these latter children was Ahmed Khan, whose family, as described in Chapter 4, became known to social services in the most florid fashion. However within days of Mrs Khan's admission to a psychiatric unit, the situation began to look less serious. Two weeks later mother and child were reunited at home under an Interim Supervision Order, the family agreed to the provision of supportive services and at the end of six weeks the local authority's application for an order of No Order was agreed.

Natalie and David Pallister, whose baby James had been so seriously injured, had co-operated throughout and it was considered that there were enough safeguards within the family network for anything more than a Supervision

Order to be unnecessary. There were three other applications for Supervision Orders in this group, one governing a placement with an estranged parent, one with relatives and the other rehabilitation of teenage children. Care Orders were applied for in six cases, four with the intention that the children should remain in public care and one with the children living with their extended family. Only Liam, who had suffered serious unexplained injuries, was to remain with his parents while assessment continued.

Only a tiny fraction of these 'off the street' cases, therefore, ended with the intent to remove permanently. However in almost all ongoing involvement was considered necessary, most commonly on a statutory basis.

Contingent objective: local authority involvement less than three months (14 cases)

In this group too, proceedings had often had to encompass a period of assessment before the application was finalised. After a legal process lasting between 14 and 64 weeks (median 25), nine of the 14 ended in an application for a Care Order. In five of these long-term substitute care outside the family was envisaged, the remainder being placed with relatives (2), one parent only (1), or at home with the parent(s) who had previously had care (1).

The local authority's plans for Robert Barnes never got beyond first base. Although things had started off well, Doreen's contact soon fell away and Jack's had always been sporadic. Thus the attachment which the mother and baby home considered the *sine qua non* for admission never developed. As the prognosis for Robert's development became increasingly gloomy it became apparent that his parents would not be able to supply this and that a very special long-term placement was urgently required.

In contrast the case concerning 3-year-old Sophie Farrow, as we saw in the previous chapter, had moved in quite the opposite direction. After Sophie returned home, surrounded by a protective framework of orders, directions and undertakings, Lisa seriously addressed her drinking problem and no further incidents were reported. By the end of proceedings the local authority, which had been so anxious about Sophie returning home, decided not to apply even for a Supervision Order. Three other cases also ended without any application for a public law order, and the children staying with at least one parent. There were no Supervision Orders in this group of cases at all.

Thus though public law orders were being sought in almost two-thirds of this group of cases, most children were to remain within their family network, usually with at least one parent.

Contingent objectives: local authority involvement more than three months (21 cases)

These remaining cases lasted between eight and 78 weeks (median 25). Thirteen ended in an application for a Care Order, 11 with the intention of arranging long-term substitute care outside the family. Only one child was expected to go to relatives on a Care Order and one to remain with a parent during a period of treatment.

The conclusion of Ben's case seems to have been one of the more inevitable: an application for a Care Order with no plans for rehabilitation. As commented in Chapter 7, given that 17 months intensive input had failed to make any sustained impact on Millie, the prospects of Ben returning home seemed minimal from the beginning; from social services' perspective this was a last ditch attempt to avoid care. The shock of proceedings, however, did not galvanise Millie into accepting treatment for her alcoholism and though the family underwent a further period of specialist assessment the report was extremely gloomy both about the future and the harm Ben had already suffered.

In contrast social services did expect to be able to rehabilitate the Symons children and there seemed to be every hope that proceedings would help to unstick the case. Sadly, as we described in Chapter 10, this initial optimism proved unfounded and, by the end of proceedings, Care Orders and leave to terminate all family contact was being sought as a prelude to adoption.

Christopher O'Brien moved to live with his grandmother following the events described in Chapter 11 and at the final hearing the local authority applied for a Supervision Order to monitor his care under a Residence Order. Only one other case, however, ended in an application for a Supervision Order.

In the six remaining cases no public law order was being sought although Residence Orders were expected to be made in two. Jenny Grayson was to remain with her grandparents because of her mother's continued stay in psychiatric hospital and Jamie Harris with his father and his new stepmother.

In all the cases where there was to be no court order at all the children were returning or remaining at home with the parent(s) who had previously had care. Michael and Elizabeth Cooper, for instance, were successfully rehabilitated and a more effective working relationship established with their parents.

• •

Sammi Collins stayed at home throughout proceedings. His parents agreed to accept a package of services and although a second medical opinion confirmed the original diagnosis of non-accidental injury it was considered there had been sufficient change in the family for Sammi to remain at home safely. Social services would have preferred a Supervision Order but given parental opposition to this and readiness to accept continued involvement on a voluntary basis agreed, somewhat reluctantly, to withdraw the application.

• •

Thus though a public law order was being sought in the majority of these cases (15) only just over half the children (11) were to be placed in public care.

In all, as Figure 15.1 shows, by the time of the final hearing the local authority was no longer seeking a public law order in a just over a fifth of the sample cases. Where an application was still alive, however, there were almost four times as many applications for Care Orders as there were for Supervision Orders.

Figure 15.1 *Local authority application at final hearing*

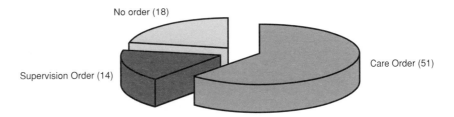

No order (18)

Supervision Order (14)

Care Order (51)

Although a Care Order application most often meant placement outside the family altogether, this was not invariably so (Figure 15.2) and overall less than half the case plans were of this nature (Figure 15.3). In just over a quarter it was planned that the child would return to or remain with the parent(s) who had previously had care while ten children were to live with one parent only.

Figure 15.2 *Orders and plans*

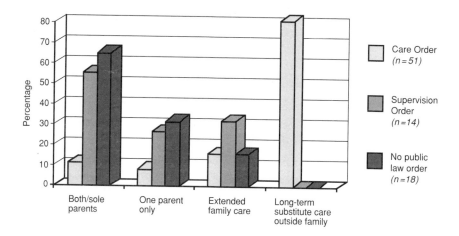

Legend:
- Care Order (n = 51)
- Supervision Order (n = 14)
- No public law order (n = 18)

Figure 15.3 *Local authority plans if application successful*

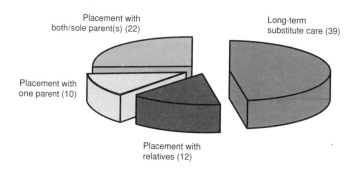

Placement with both/sole parent(s) (22)

Long-term substitute care (39)

Placement with one parent (10)

Placement with relatives (12)

Variation by area and ethnicity

There were some differences between the three research areas both in the legal orders being applied for and the plans for the children. Thus:

♦ Area A had the lowest proportion of applications for public law orders;

♦ the ratio of Care to Supervision Order applications was highest in C;

♦ plans in C were more likely to involve substitute care outside the family and slightly less likely to involve placement with a parent; and

♦ Area A tended in the main to use Care Orders for cases where the plan was for placement outside the family. Where family placement was the plan, this area was less likely than the other two areas to be applying for a Care Order and most likely to be seeking no public order at all.

Applications for Care Orders were rather more likely where either a child or an adult came from an ethnic minority, particularly a non-European, group. Such children were also less likely to remain within their nuclear families though more of the remainder were being placed with relatives. Thus overall, although a somewhat higher proportion of children from non-European families were destined to live outside their family network the difference between the two groups was less marked.

Kinship care

In all there were 12 cases in which the plans for the child involved placement with a member of the extended family. There was considerable variation, however, in the legal underpinnings sought for this arrangement. A Care Order, for example, was being applied for on Marcus, who was going to live with his aunt. Louise Milsom was to be subject to a Supervision Order supporting a package of Section 8 orders. In the case of Jenny Grayson, however, no public law order was considered necessary, the court merely being invited to make a Residence Order in favour of her grandparents.

To an extent the nature of the case will determine the degree of statutory involvement considered necessary. It was also clear, however, both from the sample cases and the interview material, that the level of support which might be forthcoming from the local authority, financial as well as other less tangible forms, is also relevant. Relatives may well be reluctant to take on the care of their young kin unless they can be guaranteed an allowance, which is currently only possible under a Care Order, or unless they can be assured of ongoing help with, for example, contact difficulties, which is at least more likely under a public law order, even if, worryingly, it cannot be assured. The increasing emphasis which the Act places on the role of the extended family, an emphasis which this research demonstrates has raised the profile of non-parent relatives in care proceedings, has generated a whole tranche of issues which need to be thoroughly explored.[22]

Section 34 Contact Orders

Once a Care Order was made under the Children and Young Persons Act 1969, contact between the child and any other person was within social services' discretion. The issue could come before a court only if it were proposed to terminate parental contact altogether and parents objected. In addition to the injustice this represented there was some evidence that a number of parental applications to discharge Care Orders were in effect disguised contact applications. Under wardship the court had the power to make orders regulating contact at the same time as making a Care Order or subsequently. Parents could also bring the matter back to court. The Children Act adopted the wardship model.

In the 52 sample cases involving Care Order applications there were only 16 in which social services were also applying for one or more Contact Orders under Section 34. Most of these (11) involved applications for leave to refuse contact by one or both parents. In three of the four cases where contact with only one parent was to be terminated orders were also sought giving the local authority powers to regulate contact by the other. There were only five cases in all where the most restrictive order was either contact at the discretion of the local authority or some definition of the contact conditions, usually that it be supervised. Orders regarding contact by siblings or other persons were also sought in four cases.

The position of the other parties

Agreements and contest

Our most reliable data, that collected on the observed cases, indicate that by the time the final hearing was reached three out of every five cases were no longer disputed while in the sample as a whole 46 were known not to be contested. As might be expected almost all the cases still in dispute involved applications for Care Orders. In 29 of these the order itself was disputed while in a further two the disagreement was only about contact. In contrast only two of the 14 applications for Supervision Orders were contested and none of the applications for an order of No Order or withdrawal of the proceedings.

Every one of the contested cases was opposed by at least one of the child's parents and, where both were involved, usually both. There were however a handful of cases where other relatives also opposed the local authority, usually on the issue of contact. This too was the topic on which Guardians ad Litem, if they disputed anything at all by this stage, were likely to take issue.

There was not a single case in which the child's representatives formally opposed the primary application at the final hearing. However it should be emphasised that there were a number in which it was evident that the guardian's approach had significantly influenced the direction of the case, sometimes from the very start. Zara's case is probably the most notable example of this. It is also extremely unlikely that the court would have allowed James Pallister to go to his aunt or Sammi Collins to remain with his parents had the guardian supported the application for an Interim Care Order at the first hearing. Sophie Farrow would certainly not have been allowed to go home mid-proceedings, despite her distress, if the guardian had not only argued for that course of action but set up the monitoring by a local community worker which allowed the risks to be contained. There were also several cases in which guardians were influential in the child going to live with relatives.

● ●

Prior to proceedings Marcus had stayed for a time with his maternal aunt, with whom he enjoyed a good relationship. There had been conflict between the sisters, however, resulting in Marcus's removal and placement in a foster home.

Four months into proceedings social services had concluded rehabilitation was not possible and long-term foster care would be necessary. This was likely to prove difficult because of the lack of culturally appropriate placements locally. Marcus himself repeatedly asked that he should go back to live with his aunt and at length social services began to explore this. By the final hearing, however, the assessment had not proceeded very far and the psychiatrist advising social services opposed the idea. The guardian was in favour but extremely doubtful that once a Care Order was made the placement would come about. Accordingly she applied for and obtained, an adjournment of the final hearing.

Four months later Marcus's mother had come round to the idea, a reconciliation of sorts had been effected and both the child psychiatrist and social services were more comfortable with the prospect. However the formal approval process had still not been completed. The guardian indicated that in view of the delay she would not be able to recommend a Care Order at the final hearing. The process was expedited, Marcus was placed and a Care Order made.

● ●

The wishes and feelings of the children

An important factor influencing the guardian in this case were the views of Marcus himself. His clear attachment to his mother and wish to remain in frequent contact with her, however, were secondary to the guardian's judgement that rehabilitation home was too risky. Placement with the aunt was therefore a compromise for both the guardian and for Marcus. Although this was therefore potentially a case where separate representation would have been appropriate it appears there was never a point at which this was seriously considered. As we reported in Chapter 9 there were only two cases in the sample where the guardian and the child's solicitor parted company.

Marcus, of course, was just 10 and most of the case children, who were even younger, could not have been considered competent to instruct even where it was apparent that they held divergent views. Indeed half appear to have been deemed too young for their wishes and feelings to be even recorded. Evidence as to the wishes and feelings of the child was recorded in only 40 of the sample cases, all submitted through the agency of others, usually guardians and social workers, although 17 other professionals and 12 family members also contributed. Accounts of the children's views were inconsistent in only eight cases. Only one, which concerned contact, involved different professional perceptions (between the guardian on the one hand and the social worker and foster carer on the other). In four cases a parent's account of the children's wishes differed from that of the guardian and/or social worker while in one case there was disagreement between family members. In the remaining two cases the children's wishes were fluctuating and hard to ascertain by anyone.

Uncontested cases

Twenty-three of the 49 cases which were not finally contested had been contested at earlier hearings. Indeed five of them had already been through at least one contested abortive *final* hearing: the Cooper children for instance, Christopher O'Brien, Sam Phillips, Marcus and, of course, Zara. Moreover in most cases, even if neither interim nor final hearings were actively contested (23 cases) it would be comparatively unusual for a care case to be *agreed* (as distinct from not opposed) by all parties throughout, although there were a small number of such cases, such as that of the Dinmore family.

What accounts for the relatively low rate of disputed final hearings? Does lack of opposition signify genuine agreement, reluctant compromise or one party giving up? The answer, of course, is that examples of all three scenarios can be found, sometimes in the same case. Andy Harris, for instance, was very satisfied that the outcome of proceedings was not a Care Order leading to adoption, as had seemed very likely at the outset, but a Residence Order under which Jamie moved to live with him and his new wife. Jamie's mother Frances, on the other hand, took no part in proceedings at all.

The incidence of genuine agreements was probably highest in those cases where social services were no longer seeking a public law order. This shift in position was usually readily made in response to changes within the family and/or to changes in the way the family was perceived. There were only two cases in which the decision to abandon the application was related to doubts that the criteria could be satisfied.[23] However in both, it should be noted, there were no longer concerns about the child's safety. In a small number of other cases, however, the local authority's position shifted with varying degrees of reluctance. In the case of Sammi Collins, for instance, it was only with considerable misgivings that social services settled for working with the level of parental co-operation that would be forthcoming on a voluntary basis rather than force the issue with a Supervision Order.

Cases involving applications for Supervision Orders tended to show the greatest polarity. There were cases like Zara's for instance, where social services were dragged kicking and screaming to the final settlement and Christopher's, where they agreed a Supervision Order as the only way to keep a foot in the door of what they predicted would be a disastrous placement with Vera. On the other hand it had always been hoped to keep the Phillips children with their mother. Whatever Joanne's real feelings on continuing social services involvement, given that ten months earlier she had been at risk of losing the children entirely, it seems likely she considered she had had a lucky escape.

Indeed in many instances Supervision Orders are probably not contested by parents because they are seen as the lesser evil: if the local authority is confident enough in its evidence to pursue an application for a public law order but is content with a Supervision Order it is a high risk strategy to contest. Most parents would no doubt prefer social workers out of their lives altogether. However since they are unlikely to achieve this even without a Supervision Order (since they would usually be expected to enter into a written agreement to work on a voluntary basis) little would be gained even by successful opposition. There were certainly several examples of this sort of *agreement* among the sample cases.

However there were also a few cases where relatives taking on the care of children (for example Louise's grandparents) positively wanted the ongoing social work assistance which a Supervision Order appeared to promise. There was even one parent, Josie Dinmore, who after an extended period in a residential unit, was still anxious to ensure social workers would continue to visit. Her needs for support and social services' need to monitor thus meshed perfectly. In a better resourced authority, of course, there would have been no need for an order at all.

Among parents not contesting a Care Order three main groups could be identified. There were those prepared to agree because the care plan involved either rehabilitation or placement within the extended family (5). At the other end of the spectrum were seven cases where parents seem to have reluctantly bowed to what they presumably saw as the inevitable, even to the extent of ceasing to participate in proceedings. One mother actually left the country. In between these extremes there were a number of parents who seem to have made a positive decision that since they were unable to provide adequate care the application was in their children's best interests. Millie, for instance, came to terms with the inevitable sufficiently well to be able to explain to Ben why he would be remaining in care long term and start to help him deal with his anxiety about her future.

It will be apparent from the above that there was a good deal of variation in the point at which proceedings were agreed. Millie had been gradually coming round to accepting reality for some weeks but did not finally confirm her agreement until a couple of weeks before the final hearing. Josie had never opposed. Stephen's mother Jasmine was still proposing to contest until the day before, while at least five cases were settled at the door of the court. Moreover, as we shall see in the next section, a number of other cases were agreed in the course of the hearing.

Contested cases

Cases classified as contested also formed a very disparate group. The Barnes's solicitor, for instance, was told not to agree the Care Order but not to actively contest. Doreen did not turn up; Jack refused to give any instructions or to say anything to the court and spent most of the time sprawled in his seat ostensibly asleep. Gina was bitterly opposed to the Care Order but her interest were still represented by the Official Solicitor, who had instructed counsel not to contest; Matt supported her but had no alternative proposals to offer for Laurie's care. The application for a Care Order and leave to terminate all family contact with Michelle was however bitterly contested not only by her mother, Claudette, but by both grandmothers. Claudette also opposed their applications for Residence or Contact Orders.

What was being contested was also very diverse. Jemima's father, for instance, was denying the allegations of physical abuse and thus arguing the threshold conditions were not made out. Her mother, however, was mainly arguing that since social services was proposing rehabilitation to her anyway, a Supervision Order would be adequate protection. A similar argument was put in the case of Julia, who was to stay with Carmen in the residential placement until they were rehabilitated in the community. In one case involving a very serious injury to a young child significant harm could not be denied but, since the source of the injuries had never been established, mother's lawyer argued that the second limb of the threshold conditions could not be met. This argument was pursued through to appeal (where it was given very short shrift). In another very similar case, however, the issue was not even raised.

Several lines of defence were sometimes employed. In the two cases in which the child and guardian were separately represented for instance, the children's lawyers argued:

♦ that the threshold conditions were not met because the alleged physical abuse was rather reasonable chastisement for disciplinary purposes which was not over-zealous by the standards of the family's culture or religion;

♦ that the order sought (a Supervision Order in both cases) would not promote the welfare of the children and was not necessary because the family was prepared to accept help; and

♦ that the children themselves were opposed to a court order.

Arguments were not, however, always so cogently presented. As commented earlier while the nature of the concerns could be deduced from the evidence presented, many statements were largely descriptive and chronological. It was comparatively unusual to find clear arguments using evidence to establish the threshold conditions. Parents' statements tended to challenge point by point rather than setting out their overall position and using evidence to support this. Thus it was often hard to establish precisely what the issues in dispute were. This is another indication of the usefulness of a pre-trial review.

Five cases were agreed in the course of the hearing, parents conceding in three, social services in one and a compromise being reached on contact in the fifth. In the four cases where the primary application was contested it is likely that positions shifted as it became apparent which way the case was going. Indeed social services' mid-hearing capitulation[24] followed a very clear indication from the judge. Court intervention was also instrumental in achieving agreement over the issue of contact in Marcus's case, the judge essentially sending the parties out to negotiate an agreement rather than battling it out in court.

Evidence

Documentary sources

By the time the final hearing was reached an average of between 13 and 14 items of written evidence had been accumulated in the sample cases, ranging from a single statement in one case to 50 documents in another. One case in five had 20 or more different items. Of course not all these statements and reports emanated from different sources; characteristically, because of the length and mutability of care cases, repeat statements in the form of updates are common. Thus 110 parents submitted 153 statements in the course of proceedings while 226 statements were filed by the 101 social workers acting as key workers. On average each case could draw on evidence from ten different sources though there could be as many as 30. In addition, as indicated earlier, there were often also interim reports from the Guardian ad Litem.

Professional evidence

Guardians were appointed in all the sample cases and reports were filed with the court in all but four, where proceedings had not run the full course. In addition an average of between 10 and 11 items of professional evidence were submitted, ranging from one statement in the case of Samantha, which was withdrawn at the first hearing, to 46 in the complicated and ever-changing case involving the Francombe children, which lasted 18 months. In this particularly difficult case, evidence was supplied by 25 different professionals, the maximum in any case, the mean being seven.

Cases reaching the care courts now include not only those which would have been heard in wardship, where written evidence was the norm, but those where proceedings under the Children and Young Persons Act 1969 would have been appropriate, where it was unusual. It was therefore surprising to find that the *number* of professionals filing evidence in the sample cases was higher even than in pre-Act wardships[25] (mean 5). The numerical predominance of the social work profession, however, remains. As Table 15.3 shows, professional evidence most commonly came from social services staff, particularly field social workers. Moreover, as indicated in an earlier chapter, the majority of other professionals were also filing evidence in support of the local authority.

Lay evidence

Professional statements and reports dominated the written evidence. In contrast to the seven professionals submitting 11 documents which was the

Table 15.3 *Documentary evidence: professional sources*

Source	No. of documents
Local authority social worker	101
Local authority team manager	26
Previous social worker	8
Family support worker	8
Other social services staff	12
Foster carer	24
Hospital social worker	10
Field social worker/other SSD	4
Other agency social worker	13
Psychiatrist	67
Paediatrician	57
Other medical specialist	15
General practitioner	13
Other community doctor	7
Other doctor	4
Hospital nurse	6
Health visitor	23
Other nurse	5
Other health professional	9
Police	50
Probation officer	5
Schools	24
Educational psychologist	13
Nursery	24
Mother and baby home	14
Family centre	12
Children's home	6
Other institution staff	9
Other	36

average per case, a mean of 3.5 documents were filed by 2.6 lay people. Indeed the *maximum* number of lay statements (13) was only slightly higher than the *mean* number of professional. In nine cases no lay evidence was filed at all.

Lay evidence was, of course, primarily submitted by the parents themselves (Table 15.4), followed by a range of other relatives, principally grandmothers and aunts plus friends and neighbours. It should also be noted that, as reported in a previous chapter, the position of key relatives was often relayed indirectly through the guardian ad litem's report rather than through the filing of evidence.

Table 15.4 *Documentary evidence: lay sources*

Source	No. of documents
Mother	69
Father	41
Mother's cohabitee	4
Sibling	5
Maternal grandmother	12
Paternal grandmother	6
Maternal grandfather	3
Paternal grandfather	3
Aunt	16
Uncle	7
Other relative	3
Friend	13
Neighbour	6
Other non-related adult	12
Other	14

The quality of written evidence

The introduction of written evidence into proceedings under the Children Act was widely welcomed by the vast majority of practitioners and members of the judiciary interviewed. However there were many complaints about the *standard* of the documents produced. Some members of the professional judiciary, for instance, complained that the quality of written statements submitted under the Children Act was inferior to the affidavits required in wardship, reflecting an apparently lower level of legal input and often resembling, it was said, proofs of evidence rather than documents for the court. Parents' statements were criticised for not identifying the issues or being written in such a way as to give a completely misleading impression of their intellectual capacity. A few complaints were made about the length of guardians' reports although their content was generally deemed very helpful.

Most criticism, however, was directed at the prolixity, repetitiveness and lack of focus of *social workers' statements*. Some of this is a problem for professional practice which should be assisted by new guidance on report writing.[26] While anxiety remains, however, that anything which is not specifically referred to in the depositions cannot be subsequently used in court, the temptation to leave nothing out will remain. Social workers, we know, sweat blood over producing statements. Given that, as it appears from our judicial interviews, they will probably be skimmed through rather than thoroughly perused, especially if the case is fairly clear-cut, one might advise them not to bother. The primary value of such statements, however, may be to others – to the guardian for instance, in her or his investigation and to the other parties, in gauging the strength of the evidence. Indeed the availability of written evidence was often cited as a contributory factor in the high rate of settlement.

Oral evidence

To our knowledge the court files examined contained a complete record of all written evidence although in a few cases specific documents were missing. The position as regards oral evidence was much more patchy. Witness records for particular hearings were sometimes missing or obviously incomplete, which gave us less than total confidence even in the data which were available. In 16 cases we were unable to ascertain whether or not oral evidence was given at any stage and these were excluded from the data reported in the following sections. A comparison of the remaining cases against the observed sample showed only small discrepancies, largely accounted for by the distortion produced by the unusual Francombe case. We therefore considered data on this reduced sample sufficiently reliable to be used.

'Professional' witnesses

A total of 208 professionals were noted on the witness record, giving a mean of three per case with a maximum of 23. Almost three-quarters of these witnesses, not unexpectedly, gave evidence at the final hearing, although nearly two in five were called at interim hearings. Indeed 51 gave evidence *only* at such hearings. The largest group to do so were local authority social workers (21) although others were represented: Guardians ad Litem (6), medical experts (8), the police (3) and eight other groups.

Thus more than *half* the professionals appearing as witnesses at interim hearings were not called at the final hearing whilst three-quarters of those called at the final hearing had not given oral evidence earlier. It seems, therefore, that there are two principal groups of witnesses: those whose evidence is used to justify the initial application, particularly the need for interim protective arrangements, such as the social worker, police and medical practitioners involved in any precipitating crisis, and others – such as the current social workers, guardians and experts – whose evidence is relevant to the final disposal. This distinction is apparent despite several 'interim' hearings in the sample being set down and managed as final hearings but resulting in Interim Orders. Without these, it might be still more clear-cut.

Less than a third of the professionals filing written evidence gave oral evidence at any stage. The discrepancy was particularly marked in relation to those professionals classified as experts of whom only 13% were called as witnesses. Psychiatrists, for instance, accounted for only 8% of oral evidence. Local authority social workers again formed the largest single group (39%) followed by guardians (19%). No other single professional group was represented in court by more than nine witnesses (4%). Professionals giving evidence for social services outnumbered those for parents by 21 to 1.

In the observed cases the duration of oral evidence given by each type of witness was recorded. Overall professional evidence took up more than three-quarters of the time (78%) though this varied between 74% in Area B and 78% in A to 85% in C. This is likely to reflect the relative proportions of contested cases in each area. Just over half the time taken up by oral evidence was accounted for by local authority social workers (52%) with guardians in the box for about one-fifth of the time. Psychiatrists were the only other group whose evidence accounted for any substantial length of time (12%).

Lay witnesses

Similarly only a minority of lay people who had filed statements gave oral evidence (28%), an average of less than one per case. Over a third of cases had no lay witnesses with the maximum number being six. By far the largest group were mothers (44%), with fathers accounting for 22% and other relatives 11%. Lay evidence was known to be heard at a quarter of final hearings, numbers ranging from one to six with a mean of 1.9.

Evidence and contest

Not surprisingly more evidence tends to be called when cases are contested, particularly where that persists until the final hearing. On average there were 5.4 sources of documentary evidence in cases which were not contested at any point, 7.5 in those which were contested at some point and 9.1 in those which were still contested by the final hearing. Similarly 5.2 professionals gave oral evidence in cases with contested final hearings, 3.5 in those which were contested at any point and 1.5 in those which were not.

The difference in the numbers of lay sources of evidence is less marked. Thus on average two people filed written evidence in uncontested cases, 2.7 in those contested at some stage and 3.3 in those which remained contested. In these latter cases 1.6 witnesses gave oral evidence compared to 1.1 in cases with some contest. In the 14 cases not contested at any hearing there was only one lay witness in all.

Duration of the final hearing

As Figure 15.4 shows, most cases did not end in hearings stretching over many days. Fifty cases took up no more than one day of court time and 71 were completed within three days. Even among cases in which the primary application was contested just over a quarter finished in a single day, further evidence of the variation in degrees of contest that can occur. There was also variation between the three research areas, with every contested final hearing

Figure 15.4 *Duration of the final hearing (days)*

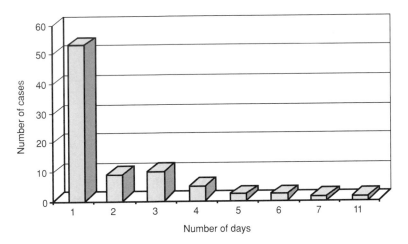

in Area B lasting for more than one day. Multi-day hearings also tended to be longest here: Area C for instance, only had four cases lasting for more than two days and Area A had five, in comparison Area B had 12. This very much reflects the pre-Act pattern in this area.

In all three areas the chances of a case taking more than one day to complete increased with the level of court. Over three-quarters of final hearings in the family proceedings court (29 of 38) took no more than one day. This fell to 60% (18 of 30) in the county court and 40% (6 of 15) in the High Court, although the very longest hearings were actually in the county court in each area. This may be purely fortuitous, or, as some practitioners suggested, reflect the degree of control exercised over the progress of the hearing.

More precise details about duration were generally only available for the 28 observed final hearings. As Table 15.5 shows, the majority of these were surprisingly short, 14 taking two hours or less and only 11 needing four hours or more, the mean being only 4 hours 37 minutes. The longest final hearing in the whole observed sample took up 19 hours of court time while the shortest was over in nine minutes.

Table 15.5 *The length of final hearings*

	Area A	Area B	Area C	All areas
Mean	5h 48m	2h 58m	4h 44m	4h 37m
Minimum	0h 15m	0h 09m	0h 15m	0h 09m
Maximum	16h 40m	8h 22m	19h 10m	19h 10m
No. taking 2 hours or less	5	5	4	14
No. taking 4 hours or more	5	3	3	11
(n=)	(10)	(8)	(10)	(28)

Legal outcomes

By the close of the final hearing only 26 cases required adjudication on any of the local authority's applications relating to any case child. In every single one of these the court's decision was in favour of the applicant, although in Ian Morse's case social services were 'happy to accept' the guardian's suggestion that a Residence Order should be accompanied by a Supervision Order.

These figures might suggest that the court is only acting as a rubber stamp. However it should be apparent from everything that has been reported in previous chapters that this would not be a valid conclusion. Rather if there is any scope for change in the position of the parties this is accomplished over the course of the case. Parents may cling on in the forlorn hope that things may go their way; social services, it seems, would rather change or withdraw applications than have judgement entered against them and courts seek to give them the opportunity to do so.

The majority of care proceedings still end, as they did pre-Act, in a public law order. As Figure 15.5 shows, 49 of the *index* children were made subject to Care Orders and a further 15 to Supervision Orders, three of which had conditions attached. Unadorned, a private law order was a fairly infrequent disposal and only occurred with Residence Orders. Six Supervision Orders, however, were made in tandem with Residence Orders, one with a Prohibited Steps Order and one with a Specific Issue Order.

Figure 15.5 *Final orders made: index child*

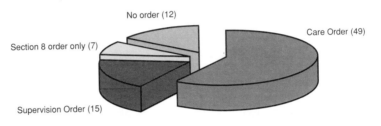

Thirteen cases ended with Residence Orders: seven to relatives and five to one parent, while the order relating to Ian Morse stipulated he should live with his mother at his grandparents' house. Of the six which were buttressed with Supervision Orders, four also had some form of additional protection: conditions on the Supervision Order (1), a Prohibited Steps Order (3); Section 8 Contact Order (2). Four of the remaining seven were also supported with other provisions: conditions on the order (1), Family Assistance Order (2), Section 8 Contact Order (2).

None of the sample cases ended in a Prohibited Steps Order alone and in comparison with its use as an interim measure, it was rare even combined with other orders, only four being made in all. Section 8 Contact Orders were also fairly unusual, being made in a total of seven cases, five of which also involved Supervision Orders.

In contrast Section 34 Contact Orders were made in 23 of the 49 cases ending in Care Orders while on a further three the issue was still outstanding, two partly motivated by the desire to keep the guardian involved. The majority of orders gave social services leave to refuse contact to both (8) or one (5) parents. A further five made contact a matter for their discretion. *Reasonable contact*, ordered in four cases, would seem to add nothing to the local authority's obligations under the Act. There were only four cases in which the terms under which contact was to operate were defined.

A considerable number of these Care Order cases involved plans for adoption. However there were only two cases in which a Freeing Order was made alongside the Care Order. In pre-Act wardships, in contrast, it was very common for this issue to be dealt with to the extent of granting leave to place.[27]

At the other end of the spectrum, 12 of the sample cases ended with no order at all. However there were only two in which the court made an order of No Order indicating that the threshold conditions had been met but an order was unnecessary. In all the remaining instances the application was withdrawn. In only two of these were difficulties anticipated in meeting the threshold conditions. In most the feeling seemed to be that even if no objection was forthcoming from parents nothing would be gained by an order, while if it were it would be distinctly counter-productive.

It was intended, however, that social services would remain involved with all these families. Usually agreements to this effect had been worked out prior to the final decision and were often attached to the court papers, while in two cases formal undertakings were accepted by the court. While one presumes these were more acceptable to parents than a Supervision Order, the nature of the commitments they were making seemed on the face of things to involve at least an equivalent level of control. Thus while statutory intervention in the family was no longer deemed to be warranted, the care which these children were likely to receive within their families was still a matter of public concern. Moreover, it should be emphasised, none of these cases ended with the local authority's application being dismissed. The spectre of Cleveland and Orkney, of draconian intervention which is later thrown out by the courts, finds no reflection in the everyday cases which form the typical workload of the care courts under the Children Act 1989.

Legal outcomes: a pre- and post-Act comparison

It is important to note, however, that in these authorities it was very rare, even before the Act, for cases to be dismissed. This only occurred in one of the sample cases brought in pre-Act care proceedings. Moreover the application was rejected on the care or control test not the primary grounds. As Figure 15.6 indicates, however, there are quite considerable changes in the balance of orders made under the old and new legislation, with a substantial increase in the proportion of cases ending in Care Orders and no public law order and a drop in the proportion of Supervision Orders. This shift is apparent whether one compares care or wardship proceedings (Table 15.6) and is generally maintained across all three authorities although the degree of change, obviously, varies. The only exception is that the proportion of cases ending in no order in Area B (highest of all pre-Act) has remained the same.

Figure 15.6 *Legal outcomes pre- and post-Act*

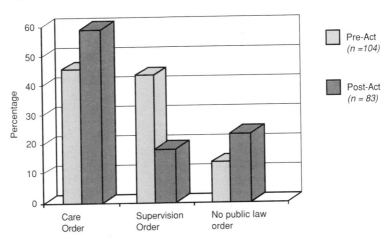

Table 15.6 *Comparative outcomes by area*

	Area A		Area B		Area C	
	Pre-Act %	Post-Act %	Pre-Act %	Post-Act %	Pre-Act %	Post-Act %
Care Order	29	55	51	60	58	71
Supervision Order	61	17	29	20	33	13
No public law order	10	28	20	20	8	17
(n=)	(41)	(29)	(36)	(30)	(27)	(24)

Back on the road

The final hearing in a care case, then, far from being the dramatic last act in a drama is very often an anti-climax. The real action will have taken place in the preceding months and the potential for an unforeseen twist in the story is very limited.

At the same time the closing of the courtroom door merely marks the ending of a particular and highly artificial episode in the lives of the families concerned and a punctuation mark in their relationship with welfare agencies. Very few could expect to resume their lives outside the spotlight of social services scrutiny. All would have to incorporate the experiences of the past months into their images of themselves and their family life; some begin to face up to permanent loss; others to changed relationships with children living in foster care or with relatives or even to learn to live again with children who had been returned. For all of them perhaps, the spectre of future compulsory intervention would always, however faintly, be there.

For the researchers who had become so familiar with these cases, the burning question was what happened next? It was already apparent in the course of the fieldwork that the fluidity which was so marked during care proceedings continued after their completion. Indeed several cases came back to court even before the research was over. We were aware, for instance, of Care Orders being sought in five cases which had ended in Supervision Orders; of proceedings being instituted on new babies and, at the other extreme, of children lingering in foster care still awaiting adoption.

The Department of Health subsequently provided further funding to follow-up the children involved in this research for at least 18 months after the final hearing.[28] In seeking to evaluate the changes the Children Act has made in the legal framework for protecting children the key question has to be whether they work in the interests of children. The new study will, we hope, move us a little further towards an answer.

Summary

The extended range of final disposals available to the courts was generally recognised by practitioners to be a considerable improvement on the Children and Young Persons Act 1969. The facility to make private law orders within public law proceedings was the most widely appreciated reform. By not conferring the broad order-making powers of the wardship jurisdiction allowing tailor-made remedies, however, the Act has not entirely lived up to expectations.

Three principal issues emerged: the power conferred on local authorities under a Care Order; the diminishing value of Supervision Orders and restrictions on who may apply for certain orders and in which court.

Disquiet about Care Orders was a dominant theme among all practitioner groups, amounting, among those practising primarily within the court system, to substantial rejection of the new boundaries established between the executive and judicial domains. This has prompted attempts to circumvent the clear intention of the legislation and generated considerable frustration as these have been repeatedly stamped on by the appeal courts. It is strongly recommended that this issue be reconsidered.

The remodelled Supervision Order has proved a disappointment, widely seen by practitioners as irrelevant and/or ineffective. It is suggested that clarification of the powers available under a Supervision Order and opportunities to explore their potential may help to prevent the order falling into disuse. It is also recommended that further consideration be given to strengthening the order itself.

The third main source of dissatisfaction centred on restrictions on the local authority's ability to apply for Section 8 orders, particularly decisions in case law preventing the use of Prohibited Steps Orders to oust and prevent contact with an alleged perpetrator. The provisions of the 1996 Family Law Act do not appear to fully address these difficulties and it is urged that further consideration should be given to the whole issue.

By the time of the final hearing public law orders were no longer being sought in one case in five. In the remainder there were four times as many applications for Care Orders as there were for Supervision Orders. Cases involving ethnic minorities, particularly non-European families, were more likely to end in a public law order, almost always a Care Order. This further reinforces the need to examine the issue of ethnicity in the context of child protection practice.

Even Care Orders did not invariably mean placement outside the family altogether and this was the plan in less than half the sample overall. Just over a quarter of the index children were to return to or remain with the parent who had previously had care. More children from non-European families were to be placed outside the nuclear family. Although a higher proportion of those separated were to live with relatives, such children were still more likely to be placed in long-term substitute care.

Placement within the extended family was the intended outcome for 15% of cases involved. The legal underpinning for such placements varied. Research is needed into the services needed to support such placements. There was variation between the study areas in the balance of legal orders being applied for and the plans for the children under such orders.

Three in ten Care Order applications also involved local authority applications for a Contact Order, usually for leave to refuse contact to one or both parents.

Only two in five cases were still disputed by the final hearing. Almost all involved applications for Care Orders contested by the parents and, occasionally, other relatives. There was not a single case in which the primary application was formally opposed by the representatives for the child. However, there was much evidence of those representatives affecting the position finally adopted by social services. Lack of contest ranged from full agreement between the local authority and parent to one side or other conceding defeat.

Almost half the cases which were not disputed at the final hearing had been disputed at earlier hearings. There was a great deal of variation in the point at which they ceased to be contested. Five cases settled at the door of the court. A contested final hearing could mean anything from a parent not giving formal agreement to a full-blown courtroom battle lasting several days. The matters at issue were also varied though few concerned the application of the threshold conditions.

The sample cases were supported by voluminous documentary evidence. One case in five had more than 20 items. On average, evidence was submitted by ten different sources in addition to the guardian's report. Written evidence was overwhelmingly submitted by professionals, mainly on behalf of the local authority. The number of professionals filing evidence was higher even than in pre-Act wardships. Professionals giving evidence for social services outnumbered those for parents by 21 to one.

The introduction of written evidence into care proceedings was widely perceived as a considerable improvement on the largely oral procedures under the Children and Young Persons Act 1969. There were, however, many complaints about the standard of written evidence, particularly the prolixity, repetitiveness and lack of focus of social workers' statements.

Less than a third of the professionals filing written evidence gave oral evidence at any stage. Almost a quarter of those who did were called only at interim hearings. Local authority social workers were the largest single group of witnesses, followed by guardians and psychiatrists. Just over a quarter of lay deponents gave oral evidence and over a third of cases had no lay witnesses at all. Lay evidence was taken at only a quarter of final hearings.

Most of the sample cases did not end in long hearings, the mean being just over $4^{1}/_{2}$ hours. Six out of ten were completed within one day and 17 out of 20 within three days.

By the close of the final hearing less than a third of the sample cases required adjudication on any of the local authority's applications, five cases having settled in the course of the hearing. Every single adjudication went in favour of the local authority.

The majority of cases ended in a public law order, most commonly a Care Order. Private law orders on their own were a fairly infrequent disposal though a number of Supervision Orders were made in support of Residence Orders. There were 15% of cases which ended with no order at all. It was intended that social services would remain involved with all these families on a voluntary basis. Although there might no longer be a need for compulsory intervention there remained concerns about the welfare of children.

The proportion of cases ending in a Care Order is larger than in the pre-Act sample as is the fraction in which no public law order was made at all. There has been a marked drop in the use of Supervision Orders.

NOTES

1 DHSS (1985): *Review of Child Care Law Report to Ministers of an Interdepartmental Working Party*. HMSO.

2 DHSS (1985): op. cit.

3 House of Commons (1984): *Second Report of the All-Party Parliamentary Select Committee on Social Services* (Session 1983-84): Children in Care (The Short Report). HMSO.

4 This amendment, which was not among the recommendations of the Child Care Law Review, was made late in the Bill's Report stage.

5 Hunt J (1993): *Local Authority Wardships before the Children Act: The Baby or the Bathwater?* HMSO.

6 Masson J; Morton S (1989): The Use of Wardship by Local Authorities. *Modern Law Review*, November.

7 Kent County Council v C [1993] 1 FLR 308; Re B (A Minor) (Care Order: Review) [1993] 1 FLR 421; Re T (A Minor) (Care Order: Conditions) [1994] 2 FCR 721; Re L (Sexual Abuse: Standard of Proof) (1995) *The Times*, 3 July. CA.

8 White R et al. (1995): *The Children Act in Practice*. 2nd edition. Butterworths.

9 According to Butler-Sloss L J, this 'allows the local authority to keep in force a supervision order for 3 years as before but under the greater control of the courts, part of the philosophy of the Act'. Re A (A Minor) (Supervision Order: Extension) [1995] 1 FLR 335.

10 The implementation of Care Orders has subsequently been the subject of two DoH funded research projects, our own (Hunt J; Macleod A (forthcoming): *The Best-Laid Plans: Outcomes of Judicial Decisions in Child Protection Cases*. The Stationery Office) and one at the University of Sussex (Implementation of Care Plans). The SSI have also conducted an investigation into the issue: Social Services Inspectorate (1998): *Care Planning and Court Orders*. DoH.

[11] Case law also suggests this view is shared by the judiciary: Re T (A Minor) (Care or Supervision Order) [1994] 1 FLR 103; Re D (A Minor) (Care or Supervision Order) [1993] 2 FLR 423; Re S(J) (A Minor) (Care or Supervision Order) [1993] 2 FLR 919.

[12] Solicitor-General. Second Reading of the Children Bill. House of Commons, 27 April 1990.

[13] [1993] 3 All ER 815.

[14] D v D 919930 2 FLR 804.

[15] Parry M (1994): *Panel News* 7(2).

[16] This was certainly not the line taken by early governmental guidance and White et al. (1995): *The Children Act in Practice* have argued that the Nottingham decision was wrong.

[17] Re H (Prohibited Steps Order) 1 FLR 638.

[18] White et al. (1995): op. cit.

[19] Schedule 2, para. 5 permits the local authority to assist an alleged perpetrator to find alternative accommodation, a provision made in response to a recommendation in the Cleveland Inquiry Report (Cm 412, 1988).

[20] Section 43(1).

[21] Section 44(1)(a).

[22] The topic was partially covered in a recent study by the SSI (DoH (1995): *Residence Orders*. HMSO). The researchers hope to pursue the issues further in subsequent research.

[23] In one of these the original concern had been emotional harm while mother was in the acute stage of a psychiatric illness. Although the mother had substantially recovered and the child was returning home, the House of Lord's judgement in Re M should have allowed the threshold to be satisfied. The second case was more worrying, since proceedings had been brought because of the death of a baby after he had been struck by his father. The difficulty was that it could not be shown that the blow, which had not directly resulted in injury, was the cause of the child's death. The family had been co-operative throughout the investigative process and were agreeing to further assessment. Moreover, as we indicated in Chapter 7, the instigation of proceedings might have been regarded as somewhat unnecessary in relation to the surviving children, who were less vulnerable because of their age. Thus purely in terms of the welfare of the case children withdrawal of proceedings was reasonable. However, were the family to cease being co-operative and another baby be born, or were the father to form a new family, one wonders how difficult it would be to invoke the courts to provide protection without a finding in the sample case.

[24] An unusual case in which DNA tests showed that the child's 'father' was not biologically related. The child had been placed with him early in proceedings but the level of conflict with mother remained high. The local authority, supported by the guardian, applied for a Care Order; the judge indicated he would take a great deal of persuading not to make a Residence Order.

[25] Hunt (1993): op. cit.

[26] Plotnikoff J; Woolfson R (1997): *Reporting to Court: A Handbook for Social Services*. SSI.

[27] Hunt (1993): op. cit.

[28] Hunt J; Macleod A (forthcoming): *The Best-Laid Plans: Outcomes of Judicial Decisions in Child Protection Cases*. The Stationery Office.

16 Moving on

It is doubtful if any piece of legislation could live up to the euphoria and hyperbole which surrounded the introduction of the Children Act. In the preceding chapters we have identified a number of aspects of the Act or its operation which need further consideration and thus inevitably have at times dwelt on the defects and the difficulties. Entry to and exit from the legal process have been shown to be points of tension under the Act and the period in between unreasonably long. Indeed at almost every stage of the process there has been something to criticise, something to change, something causing difficulty to someone.

Notwithstanding, as far as the compulsory protection of children is concerned, the Act has to be regarded as a substantial achievement which has had an enormous impact on practice. Indeed it was noticeable that many of the practitioners we interviewed, even those who had been most critical of certain aspects of the new legislation, were concerned to put on record their overall approval. In this concluding chapter, then, it is appropriate to start by emphasising how far the system has moved.

One set of criteria, rather than a plethora, now governs state intervention into family life. These are unequivocally seen to be a vast improvement on those governing care proceedings under the Children and Young Persons Act 1969, previously the principal statutory route. Regrets remain for the ease with which protective powers could be invoked through the broad discretion of the wardship jurisdiction. However fears that their removal would leave children seriously unprotected have not materialised to any real extent.

The wording of the criteria may yet prove a fertile ground for legal argument. As yet, however, this has not happened. Moreover the concepts to which the conditions give expression are widely accepted as valid and providing a more structured and rigorous framework for decision-making, both in demonstrating the justification for and estimating the effects of intervention. Throughout the system practice is seen to have become more thoughtful and measured.

Care proceedings are now more likely to be brought only when lesser alternatives have been explored, thus realising one of the key objectives of the legislation. Fewer are instigated in the wake of a crisis. Emergency Protection Orders are not being used as a routine way to begin proceedings, which was said to be the case with Place of Safety Orders, and alternatives to such draconian intervention are being more thoroughly investigated. Clearer and more demanding criteria, shorter time limits and rights of challenge all afford better protection to family integrity while the local authority's powers under an order have been clarified and their use made more accountable to the court.

The court framework has been transformed. It may not be integrated but it is more interconnected. Most remedies are available at all levels of court and all child matters concerning the same family can be dealt with together; it is no longer necessary to have several sets of proceedings running in parallel. The availability of private law orders in public law proceedings in particular offers a degree of flexibility hitherto only available in wardship. The level of court at which a case is heard is no longer determined by the nature of the initial application. Anxieties that access to the expertise of the professional judiciary would be restricted have proved unfounded. Transfers between court levels work remarkably smoothly.

The new structure incorporates some of the best elements of its component parts. Children subject to proceedings are now entitled to legal representation and, importantly, of a type which can accommodate both their rights and their needs, as they were previously only under the Children and Young Persons Act 1969. As in wardship, anyone who can demonstrate a legitimate interest in the child's welfare can participate in proceedings. Written depositions and advance disclosure have replaced the oral procedures characteristic of the magistrates' summary jurisdiction and rules of evidence are more like those previously only considered appropriate for a professional judiciary.

The persistence of delay remains the most glaring failure. Yet even here the Act has had a significant impact in re-framing delay as a problem to be identified and addressed rather than tolerated or ignored. The strategies to control and monitor case progress may not go far enough but they are a sound basis for further development.

Perhaps most significantly of all, mechanisms were put in place to monitor implementation, notably the Children Act Advisory Committee. While not quite the superordinate structure advocated by some commentators[1] it provided for a degree of overall co-ordination previously unheard of. The local committees may not have been as successful as had been hoped,[2] but they too constituted an advance, providing a conduit through which information about problems and positive as well as ineffective practice could be communicated. The annual reports of the Committee not only provided a regular audit of the operation of the system but a means of shaping it coherently. The demise of this Committee is to be much regretted: it remains to be seen whether its successor, the Advisory Board on Family Law, will prove as effective.

It is in the nature of reform, however, that it throws into relief areas where change is still needed; indeed can generate impatience with the unevenness and the pace of change. We turn now to the examination of some of the outstanding or emergent issues.

The substantive law

There are only two aspects of the *substantive* law, the research suggests, which need reconsideration. The first, and relatively minor aspect, is the duration of Emergency Protection Orders. Here, we would argue, the Children Act has over-corrected the imbalance in the previous legislation, under which neither children nor parents had any rights under a draconian order which could last for up to 28 days. Now that children can be represented, parents have the right of challenge and local authorities are accountable to the court for the management of such crucial issues as contact and medical examinations, the need for quite such a tight time-scale is less evident. Other changes brought about by the Act, moreover, mean that the period of the Emergency Protection Order is dominated by preparation for the first care hearing rather than an opportunity to work with a family in crisis which, particularly in new cases, might render court action unnecessary. Thus we would suggest that the maximum duration of an initial order be extended to the 15 days which is currently only permissible via an extension.

The second aspect of the law which does not appear to be entirely satisfactory relates to the orders available. Concerns were identified with the Supervision Order, which, contrary to intention, seems to have become even less attractive as a disposal, and with the restrictions on local authority access to certain private law orders. The much vaunted extended menu of orders is in reality fairly restricted and certainly does not offer the flexibility previously available under wardship. The really major issue, however, is clearly the Care Order, whose Children Act formulation, in contrast to the version applied in wardship, hands decision-making power to the local authority. The boundary thus drawn between domains remains one of the most contentious aspects of the legislation even several years into the Act. This alone would seem to justify re-examination of the question.

Structural change

Reform of the substantive law, it was said when the Children Bill was before Parliament, had to precede any reform of the court structure. The system of concurrent jurisdictions set up by the Children Act, which could be seen as an imaginative strategy to deflect calls for more radical change, has undoubtedly brought about major improvements in the management of child protection cases by the legal system. It is, none the less, a rather cumbersome framework, whose joints need constant oiling. Thus while it has to be conceded, on the evidence of this research, that the system on the whole works surprisingly well, we would still regard it as a poor substitute for a properly integrated court system and would urge that the issue be dusted off and given fresh consideration in the light of what has been learned since 1991.

It may well be that this has to be a medium- or even long-term objective, given the resource implications of establishing a one-roof Family Court. A start might, however, be made by amalgamating local administrations. Though we do not underestimate the problems this would present, the changes already brought about in relation to the Act (such as the creation of the family proceedings court and transfer of central responsibility for its administration to the Lord Chancellor's Department) make the task rather less Herculean.

It could be argued, of course, that the skeleton of a Family Court could be created quite simply and swiftly by transferring all family business to the care centres and eliminating the jurisdiction of the lay magistracy. There are arguments in favour of such a move and it would undoubtedly receive support from some quarters. However there appears to be no groundswell of opinion in favour of such change at the moment. Moreover the resource situation makes it most unlikely that family business could afford to bypass the lay magistracy in the near future. Thus consideration would have to be given to their role and to the further separation of the work of the family justices from the criminal jurisdiction. This would allow for the establishment of a more dedicated magistracy, perhaps making greater use of those with relevant professional experience, and restricted to those who have a particular commitment to and an aptitude for the work.

We have also argued that the creation of a single court structure would provide a much needed opportunity to reallocate responsibility for the Guardian ad Litem panels, whose organisational relationship with the local authority has long been a concern of ours.[3] Irrespective of the attempts to secure the independence of the panels and the continuing lack of evidence that guardians have not acted independently they remain compromised by their organisational arrangements. This too, was an issue we were told would be receiving consideration under the then government's rolling programme and one which we hope will be not much longer deferred.[4]

The challenge to practice

Changes within the substantive law and the court framework have enormously increased the demands made on all those practising within the system. The new criteria for statutory intervention, for instance, and the emphasis on partnership with parents, place a premium on the capacity of social workers and their managers to evaluate evidence and manage risk, to develop skills at working within a voluntary framework and judging the point at which that is not viable. Once a case comes to court the social worker is expected to be able to present coherent written evidence on what may well now be a more complex involvement with the family, be au fait with court procedures and be a competent witness even though the opportunities to accumulate court experience are less frequent.

The Guardian ad Litem's role now includes not only the duty to represent the child and provide independent advice to the court but to assist in managing the progress of the case through the legal process. Moreover, the investigative task is now more complex because of the issues which have to be considered and the options which have to be explored.

The same factors require a more thorough approach by lawyers representing parents, who additionally have to grapple with helping their clients to comply with the procedural requirements of the court in the form of written statements and timetabling and to work within a court culture which is moving ever further away from the traditional adversarial and confrontational approach.

Justices' Clerks, magistrates and the professional judiciary are all having to adjust to expanded roles. Clerks are now primarily responsible for setting and policing the case timetable, liaising with the care centre, and helping magistrates formulate their reasons, as well as their traditional role in providing legal advice to the lay Bench. The requirement that all substantive decisions should be supported by reasons is an entirely novel accretion to the magisterial role. Within the higher courts the judicial role is no longer merely one of adjudicating or ratifying agreed decisions but incorporates key responsibilities for case management.

Specialisation

The critical importance of the knowledge, skills, understanding and aptitude of those operating the new legislation has been a persistent theme throughout the research report and we have had occasion to comment on the diversity of standards of performance that obtain. Indeed as far as representation for parents is concerned we have argued that the increased demands of the Act make it imperative that, like lawyers for children, only those who can demonstrate an acceptable level of competence in this work should be able to practise in care proceedings.

We would also support the development of a more specialised judiciary, both lay and professional. Dame Margaret Booth's research for instance suggests that some judges who currently hold a care ticket, but are not fully committed to the work, should be encouraged to withdraw. The Association of Lawyers for Children has also pointed out the peculiarity of requiring both magistrates and county court judges practising in family law to have experience in adult criminal justice.[5] The logic of creating a judiciary with experience in family matters has been recognised in recent years in the constitution of the Family Division Bench and we see no reason why a similar philosophy should not pertain throughout the system. Indeed, with respect to the professional judiciary, perhaps it would not be too fanciful to hope that the establishment of the Law Society Child Care Panel (now the Children Panel), which has so transformed the representation available to children, can be capitalised upon. The creation of an equivalent panel for the Bar would carry a similar long-term potential benefit.

Such developments seem increasingly feasible as family justice emerges from obscurity and separates itself out from other forms of law. As yet a more radical approach, such has been adopted in France with the creation of the *Juge des enfants*, seems inconceivable, since it challenges the traditional principle of progress to judicial status through prowess as an advocate as well as the virtues of genericism.

Professional development

The need for ongoing training for all groups has been evident throughout the report, whether this is to refine traditional competencies or develop new ones. The initial massive Children Act training initiative was almost universally positively regarded. A persistent complaint among our interviewees, however, was not only the need for updating on developments in the law but for reviewing and comparing practice in the light of experience. Many practitioners, for instance, told us that the research interview was valuable to them as an opportunity to reflect on what they were doing; indeed for some, it was sadly apparent, it was the only occasion they had had to do so.

The professional matrix

Effective implementation of the Children Act makes it even more vital that the core practitioners (lawyers, guardians, social workers and court personnel) should be able to work together, whatever their professional discipline, whatever their agency or party allegiance, whatever their role in the process. The research, of course, was not directly concerned with such issues. However it has revealed, in passing, instances of conflict between social workers and local authority lawyers, between local authorities and guardians; between local authorities and the courts. Uncertainties were apparent in the Guardian ad Litem's working relationship with counsel and the professional judiciary. Relationships between the different levels of court, even between courts at the same level, and between courts and the local authority were not always free from suspicion.

Such difficulties should not surprise us. The impediments to multi-disciplinary practice have become a major theme in the family justice literature.[6] The Act, moreover, has shifted familiar boundaries, redefined institutional domains and professional roles, created a new pattern of relationships in which issues of status, power and control, of inclusion and exclusion have to be reworked.

The emphasis in the Act on the avoidance of delay highlights the need for core personnel to collaborate on process issues. Moreover, as we have sought to demonstrate, the progress of care cases through the legal process is inherently a highly dynamic one. A key theme in the report has been the diversity of the cases passing through the court, all under the Section 31 banner. The legal process is still formally structured around an adjudicative model. Yet as we have demonstrated, only a minority of care cases require final adjudication and at the point of entry to the process it is very often unclear *on what* the court might be asked to give judgement. Thus in a large proportion of cases the role of the court is to provide a framework for welfare investigation, assessment and the encouragement of change. Problem resolution,[7] therefore, a concept which is probably more familiar within the realm of private law, might be regarded as at least a parallel if not a dominant mode.

Reconceptualising care proceedings in this way, however, requires changes in working practices and roles and the development of new skills. The interim period in care cases is still dominated by court hearings even when there is no issue to be argued. These are the occasions on which the parties and their representatives assemble, bring each other up to date on what has happened and generally seek the approval, or very occasionally the arbitration of the court. This episodic approach is ill-matched to what is essentially a continuous developmental process.

Thus we would see practitioners being much more engaged with each other in between hearings and much less business being transacted in court corridors. This means a more hands-on approach for all concerned and a move away from the legal culture of last-minutism and door of the court bargaining. It suggests a greater emphasis on skills of problem definition and dispute resolution alongside those of advocacy. The Guardian ad Litem's covert role in brokering change[8] could be explicitly recognised. Over this process we would envisage the court maintaining a consistent rather than a periodic surveillance. Such through-monitoring, we have argued in the context of the avoidance of delay, is necessary in order to realise the new ideal of court control of the pace of proceedings. The concept of a judicial case officer, however, which we suggested would facilitate such monitoring, is equally relevant to the task of problem resolution.

Parental participation

Such a shift away from a court-centred process, of course, carries a risk that parents will be even more excluded from the process than they are under current arrangements when at least they will normally be present at the court hearing (even if ignored) and aware of (even if usually left out of) professional discussions. Recognising the problem resolution strand in care proceedings more explicitly, however, both suggests the need for changes in the organisation of court hearings and offers an opportunity to move towards a less formal, more participatory approach. As we note elsewhere:

> Highest levels of satisfaction (with the court process) were expressed when the judiciary had directly addressed parents, listened patiently and sympathetically to what they had to say, shown an interest in the children and displayed respect, warmth and humanity towards them. These are not qualities which would be seen as critical to the performance of the judicial role in most other types of proceedings but, judging from this survey, they are clearly vital to judges and magistrates hearing these very difficult and sensitive family matters.[9]

This research is by no means unique[10] in commenting critically on the marginalisation of parents in court hearings by a professionally dominated and formally structured process. Where the issue before the court is the adjudication of a substantive issue, particularly a contested Care Order, the justification for formal procedures and a lawyer-led process is strongest. Where only non-contentious or process issues are being dealt with, however, or the task is to work out how to go forward, the opportunity exists to develop a different approach.

Participatory justice may be an inherently difficult concept,[11] and the UK legal culture a peculiarly hostile culture for its development. The philosophy of the Children Act, however, with its emphasis on parental responsibility, on agreement, on partnership and, within the child welfare system at least, on participation, strongly suggests that efforts have to be made in this direction.

Reconstructing even directions hearings in this way, of course, requires a radically different approach on behalf of both the court and lawyers. Such hearings already, at least in the higher courts, tend to take the form of an interchange between the judge and the lawyers, rather than a series of monologues. They almost never, however, involve the parents, even on straightforward matters of fact where a direct question would be the obvious approach. Indeed in most hearings one cannot help wondering why the parents are there at all. Moving towards a format whereby the judiciary communicate directly with parents and the role of lawyers is to assist parents take part, rather than render them superfluous, would thus represent an enormous cultural leap.

Ensuring continuity of the tribunal, which we have also argued for in the context of reducing delay, would facilitate this process. Parental diffidence would be expected to diminish with acquaintance, while a judge who is familiar with the facts of the case will be less dependent on the lawyer as informant and intermediary.

Marginalising the court

Rather than seeking to shape the court process, however, it may be argued, the way forward is to keep more cases out of the court system altogether. The research indicates some of the unfortunate consequences of the emphasis on minimising statutory intervention in the early years of the Act, which was perceived as constructing the legal process in entirely negative terms and erecting hurdles against its use. This overtly denies the possibility that, as we saw in a number of the sample cases, coercion can be effective in producing change. Moreover, because covertly the need for coercion/control in some cases *is* recognised, it can also subvert the principles of voluntarism. So we have the paradox of enforced accommodation and the ambiguity of voluntary agreements.[12]

A cynic might see these efforts to keep more cases out of court, thus shifting the locus of decision-making, just at the point when parents had acquired more rights *in* court, as evidence of the social welfare system defending its threatened power superiority. While we would not concede the intent, the effect, on occasion, may be the same, as parental reports and practitioner concerns attest. Thus the justice/welfare debate, out of which the improvements in due process over the past decade grew, is set to expand beyond the court forum.

The response to such changes is likely to be greater pressure for lawyers or para-legals to penetrate the welfare domain. Whether that would be to positive or negative effect depends a great deal on the approach of the advocate and the responses of welfare professionals. At the moment, while these developments remain embryonic, both are individualised and experiences are mixed. Yet while there is legitimate anxiety about the further legalisation of welfare issues, there is also, it would appear, a potential for facilitating a more constructive relationship between parents and agency.

Another approach might be to explore the potential for brokering change in cases which appear to have become deadlocked through the involvement of another worker or even another agency in a *mediating* role. The research suggests that while parents are frequently reluctant to accept social services concerns in their entirety they often accept there are problems which need addressing. This small area of congruence may provide the basis for a more co-operative relationship.

The Children Act has substantially raised the profile of non-parent relatives within court proceedings, and the research evidence suggests that social workers are taking the kinship network more thoroughly into account pre-court. None the less some of our sample cases might still have been diverted from court had potential carers within the extended family been more fully explored. Greater attention to kinship resources, particularly perhaps the use of family group conferences, suggests yet another strategy through which children might be protected without the need for statutory intervention.

In the fullness of time, of course, one hopes that changes in policy and practice within the social welfare system aimed at assisting children in need and developing services which support families will have the desired effect of reducing the need to bring court proceedings. The research suggests that while at the point the sample cases came to court a good deal more had been done to explore alternative options there were still instances where the provision of the appropriate services in the past might have altered the direction of the case. The profile of our case sample suggests that particular social problems – psychiatric illness or disability, substance abuse, domestic violence, lone parenthood, poverty – make affected families particularly vulnerable to statutory intervention and the risk of children being lost into care. Attention to the special needs of such families would, therefore, seem a logical imperative.

The need for resources

Implementation of a thorough-going preventative policy, however, without prematurely running down the protective services, would inevitably demand increased funding. Yet lack of resources has been a persistent theme in this report. Resource difficulties within the court system and the services on which it depends, professional and administrative, contributed substantially to the dashing of hopes that the Children Act would deal with the problem of delay. While we have devoted considerable space in this report to suggesting ways in which the resources which are available might be used more economically, it cannot be denied that simply being able to operate in less straitened circumstances would be the most effective remedy. Indeed some of our ideas for tackling delay, such as local monitoring, are not resource-neutral.

The question which might be posed, therefore, is whether the level of sophistication which characterises child protection proceedings under the Act and which makes them such a resource-intensive process, is necessary in all cases.

Multi-tracking

Care proceedings are formally geared to the trial process, in which the ultimate sanction, a Care Order, can result in the permanent removal of a child. Such a context supports the emphasis on the protection of rights, the meticulous construction and evaluation of a legal case, and tight criteria for the breaching of family integrity. Yet as the research has demonstrated, care proceedings are actually a multi-track process, in which only a minority are following the Care Order route from the start. In many more cases, what is being sought is a legally protected period during which the options can be fully explored and a degree of pressure put on parents to respond to agency concerns. Under current legislation such a period, which would usually need to be substantially longer than that provided by the Child Assessment Order (unused largely for this reason), can only be obtained via an Interim Order after an application for a Care or Supervision Order has been lodged. The full machinery of the legal process is thus engaged and parents and local authority are cast as adversaries.

An alternative option, however, might be to make this available as a discrete, short-term order under which certain activities would be authorised or directed. The duration of the order would depend on the purpose for which it was sought. Those which were essentially an extension of child protection investigations, for instance, might be only four weeks; those which depended on a specialist assessment of some form, or a parent undertaking specific treatment, might be for a maximum period of say six months, renewable by consent.

Such an order might be simply added to the range of orders available to the court system as currently constructed. It might become the principal child protection function of the lower courts. More radically it might be an appropriate disposal around which could be constructed a different type of tribunal, less legalistic, more welfare-orientated and more participatory.

Such a tribunal might help to relieve some of the pressure on other parts of the court system. It could also offer a strategy for action in those difficult cases where currently parents feel forced into voluntary agreements and/or workers feel immobilised by the constraints of the law. It could allow for the development of a more constructive relationship between the judiciary and local authorities.

The complexity of the issues such a change of approach would have to negotiate are evident. It may also be seen as quixotic to begin this chapter by praising the Children Act reforms for bringing the previous disparate jurisdictions together and providing consistent remedies throughout the court system and ending it by raising the possibility of creating a new tribunal or an order whose use might come to define the domain of the lower courts. However, as already indicated, these ideas are offered not as a blueprint for reform but as a topic for debate. We are equally aware of an alternative perspective which would point to the multi-tracking which was so striking a feature of our sample cases as demonstrating the flexibility of the whole system and its capacity to accommodate diversity.

Systems in transition

Perhaps the dominant theme in this research report, however, has been that of a system in the process of evolution. The Children Act sought to change far more than the legal framework, encapsulating a new philosophy about the relationship between families, the state and the courts and requiring, as the Lord Chancellor expressed it, all of those involved in its implementation: 'to be prepared to throw off many familiar and perhaps comfortable habits of both mind and practice'.[13]

Some of the tensions and conflicts generated or exposed by that process have been documented in this report. As we have also sought to show, at the point the research was undertaken the system was assuming a variety of forms on the ground via the interpretations of a host of practitioners while from the centre a range of influences were being brought to bear (via the higher courts, government sponsored reports and the Children Act Advisory Committee) which sought to identify problems and shape developments. The system of family justice which appears to be emerging from this process may not yet be a coherent whole, indeed in some respects might be considered to be riven with contradictions. Implementation of the Act, however, must surely be seen as a significant advance while the existence of mechanisms through which the effectiveness and impact of the Act can be evaluated provide a means of continuing to move forward. By dissecting the processes by which child protection cases are brought to and are managed by the courts under the Children Act, as well as through making specific recommendations for further change, we hope this report will contribute to that process.

NOTES

[1] Murch M; Hooper D (1992): *The Family Justice System*. Family Law.

[2] Wells A (1993): *Family Court Services Committees: A Review of their Function with Respect to their Terms of Reference. Report to Children Act Advisory Committee.* Council for Family Proceedings.

[3] Hunt J; Murch M: (1989): *Speaking out for Children*. The Children's Society; Murch M et al. (1991): *Representation of the Child in the Civil Courts: Summary and Recommendations to the Department of Health.* Socio-Legal Centre for Family Studies, University of Bristol.

[4] Since this report was completed the new Labour government has issued a consultative document on the reorganisation of welfare services for the courts – DoH et al. (1998): *Support Services in Family Proceedings: Future Organisation of Court Welfare Services.* DoH.

[5] Association of Lawyers for Children (1995): *Response to National Committee of Inquiry into the Prevention of Child Abuse.*

[6] Murch and Hooper (1992): op. cit; King M; Piper C (1995): *How the Law Thinks About Children.* 2nd edition. Arena; DHSS (1988): *Report of the Inquiry into Child Abuse in Cleveland 1987.* Cm 412, HMSO.

[7] Murch and Hooper (1992): op. cit.

[8] Smith P (1995): Child Protection Research. *Family Law*, 432.

[9] Freeman P; Hunt J (1998): *Parental Perspectives on Care Proceedings*. The Stationery Office.

[10] Carlen P (1976): *Magistrates' Justice*. Martin Robertson; Murch M (1980): *Justice and Welfare in Divorce*. Sweet and Maxwell; Lindley B (1995): *On the Receiving End*. Family Rights Group.

[11] Cretney S (1990): Defining the Limits of State Intervention: the child and the courts, in Freestone D (ed.) *Children and the Law*. Hull University Press.

[12] Nelken D (1988): Social Work Contracts and Social Control, in Matthews R: *Informal Justice?* Sage.

[13] Lord Mackay, LC (1989): Joseph Jackson Memorial Lecture: Perceptions of the Children Bill and Beyond. *New Law Journal*, 14 April.

Appendix
Cases referenced in the text

Bibliography

Ackroyd W (1994): The Nature of Proceedings, the Family Court and the Selection of the Judiciary. *Family Law*, 89.

Adcock M; White R (1983): *The Administrative Parent: A Study of the Assumption of Parental Rights and Duties*. BAAF.

Adcock M; White R; Hollows A (1991): *Significant Harm*. Significant Publications.

Aldgate J (1980): Identification of Factors influencing Children's Stay in Care, in Triseliotis J (ed.): *New Developments in Foster Care and Adoption*. Routledge and Kegan Paul.

Allen N (1992): *Making Sense of the Children Act*. Longman.

Association of Lawyers for Children (1995): *Response to National Committee of Inquiry into the Prevention of Child Abuse*.

Bainham A (1990): *Children – the New Law. The Children Act 1989*. Family Law.

Ball C; Berkeley-Hill B (1994): *The Welfare of the Child: Assessing Evidence in Children Cases*. The Magistrates Association.

Bell M; Daly R (1992): Social Workers and Solicitors: working together? *Family Law*, 257.

Bentovim A (1991): Significant Harm in Context, in Adcock M; White R; Hollows A: *Significant Harm*. Significant Publications.

Bissett-Johnson A (1995): Scottish Office White Paper: Scotland's Children – Proposals for Child Care Policy and Law: a critical analysis. *Journal of Social Welfare and Family Law*, 17(1).

Booth, Dame Margaret (1995): *Avoiding Delay in Children's Cases: Preliminary Report*. Lord Chancellor's Department.

Booth, Dame Margaret (1996): *Avoiding Delay in Children Act Cases*. LCD.

Borkowski A (1995): Police Protection and Section 46, *Family Law*, April.

Bowlby J (1971): *Attachment and Loss*. Penguin.

Bracewell, Mrs Justice (1995): Comment. *Family Law*, February.

Brasse G (1993): The Section 31 Monopoly. Nottinghamshire County Council v P Considered. *Family Law*, 691.

Brasse G (1994): A Tightly Run Procedure? Interim Care Orders under strain. *Family Law*, 261.

Braye S; Preston-Shoot M (1992): Honourable Intentions: Partnerships and Written Agreements in Welfare Legislation. *Journal of Social Welfare Law*, 511.

Brophy J (forthcoming): Guardians ad Litem, experts and care proceedings. The Stationery Office.

Caplan G (1964): *The Theory and Practice of Mental Health Consultation. Principles of Preventative Psychiatry*. Basic Books.

Carlen P (1976): *Magistrates' Justice*. Martin Robertson.

Children Act Advisory Committee Annual Reports 1991–92, 1992–3, 1993–4. LCD.

Church T W Jr (1979): Civil Case Delay in State Trial Courts. *Justice System Journal*.

Clark D (1995): Roundabouts and Swings - Recent Court Decisions about the Representation of Older Children. *GAL Panel News*, 7(4).

Cleaver H; Freeman P (1995): *Parental Perspectives in Cases of Suspected Child Abuse*. HMSO.

Cobley C (1995): *Child Abuse and the Law*. Cavendish Publishing Limited.

Collins P (1994): Does the System Protect Children? *Family Law*, 686.

Cooper A; Hetherington R; Baistow K; Pitts J; Spriggs A (1995): *Positive Child Protection: A View from Abroad*. Russell House Publishing.

Corby B (1993): *Child Abuse, Towards a Knowledge Base*. Open University Press.

Cretney S (1990): Defining the Limits of State Intervention: the child and the courts, in Freestone D (ed.): *Children and the Law*. Hull University Press.

Davis G (1994): Simple Quarrels. *Family Law*, 323.

Department of Health (1988): *Protecting Children: a Guide for Social Workers Undertaking a Comprehensive Assessment*. HMSO.

Department of Health (1989): *An Introduction to the Children Act 1989*. HMSO.

Department of Health (1989): *The Care of Children: Principles and Practice in Regulations and Guidance*. HMSO.

Department of Health (1991): *Patterns and Outcomes in Child Placement*. HMSO.

Department of Health (1991): *The Children Act 1989 Guidance and Regulations, Volume 1: Court Orders*. HMSO.

Department of Health (1992): *The Children Act 1989 Court Orders Study: A Study of Local Authority Decision-making about Public-Law Court Applications*. HMSO.

Department of Health (1992): *Manual of Management for GALRO Panel Managers*. HMSO.

Department of Health (1995): *Child Protection: Messages from Current Research and their Implications*. HMSO.

DoH, Home Office, LCD, Welsh Office (1998): *Support Services in Family Proceedings: Future Organisation of Court Welfare Services*. DoH.

Department of Health and Social Security (1985): *Review of Child Care Law: Report to Ministers of an Interdepartmental Working Party*. HMSO.

Department of Health and Social Security (1985): *Social Work Decisions in Child Care*. HMSO.

Department of Health and Social Security (1988) *Report of the Inquiry into Child Abuse in Cleveland 1987*. Cm 412, HMSO.

Diduck A (1995): Partnership: reflections on some Canadian experiences, in Kaganas F (ed.) *Legislating for Harmony: Partnership under the Children Act 1989*. Jessica Kingsley.

Dingwall R; Eekelaar J; Murray T (1983): *The Protection of Children*. Basil Blackwell.

Douglas J (1970): Broken Families and Child Behaviour. *Journal of the Royal College of Physicians*.

Eekelaar J (1991): Parental Responsibility: State of Nature or Nature of the State? *Journal of Social Welfare Law*, No. 1.

Eekelaar J; Dingwall R (1990): *The Reform of Child Care Law*, Tavistock/Routledge.

Family Rights Group (1994): *Family Group Conferences*. FRG.

Farmer E; Owen M (1995): *Child Protection Practice: Private Risks and Public Remedies – Decision-Making, Intervention and Outcome in Child Protection Work*. HMSO.

Farmer E; Parker R (1985): *A Study of Interim Care Orders*. School of Applied Social Studies, University of Bristol.

Fish D (1995): Acting for Parents in Care Proceedings. *Family Law*, 414.

Frankenburg C; Tarling R (1983): Time taken to deal with juveniles in criminal proceedings. Research Planning Paper 18. Home Office.

Freeman M D A (1992): *Children, their Families and the Law. Working with the Children Act*. Macmillan.

Freeman P; Hunt J (1998): *Parental Perspectives on Care Proceedings*. The Stationery Office.

Frothingham T E; Barnett R A M; Hobbs C J; Wynne J M (1993): Child Sexual Abuse in Leeds Before and After Cleveland. *Child Abuse Review*, 23.

Garbarino J; Gilliam G (1980): *Understanding Abusive Families*. Lexington Books.

Gibbons J; Conroy S; Bell C (1995): *The Operation of Child Protection Registers*. HMSO.

Goldstein J, Freud A, Solnit A (1979): *Beyond the Best Interests of the Child*. Free Press, New York.

Hale, Mrs Justice (1995): Foreword, in White R; Carr P; Lowe N: *The Children Act in Practice*. Butterworths.

Hallett C (1995): *Inter-agency Co-ordination and Child Protection*. HMSO.

Harris P (1995): Representing Children. *Representing Children*, 8(2).

Harwin J (1992): Child Protection and the Role of the Social Worker under the Children Act, in Parry M (ed.) *The Children Act 1989: Conflict and Compromise*. Hull University Law School.

Hildgendorf L (1980): *Social Workers and Solicitors in Child Care Cases*. Tavistock.

Hoggett B (1992): Ten Years of Family Law Reform. Paper delivered at the Annual Conference of the Socio-Legal Studies Association, April 1992. *SLSA Newsletter*, Winter 1992.

Home Office (1989): *Scrutiny of Administrative Arrangements in Magistrates' Courts*. HMSO.

Home Office, Department of Health, Department of Education and Science, and Welsh Office (1991): *Working Together: A Guide to Arrangements for Inter-agency Co-operation for the Protection of Children from Abuse*. HMSO.

House of Commons (1984): *Second Report of the All-Party Parliamentary Select Committee on Social Services* (Session 1983–84): Children in Care (The Short Report). HMSO.

Hunt J (1986): The Grounds for Care. Report to DoH (unpublished).

Hunt J (1986): The Role and Practice of the Guardian ad Litem. Report to DoH (unpublished).

Hunt J (1992): Avoidable Delay in Child Care Proceedings. Paper delivered at Socio-Legal Centre Conference.

Hunt J (1993): *Local Authority Wardships before the Children Act: The Baby or the Bathwater?* HMSO.

Hunt J; Macleod A (1993): *Child Protection Proceedings before the Children Act: A Case for Change?* Report to DOH (unpublished).

Hunt J; Macleod A (forthcoming): *The Best-Laid Plans: Outcomes of Judicial Decisions in Child Protection Cases*. The Stationery Office.

Hunt J; Murch M (1989): *Speaking Out for Children*. The Children's Society.

Kaganas F (1995): Partnership under the Children Act 1989 – an overview, in Kaganas F; King M; Piper C: *Legislating for Harmony: Partnership under the Children Act*. Jessica Kingsley.

King M (1995): Law's Healing of Children's Hearings: the paradox moves north. *Journal of Social Policy*, 24(3).

King M; Piper C (1990): *How the Law Thinks About Children*. Gower.

King M; Piper C (1995): *How the Law Thinks About Children*. 2nd edition. Arena.

Law Commission Report No. 172 (1988): *Family Review of Child Law: Guardianship and Custody*. HMSO.

Lindley B (1995): *On the Receiving End*. Family Rights Group.

London Borough of Brent (1985): *A Child in Trust: Report of the Panel of Inquiry Investigating the Circumstances Surrounding the Death of Jasmine Beckford*. London Borough of Brent.

London Borough of Greenwich (1987): *A Child in Mind: Protection of Children in a Responsible Society, Report of the Commission of Inquiry into the Circumstances Surrounding the Death of Kimberley Carlile*. London Borough of Greenwich.

London Borough of Lambeth (1987): *Whose Child? The Report of the Public Inquiry into the Death of Tyra Henry.* London Borough of Lambeth.

Lord Chancellor's Department (1986): *Interdepartmental Review of Family and Domestic Jurisdictions.* LCD.

Lord Chancellor's Department (1988): *Improvements in the Arrangements for Care Proceedings.* LCD.

Lynch M A; Roberts J (1982): *Consequences of Child Abuse.* Academic Press.

Lyon C M (1995): Representing Children, towards 2000 and beyond. *Representing Children,* 8(2).

Lyon C; de Cruz P (1993): *Child Abuse.* 2nd edition. Family Law.

Mackay, LC, Lord (1989): Joseph Jackson Memorial Lecture. *New Law Journal,* 139.

Macleod A (1993): *Servicing Social Services: Local Authority Representation in Child Care Cases.* HMSO.

Macleod A; Malos E (1984): *Representation of Children and Parents in Child Care Proceedings.* Socio-Legal Centre for Family Studies, University of Bristol.

Masson J; Morton S (1989): The Use of Wardship by Local Authorities. *Modern Law Review,* November.

Masson J; Oakley M (1997): Out of Hearing: the representation of children by Guardians ad Litem and solicitors in public proceedings. Research report. Faculty of Law, Warwick University.

Matza D; Sykes G (1957): Techniques of Neutralization: a theory of delinquency. *American Sociological Review,* 22.

Millham S; Bullock R; Hosie K; Haak M (1985): *Lost in Care: The Problems of Maintaining Links between Children in Care and their Families.* Gower.

Mnookin R (1979): Bargaining in the Shadow of the Law: the case of divorce. *Yale Law Journal,* 88.

Montgomery J (1989): The Emotional Abuse of Children. *Family Law,* 19, 25–9.

Murch M (1980): *Justice and Welfare in Divorce.* Sweet and Maxwell.

Murch M; Borkowski M; Copner C; Griew K (1987): *The Overlapping Jurisdiction of Magistrates' Courts and County Courts.* Socio-Legal Centre for Family Studies, University of Bristol.

Murch M; Hooper D (1992): *The Family Justice System.* Family Law.

Murch M; Hunt J; Macleod A (1991): *Representation of the Child in the Civil Courts: Summary and Recommendations to the Department of Health.* Socio-Legal Centre for Family Studies, University of Bristol.

Murch M; Lowe N; Borkowski M; Copner R; Griew K (1993): *Pathways to Adoption.* HMSO.

Murch M; Mills E (1987): *The Length of Care Proceedings.* Socio-Legal Centre for Family Studies, University of Bristol.

Murch M; Thomas C (1992): *Feedback from Family Court Business Committees.* Socio-Legal Centre for Family Studies, University of Bristol.

Nelken D (1988): Social Work Contracts and Social Control, in Matthews R: *Informal Justice?* Sage.

O'Hagan K (1993): *Emotional and Psychological Abuse of Children.* Open University Press.

Owen M (1992): *Social Justice and Children in Care.* Avebury.

Packman J; Hall C (1998): *From Care to Accommodation.* The Stationery Office.

Packman J; Randall J; Jacques N (1986): *Who Needs Care?: Social Work Decisions about Children.* Blackwell.

Parker J; Burrows D (1993): Identify the Issues in Cases Relating to Children. *Family Law*, November.

Parry M (1992): The Children Act 1989: a Conflict of Ideologies?, in Parry M (ed.): *The Children Act 1989: Conflict and Compromise.* Hull University Law School.

Parry M (1994): *Panel News*, 7(2).

Parton N (1991): *Governing the Family: Child Care, Child Protection and the State.* Macmillan.

Plotnikoff J (1992): *The Timetabling of Care Proceedings before the Children Act.* HMSO.

Plotnikoff J; Woolfson R (1997): *Reporting to Court: A Handbook for Social Services.* SSI.

Purcell T (1995): Technology's Role in Access to Legal Services and Legal Information, in Smith R (ed.): *Shaping the Future: New Directions in Legal Services.* Legal Action Group.

Report of the Committee on One Parent Families (1974). CM 5629, HMSO.

Robertson I (1995): Comment. *Family Law*, 393.

Rowe J (1985): *Social Work Decisions in Child Care – Recent Research Findings and their Implications.* HMSO.

Rowe J; Hundleby M; Garnett L (1989): *Child Care Now.* BAAF Research Series 6.

Rutter M (1972): *Maternal Deprivation Re-assessed.* Penguin.

Rutter M (1985): Resilience in the Face of Adversity: protective factors and resistance to psychiatric disorder. *British Journal of Psychiatry*, 147, 598–611.

Ryburn M (1992): Family Group Conferences, in Thoburn J (ed.): *Participation in Practice: Involving Families in Child Protection.* University of East Anglia.

Salgo L (1993): *Der Anwalt des Kindes: Die Vertretung von Kindern in zivilrechtlichen Kindesschutzverfahren – eine vergleichende Studie.* Bundesanzeiger.

Saves D (1996): Parental Participation in Case Conferences. *Child and Family Law Quarterly*, 8(1).

Smith P (1995): Child Protection Research. *Family Law*, 432.

Smith R (1995): Lawyers, Courts and Alternatives, in Smith R (ed.): *Shaping the Future: New Directions in Legal Services*. LAG.

Social Services Committee: Children in Care in England and Wales. House of Commons Paper 88/89 No 84. Memoranda to Committee.

Social Services Inspectorate (1995): *The Challenge of Partnership in Child Protection: A Practice Guide*. HMSO.

Thoburn J et al. (forthcoming): *Safeguarding Children with the Children Act*. The Stationery Office.

Thomas C; Hunt J (1996): *The Care Workloads of the Civil Courts under the Children Act*. Report to DoH. Centre for Socio-Legal Studies, University of Bristol.

Thoburn J; Lewis A; Shemmings D (1995): *Paternalism or Partnership? Family Participation in the Child Protection Process*. HMSO.

Thomas C; Murch M; Hunt J (1993): *The Duration of Care Proceedings: A Replication Study*. HMSO.

Thomas N; Beckett C (1994): Are Children Still Waiting? *Adoption and Fostering*, 18(1).

Vernon J; Fruin D (1986): *In Care, A Study of Social Work Decision-making*. National Children's Bureau.

Wald M (1982): State Intervention on Behalf of Endangered Children – a proposed legal response. *Child Abuse and Neglect*, 6, 3–45.

Wall, The Honorouble Mr Justice (1995): The Use or Misuse of Experts: a judicial perspective. Paper given at NALGRO conference. 29 March 1995.

Wedge P; Mantle G (1991): *Sibling Groups and Social Work*. Avebury.

Wells A (1993): *Family Court Services Committees: A Review of their Function with Respect to their Terms of Reference. Report to Children Act Advisory Committee*. Council for Family Proceedings.

White R (1996): Reasonable Doubt. *Community Care*, 8 February, Issue 1105.

White R; Carr P; Lowe N (1990): *A Guide to the Children Act 1989*. Butterworths.

White R; Carr P; Lowe N (1995): *The Children Act in Practice*. 2nd edition. Butterworths.

Wingham G (1995): Choice or Change. *Child Care Forum*, Issue 5.

Wolkind S; Rutter M (1973): Children Who have been in Care – an epidemiological study. *Journal of Child Psychology and Psychiatry*, 14.

Woolf, Lord Justice (1996) *Access to Justice*. HMSO.

Index

welfare service, need for court-based 174,
185
welfare system 37, 116, 152
Working Together 90–1
written statements 215, 260

Index by Mary Norris